The Anthem Companion to Max Weber

ANTHEM COMPANIONS TO SOCIOLOGY

Anthem Companions to Sociology offer authoritative and comprehensive assessments of major figures in the development of sociology from the past two centuries. Covering the major advancements in sociological thought, these companions offer critical evaluations of key figures in the American and European sociological tradition and will provide students and scholars with an in-depth assessment of the makers of sociology, charting their relevance to modern society.

Series Editor

Bryan S. Turner – City University of New York, USA, and Australian Catholic University, Australia

Forthcoming titles in this series include:

The Anthem Companion to Hannah Arendt
The Anthem Companion to Auguste Comte
The Anthem Companion to Everett Hughes
The Anthem Companion to Karl Mannheim
The Anthem Companion to Robert Park
The Anthem Companion to Talcott Parsons
The Anthem Companion to Phillip Rieff
The Anthem Companion to Georg Simmel
The Anthem Companion to Gabriel Tarde
The Anthem Companion to Ferdinand Tönnies
The Anthem Companion to Ernst Troeltsch
The Anthem Companion to Thorstein Veblen

The Anthem Companion to Max Weber

Edited by Alan Sica

ANTHEM PRESS

Anthem Press
An imprint of Wimbledon Publishing Company
www.anthempress.com

This edition first published in UK and USA 2016
by ANTHEM PRESS
75–76 Blackfriars Road, London SE1 8HA, UK
or PO Box 9779, London SW19 7ZG, UK
and
244 Madison Ave #116, New York, NY 10016, USA

British Library Cataloguing-in-Publication Data
A catalogue record for this book is available from the British Library.

Library of Congress Cataloging-in-Publication Data
Names: Sica, Alan, 1949– editor.
Title: The Anthem companion to Weber / edited by Alan Sica.
Description: New York : Anthem Press, 2016. |
Includes bibliographical references and index.
Identifiers: LCCN 2016029231 | ISBN 9781783083794 (hardback : alk. paper)
Subjects: LCSH: Weber, Max, 1864–1920—Political and social views. |
Sociology—Philosophy.
Classification: LCC H59.W4 A58 2016 | DDC 301—dc23
LC record available at https://lccn.loc.gov/2016029231

ISBN-13: 978-1-78308-379-4 (Hbk)
ISBN-10: 1-78308-379-4 (Hbk)

This title is also available as an e-book.

CONTENTS

Chapter 1

MAX WEBER INVENTS HIMSELF

Alan Sica

"Those who would think about the nature of society and history in our time have been living off the big men of the nineteenth century. There has not yet appeared any twentieth-century political theorist, sociologist, historian, or economist whose work is truly up to their level." C. Wright Mills, "Introduction" to W. E. H. Lecky's *History of European Morals from Augustus to Charlemagne* (Mills, 1955)

The Budding Classicist

Max Weber fashioned himself into a historian and economist of ancient Rome by means, it can be argued, of pointed scholarly disputes with a set of accomplished and much older scholars – one in particular. This protracted, genteel set of disagreements amounted to a modified Oedipus tale not unlike, yet more important for his research than the famous one that erupted between Weber and his father when he evicted Max Weber Sr. from his home in 1897, six weeks before the latter's sudden death in a foreign city. As is well documented (Marianne Weber, 1975: 230–264; Radkau, 2009: 64–69, 145ff), the latter dispute ignited endless emotional trouble for Weber during the remaining 22 years of his life. Yet the former set of disagreements, I think it can be shown, inspired his early writing and gave him a lifelong impetus to work extremely hard at his scholarship.

A hint of all this comes from his wife's indispensable biography:

At the beginning of 1877, before his fourteenth birthday, Max wrote – evidently as a belated Christmas present – two historical essays "after numerous sources," one "About the Course of German History, with Special Regard to the Positions of the Emperor and the Pope," the other "About the Roman Imperial Period from Constantine to the Migration of Nations"; the latter was "Dedicated by the Author to his Own Insignificant Self as well as to his Parents and Siblings." The text of the second essay is illustrated with a sketch of Constantinople, the family tree of Constantius Chlorus [Constantius I, "The Pale"] and daintily drawn heads of the *Caesares* and *Augusti,* apparently copied from antique coins the boy was collecting at the time. (Marianne Weber, 1975: 46)

All the key ingredients of his modus operandi are here if one were to work backward in Weber's life from his *Agrarian Sociology of Ancient Civilizations* (1909) to these memorable pieces of juvenilia 32 years before. Marianne records the reading habits of the precocious scholar, which by modern standards seem quite improbable: "But books were the most important thing in his rich boy-hood" (45). He absorbed Spinoza, Schopenhauer, Kant, Machiavelli, Luther, histories by Curtius, Mommsen, Treitschke, all of Goethe's works, and so on. "I don't daydream, I don't write poetry, so what else shall I do but read? So I am doing a thorough job of that … My progress is slow, because I make many notes as I read" (46; 49–50). As Marianne also observes, "His judgments on the Greek and Latin classics – Homer, Herodotus, Virgil, Cicero, Sallust – show precocious, independent mental activity and astounding intellectual intensity" (50). In defending his negative appraisal of Cicero, unorthodox at the time, Weber claims that neither his teachers nor books influenced his atti-tude toward the great orator, "for I have only recently looked this period up in important works, such as Mommsen's history of Rome" (54).

The Looming Family Friend

By the time Theodor Mommsen (1817–1903) won the second Nobel Prize for Literature in 1902, only 11 months before his death at 85, he was the most important humanist scholar in Germany, perhaps anywhere, and surely the leading classicist in an era when ancient historiography crowned the humani-ties. The first Prize winner in 1901 had been Sully Prudhomme, a French poet of whom there is no mention in the *New Oxford Companion to Literature in French* (1995). The 1903 winner was Bjørnstjerne Martinus Bjørnson, another for-gotten Norwegian poet. Mommsen, however, is as pertinent today as he was then, especially when considering the early scholarship of Max Weber – who was 38 when Mommsen received the Nobel Prize and who was still enduring the agonies of mental collapse that had begun several years before. One of Mommsen's four sons, Karl, had been a close friend of Max while they were schoolboys, and another, the physician Ernst, married Weber's younger sister, Klara ("Klärchen" or "Mädi"), in 1894. Mommsen was a regular visitor to the Weber household when Max was growing up and had already become inter-nationally famous for his *History of Rome* (1854–1856), years before Max was born. He enjoyed very much the company of Weber's mother and also argued with the young Weber about historical matters but "bore him no grudge even after heated encounters" (Marianne Weber, 1975: 35, 48, 194). Arnaldo Momigliano,the leading classical scholar of our own time had this to say in 1982 about the relationship between Mommsen and Weber: "Max Weber could boast (if he had ever been inclined to boast) of being the favorite pupil of both Theodor Mommsen, the greatest authority on Rome, and of August Meitzen, the greatest authority on medieval land-tenure" (Momigliano, 1994: 248).

The Nobel Prize speech regarding Mommsen's achievement called him "the greatest living master of the art of historical writing, with special reference to his monumental work, *A History of Rome*." After explaining that the Prize in its second year of existence would go to a historian rather than a litterateur, the spokesman for the Swedish Academy explained their rationale:

A bibliography of Mommsen's published writings, compiled by Zangemeister on the occasion of his seventieth birthday, contains nine hundred and twenty items. One of Mommsen's most important projects was editing the Corpus Inscriptionum Latinarum (1867–1959), a Herculean task despite the assistance of many learned collaborators, for not only did Mommsen contribute to each of the fifteen volumes but the organization of the total work is his lasting achievement. A veritable hero in the field of scholarship, Mommsen has done original and seminal research in Roman law, epigraphy, numismatics, the chronology of Roman history, and general Roman history." (Nobel Prize Committee, 1902)

The Nobel Prize aside, encomia for Mommsen during his lifetime and afterwards have been endless in their variety and depth. Gilbert Highet's estimate in *The Classical Tradition* is typical: "The greatest classical historian of the nineteenth century was Theodor Mommsen ... he edited the huge *Corpus of Latin Inscriptions* – a task which demanded as much energy and organizing ability as building a transcontinental railway, to say nothing of his unrivalled knowledge Mommsen brought to bear on it" (Highet, 1949: 474). G. P. Gooch's (1913/ 1959) standard work devotes a chapter to "Mommsen and Roman Studies" that is thoroughly complimentary: "The history of Roman studies since the death of Niebuhr is largely the record of the amazing activities of a single man ... The most important of the books written during his occupation with the *Corpus* was the treatise on *Roman Public Law*. Double the length of his *Roman History*, the *Staatsrecht* was regarded by the author as the greatest of his achievements ... It is perhaps the greatest historical treatise on historical institutions ever written" (459).

To this Gooch felt obliged to add the inevitable comparison: "Mommsen and Ranke stand together and alone in the first class of nineteenth century historians ... Mommsen earned fame not only as a master of narration but as an interpreter of institutions and an editor of inscriptions and texts. They resembled each other in their productiveness and their combination of critical technique with synthetic vision … Mommsen's publications extended over sixty years. There is no immaturity in his early work and no decline in his later. He alone achieved the complete assimilation and reproduction of a classic civilization for which scholars have struggled since Scaliger. Rome before Mommsen was like modern Europe before Ranke. *Latericium accepit, marmoream reliquit*" (Gooch, 1913/1959: 459, 464, 469). And 45 years later while reviewing Alfred Heuss's study of Mommsen, Gooch points, perhaps unknowingly, to strong similarities with Max Weber: "Waging lifelong war against 'dilettantism,' he touched nothing in the vast field of Roman history, institutions and law which he did not adorn" (Gooch, 1958). Also remembered was Mommsen's strong resistance to the authoritarian direction Bismarck had taken, producing what Mommsen called "the land of obedience," in which he "had made Germany great and the individual German small" (376).

Of course, the most picturesque and widely known documenting of Mommsen's "royal status" among scholars comes from Mark Twain, writing for the *Chicago Daily Tribune* and other papers on April 3, 1892. Twain witnessed the spontaneous response of a thousand attendees at the University of Berlin, who stood to attention, held their swords high and "shouted and stamped and clapped, and banged the beer mugs" during a ceremony (honoring other scholars) when Mommsen entered the large hall. Clemens continued:

> It surely seemed to me that I had reached that summit, that I had reached my limit, and that there was no higher lift desirable for me … Then the little man with his long hair and Emersonian face edged his way past us and took his seat. I could have touched him with my hand – Mommsen – think of it! This was one of those immense surprises that can happen only a few times in one's life. I was not dreaming of him; he was to me only a giant myth, a world-shadowing specter, not a reality. The surprise of it all can be only comparable to a man's suddenly coming upon Mont Blanc, with its awful form towering into the sky … I would have walked a great many miles to get a sight of him, and here he was, without trouble or tramp or cost of any kind … carrying the Roman world and all the Caesars in his hospitable skull, and doing it as easily as that other luminous vault, the skull of the universe, carries the Milky Way and the constellations. (Twain, 1960: 218)

Samuel Clemens was simply authenticating common knowledge. In 1901, when Mommsen was 84, one classicist committed 72 pages of *The English Historical Review* to analyzing his *Römisches Strafrecht* (1899): "This great work, extending over a thousand pages, and dealing with a subject which bristles with problems and difficulties ... [is] justified by a lifetime of scholarly labour ... Future labourers will take Mommsen's work as a basis and starting point for their own" (Strachan-Davidson, 1901: 219). (Decades later the companion volume won this matter-of-fact endorsement from Arnaldo Momigliano: "In 1871 Mommsen published the first volume of his *Römisches Staatsrecht*, possibly the greatest descriptive work of modern historiography" [Momigliano, 1982b: 296]. Momigliano was famously cautious in his praise and therefore trusted implicitly for his scholarly judgements.)

In a long obituary in the same journal, F. Haverfield celebrated Mommsen in detail and with sentiments which could in part as easily be applied to the young Max Weber:

> This was the century of Buckle, Grote, and Stubbs, of Niebuhr and Mommsen, of Ranke and Treitschke, and a noble host of colleagues, numerous and active all over Europe. New lines of work ... and new possibilities for future research were in quick succession opened out ... Across all this period stands the figure of Mommsen ... *He was sensitive to external impressions, excitable even to vehemence, liable to be betrayed into hasty words, still more apt to display a superb vivacity, and astonishing intellectual alertness* ... he combined that very different form of genius which is the infinite capacity for taking pains. His control over detail, his aptitude for drudgery, were supreme. He could plod unwearyingly through laborious days of indexing and statistic-gathering, and finally reduce to order the million items. In particular his accuracy was almost infallible ... Such accuracy cannot be maintained simply by the use of friends or secretaries: it is genius ... Mommsen surpassed Gibbon in his critical faculty. (Haverfield, 1904: 81; emphases added)

Two months later Jesse Benedict Carter wrote in *The Atlantic Monthly*, also at length but for the American audience, simply declaiming, "None of us will ever again see the like of Theodor Mommsen ... He was certainly the greatest scholar of our time, and in point of toilsome erudition turned into knowledge, it is doubtful if the world has ever seen his superior" (Carter, 1904: 373, 377). He recounts Mommsen's unlikely early career during which he went to Italy on a Danish government stipend, stayed for three years gathering inscriptions, returned to Leipsic (*sic*) at 31 for a professorship in law but promptly lost that job when he sided loudly with revolutionaries in 1848. Breslau and then Zurich took him on as an expert in Roman law in 1854, after which came Berlin in 1857, where he stayed. He enlisted his brother, Tycho, to help him collect inscriptions, along with dozens of other young researchers, and created enough folio volumes to fill eight linear feet of shelving, listing and annotating 83,000 inscriptions (the first volume of which appeared in 1863, the year before Max Weber's birth). One of his key achievements was to eliminate many forged inscriptions from the historical record, insisting that all collected data be examined by his underlings or himself, and not be included in the *Corpus* otherwise. He founded scholarly journals, wrote definitive works on Roman public and criminal law thousands of pages long, also on numismatics and epigraphy, was active politically against Bismarck's protective tariff policy – and meanwhile, he and his wife produced 16 children.

Carter notes, "Mommsen's biography is more than a bibliography, for, wonderful as were his works, he was more man than book. We instinctly apply to him his own words: 'Each one must specialize in one branch of learning, but not shut himself up in it. How miserable and small is the world in the eyes of the man who sees in it only Greek and Latin authors or mathematical problems!'" In fact, Carter believed that "Mommsen possibly set more store by his political work than by his scholarship or his letters, and probably he would rather go down in history as a great statesman than as a great scholar" (Carter, 1904: 376). The clear parallel here with Weber needs only to be mentioned in order to register. It is also worth noting that early in his career, at about the same age as was Weber when the latter wrote his habilitation, Mommsen "published a learned work on Roman surveying," precisely anticipating and in part inspiring Weber's own work 40 years later (374).

After the shock of his death began to fade, other experts weighed in with their evaluations of Mommsen's lasting achievements. W. Warde Fowler at Oxford lectured in October 1909 on Mommsen's life and work: He "was by general consent the greatest figure in the region of classical learning that the nineteenth century produced." Fowler recalled meeting Mommsen at Oxford in 1886, noting his companionable nature, his love of scholarly discussion, avid pursuit of books in English and his "needing friendship more than anything in this life. But all his day was spent in persistent work. At Oxford he was found waiting at the Bodleian at seven in the morning, and indignant when he found that it did not open till nine" (Fowler, 1920: 251–252). Again this foreshadows one of Weber's repeated themes: "[W]ith an iron will which mastered easily all petty obstacles, with the utmost contempt for all half-work and dilettantism, he worked on incessantly for more than sixty years" (253). We recall that one of Weber's most damning criticisms was to accuse a scholar or functionary of practicing "mere dilettantism" (e.g., Weber, 1946: 222; 224, regarding Frederick the Great's amateurish opinions). Fowler also brings up the tragic fire in Mommsen's home on July 7, 1880, which not only burned the scholar himself as he tried to rescue manuscripts but also destroyed materials he had borrowed from major libraries. A call went out over Europe for replacement volumes so that Mommsen could continue his writing (263).

Finally, another patent characterological similarity with Weber: "The perfectly clear insight, the unerring judgement, which he possessed to an extraordinary degree in the world of learning, were never at his command in the world of practical politics. But his passionate feeling, however unfortunately expressed, was always honourable to himself, for it was based … on a deep and intense conviction of right and wrong" (265). As Mommsen did polemical battle with the Iron Chancellor, and was sued for it, Weber demanded in public that Kaiser Wilhelm II resign and was threatened with similar punishment. Privately Weber told friends that the Kaiser, "a conceited dilettante," should be executed (Radkau, 2009: 337).

Even the astringent 11th edition of the *Encyclopaedia Britannica* (1910) could not restrain itself:

> There is probably no other instance in the history of scholarship in which one man has established so complete an ascendancy in a great department of learning. Equally great as antiquary, jurist, political and social historian, he lived to see the time when among students of Roman history he had pupils, followers, critics, but no rivals. He combined the power of patient and minute investigation with a singular faculty for bold generalization and the capacity for tracing out the effects of thoughts and ideas on political and social life. Partly, perhaps, owing to a philosophical and legal training, he had not the gift of clear and simple narrative, and he is more successful in discussing the connexion between events than in describing the events themselves." (*Encyclopedia Britannica*, 1910, vol. 17/18: 684)

Without too much effort, one could substitute the name "Max Weber" where the *Britannica* writes "Mommsen," though Weber himself would likely not have entertained such a notion.

One of the longest and least admiring analyses of Mommsen's accomplishments was written in 1915 by the Swiss intellectual historian, Antoine Guilland whose *Modern Germany and Her Historians* offers extended treatments of Niebuhr, Ranke, Mommsen, von Sybel and Treitschke. Though impressed as was everyone else with Mommsen's lifework, he does not worship at the German's feet: "Mommsen's *History of Rome* is two things: it is in the first place the most illuminating summary, the most exact and vivid of the conclusions arrived at by historical science on Roman affairs; next it is an extraordinarily partial judgment on Roman politics. And these two things, each having an absolute character, are as opposed one to the other as much as it is possible for things to be opposed" (Guilland, 1915: 138).

In an eerie anticipation of Wolfgang Mommsen's attack on Max Weber's politics decades later (Mommsen, 1959), Guilland insists that the elder

Mommsen's work be evaluated along political lines, where he found it decidedly wanting. On the other hand, "Few historical works have had a more resounding success than Mommsen's *History of Rome*. When it appeared, in 1854, the effect was immense and re-echoed far through the nation. The Universities, it is true, were not pleased with it. The historian, in his work, overthrew all accepted opinions and treated with an absolute lack of respect men whom they had been wont to venerate. Cicero, for example, was treated therein as a coward ... Mommsen had accomplished a miracle: that of making Roman history an actual and living thing." Guilland then quotes Treitschke, Mommsen's only real competitor: "The *History of Rome* is one of the finest things ever written in our language, and there should be no young man or soldier who would not be delighted with his descriptions of Hannibal and Caesar" (163–164).

More recently the preeminent expert on Victorian cultural life, Peter Gay, and a junior colleague had this to say in a widely used sourcebook: "Mommsen was, first of all, the most skilled and professional scholar of his time and, in addition, to history, he was a master of no fewer than five ancillary fields, including epigraphy, numismatics, civil and constitutional law, archaeology, and early Italian philology ... Any reader of his *History of Rome* will be quickly convinced that Mommsen can equal Macaulay or Parkman at their rhetorical best. Not since Gibbon had critical skill and literary flair met in such a felicitous combination" (Gay and Wexler, 1975: 271). Even more topically interesting today, and of special concern for Gay as a refugee from Nazism, is this rare observation: "Mommsen deplored the decay of his university and of the imperial Germany. In his rectoral address of 1874, he predicted that the anti-Semitic movement would destroy the very purpose for which the University existed: 'the unfettered search for truth'" (274). Thus Mommsen anticipated the Dreyfus Affair in France by 20 years, not to mention the catastrophe of the Third Reich.

Lest Mommsen be misconceived as a Roman god who could do no wrong, there is the outstandingly bitter response to his *History of Rome* by the Swiss philologist, Johann Jakob Bachhofen, best known for his *Mutterrecht* idea. His "passionate and enduring hatred" of Mommsen sprang from the latter's attitude toward Rome historiography:

> The rough hands of this northern rationalist had violated and degraded the sanctity of the myths in which Bachofen perceived the fragile remnants of a past more remote, more beautiful, more glorious, and of far vaster significance than the surface history of class and political struggles, to which the critical historians, as he saw it, had reduced ancient Greece and Rome ... antiquity was being stripped of its glory, of everything that made it unique and different from

the present, greater, more richly human, more heroic. It was being remodeled to conform with the pettiness and fragmentariness of contemporary Berlin, and with the narrow interests, the egotism and the unbridled lust for power of modern societies. (Gossman, 1983: 1, 21)

Clearly from the worldwide sales and approbation that Mommsen's Roman history received, Bachofen's voice occupied a very small niche and likely never even registered with the author himself.

In keeping with the mainstream, one of America's leading historians and "public intellectuals," Anthony Grafton, recently reintroduced Mommsen's *History of Rome* (the 1958 one-volume abridgement by Saunders and Collins) to a new audience, with a concise and unambiguous appreciation. Recalling Mommsen's easy interaction with nonscholars, Grafton characterizes him as being constituted of "an organic connection between the tireless scholar and the steely public man," unafraid to confront Treitschke publicly over his anti-Semitism or Bismarck over his foreign policy, while befriending and enchanting his friends and casual acquaintances. Referring to his youthful Roman history, Grafton observes that "the book has never been out of print in Germany, and rarely abroad. Like the works of Darwin and Marx, Mommsen's *History* continues to offer a model of synthesis on the very grand scale: an intellectual achievement based on a staggeringly deep and broad command of details, all of them systematically and elegantly deployed in the service of a general idea, and clothed in a brilliant, powerful style" (Grafton, 2006: 48, 49).

Weber Probes Roman Surveying Techniques

Mommsen wrote his three-volume *History of Rome* between the ages of 37 and 39 (1854–1856) at the request of a publisher (his father-in-law, Karl Reimer) who asked for a much shorter work. He dropped a candle causing a fire in his home on July 7, 1880, destroying many precious documents, including the manuscript of his promised fourth volume, which would have advanced the story from July 46 BC, where he had left it. A companion volume appeared in 1885 treating the provinces of the Empire, but he was emotionally unable, so it was hypothesized, to write about Julius Caesar's death, so the Roman history as such ended prematurely. Only in 1980 were a complete set of lecture notes, taken by Sebastian and Paul Hensel, discovered in a Nuremburg used bookshop, and subsequently published in 1992. Thus the "missing fourth volume" appeared in the same way that George Herbert Mead's books or Weber's *General Economic History* presented themselves – purely as the result of expert student note-taking (Mommsen, 1996).

The related question before us is apparently straightforward, but only seemingly: To what extent was Weber's habilitation, *Die römische Agrargeschichte in ihrer Bedeutung für das Staats- und Privatrecht* (1891; 1962; 1986), at least in part, a strategic response to Mommsen's extraordinary scholarship, implicitly and explicitly? To be sure there were many other scholars who guided Weber, either by his having attended their lectures or by reading their works. Lutz Kaelber in his chapter of this book lists no fewer than 28 senior scholars whom Weber himself names as having influenced his early work. Yet Mommsen occupied a separate and superior category, as Kaelber also discovered: "Mommsen had a large impact ... [he] provided for Weber the substantive substratum of knowledge in his well-known and well-received general studies of Roman law and history ... Weber relied extensively on Mommsen's studies, sometimes without direct acknowledgement." And later in the same chapter, "The main influence on Weber for his *Habilitation* was a historian, Mommsen, who took ... a 'social historical approach' to the study of Roman agrarian history" (see chapter 2: p. 30). In point of fact, Weber was not shy about giving Mommsen his due as measured simply by overt references to his person or work. In the English translation of the habilitation, Mommsen is named 32 times (some of which are not properly indexed), and in the German edition there are indexed more than 100 references to the great scholar. No other scholar comes close, even the Berlin economist, August Meitzen, to whom Weber dedicated the work.

From the 70th birthday celebratory bibliography two years before, it was known that Mommsen's writings already numbered over 900 items, not to mention the several new fields of learning he had created. Weber at 27 had published almost nothing except his dissertation (Käsler, 1988: 243). Had Mommsen been a malevolent force in German scholarship, the image of David and Goliath would present itself. But a more apt analogous image lies within reach: the best and most senior athlete in a given sport is tested by an energetic, gifted novice. The senior champion is naturally expected to prevail, but only after the newcomer has inflicted praiseworthy damage to the elder's reputation and dominance. It is clear from the preceding commentaries about Mommsen's achievements that he had constructed a virtually impregnable reputation among humanist scholars, and it was surely not Weber's intention nor desire at 27 to dethrone the emperor, as it were. Yet Weber at that age was nevertheless himself, frankly stating his case wherever the data led him, regardless upon whose silken slippers he might be stepping. In this very attitude, if not otherwise, one could say he was indeed Mommsen's acolyte.

The habilitation has rarely been studied assiduously, nor has it served as a launching pad for much subsequent research in the way that so much of Weber's later writing did. It reached English very late (2008; revised 2010) and soon went out of print along with its defunct publisher, and since has become a rare and expensive volume. Its structure, language(s) and relentless exploration of arcane terminology and data almost make it Weber's own anticipatory parody of his older self. Meaningful references in English to *Die römische Agrargeschichte* in chronological order of composition are these: Marianne Weber, 1926/1975: 164, n.15; Honigsheim, 1949/2000, 59–64, 92; Momigliano, 1982b: 248–251; Mueller, 1986, 9–14, 19–20; Käsler, 1988: 28–31, 32–36; Love, 1991: 13–22; Dilcher, 2008: especially 178–183; Whimster, 2008, especially 251–252, 256; Harvey, 2009; Radkau, 2009: 72–76; and Sampson, 2009. None of them is a penetrating, thorough, or even an argumentative assessment of Weber's book. Most are brief summaries of a few key points Weber was apparently trying to make, but none meet him on his own terms.

When Marianne Weber elected to ignore the work except for one brief reference, she perhaps inspired Reinhard Bendix to do the same in his early and widely influential *Max Weber: An Intellectual Portrait*. In this long book Bendix confines himself to these paltry remarks: "By examining the methods of land surveying in Roman society, the different terms used to designate the resulting land units, and the extant writings on agriculture by Roman authors, Weber analyzed the social, political and economic developmnts of Roman society" (Bendix, 1962: 2). This summary would equate with referring to *Das Kapital* as "a study of the origins and circulatory nature of capital using examples from mid-nineteenth century Europe and her colonies." Given that there are thousands of scholarly works dealing principally with Weber's works and ideas (Sica, 2004), why are there so few which delve even minimally into the habilitation? Is it enough to say that working under Levin Goldschmidt when writing his dissertation on medieval trading companies in Italy and Spain (Weber, 1889/2003), he thus became "qualified ... in German law" (Frank in Weber, 2008; vii–viii) and after which, seeking teaching credentials in Roman law, he wrote the habilitation more or less "under" Mommsen? Probably not, though this small-bore biographical note typically stands in for actual analysis of the book itself.

The simple fact is that *Roman Agrarian History*, whether in German or the recent English version, is not fun to read, nor easy to digest. His most recent biographer says that Weber "tried to astound the reader with legal and agronomic shop-talk, to such a degree that today even a well-versed historian does not find it easy to understand what was the real point of the exercise" (Radkau, 2009: 73). Similarly, the book's English translator opens his "preface" by quoting Heuss's famous denunciation of the study in 1965: "The present work has been described by a distinguished German Romanist as 'hard to understand because of its dry and remote subject matter' and [is] 'generally neglected by historians'" (Weber, 2008: vii). Another reviewer of the English

translation reported that it "does leave the reader jolted," and is "an introduction to a large number of different topics, some of which are highly technical
... without finding a central theme to link them together." It also "covers a
broad range of topics, some in great technical detail, albeit in a brief and
somewhat breathless manner ... the title is somewhat of a misnomer with
the discussion ranging far wider than the reader might assume." He ends by
admiring the quality of scholarship and ambition Weber displayed but also
notes the "frustration" of the reader owing to "the constant failure to develop
points in any depth and the endless jumping back and forth between topics ...
a huge jumble of ideas and thoughts but with little structure ... the misleading chapter titles, which do not give the reader the scope of the subjects and
concepts within" (Sampson, 2009). If most of Weber's work reads poorly in
any language, his early studies – composed in obvious competition with far
more senior scholars and promoting his claim of expert status in disparate
fields of learning – stretch the tolerance of even those readers who come to
his juvenilia with happy anticipation.

If one were to attend to *Roman Agrarian History* with the kind of dedication required for complete understanding, for hermeneutic clarity, the first
prolegomenal texts kept ready to hand would be several recently made available that explain Roman surveying techniques and the complex, often contradictory jargon that arose from them. Richard Frank, the translator, helpfully
names a few while also pointing out that Weber's own investigation of these
changing techniques was primarily made possible with the publication in 1848
of Karl Lachmann's *Die Schriften der römischen Feldmesser* (Berlin), a collection
of original documents. To this book four years later was added a companion volume of essays, also edited by Lachmann. In 2000 Brian Campbell,
an Irish classicist, issued an extraordinarily helpful volume, *The Writings of the
Roman Land Surveyors: Introduction, Text, Translation and Commentary*. This unique
source (Latin texts on one page, English translations on the next) not only
reproduces Lachmann's collection of original texts – the *agrimensores*, or, more
formally *Corpus Agrimensorum Romanorum*, plus indispensable illustrations (278–
316) – but adds a very large index of Latin terms (533–552), maps and aerial
photographs.

All of this and more is required to decipher Weber's text since "Weber's
references to the *Digest* [*Pandects* of Justinian] are often incomplete and/or
inaccurate. This is the more surprising as his references to Lachmann and
other sources are invariably quite accurate" (Weber, 2008: xiii). Another key
to understanding Weber's cryptic reference system is O. A. W. Dilke's *The
Roman Land Surveyors: An Introduction to the Agrimensores* (1971), part of which
inspired Campbell's larger collection. More generally one can put to use
Kain and Baigent's *The Cadastral Map in the Service of the State: A History of*

Property Mapping (1992) in order to situate Weber's study in its naturally larger context. And in pursuing Weber's constant references to the "CIL" (*Corpus Inscriptionum Latinarum*), one of Mommsen's greatest achievements, John Sparrow's *Visible Words: A Study of Inscriptions In and As Books and Works of Art* (1969) and Peter Liddel and Polly Low's *Inscriptions and Their Uses in Greek and Latin Literature* (2013) prove especially illuminating. Lastly, and unsurprisingly, the very large articles on Roman Law and Roman History in the 11th edition of the *Encyclopaedia Britannica*, especially given that Mommsen's influence remained profound in 1910 when they were published, have shown the way for a century. They would have likely duplicated the outline of Weber's consciousness regarding Roman culture and politics given their very high quality and detailed nature.

Weber's overall scholarly goal in writing his habilitation has been ably summarized not only by Kaelber in the present book but also by other experts like Sam Whimster and Dirk Käsler. Aside from highly technical questions of the kind which Weber and Mommsen debated, the largest question revolved around Germany's sense of itself in Bismarck's period – remembering that Weber's father was politically involved in the creation of the new country, which gave the work special meaning indeed. As Kaelber writes: Weber "joined Meitzen in the – as is now known: historically untenable – assumption that this type of primordial communitarian local commune (*Flurgemeinschaft*) reflected a Germanic (egalitarian) rather than Celtic (hierarchical) social organization." Mommsen and others wanted to know how land-procuring practices, including imperialism, surveying and taxation, affected the Romans' legal and cultural understanding of property, particularly real estate.

For citizens of modern societies, obsessed as they are with such questions, it may seem quaint to worry about the origins of what they take for granted, but for Mommsen, Weber, and many other experts at the time, much more was at stake than merely knowing who owned what when. This is because all Roman land initially was *ager publicus*, so the interesting question was when, how and with what results did it slowly transmogrify into *ager privatus*. How, in short, did individuals begin to profit from the sale of, and later speculation in, real estate once it was alienated from its earliest usage? Put another way, when exactly did elites form, founded on real estate holdings, which eventually led to absentee ownership and the eroding of social structure that helped propel Rome's collapse in the fifth century CE? Inquiries such as these obviously led to Weber's mature theory of stratification, and what better historical data to invoke than Rome's. As Kaelber summarizes: "In his *Habilitation*, Weber traced the development of private and public lands, and the privatization of the latter, for commerical use from an original communitarian condition in ancient Rome in which land was neither privately held nor a market commodity."

In *Economy and Society*, as well as in the lectures which made up *General Economic History*, Weber introduced his readers and auditors to "tax farming" as an international and historical phenomenon. Because of his training in law and in historical economics, in addition to his extended family's participation in global trade, Weber knew a great deal about capital and commodity markets and also about taxation practices. He wrote about Asian techniques of raising government money, as well as Roman and medieval taxation systems in Europe. The reason, then, that the development of surveying was so important in Rome was because citizens generally escaped taxation while noncitizens in Italy and in the colonies did not. The more land was grabbed by the elite, the less tax revenue was raised, a persistent problem then as now. And naturally, if taxes were linked to land ownership just as they are today, and because early on taxation by a central authority was an experimental and novel procedure, ever-increasing precision in surveying became a socioeconomic and legal necessity. It is no accident that the ingenious popular historian, Will Durant, entered "taxation under Rome" in the index of his *Caesar and Christ* no fewer than 63 times, often with multiple pages indicated (Durant, 1944: 51, 58, 68, 80–81, 89, 91, etc.). The endless gaming of the tax system is one of the key ingredients to understanding Rome's rise and fall, of course.

Sam Whimster (2008) helpfully simplifies Weber's explanation of how and why all this happened, opining that *Roman Agrarian History* is "an audacious piece of scholarship" (251):

> Weber argued that the key to understanding the agrarian economy and its legal forms was through Roman survey methods and cadastral registers. Weber goes into detail here and the reader has to follow him closely. There were two types of survey method. One was a numbered grid of the land surveyed with the grid lines oriented as accurately as possible to the east-west meridian with the north-south fixed from the stars. The names of possessors of the land and their plots were marked to the grids but with only a vague depiction of boundaries or geographical features ... The other survey method was a more accurate map of settlements with the plots abutting one another as rectangles. This survey map had all the boundaries of the plot marked, and accurately measured in *actus* (about 35 meters) ... the first method ... was indicative that this land had been given with no great concern about boundaries and taxable acreage. The land was assigned to Roman citizens who paid no tax (excepting inheritance tax). The other method (*ager per scamna et strigas* – the widths and lengths of the plot) was exact because the land was subject to taxation obligations. This was public land distributed in the provinces outside Italy and subject to rent, taxes, and levies of various kinds ... One can sum up the developments as follows: the expansion of Rome's sphere of economic activity, in particular its public lands,

so that eventually the Roman *ager publicus* came to include a large portion of Italy. The question then naturally arises: what use was made of this enormous area? (Whimster, 2008: 251–252)

Stated this way, the issue seems simple and hardly worth an entire, dense monograph. The reason Weber took such pains with this work, and was willing to debate Mommsen in public about its technical details, is because the historical record, the "evidence," which historians after Ranke began to pursue with innovating vigor, was ambiguous. A great deal had to be imagined, hypothesized, wondered about, leaving plenty of hermeneutic room for those who cared to debate how Rome was formed, in terms of property relations, and how it eventually fell apart, as more and more of the elite excused themselves from taxation and legally shifted the burden to nonelite members of the Empire. A very old story, to be sure, and one that lives today with political-economic consequences not unlike those which regularly afflicted Rome.

As hinted above, adequate assessment of *Roman Agrarian History* requires knowledge of Roman history, Latin legal terms, evolving surveying techniques and perhaps, most importantly, the intimately experienced scholarly arguments of the time, many of which were instigated and prolonged by some of Weber's own professors. In our era of overdocumentation, when the endnotes to a monograph can equal in length the study itself, Weber's work seems almost mysterious in inspiration and intent. Not only does he casually refer to classical sources as if they are as commonly known as yesterday's newspaper accounts, but his references to these sources are seldom spelled out in detail.

A small sense of this unrelentingly peculiar style of scholarship, so foreign to our own practices, appears in the "Appendix: The Arausio Inscription." Whimster closes his review-essay of the habilitation by claiming that "A major thesis of Weber's *Roman Agrarian History* turns on the correctness of the reading of this inscription" (Whimster, 2008: 256). This is how Weber opens his "appendix":

Following this analysis I print drawings of fragments of an inscription from the French town of Orange, the ancient Arausio (CIL XII.1244). In the upper panel on the left side is the most important figure, two fragments put together. The originals are in the possession of Professor Otto Hirschfeld, who has kindly let me examine them. The dimensions of the pieces are not given by CIL, which is why I print this drawing. I should note that the drawing is not entirely accurate, but that is not important since the reading is secure. The fragment on the right is from CIL Supplement; Professor Hirschfeld gave me only a sketch of it. The dimensions of this second fragment are not known to me, but it seems likely to me that it fits in the gap at the lower right of the first, if the dimensions fit. The reading of its top line is doubtful. I have not joined the two fragments because I haven't examined both. (Weber, 2008: 173)

If however, the proposed combination is correct, then the inscription would be an almost complete record of a centuria and would read as follows:

S.D.X.C.K.X. Ex tr. XII. Col. XcVIII. (=XC.VIII?)
Colvarius (= col. Varus?) Calid. XX.a. II.x.*
XXVI. n.a. II
XII. Appuleia Paulla XLII.a.II.x*.II
a.IIXII.
Valer. Secundus IV.a.IIX.*II.
...Interpretation of the inscription is of great importance, for it is a key to the tax system and to methods used in surveying land in the provinces (Weber, 2008: 173–174).

If this seems inscrutable, it may explain in part why Weber's habilitation is seldom read. Keep in mind that Campbell's indispensable anthology of surveying methods (the *Corpus Agrimensorum Romanorum*) helpfully concludes with an "Index of Latin Words" that fills 20 large pages listing over 1,000 different terms. He also notes that "Mommsen's scheme requires two *scamna* and one *striga* between the *kardo maximus* and the second *limes* (C 163.10), and six *strigae* and four *scamna* between the *decumanus maximus* and the second *limes* (see Diagram 16)" (Campbell, 2000: 400).

Weber continues in his "appendix" to calculate dimensions in *iugera* of taxable land based on his reading of this inscription. He cannot resist baiting his great teacher, sometime houseguest and family friend: "Mommsen has suggested that 'a.' stands for the plural of the copper coin as [*sic*]. Very likely however it doesn't. In any case I think the numbers following the names indicate the shares of land (*modus agri*) given each person. One can see in the left fragment that the shares on it run through several centuries" (Weber, 2008: 174). Weber does not say why Mommsen's interpretation is incorrect, only that it is – an astonishingly bold statement from a very junior scholar.

There are no easy stretches of readily comprehensible text in Weber's habilitation. More than anything else, it reads like a research memo directed at those very few specialists with enough complementary knowledge to appreciate and evaluate its arguments – that is, as a dissertation of a high order. From the first chapter, "Roman Surveying and Roman Lands," we learn a great deal, e.g.: "As for public law, I think – following the argument of Mommsen.... – that the legal status of *ager quaestorius* was similar to that of the *trientabula*. On the origin of the *trientabula* in 200 B.C. we have the following explanation from

Livy 31:13...." This calls for knowledge of Roman law, of Mommsen's viewpoint, of Livy's history and so on. Weber continues:

> Mommsen argued that the sale of *ager quaestorius* was simply a device to remedy the treasury's temporary shortage of money... very similar to the practice of purchase and redemption used in medieval finance. Just as in medieval cities, up until they developed the use of selling annuities, so in ancient Rome there were only two ways of raising money for emergencies: forced loans (equivalent to *tributum*) and mortgages in the form of sale of land subject to redemption. In addition, the sale of *ager quaestorius* was, as is indicated by the surveying handbooks, also the legal procedure by which conquered land was used to raise money quickly.

> We have tried to demonstate that the Roman state probably had the right to redeem land it had sold. If true, that amounted to a right to expropriate property, which was otherwise unknown in Roman law so far as concerns *ager privatus*. Where it existed in regard to colonial land, for example for the construction of an aqueduct, that was explicitly stated in the colony's foundation statute. An example is in the *Lex col. Genetivae*, c.99 (*Eph.Epigr.* II, p. 22ff). When the Triumvirs carried out expropriations with compensation they may have based their actions on existing authorizations in the case of *ager quaestorius*, or else on the revocable status of *possessiones* in the *ager publicus*, or they may have used their extraordinary powers to extend the state's right of redemption – illegally – to *ager privatus*. (Weber, 2008: 30–32)

Weberians will recognize themes that occupied him throughout his 30 years of scholarly writing: power, legitimacy, property, finances, imperialism and so on. And Weber seldom hedges, even when evidence is thin:

> The conclusions advanced above are hypothetical. But if they are compared with ... Livy, then they seem to make sense ... From the above I conclude that in earlier times the surveying procedure *per scamna et strigas* was for land granted by the censor, which was held by right of rental (*locatio*). It was also used for land granted by the quaestors in the form of squared *laterculi* with *limites*, which was held by the right of sale (*venditio*) and was of lower status. The only land surveyed *per centurias* was that granted with full rights of ownership by *assignatio*. (32)

Throughout the work Weber repeatedly mentions Mommsen by name or by implication. Under the subheading "Character of Roman Colonization," he observes that "Roman colonization took two forms: either the foundation or transfer of a city (*deductio coloniae*), or unorganized settlement in single homesteads (*viritim assignatio*). Mommsen thought the *colonia* was a community of farmers … but it was also organized to defend itself behind fortifications – in short, a city" (40). In a heroic endnote that covers most of two pages, Weber writes without contrition: "In the course of my public examination for the doctorate, I had the honor of attempting to defend the views given here [Chapter Two] against our great master, Professor Mommsen. He rightly argued then and later that what I proposed was only an hypothesis without clear support in the evidence. I would contend, however, that in looking at the larger context I have come to a view which has a certain probability" (196). He then delivers an instructive mini-thesis (not unlike some of the longer notes to *The Protestant Ethic*), which politely but firmly maintains his beliefs against those of "the master."

If Whimster is correct in calling *Roman Agrarian History* an "historical gem … a must-buy purchase for historians and historical sociologists for its unrivalled combination of method and speculation," not to mention the "depth of Weber's scholarship [and] the laconic way in which he conducts his arguments" (Whimster, 2008: 256), then modern social scientists must reappropriate the extraordinary learning possessed by German classicists c. 1890 if they wish to follow Weber down this path. Not a likely event, but one which would indeed yield unique fruit for those who have the stomach for it.

* * *

The authors whose chapters fill this book were invited to write about Weber on a topic of their choice because they are internationally recognized as part of the top cadre of Weberian scholars whose work appears principally in English. Most have published lauded studies of Weber for decades. Very few other experts (most notably Peter Ghosh and Guenther Roth) meet the criteria for inclusion in this book. As such their commentaries do not require much by way of introduction to the likely audience for a volume such as this one. Nevertheless, it is customary for an editor of a scholarly handbook to say a few words about its contents.

Lutz Kaelber has made himself the leading expert on Weber's early work, specifically his dissertation, *The History of Commercial Partnerships in the Middle Ages* (Weber, 2003), which was known only by title until he translated and introduced it, at length, to English language readers. In his chapter in this book he has added a sensible approach to Weber's habilitation (the second dissertation required for certification in Germany at the time if a scholar wished to teach). The question he poses to himself is to what extent Weber's early works point conceptually to ideas that he later developed at great length, for example, the Protestant ethic's connection to capitalist development, the meaning of association and community (the *Vergemeinschaftung-Vergesellschaftung* distinction), ideal-types and so on. In short, he provides a handy, informed road map into these works that will aid scholars as they navigate these dense monographs.

Elaborating on work originated in English by Paul Honigsheim in the 1940s and carried on by Keith Tribe 25 years ago, Christopher Adair-Toteff offers a precise historiographical account of Weber's role as an expert in the transformation of large-scale German agriculture. Adair-Toteff is an unusual source of Weberian scholarship in that, though American by birth and education, he lives in Germany and is fully conversant with the ever-enlarging "Weber industry" built around the monumental Weber *Gesamtausgabe*, in process for over 30 years. He points out that visualizing Weber, at 40, as "merely" the author of *The Protestant Ethic and the Spirit of Capitalism* is incorrect, since he was already by that time a renowned resource for those politicians and strategists wondering how other countries' agricultural production would eventually affect German agribusiness. By carefully analyzing practices of the large-scale landowners in what is now Poland, the Prussian "Junker" class, Weber began to understand how social class affiliation would affect national and international policy priorities. Eventually the intransigent conservatism of the agricultural aristocracy led to economic crises, and similar sentiments 30 years later helped the National Socialists attain office. Put another way, the socioeconomic and political analyses that Weber carried out during the "agrarian crisis" years became a conceptual platform from which he launched his large-scale comparative sociology during the last decade of his life. Understanding of Weber's final work, so Adair-Toteff's chapter strongly suggests, begins in the 1890s when he undertook what today would be called "contract survey research" for "clients" desperate to know the direction of large-scale German agriculture. This is not the conventional view of Weber's labors as a young scholar.

In the library at the University of Wisconsin's main campus there sits an 1,100-page dissertation called *Authorities, Deities, and Commodities*, finished by David Norman Smith in 1988. If it is not the longest sociology dissertation in recent disciplinary history, it must be among the most complex, theoretically speaking. Just as Smith's dissertation was twice the length of even ordinarily long ones, his chapter in this book consumes twice as many words as do most of the others. It bears the scholarly hallmarks for which Smith has become well-known: extraordinarily conscientious attention to bibliographic detail, copious endnotes, multilingual sources, strong theoretical projection and a subtlety in the use of evidence and argument that is simply not often found in modern social science. As he writes, "we can only fully appreciate that point [capitalism as a revolutionary force] if we grasp that Weber's notions of charisma and capitalism are counter-intuitively subtle and complex." He takes the topic of "charisma," which it would seem has been analyzed so thoroughly that nothing new could be said about it, and invests it with fresh insights regarding capitalist development in India and China by means of "discipleship." In short, he aims to decentralize the notion of charisma as personal magnetism conferring rare authority on few leaders by following Weber's notion about groups, "a charisma of disciples." This is an unusual claim and typical of Smith's innovative work.

Becoming a true Weberian, one who studies Weber's own writings and those of other scholars equally addicted to his way of thinking, seems to require long-term commitment. Stephen Kalberg's 1978 dissertation was about Weber, and his career ever since has revolved principally around a specific component of Weber's thinking which Kalberg has truly made his own. Beginning with books and articles over 20 years ago, Kalberg has argued persuasively that the most fruitful and contemporarily useful aspect of Weber's thinking involves a comparative view of civilizations. He leaves behind previous versions of Weberianism that prevailed following World War II, including those which marked *The Protestant Ethic* as his major achievement (even though Kalberg has translated and edited the work himself in several editions), fascination with bureaucratic theory, power, charisma and so on, or an apotheosis of "Western rationalism" when compared with other major cultures. In their place Kalberg posits a "systematic sociology of civilizations" constructed around six key terms and their supporting arguments regarding Weber's version of comparative analysis: anti-organicism, subjective meaning, multi-causality, patterned action, the link between past and present and social carriers. Given the recent success with which Kalberg has applied this orientation to the United States and other civilizations, his chapter allows scholars to leap into a Weberian style of comparison without wasting time with preliminaries that in the end, so Kalberg believes, diverge significantly from Weber's intentions.

Another scholar whose attentions to Weber began in the 1970s, Stephen Turner in his chapter offers a novel and thus far little-examined component to what has become "the Weber legend." There are those who believe that had Weber lived beyond the age of 56, dying in 1920 during the influenza pandemic, he could have made a substantial difference to politics during the Weimar period, and might even have helped stymie the Nazis before they took power in 1933. Others, less entranced with Weber as a political actor, see this as hagiography without much empirical basis. Turner does not add to this debate by mere hypotheses but instead mines several key documents in order to find out how effective Weber actually was during two late episodes in his political life. The more important was Weber's contribution to debates at the Versailles peace talks following World War I, particularly concerning at whose feet responsibility for the war should be laid, and who therefore should bear the costs of reparation. Turner carefully analyzes several key texts, especially Alma Luckau's *The German Delegation at the Paris Peace Conference* (1941) and Friedrich Naumann's *Central Europe* (1915/1971). By examining the documentary evidence these sources provide, and comparing it judiciously with Wolfgang Mommsen's celebrated study, *Max Weber and German Politics* (1959/1984), Turner is able to provide a closely reasoned portrait of Weber doing his political best and putting into practice some of the themes made famous in his lecture of January 1919, "Politics as a Vocation." Turner concludes that Weber in essence anticipated Hitler's ascent long before anybody knew his name, mainly because the Versailles Treaty gave any dictator-in-waiting the ideological ammunition he needed to start another war.

Ever since publishing his first article about Weber in 1973, Lawrence Scaff has been at the forefront of Americans working within this crowded zone of social thought. In addition to many other works, he has written the only extended treatment of Weber's epochal trip, with his wife, to the United States in 1904. His work has always been characterized by graceful English prose mixed with careful analysis of Weber's "unbelievably bad handwriting," as he once termed it. He is one of the few Americans who has spent considerable time laboring in Weber archives in Germany. As he wrote elsewhere in his first Weber book, "My interest, then, is in that 'other' Weber, the man we have not known, the thinker we have missed in the rush to establish the conceptual boundaries and methodological foundations of the social sciences. I have tried to read him afresh, unburdened by the old controversies or interpretations, and with a mind open to the possibilities of his thought" (Scaff, 1989: x). In the present chapter, Scaff condenses and restates observations made in previous works regarding two, linked phenomena: Weber's extended tour of the United States (*Amerikareise*) and the way his ideas were taught, absorbed, perverted and repackaged over the subsequent century (*Rezeptionsgeschichte*) in the country he found fascinating and inspiring. According to Scaff, Weber's institutionalization in the United States (and elsewhere, for that matter) occurred "for reasons having little to do with authorial intentions." Speaking with rare authority, Scaff's chapter offers the best available brief guide to this unique intellectual transplanting of intensely Germanic ideas into US soil.

In his short, dense chapter, Sven Eliaeson recreates out of disparate texts Weber's attitude toward Russian politics between 1895 and his death in 1920. Even though Leon Trotsky himself wrote a long study of the 1905 "revolution" in Czarist Russia – a "practice session" for the Bolshevik Revolution a dozen years later – that failure of peasant enthusiasm for change has not registered as particularly important to Weber or to many of his followers. Eliaeson shows that this lacuna should be filled. Weber's wife tells the story in her biography about Weber hiring Russian emigrés, who had fled to Heidelberg in

1905, to tutor him in their language. He allegedly mastered Russian within six weeks or so sufficiently well to enable him to read contemporary accounts of the "revolution" in Russian newspapers. Out of this reading he produced two long essays at the time (finally translated into English in 1995), and according to Victoria Bonnell's review of the translation, they hold up remarkably well despite being written so closely to the events analyzed therein. Eliaeson expands on Weber's adventure in rapid scholarship-as-journalism and illustrates how wary thinkers of Weber's background and affiliations were concerning Russian culture and politics. "Russophobia" is perhaps not too strong a term to apply to such attitudes, whether voiced by Weber or many of his contemporaries. Fear of unwanted russofication of Germany, whether in the 1890s during the "agrarian crisis" or the political upheavals following World War I, is an undeniable part of the German mindset at the time. One could argue it has never disappeared, particularly after the unhappy events of the next "great war." In any case, understanding Weber's attitude and knowledge about Russia's march out of feudalism and into modernity, as analyzed by Eliaeson, adds a necessary bit of *realpolitik* to what could otherwise become an idealized sense of Weberian international relations.

Assessing the lasting value of Weber's main books – all of them published as such posthumously – requires specialized knowledge across a number of fields that very seldom nowadays cohere in a single scholar. This of course accounts in part for Weber's continuing international and intercultural appeal among social scientists, the fact that he became in essence a one-man research faculty. Ever since 1980 when Jack Barbalet published his first article on Weber, he has been probing components of Weberian thought along a number of intriguing avenues, not least of which has been his willingness to pursue social-psychological topics partially by means of the Weberian lens. In his chapter he reexamines one of Weber's boldest and most carefully scrutinized volumes in his comparative religion series, *The Religion of China*. English readers have been tethered to the Hans Gerth translation for 65 years, and Barbalet notes that the German variorum edition (1991) corrects substantial bibliographical errors in the original version from 1916 that Gerth reproduced. But aside from technical matters such as these, Barbalet asks more fundamental questions about Weber's understanding of Chinese civilization, particularly as it was rooted in Confucianism. The largest question which sinologists have long been asking is whether or not Weber's claim that Confucian doctrine inhibited "the capitalist spirit" is accurate given alleged improvements in historical re-creation since Weber's time. He did his best to absorb the latest findings of specialists at the time, and was successful to an astonishing degree, but given that a century has passed since he published the study, Barbalet and others are right in questioning Weber's conclusion about religion and capitalist development, especially as applied to the special case of China. Only a scholar such as Barbalet, equally comfortable as a Weber specialist and also sinologist, can reasonably judge this issue which, given China's position in the global economy, has become more important than Weber could have imagined.

One of the most highly praised members of the latest cohort of Weber specialists, the American, Joshua Derman, studied at Harvard and Princeton, spent two years in Germany and Italy and now works at Hong Kong University. As such he represents the globalization of knowledge that particularly suits the "world according to Weber." As an intellectual historian Derman is keenly aware of subtle changes in terminology and conceptualizations as they shift from one culture or historical period to another. In his chapter he has taken on a favorite term among Weber's readers, *Entzauberung*, and examined its original meanings for Weber himself, and subsequent reappropriations. He argues that Weber understood the word – which Derman prefers to translate literally as "demagification" rather than following the more standard "disenchantment" – in at least two ways. When writing sympathetically about religious experience, he meant that magical thinking and ritual, originally created in order to stave off the unpredictable and undesirable, had been slowly extracted from religious dogma, as well as everyday life. But when addressing politics, however, he used the term almost in disparagement, as a key to understanding the link between beliefs and material interests, that is, self-serving ideologies. The virtue of Derman's quest is to understand such conceptual subtleties so that hermeneutic precision can be linked fruitfully with practical application of Weber's original ideas. As such he is reinvigorating notions broached some time ago (e.g., by Stephen Turner in 1984) and updating them to suit his own generation of researchers.

A young Canadian political theorist, Terry Maley situates his interpretation of Weber's role within today's environment by recapturing in abbreviated form the history of recent Weberianism. He makes creative use of Robert Antonio's "homogenization-regimentation" scheme for understanding how Weber was used by American social science, even when such use required significant misinterpretation of his key texts and ideas. Maley's quick trot through the history of Weberian adaptations will be useful for readers in need of that information, concisely expressed. From here Maley moves to the latest developments in democratic theory as informed by Weber, especially Peter Breiner's 1996 book, which helped inspire Maley's own monograph in 2011. By moving systematically through works by David Held, Jeffrey Green, Tracy Strong, Andreas Kalyvas and other political theorists, Maley shows that Weber's thoughts about modern political organization continue to thrive. This is very good news for those who still value the Weberian legacy since the measure of any theoretical perspective is the degree to which succeeding generations find in it a voice worth heeding – as Maley clearly does.

References

Bendix, Reinhard 1962 [1960]: *Max Weber: An Intellectual Portrait*. Garden City, NY: Doubleday & Co.

Campbell, Brian 2000: *The Writings of the Roman Land Surveyors: Introduction, Text, Translation and Commentary*. *Journal of Roman Studies Monograph No. 9*. London: Society for the Promotion of Roman Studies.

Carter, Jesse Benedict 1904: "Theodor Mommsen." *The Atlantic Monthly: A Magazine of Literature, Science, Art, and Politics*, Vol. 93; No. 557 (March): 373–378.

Dilcher, Gerhard 2008: "From the History of Law to Sociology; Max Weber's Engagement with the Historical School of Law." *Max Weber Studies*, Vol. 8; No. 2 (July): 163–186.

Dilke, O. A. W. 1971: *The Roman Land Surveyors: An Introduction to the Agrimensores*. New York: Barnes and Noble, Inc.

Durant, Will 1944: *Caesar and Christ: A History of Roman Civilization and of Christianity from Their Beginnings to A.D. 325* (*The Story of Civilization: Part III*). New York: Simon and Schuster.

Fowler, W. Warde 1920: "Theodor Mommsen: His Life and Work." pp. 250–268 in *Roman Essays and Interpretations*. Oxford, UK: Oxford at the Clarendon Press.

Gay, Peter and Victor G. Wexler (eds) 1975: *Historians at Work*. 3 vols. New York: Harper and Row, Publishers.

Gooch, G. P. 1913 [1959]: *History and Historians in the Nineteenth Century*. Boston, MA: Beacon Press.

———1958: Review of Alfred Heuss, *Theodor Mommsen und das 19 Jahrhundert*. *The English Historical Review*, Vol 73; No. 287 (April): 376.

Gossman, Lionel 1983: *Orpheus Philologus: Bachofen Versus Mommsen on the Study of Antiquity*. *Transactions of the American Philosophical Society*, Vol. 73; Part 5. Philadelphia, PA: The American Philosophical Society.

Grafton, Anthony 2006: "Roman Monument." *History Today* (September): 48–50.

Guilland, Antoine 1915: "Theodore Mommsen." pp. 120–170 in *Modern Germany and Her Historians*. London: Jarrold & Sons. (Reprinted by Greenwood Press, 1970.)

Harvey, P. B. 2009: Review of Max Weber, *Roman Agrarian History*. *Choice*, Vol. 46; No. 6 (February).

Haverfield, F. 1904: "Theodor Mommsen." *The English Historical Review*, Vol. 19; No. 73 (January), 80–89.

Highet, Gilbert 1949: *The Classical Tradition: Greek and Roman Influences on Western Literature*. New York: Oxford University Press.

Honigsheim, Paul 2000: "Max Weber as Historian of Agricultural and Rural Life." First pub. 1949. Reissued in *The Unknown Max Weber*. Ed. and intro. by Alan Sica. New Brunswick, NJ: Transaction Publishers.

Kain, Roger J. P. and Elizabeth Baigent 1992: *The Cadastral Map in the Service of the State; A History of Property Mapping*. Chicago: University of Chicago Press.

Käsler, Dirk 1988: *Max Weber: An Introduction to his Life and Work*. Tr. by Philippa Hurd. Chicago: University of Chicago Press.

Liddel, Peter and Polly Low 2013: *Inscriptions and Their Uses in Greek and Latin Literature*. Oxford, UK: Oxford University Press.

Love, John R. 1991: *Antiquity and Capitalism: Max Weber and the Sociological Foundations of Roman Civilization*. London: Routledge.

Mills, C. Wright 1955: "Introduction" (pp. v–ix) to William Edward Hartpole Lecky's *History of European Morals from Augustus to Charlemagne* [1869]. New York: George Braziller.

Momigliano, Arnaldo 1982a: *Essays in Ancient and Modern Historiography*. Middletown, CT: Wesleyan University Press.

———1982b: "New Paths of Classicism in the Nineteenth Century." *History and Theory*, Beiheft 21, 64pp.

———1994: *A. D. Momigliano: Studies on Modern Scholarship*. Ed. by G. W. Bowersock and T. J. Cornell. Berkeley: University of California Press.

Mommsen, Theodor 1996: *A History of Rome Under the Emperors*. London: Routledge.

Mommsen, Wolfgang 1984 [1959; 1974]: *Max Weber and German Politics, 1890–1920*. Tr. by Michael Steinberg. Chicago: University of Chicago Press.

Mueller, G. H. 1986: "Weber and Mommsen: Non-Marxist Materialism." *British Journal of Sociology*, Vol. 37; No. 1 (March): 1–20.

Nobel Prize Committee 1902: "Presentation Speech by C.D. af Wirsén." http://www.nobelprize.org/nobel_prizes/literature/laureatest/1902/press.html.

Radkau, Joachim 2009: *Max Weber: A Biography*. Tr. by Patrick Camiller. Cambridge, UK: Polity Press.

Sampson, Gareth C. 2009: Review of Max Weber, *Roman Agrarian History*. *Bryn Mawr Classical Review*, 08.42. (http:bmer.brynmawr.edu/2009/2009-08-42.html).

Scaff, Lawrence A. 1989: *Fleeing the Iron Cage: Culture, Politics, and Modernity in the Thought of Max Weber*. Berkeley, CA: University of California Press.

Sica, Alan 2004: *Max Weber: A Comprehensive Bibliography*. New Brunswick, NJ: Transaction Publishers.

Sparrow, John 1969: *Visible Words: A Study of Inscriptions In and As Books and Works of Art*. Cambridge, UK: Cambridge University Press.

Strachan-Davidson, J. L. 1901: "Mommsen's Roman Criminal Law." *The English Historical Review*, Vol. 16; No. 62 (April): 219–291.

Twain, Mark 1960 [1892]: "Mommsen, Wagner, and the Jubilees." pp. 218–219 in *Mark Twain Himself: A Pictorial Biography*, produced by Milton Meltzer. New York: Thomas Y. Crowell.

Weber, Marianne 1975 [1926]: *Max Weber: A Biography*. Tr. and ed. by Harry Zohn. New York: John Wiley-Interscience.

Weber, Max 1891: *Die römische Agrargeschichte und ihrer Bedeutung für das Staats- und Privatrecht*. Stuttgart: Ferdinand Enke Verlag. (Reprinted by P. Shippers, Amsterdam, 1962)

———1946: *From Max Weber: Essays in Sociology*. Ed. and intro. by Hans Gerth and C. Wright Mills. New York, NY: Oxford University Press.

———1986: *Die römische Agrargeschichte und ihrer Bedeutung für das Staats- und Privatrecht. Max Weber Gesamtausgabe, Abteilung I: Schriften und Reden, Band 2*. Ed. by Jürgen Deininger. Tübingen: J.C.B. Mohr (Paul Siebeck).

———2003: *A History of Commercial Partnerships in the Middle Ages*. Translated and introduced by Lutz Kaelber. Lanham, MD: Rowman and Littlefield Publishers, Inc.

———2008: *Roman Agrarian History in its Relation to Roman Public & Civil Law*. Translated and introduced by Richard I. Frank. Claremont, Calif. : Regina Books.

Whimster, Sam 2008: Review-essay on Max Weber, *Agrarrecht, Agrargeschichte, Agrarpolitik* and Max Weber, *Roman Agrarian History*. *Max Weber Studies*, Vol. 8; No. 2 (July): 249–256.

Chapter 2

WEBER'S DISSERTATION AND *HABILITATION*

Lutz Kaelber

Introduction

Except during a brief period after their publication, Max Weber's two earliest book-length studies, in 1889 and 1891, have not left much of a mark on social science, and even in Weberian scholarship they have remained largely obscure. When Reinhard Bendix published *Max Weber: An Intellectual Portrait* to introduce the scholar to an American audience, he began his chapter "Weber's Early Studies and the Definition of His Intellectual Perspective" with a discussion of Weber's agrarian studies for the *Verein für Sozialpolitik* and his work on the stock exchange. Weber's dissertation and *Habilitation* were barely mentioned in the biography section (Bendix, 1960: 1–2). Recently, as part of his over-all attempt of meshing Weber's writings with his family and personal history, Joachim Radkau termed Weber's dissertation to be about "tedious material" (*öde Materie*), an "unlucky start to his career," claiming that Weber's own youthful experiences with his large extended family provided the "key to [Weber's conceptualization of] economic history," even his understanding of the beginnings of capitalism itself (2005: 39–40). The Weber biographer is more generous in his assessment of the academic success of *Weber's Habilitation*, but in pursuing the elusive goal of characterizing its content, Radkau ultimately considers it an attempt by Weber to root his fledgling sociological understanding of history in a type of naturalism, namely, an interest in the "soil basis of human civilization" (124–128; the phrase is taken from the English translation: Radkau, 2011: 72).

Such confounding remarks and dubious characterizations have not helped generate more interest in Weber's earliest studies, but the marginal status of these two studies, which have been said "to have met little interest especially in German-speaking areas" (Dilcher, 2008: 167; for the dissertation) and to have garnished so little attention by scholars of Antiquity "as if Weber had not existed at all" (Heuss, 1965: 554; for the *Habilitation*), might also be explained by the fact that for a long time no English translations were available, which reduced the audience to readers conversant in both German and the arcane technicalities of medieval mercantile law and agrarian structures in Roman antiquity – an uncommon combination. Only now have English translations of the entire studies become available (Weber, 2003; 2010), both of which have the advantage of including translations of numerous passages in Latin and other languages in the original. Moreover, the critical editions of these studies as part of the *Max Weber Gesamtausgabe*, which have contributed immeasurably to our understanding of Weber and his work, did not appear until 1986 and 2008, respectively (Weber, 1986; 2008). In their wake, a more nuanced understanding of the contents and the implications of Max Weber's earliest studies has arguably emerged. Rather than provide a detailed exposé of their contents, I will limit my remarks to the following: 1) brief accounts of the main arguments of Weber's dissertation and *Habilitation* and of scholarly influences on them; and 2) an assessment of the "sociological elements" in his early writings. These elements, which I will call "micro-themes," include attention to the embeddedness of human action, interdependence of social spheres and the comparative method, as well as "sociogenetic explanation" and consideration of human interests, capitalism(s) in Antiquity and the Middle Ages, the ideal typical method and the pair of concepts "Vergesellschaftung – Vergemeinschaftung." Given the confines of space, it is not possible to address the impact of Weber's earliest studies on his conceptualization of the "city" (Nippel, 2000: 247–255), the entire body of his later sociology of law (Dilcher and Lepsius, 2008: 67–70), his sociology of Antiquity (Love, 1991), his later agrarian studies (Capogrossi Colognesi, 2004), or his sociology more generally (Kaelber, 2003a: 27–36).

Weber's Studies: Scholarly Contexts and Main Arguments

Given that both Weber's dissertation, entitled *Zur Geschichte der Handelsgesellschaften im Mittelalter: Nach südeuropäischen Quellen* (Weber, 1889a; technically first presented in summer 1889 in the form of a pamphlet containing the third chapter of the entire study and entitled *Entwickelung des Solidarhaftprinzips und des Sondervermögens der offenen Handelsgesellschaft aus den Haushalts- und Gewerbegemeinschaften in den italienischen Städten* [Development of the Principle of Solidary Liability and a Separate Fund of the General Partnership Originating in Household and Trade Communities in Italian Cities]; Weber 1889b), and *Habilitation*, entitled *Die römische Agrargeschichte in ihrer Bedeutung für das Staats- und Privatrecht* (Weber 1891), were in the field of law, it is not surprising that Weber credited mostly legal scholars as having trained him and shaped his thought. For his dissertation and *Habilitation*, as the relevant volume of the MWGA now has revealed (Weber, 2008: 352–356; superseding information provided in studies such as Marra, 1992), Weber submitted three different versions of his *Lebenslauf* (curriculum vitae) in 1889 (twice) and 1891. In them, he recognized professors Ernst Immanuel Becker, Otto Karlowa, Karl Heinze and Hermann Schulze at the University of Heidelberg; Rudolph Sohm, Franz Bremer and Hermann Baumgarten at the University of Strasbourg; Georg Beseler, Heinrich Dernburg, Heinrich Rudolf von Gneist, Heinrich Brunner, Ludwig Aegidi and Alfred Pernice at the University of Berlin; and Richard Dove, Karl von Bar, Ferdinand Frensdorff, Ferdinand Regelsberger and Richard Schröder at the University of Göttingen. Among the scholars whose expertise was not (primarily) in the field of law, he credited the philosopher Kuno Fischer, the economist Karl Knies and the historian Bernhard Erdmannsdörffer at the University of Heidelberg, as well as the economists Adolph Wagner and August Meitzen at the University of Berlin. That Weber studied with the latter group is an indication that his interest as a student went far beyond the narrow field of legal scholarship, but for his own studies, he engaged with a largely different group of scholars.

Leading up to his dissertation, Weber had attended a seminar by the seminal expert on commercial law, Levin Goldschmidt, whose writings spanned the gap between the distinct camps of Romanists and Germanists, as Weber's own scholarship would as well. Goldschmidt was generally disinclined to adduce distant legal-doctrinal precedents in Roman or Germanic law as proximate explanations of specific medieval commercial practices and their legal counterparts, as he, in line with the Historical School of Law, saw law as socially, culturally and economically contingent (see Dilcher, 2008). Contingency dictated a methodology that was historical and comparative, and more in line with the Germanists than the Romanists. In current sociological parlance, to use Charles Tilly's (1984) terms, Goldschmidt often preferred an individualizing and variation finding approach to an encompassing and universalizing one – a general tendency also present to a significant extent in Weber's dissertation, in regard to the study of law in some of the most advanced commercial practices in Europe in the late Middle Ages: urban trade in Italian cities. Weber compared Florence to Pisa as his main cases, but he included the analysis of many other cities and regions in his study, including Genoa, Venice and even southern France and Spain. Beyond the looming presence of Goldschmidt in Weber's dissertation, the imprint of other scholars is also clear: these include Gustav Lastig, Paul Laband, Wilhelm Endemann and Wilhelm Silberschmidt, as well as, to a lesser degree, Otto Gierke (see Dilcher and Lepsius, 2008: 30–41). The first two scholars composed compendia on the history of trading companies: Endemann on the imprint of religious doctrine on law and commercial practice and Silberschmidt on the historical roots of the commenda. The Germanist Gierke, who had been a student of Weber's teacher Beseler and next to Goldschmidt came to be an evaluator of the full version of the dissertation as it was submitted as part of Weber's *Habilitation* procedure (see Dilcher and Lepsius, 2008: 77), proposed, in line with Weber's view on the origins of the general partnership in conditions present in Langobardic–Germanic households, that much of the German law of association originated in communal practices of premodern small groups. He also was influential in emphasizing the importance of "joint hands" in Germanic law, which is a concept that Weber adopted. It is important to note, using Dilcher and Lepsius's (2008: 31) poignant assessment, that Weber's dissertation was situated within a specific and well-articulated line of research that was "in full bloom" and of (particularly) "high quality" at the precise time the dissertation was composed.

In regard to Weber's *Habilitation*, analogous to Levin Goldschmidt's role in Weber's dissertation, the historian Theodor Mommsen had a large impact. Mommsen, the doyen of Romanist scholarship, provided for Weber the substantive substratum of knowledge in his well-known and -received general studies of Roman law and history, and like Goldschmidt he was at a very advanced state in his career. Further, Mommsen and Goldschmidt shared a conviction in the sociocultural and socioeconomic situatedness of the law. Weber relied extensively on Mommsen's studies (sometimes without direct acknowledgement; see Deininger 1986b: 86), and doing so provided an obvious indication that this study (in contrast to Weber's dissertation) was associated with the Romanist camp. Even though Weber did not mention Mommsen in his CVs, he had attended Mommsen's seminar on Roman public law as a *Referendar*, at least partially, and excerpted his major study of Roman public law liberally. Their exchange and Mommsen's remarks about Weber during the oral disputation of Weber's dissertation have become somewhat legendary (Deininger, 1986a: 9, 22–4; Dilcher and Lepsius, 2008: 4–5). Rather than to the faculty of law, like Goldschmidt, however, Mommsen the historian belonged to the faculty of philosophy, as did another scholar at the University of Berlin whom Weber dedicated his *Habilitation* to and called his "revered teacher": August Meitzen. Meitzen was a statistician and economist, who apart from his publications on statistics was an expert on settlements. He combined historical with geographical studies in using land surveys as source of information to determine patterns of land ownership and their practical implications for the law, focusing on Germanic history. Weber would use Meitzen's methodological approach while extending Meitzen's agrarian studies backward in time, but in doing so Weber used the approach of another national economist, the long-dead Johann Karl Rodbertus. Though critical of Rodbertus's substantive arguments, Weber would embrace Rodbertus's approach of employing economic and fiscal considerations in the study of ancient history, including taxation and the relevance of economic interests (Deininger, 1986a: 13–24). In these regards, Weber's approach and methodology in his *Habilitation* were both more innovative but perhaps also more speculative when compared to his earlier study.

In his dissertation Weber's core interest was how major forms of economic partnership in Europe emerged, particularly the general partnership but also the limited partnership, known as the *Offene Handelsgesellschaft* and *Kommanditgesellschaft* in German law and existent in various iteration on the European continent this day (Kaelber, 2003a, 2003b; Dilcher and Lepsius, 2008; see Kaelber, 2016 for a more extensive version of the following section). Weber quickly excluded the Roman *societas* as the institution from which these partnership developed, as, in contrast to the general partnership, it had no "separate fund" distinct from the liable assets of the individual partners. Moreover, unlike the *societas*, when contracting with a third party, the general partnership's partners act "on behalf of the partnership," resulting in joint and several (solidary) liability toward creditors for debts and obligations. As a "firm," it also has a joint name under which it conducts business. In contrast to the general partnership, in a limited partnership the limited partners do not partake in the daily operation of business and the amount of their capital contribution sets a limit to their legal liability.

Predecessors to these types of modern partnerships existed, Weber argued, in the form of medieval Italian partnerships known as *commendas*, in which a sedentary investor invested capital in a business run by a partner who conducted it on behalf of the partnership. In a bilateral *commenda* both parties contributed capital to the business, whereas in a unilateral *commenda* only the sedentary partner did. After conclusion of business, the managing partner was to account for the business's successes and failures to the sedentary investor, and any profit was divided after the deduction of expenses and the original capital contribution according to the specifications in their business contract. In the bilateral *commenda*, the managing partner would typically assume some risk of financial failure, whereas in the unilateral *commenda*, the contributor of capital carried that risk of loss of capital alone.

Yet in exploring the legal underpinnings of several forms of commercial partnerships in medieval Italy, Weber rejected the notion that the limited and the general partnership had directly descended from them. Constitutive elements of liability and assumption of risk were crucially different. Weber rejected Silberschmidt's assertion that the historically older unilateral *commenda* was the original incubator of the modern limited partnership because the managing partner had no capital of his own invested and merely participated in the business as an agent of a principal, buying and selling goods in his own name on account of the latter, while assuming no risk for the loss of capital on his own. Weber further rejected Silberschmidt's argument of the modern general partnership's descent from the *societas maris* (a commercial venture at sea in the form a bilateral *commenda*), for the contributing partners did not fully assume joint liability and only traces of a legal construct of a separate fund existed, as was the case in Genoa. Yet in the partnership called *societas terrae* or *compagnia di terra* in Piacenza, some partners had unlimited liability while other partners' liability was capped at their capital contribution, and in Pisan commercial statutes concerning the *societas maris*, Weber saw evidence of the historical origins of the modern limited partnership in the form of both a separate fund and the conduct of business in the name of a firm, whereas (full) solidary liability did not exist.

Medieval Florence was the incubator of the modern general partnership: its *corpo della compagnia* constituted a separate fund representing the joint equity of a partnership, the partnership operated as a "firm," and the partners were solidarily (jointly and severally) liable for partnership debt, including debt encumbered by other partners acting on the partnership's behalf and in its name.

In contrast to these explorations of some early medieval Germanic and mostly high-to-late medieval Italian law Weber's *Habilitation* takes the reader back to ancient Roman times. Weber's overarching interest was in the transformation of soil from being jointly and communally owned, owned to becoming, at least for some time, the object of capitalist speculation and foundation of political power. The development of private property in land, Weber posited, followed a general trajectory of development that drew to a conclusion at the end of the Roman empire with the decline in commercial exchange and market production and ultimately resulted in the emergence of a system of seigneurial ownership (*Grundherrschaft*) in the Middle Ages (for more detailed treatments, see Love, 1991; Deininger, 1986a; Käsler, 1988).

Weber assumed, based on Meitzen, that a relationship could be established between the ways in which land surveys were conducted and the prevalent type of landholding and soil ownership. With Mommsen, he projected into the distant past a form of agrarian communism, in which the alienation of Roman land was scarcely if at all possible by individuals. He joined Meitzen in the – as is now known: historically untenable – assumption that this type of primordial communitarian local commune (*Flurgemeinschaft*) reflected a Germanic (egalitarian) rather than Celtic (hierarchical) social organization. According to Weber, the restrictions on land alienation were only gradually loosened but came to full fruition in the concept of the *ager privatus* as commercial property. It culminated in

> removing legal limitations on property by having individual properties registered in the public cadaster as part of the organization by centuries established

by the Servian constitutions, and also by the grant of complete freedom of contract in the Twelve Tables [after 451 BCE]. ... [It constituted] economic emancipations of land from patrimonial and collective limitations ... [and] dissolution of the common lands by dividing them into parcels to be held with full private property rights. This concept of unlimited private property rights was ... taken from what existed and applied to landed property. (Weber, 1985: 205; 2010: 79)

Weber used evocative terms to convey the main point, namely, that the creation and even "unleashing" (*Entfesselung*) of personal private property in land gave "landowners complete independence in the economic and legal disposition of their properties." In a "revolutionary transition," it made "property as marketable and liquid as possible," turning Rome into the [Western] world's preeminent "real estate exchange" (Weber, 1986: 187, 201, 206; 2010: 68, 76–77, 80; translation altered).

Apart from this transformation of the *ager privatus*, for which this legal arrangement applied to citizen colonies on Italian soil but not its provinces (its colonies), the legal status of the *ager publicus* underwent significant changes. The issue of property rights came into sharp relief when Roman imperialism and consolidation of Continental rule yielded significant gains in conquered land. This new territory was formally in the hands of the Roman state but allowed for novel forms of ownership. It allowed for the emancipation from patrimonialism, but the opportunities that arose, when "all citizens were given equal access to the public lands, in that all had equal right to use public lands for grazing and equal right to settle on them," transformed into a gift to wealthy capitalists, who came out victorious in a fierce struggle over the *ager publicus* and were able, as Weber put it, to use it as objects of speculation and economic exploitation (Weber, 1986: 216; 2010: 86). This period came to an end with a decreasing supply of slaves and an increased interest of large land owners in the economic use of their estate through the use of peasants owning labor services next to the slaves. The decline of cities and the emergence of autarchic manors signaled the transition to the Middle Ages.

Sociological Elements in Weber's Early Studies

Embeddedness of human action, interdependence of social spheres and the comparative method

In both Weber's dissertation and his *Habilitation*, the reader is able to detect sociological approaches to the study of the respective subject matter. From the onset, Weber's studies were steeped in an approach that considered law as economically and socially contingent, as well as culturally. Weber's dissertation supervisor, Goldschmidt, had moved away in his own work from a doctrinal approach to law and toward a historical, and perhaps, one might argue, even a slight sociological one. Weber echoed this approach in his dissertation. In the most general way, in his study of family business and commercial company in the Middle Ages, Weber saw the roots of the legal allocation of risk and liability in the way in which households were constituted, shifting attention away from the purely commercial and legal aspect of partnership ventures to constellations of family and kin. In doing so, he conducted a quasi-socio-logical study of household arrangements in medieval Italian cities and found particular living conditions, namely married sons and their families staying in the quarters of the sons' families of origins and continuing to work there or from there.

The main influence on Weber for his *Habilitation* was a historian, Mommsen, who took what Jürgen Deininger (1986a: 23) has called a "social historical approach" to the study of Roman agrarian history. Again, Weber was not only comfortable with this approach but mimicked it in his own writing. Here he pointed to the wide-ranging social consequences of law in shaping eco-nomic conditions as well the cultural status of entire groups of people. From the onset, Weber regarded human action as embedded in legal, cultural, economic, political and social contexts, and the various spheres were inter-dependent, in that they mutually affected one another. Weber's early studies were also expressly comparative, both synchronically and diachronically. It is therefore perhaps not an overstatement to note that in the field of legal stud-ies, Weber's approach was probably as historical-comparative as about any at the time and proceeded with an early if implicit nod to the fledgling field of sociology.

"Sociogenetic explanation" and consideration of human interests

One could also argue that early on Weber implicitly used a sociological con-cept for which another sociologist was recognized half a century later. Norbert Elias's "figurations of networks" provided what Elias termed a "sociogenetic explanation" of how larger social structures derive from particular associa-tions of people that change over time (Elias, 1986; 2000). Whereas Elias stud-ied court societies and civilizational habits among the nobility of the sixteenth and seventeenth centuries, Weber went back much further. In his dissertation, Weber discussed the early medieval Germanic Lombard laws, and unlike Elias he did not focus on patterns of status reproduction and consumption but on the side of production among the nascent urban bourgeoisie. Weber noted how essentially economic (not reproductive) conditions, namely, the necessity to be able to establish in what way different units within a larger household-based kin group can encumber household assets and increase (or decrease) their value through economic transactions with third parties, was reflected in the law.

In his *Habilitation*, he made several remarks in regard to *interests* in social relationships, to which he had not turned his attention before in his dissertation. Weber's remarks relate to the exercise of political power on the basis of class interest. Weber asked, in regard to colonial conquest, "what were the social classes and the economic interest groups which provided the political driving force behind the territorial expansion" (Weber, 1986: 101–2; 2010: 5)? And was the change from the exploitation to maritime power to increase territories "due to the conscious decisions of particular interest groups" (Weber, 1986: 102; 2010: 5)? While Weber did not attempt to answer this question directly, he alluded to the struggle over the spoils of newly available territory as "class conflict," rooted in *material interests* (political as well as economic), over control of the *ager publicus*. The result of this class struggle was the victory of the landed classes, the latifundists, who benefited from the privatization of this land and its employment for individual gain. Weber characterized this process as one by which different political parties struggled over a political goal and control over government; a struggle whose prize was the shaping of property law and attaining economic gain and social privilege: "Never in any great state has control of the government been so directly connected with financial profit" (Weber, 1986: 102; 2010: 5). Attention to personal economic and political interests as the basis of class and class interest (see similarly Käsler, 1988: 31), class as the basis of political action and politics as class struggle are topics that clearly shine through sections of Weber's *Habilitation*.

Capitalism(s)

In writing about class struggle in his *Habilitation*, Weber made references to capitalist exploitation of land. Capitalism as a concept has been a main staple of scholarship on Weber addressing where, when and how he discussed it (e.g., Mommsen, 1974; Riesebrodt, 1985; Schluchter, 1980; Swedberg, 2003). The main foil on which Weber presented other forms of capitalism was arguably *modern rational* capitalism, predominantly in *The Protestant Ethic, Economy and Society* and his lectures on "General Economic History," from which he developed a list of distinguishing characteristics that, Weberian scholars generally agree, can be divided into three main categories: the modern capitalist enterprise, the modern capitalist economic order and the modern capitalist spirit (Schluchter, 1996: 200; see also Kaelber, 2003a: 28–29; Schluchter, 2011: 19–24).

The first category, the modern capitalist enterprise, is reflected in continuous profit-seeking private enterprises, capital accounting and bookkeeping
and separation of household and business. Weber's *Habilitation* is mum about
the presence of these factors, and, in fact, in later writings, Weber strongly
argued that they were absent in Antiquity (Love, 1991). The same cannot be
said about Weber's dissertation. The types of partnerships Weber explored,
at least in their late medieval, post-*commenda* forms, were commercial enterprises, continuously oriented toward profit. This arrangement presumed not
only (once the size and scope of the enterprise had required it) a physical
separation between residence, workshop and firm but also, and more importantly, a legal separation between private wealth and the assets of the company. Capital accounting distinguished between such business assets and the
personal assets of the partners or owners, and this legal and financial division
in assets reflected an arrangement of risk and liability in which liability was
shared jointly among partners but limited to a partnership's capital assets.
While Weber did not discuss these conditions expressly in the context of a
thematization of capitalism in his dissertation, his early explorations of these
issues did therefore foreshadow his reflections in his mature sociological writings in regard to this category (see further Kaelber, 2016).

Concerning the second category, the modern capitalist order, Weber assumed
for Roman antiquity the presence of political capitalism – an important term
in this context, denoting the exploitation of market-based opportunities on the
basis of state-provided privileges or other advantages skewing the competition
(see Love, 1991; on the analytical distinction, Kaelber, 2005: 141–142); for
a modern application, Garcelon, 2005). On the basis of this presupposition,
and accepting the term "capitalist" that Mommsen and Meitzen had used to
characterize the Roman economy in it most flourishing times, he addressed
capitalism only in the context of "agrarian capitalism," to which he even dedicated a section. Weber noted the availability of the *ager publicus* "available for
settlement and capitalist exploitation" (Weber, 1986: 101; 2010: 5) and free
competition among large capitalists that helped usher in "unfettered agrarian capitalism never before heard of in history" (Weber 1986: 216; 2010: 86;
translation altered). In his dissertation, Weber eschewed the use of the term
"capitalist" in the sense of the term's connotation of a proto-modern capitalist
economic order, almost entirely. When the term "capitalist" was used, it regularly referred to the provider of capital to a commercial venture or partnership. Just as Weber did not make his *Habilitation* a study of or about agrarian
capitalism, as Jürgen Deininger correctly emphasized (1986a: 25), he did not
tie the study of medieval commercial partnerships in the flowering economic
landscapes of late medieval Italy to a conceptualization of the emergence of
modern capitalism.

The same considerations apply to the third, and perhaps most debated, category, the modern capitalist spirit. Weber, who later would famously dispute Werner Sombart's (1913) and Lujo Brentano's (1916: 132–135) assertions of the presence of a capitalist spirit before the period under consideration in the *Protestant Ethic* (see also Schluchter, 2011: 24–36), did not address the "spirit" of enterprise in his dissertation – even though the nature of his investigations, had those not been confined to a study of law, very much suggested such an analysis per se. In his *Habilitation*, he did use the actual term "capitalist spirit" (*kapitalistischer Geist*) once, namely, in reference to the law providing for the transfer for public lands into private hands in the Roman province of Africa (Weber, 1986: 239; 2010: 101; translation altered), but it denoted merely the facilitation of merchantability of land.

Ideal-typical method

While this analysis suggests that the concept of capitalism in its distinctive forms (modern, political, agrarian, craft-based, etc.) was not yet developed in Weber's early studies, two scholars have independently made the claim that roots of the ideal typical methods can be detected in them, one for his dissertation, and the other one for his *Habilitation*. Gerhard Dilcher, the editor of the critical edition of Weber's dissertation, argued that

> Weber's paramount methodological-theoretical instrument of analysis, the ideal type, is prefigured in his first major writing and his years of studies in the Historical School of Law. For Weber the ideal type ...is a scientist's conceptual construct serving to relate a variety of empirical phenomena to a research question and to make an analytic determination of their manifold manifestations. In his dissertation he used the characteristics of the fully developed modern general partnership in a very similar manner as the core criterion, to establish a measure of development along which to line up late ancient and early medieval creations that did not yet correspond to this type, and categorically to distinguish the partnership of "joint hands" from a business association merely for the purpose of a limited partner providing capital. He pursues a combination of isolating individual points of view and synthesized generalization, corresponding to the methodology used by the Pandectists following Savigny's thought in systems and, based on their own model, by the Germanists in German private law. (Dilcher, 2008: 187)

The editor of the critical edition of Weber's *Habilitation*, Jürgen Deininger, has made the same claim for his part (1986a: 51–52; also 2005: 268–270), echoing an argument made earlier by sociologist Dirk Käsler, who noted that

> Already [in his *Habilitation*] …Weber had mentioned a concept, which he was later to make into a centrally important element of his methodological delibera-tions. In explaining the relations of community property and private property, Weber established the rather considerable difference in the respective regions …, in order to assert "If one wants to formulate the tendencies of the develop-ment thus in ideal pictures [*Idealbildern*], always with the proviso that they are just tendencies … and that they will perhaps never appear at all in full purity. …" We can already discern the crude outline of the ideal-typical procedure. (Käsler, 1988: 32; cf. Deininger, 1986a: 51–52; also Deininger 2005: 268–270; the original passages appear in Weber, 1986: 340; 2010: 165; translation altered)

A bit of caution regarding the veracity of these assertions seems to be in order. For one, one of the major studies that was to influence Weber's thought on methodology and concept formation, *Die Grenzen der naturwissenschaftlichen Begriffsbildung*, by Heinrich Rickert (a student of Wilhelm Windelband), did not appear in full until 1902 (for the first three chapters, until 1896), and there is no evidence of a significant influence of Southwestern neo-Kantianism on Weber so early in his career. Consistent with this observation, there is little in Weber's dissertation that indicates the use of concepts as a synthetic con-struct. Weber's main concepts were not presented in the form of an analytical accentuation of certain features and one-sided abstractions that served as a heuristic or expository tool for the study of history, to use the characteriza-tion of the "ideal type" in Weber's famed 1904 essay (Weber, 1904; 2012a). After all, this was a study intended to establish the scholarly credentials of a young man under the tutelage of the Germany's most eminent professor of commercial law with no known ties or affinity to the Southwest German school informed by Windelband and Rickert. Overall, it is my impression that Weber knew better than to "accentuate" certain historical features to an extent that they would assume the character of one-sided exaggerations and a utopian syntheses of concrete individual phenomena. In his *Habilitation*, particularly in the early parts, Weber's writings were demonstrably much more speculative and often inferred legal changes from social and economic conditions, so much so that Deininger (1986a: 28) termed them reliant "on a series of often unverified legal-historical and agrarian-historical hypotheses." The problem was that, due to the lack of available information in the existing documents and scholarship at the time, many of these hypotheses were not only unverified but almost unverifiable. For reasons of historical necessity, not methodological procedure, Weber himself had to admit to the "constructed character" of the first three of the four chapters, for which "almost invari-ably the method of reasoning from consequences has been used" (Weber, 1986: 98, 101; 2010: 2, 4; translation altered). This was the real reason for

Weber's ample use of hypotheses and the term "developmental tendencies" (*Entwicklungstendenzen*).

Vergemeinschaftung-Vergesellschaftung

The use of the term "Vergesellschaftung" in scholarly publications had become, perhaps contrary to expectation today, not entirely uncommon by the early 1890s. Research in an archival database of German texts reveals that Theodor Mommsen himself used it in his *Roman History* in 1856; as did Karl Marx in *Capital* in 1867; Georg Simmel in *On Social Differentiation* in 1890; and Gustav Schmoller and Karl Bücher in their books on the economy in 1893 (see Berlin-Brandenburgische Akademie der Wissenschaften, 2014a). Even though he did not use this term at the time, Ferdinand Tönnies had most directly become associated with the terms *Gemeinschaft* and *Gesellschaft* by virtue of having published his main work using these terms in 1887, which, according to Alan Sica (2004: 42), was a book that had "perhaps the most immediately recognizable title of any book published by a sociologist in the nineteenth century."

Traditionally the scholarly analysis of Weber's use of the concept of "Vergesellschaftung" has focused on his mature scholarship, particularly the contrast he drew between "Vergesellschaftung" as associative form of relationship and the associated term "Gesellschaftshandeln" (action based on and oriented toward a formal rule or order), and "Vergemeinschaftung" as communal relationship and "Gemeinschaftshandeln" (communal action) (see Schluchter, 2000: 183 n. 14; Orihara, 2000: 216; Swedberg, 2005: 11–2, 246–248; but see Lichtblau, 2011). While the terms "Vergesellschaftung" and "Vergemeinschaftung" seem to have appeared together for the first time in German language in a translation of the writings of the Swedish scientist Emanuel Schwedenborg in 1776 (see Berlin-Brandenburgische Akademie der Wissenschaften, 2014b), Weber did not use the term "Vergemeinschaftung," it appears, until 1913 in his essay "On Some Categories of Interpretive Sociology" (Weber, 1913; 2012).

However, Weber did use the term "Gemeinschaft" extensively in both of his early studies, and while the term "Vergesellschaftung" does not appear in his *Habilitation*, the situation is different for his dissertation, as scholars have discovered over the past decade (Kaelber, 2003a: 25, 34; Lichtblau, 2005: 83; Kaelber, 2008; Dilcher, 2008: 185–186). The task of linking Weber's early use of the term "Vergesellschaftung" to its use(s) in the later stage of his career is a larger one than can be accomplished here, but how Weber embraced the term "Vergesellschaftung" in his dissertation, and avoided using this term – as well as the term "Gesellschaft" – in his *Habilitation*, is illuminating in itself.

In his magnum opus Tönnies (2001: 228) referred to family life in kin groups as "the general basis of life in the Gemeinschaft" subsiding in village and town life, and Weber adopted this view as a historical starting point (though not of his inquiries, which for the most part did not proceed chronologically) in both his *Habilitation* and in his dissertation, but quite differently so. In his *Habilitation*, Weber traced the development of private and public lands, and the privatization of the latter, for commercial use from an original communitarian condition in ancient Rome in which land was neither privately held nor a market commodity. His characterization of Roman society was, depending on the historical period, in reference to an "agrarian community" (*agrarische Gemeinschaft*) (Weber, 1986: 97, 173; 2010: 1, 58), to one that acquired new land in conquest as a "community" (1986: 160 n. 38; 2010: 187 n. 38), and in the later periods, when landed estates managed land for profit, to reliance on the labor of a "community" of *coloni* (peasants owning labor service and gradually turning into serfs) (1986: 324 n. 60; 2010: 229 n. 60), and to having destroyed the local patriotism of its "urban communities" (*städtische Gemeinschaften*) (1986: 352; 2010: 172; translation altered). Despite the very advanced commercialization of agriculture emphasized by Weber, he never once in the entire book used the terms "Gesellschaft" or "gesellschaftlich" in the context of Rome – which, in fact, to him appears to have been a society without "Gesellschaft," retaining its character as a "Gemeinschaft."

Weber's depiction of Roman society was therefore without a finding of processes of "Vergesellschaftung," in utmost contrast to processes he had described and analyzed in medieval cities in his dissertation. Weber used the term in his *History of Commercial Partnership* exactly five times. As he put it in his beginning chapter, "Essentially, our question is, from which of the different relations of sociation (*Vergesellschaftungsverhältnisse*) did the principles of today's general partnership derive?" (Weber, 2008: 156; 2003: 60). To this end, Weber analyzed family households: "the family is primarily a natural 'community of *production*' (*Produktionsgemeinschaft*), not, as it appears to be the rule to us, a mere 'community of consumption' (*Konsumtionsgemeinschaft*). In Italian cities especially it served as the foundation of more extensive forms of sociation (*Vergesellschaftung*)" (2008: 194; 2003: 88). One of the communities of production was the association of craftsmen, Weber noted, as "commercial labor was at first a matter of the crafts. Hence, it is here that we can find the beginnings of the formation of partnerships. At first there was little need for, and possibility of, either the creation of joint funds through the aggregation of capital or sociation (*Vergesellschaftung*) on the basis of the unilateral *commenda*" (2008: 202; 2003: 92; translation altered). In reference to a book by his academic teacher Heinrich Brunner, Weber stated that the "sociation (*Vergesellschaftung*) of relatives for commercial purposes" (2008: 208 n. 72; 2003: 95 n. 29) had existed as early as in Langobardian documents, and in the very last paragraph of the book, summarizing his findings, he concluded that the difference between the general partnership and the limited partnership "lies in the legal nature of sociation (*Vergesellschaftung*)" (2008: 332; 2003: 181).

In short, Weber does not see familial or kinship associations as the foundation of a household but rather joint residence and acquisitive activity (see Kaelber, 2003a: 25; Kaelber, 2016 for earlier remarks on the following). The formalization of household relations is pressing when they extend beyond kin, but particularly when commercial acquisition is essential to the household, as some income or expenses are joint, while others are personal. This "accounting" is a motor of *Vergesellschaftung*. As families turn to urban profit-seeking craft production, continuous profit-seeking partnerships in the craft sector replace family associations as the locus of enterprise, and the legal concept of limiting liability to those debts that were incurred on the account of the partnership spreads: that is, only debts and obligations incurred in the name of the partnership, or for the firm, make the partners liable. This notion of the operation of a continuous commercial enterprise with its own name, the presence of a firm and the practice of executing contracts in its name incurring liability for its partners, then become applicable to commercial enterprises that focused not on production, as the craft households did, but on trade. Urban profit-seeking craft production as "communities of labor," not rent-seeking by speculation and commercial trade in land as in Rome, was thus the nucleus of a legal development that would inform modern commercial law. While Roman relations remained based on *Gemeinschaft*, in medieval Italy these relations had evolved into formal sociation on a contractual basis. The distinction between joint (business) and personal assets lent itself to treating business assets as a separate fund, held liable for all debts of the association and its members. Weber's analysis of a broad range of documents shows that a household's creditworthiness related to a large extent to legal stipulations that were triggered in the case of bankruptcy, namely, solidary liability, among members of a household that forms a unit of production, and no longer solely rests on kinship. As family associations were replaced by continuous profit-seeking partnerships in the course of capitalist development in medieval Italy, there was a tendency to limit solidary liability to debts incurred on the account, and in the name, of the partnership. For Weber, this legal condition then spilled over from commercial craft associations to commercial partnership of trade. Law and commercial practice interacted and mutually informed each other (see Kaelber, 2003a: 25–27). *Vergesellschaftung* of a near-modern type had arrived.

References

Bendix, Reinhard. 1960. *Max Weber: An Intellectual Portrait*. Garden City, NY: Doubleday.

Berlin-Brandenburgische Akademie der Wissenschaften. 2014a. "Deutsches Textarchiv." (Search term: "Vergesellschaftung"). Online: http://www.deutschestextarchiv.de/ (accessed 3 March 2014).

————2014b. "Deutsches Textarchiv." (Search terms: "Vergemeinschaftung" and "Vergesellschaftung"). Online: http://www.deutschestextarchiv.de/ (accessed 3 March 2014).

Brentano, Lujo. 1916. *Die Anfänge des modernen Kapitalismus*. Munich: Verlag der Akademie der Wissenschaften.

Capogrossi Colognesi, Luigi. 2004. *Max Weber und die Wirtschaft der Antike*, translated by Brigitte Szabó-Bechstein. Göttingen: Vandenhoeck & Ruprecht.

Deininger, Jürgen. 1986a. "Einleitung." In Max Weber, *Die römische Agrargeschichte in ihrer Bedeutung für das Staats- und Privatrecht* (Max Weber Gesamtausgabe I/2), pp. 1–54, edited by Jürgen Deininger. Tübingen: Mohr.

————1986b. "Editorischer Bericht." In Max Weber, *Die römische Agrargeschichte in ihrer Bedeutung für das Staats- und Privatrecht* (Max Weber Gesamtausgabe I/2), pp. 55–90, edited by Jürgen Deininger. Tübingen: Mohr.

————2005. "Zweierlei Geschichte des Altertums: Max Weber und Theodor Mommsen." In *Theodor Mommsen: Wissenschaft und Politik im 19. Jahrhundert*, pp. 259–81, edited by Alexander Demandt, Andreas Goltz, and Heinrich Schlange-Schöninge. Berlin: de Gruyter.

Dilcher, Gerhard. 2008. "From the History of Law to Sociology: Max Weber's Engagement with the Historical School of Law." *Max Weber Studies* 8, no. 1: 165–88.

————and Susanne Lepsius. 2008. "Einleitung." In Max Weber, *Zur Geschichte der Handelsgesellschaften im Mittelalter: Schriften 1889–1994* (Max Weber Gesamtausgabe I/1), pp. 1–97, edited by Gerhard Dilcher and Susanne Lepsius. Mohr: Tübingen.

Elias, Norbert. 1983. *The Court Society*, translated by Edmund Jephcott. New York, NY: Pantheon.

————2000. *The Civilizing Process: Sociogenetic and Psychogenetic Investigations*, edited by Eric Dunning, Johan Goudsblom, and Stephen Mennell; translated by Edmund Jephcott. Revised edition. Oxford: Blackwell.

Garcelon, Marc. 2005. *Revolutionary Passage: From Soviet to Post-Soviet Russia, 1985–2000*. Philadelphia, PA: Temple University Press.

Heuss, Alfred. 1965. "Max Webers Bedeutung für die Geschichte des griechisch-römischen Altertums." *Historische Zeitschrift* 201, no. 3: 529–56.

Kaelber, Lutz 2003a. "Introduction: Max Weber's Dissertation in the Context of His Early Life and Career." In Max Weber, *The History of Commercial Partnerships in the Middle Ages*, pp. 1–47, translated by Lutz Kaelber. Lanham, MD: Rowman and Littlefield.

————2003b. "Max Weber's Dissertation." *History of the Human Sciences* 16, no. 2: 27–56.

————2005. "Rational Capitalism, Traditionalism, and Adventure Capitalism: New Research on the Weber Thesis." In *The Protestant Ethic Turns 100: Essays on the Centenary of the Weber Thesis*, pp. 139–163, edited by William H. Swatos and Lutz Kaelber. Boulder, CO: Paradigm Publishers.

————2008. "*Vergesellschaftung* and *Berufsmenschentum*: Max Weber on Religion and Rationalism in the Middle Ages." In *Max Weber Matters*, pp. 191–204, edited by David

A. Chalcraft, Fanon Howell, Marisol Lopez Menendez, and Hector Vera. Aldershot, VT: Ashgate.

———2016. "Max Weber's Dissertation: An Analysis (and a Comparison to his *Habilitation*)." In *The Foundation of the Juridico-Political: Concept Formation in Kelsen and Weber*, pp. 207–25, edited by Ian Bryan, Peter Langford, and John McGarry. London: Routledge.

Käsler, Dirk. 1988. *Max Weber: An Introduction to His Life and Work*, translated by Philippa Hurd. Cambridge: Polity Press.

Lichtblau, Klaus. 2005. "Von der 'Gesellschaft' zur 'Vergesellschaftung': Zur deutschen Tradition des Gesellschaftsbegriffs." In *Weltgesellschaft: Theoretische Zugänge und empirische Problemlagen*, pp. 68–88, edited by Bettina Heintz, Richard Münch, and Hartmann Tyrell. Stuttgart: Lucius & Lucius.

———2011. "*Vergemeinschaftung* und *Vergesellschaftung* in Max Weber: A Reconstruction of His Linguistic Usage," translated by Keith Tribe. *History of European Ideas* 37: 454–65.

Love, John R. 1991. *Antiquity and Capitalism: Max Weber and the Sociological Foundations of Roman Civilization*. London: Routledge.

Mommsen, Wolfgang. 1974. "An Alternative to Marx: Dynamic Capitalism Instead of Bureaucratic Socialism." In his *The Age of Bureaucracy: Perspectives on the Political Sociology of Max Weber*, pp. 47–71. Oxford: Blackwell.

Nippel, Wilfred. 2000. "From Agrarian History to Cross-Cultural Comparisons: Weber on Greco-Roman Antiquity." In *The Cambridge Companion to Weber*, pp. 240–55, edited by Stephen Turner. Cambridge: Cambridge University Press.

Marra, Realino. 1992. *Dalla comunità al diritto moderno: La formazione giuridica di Max Weber, 1882–1889*. Turin: G. Giappichelli.

Orihara, Hiroshi. 2000. "Max Webers Beitrag zum Grundriss der Sozialökonomik: Das Vortragsmanuskript als integriertes Ganzes." In Wolfgang Schluchter, *Individualismus, Verantwortungsethik und Vielfalt*, pp. 211–225. Weilerswist: Velbrück.

Radkau, Joachim. 2005. *Max Weber: Die Leidenschaft des Denkens*. Munich: Hanser.

———2011. *Max Weber: A Biography*, translated by Patrick Camiller. Cambridge: Polity Press.

Rickert, Heinrich. 1902. *Die Grenzen der naturwissenschaftlichen Begriffsbildung: Eine logische Einleitung in die historischen Wissenschaften*. Tübingen: Mohr.

Riesebrodt, Martin. 1985. "Vom Patriarchalismus zum Kapitalismus: Max Webers Analyse der Transformation der ostelbischen Agrarverhältnisse im Kontext zeitgenössischer Theorien." *Kölner Zeitschrift für Soziologie und Sozialpsychologie* 37, no. 3: 546–567.

Schluchter, Wolfgang. 1980. "Der autoritär verfasste Kapitalismus: Max Webers Kritik am Kaiserreich." In his *Rationalismus der Weltbeherrschung*, pp. 134–169. Frankfurt: Suhrkamp.

———1996. *Paradoxes of Modernity: Culture and Conduct in the Theory of Max Weber*, translated by Neil Solomon. Stanford, CA: Stanford University Press.

———2000. "Vorbemerkung: Der Kategorienaufsatz als Schlüssel." In his *Individualismus, Verantwortungsethik und Vielfalt*, pp. 179–189. Weilerswist: Velbrück.

———2011. "Einleitung." In Max Weber, *Abriss der universalen Sozial- und Wirtschaftsgeschichte: Mit- und Nachschriften 1919/20* (Max Weber Gesamtausgabe III/6), pp. 1–45, edited by Wolfgang Schluchter. Tübingen: Mohr.

Sica, Alan. 2004. *Max Weber and the New Century*. New Brunswick, NJ: Transaction Books.

Sombart, Werner. 1913. *Der Bourgeois: Zur Geistesgeschichte des modernen Wirtschaftsmenschen*. Munich: Duncker & Humblot.

Swedberg, Richard. 2003. "The Economic Sociology of Capitalism: Weber and Schumpeter." *Journal of Classical Sociology* 2, no. 3: 227–256.

———2005. *The Max Weber Dictionary: Key Words and Central Concepts*. Stanford, CA: Stanford University Press.

Tilly, Charles. 1984. *Big Structures, Large Processes, Huge Comparisons*. New York, NY: Russell Sage Foundation.

Tönnies, Ferdinand. 2001. *Community and Society: Gemeinschaft und Gesellschaft*, edited and translated by C. P. Loomis. Mineola, NY: Dover Publications.

Weber, Max. 1889a. *Zur Geschichte der Handelsgesellschaften im Mittelalter: Nach südeuropäischen Quellen*. Stuttgart: Enke.

———1889b. *Entwickelung des Solidarhaftprinzips und des Sondervermögens der offenen Handelsgesellschaft aus den Haushalts- und Gewerbegemeinschaften in den italienischen Städten*. Stuttgart: Kröner.

———1891. *Die römische Agrargeschichte in ihrer Bedeutung für das Staats- und Privatrecht*. Stuttgart: Enke.

———1904. "Die 'Objektivität' sozialwissenschaftlicher und sozialpolitischer Erkenntnis." *Archiv für Sozialwissenschaft und Sozialpolitik* 19, no. 1: 22–87.

———1913. "Über einige Kategorien der verstehenden Soziologie." *Logos* 4, no. 3: 253–294.

———1986. *Die römische Agrargeschichte in ihrer Bedeutung für das Staats- und Privatrecht* (Max Weber Gesamtausgabe I/2), edited by Jürgen Deininger. Tübingen: Mohr.

———2003. *The History of Commercial Partnerships in the Middle Ages*, translated by Lutz Kaelber. Lanham, MD: Rowman and Littlefield.

———2008. *Zur Geschichte der Handelsgesellschaften im Mittelalter: Schriften 1889–1994* (Max Weber Gesamtausgabe I/1), edited by Gerhard Dilcher and Susanne Lepsius. Mohr: Tübingen.

———2010. *Roman Agrarian History: The Political Economy of Ancient Rome*, translated by R. I. Frank. Revised edition. Claremont, CA: Regina.

———2012a. "The 'Objectivity' of Knowledge in Social Science and Social Policy." In *Max Weber: Collected Methodological Writings*, pp. 100–138, edited by Hans H. Bruun and Sam Whimster; translated by Hans H. Bruun. New York, NY: Routledge.

———2012b. "On Some Categories of Interpretive Sociology." In *Max Weber: Collected Methodological Writings*, pp. 273–301, edited by Hans H. Bruun and Sam Whimster; translated by Hans H. Bruun. New York, NY: Routledge.

Chapter 3

MAX WEBER AND THE "AGRARIAN CRISIS" 1892–1902

Christopher Adair-Toteff

Introduction

Max Weber published the first installment of the "Protestant Ethic and the Spirit of Capitalism" in 1904 and by then he was 40 years old. While it was primarily this work that made Weber famous, he was already a well-known and well-respected figure. It was neither because of his work on modern capitalism nor on his writings on the importance of rationalism; rather, it was because of his work on agrarian history. He began the last decade of the nineteenth century as a jurist, but he ended it as one of the leading authorities on Germany's agrarian history (Aldenhoff-Hübinger, 2008: 1–2). While Weber was interested in agricultural history, he was more concerned with what was referred to as the "agrarian crisis" (Riesebrodt, 1984a: 15). This topic may seem to be of limited interest, but it should not be regarded as such. Instead, Weber's work on the agrarian crisis is important for several reasons: first, it was during this period that Germany was undergoing considerable economic, political and social changes. During the second half of the nineteenth century, Germany was undergoing a massive transformation in the agricultural regions. The introduction of machinery and other improvements in farming meant that the need for agrarian workers was being fundamentally altered. Many people left the land and many others were replaced by seasonal workers. The old patriarchal society was being supplanted by a modern industrial economy. In addition, Germany was moving from being a major exporter of grain to a major importer – North America and Russia were undercutting the German prices, prompting a further rethinking of Germany's role in the world. While many people were well aware of these changes, Weber was one of the most acute observers of them (Tribe, 1989c: 85). Second, Weber was one of the best of the best political minds so he was well positioned to formulate political and social solutions to Germany's problems. Third, while the agrarian crisis affected Germany at the end of the nineteenth century, many of its causes can be attributed to the tendency of human beings to act in certain ways; thus, Weber's account of the agrarian crisis and his various solutions to it are not only of historical interest. As with much of Weber's work, his writings on the agrarian crisis continue to have current relevance. Finally, Weber's work on the agrarian crisis is helpful for understanding many of his later writings, but it is indispensible for understanding his famous "Protestant Ethic."

The agrarian crisis was the crisis that affected the agricultural regions of much of Germany in the last three decades of the nineteenth century. The crisis was particularly acute in the area east of the Elbe River because of several interconnected reasons. Agriculture in the region was no longer financially feasible primarily because its agricultural practices were outdated. In addition, governmental policies were no longer viable. As a result of these and other problems many people left the region in the search for better lives. Politicians and scholars had grappled with the problems which had led to the agrarian crisis, but without any real success. By 1890, conditions had worsened, so the agrarian crisis drew even greater attention (Tribe, 1989c: 92).

Max Weber devoted most of his work in the 1890s to the examination of the agrarian crisis and to offering political answers to it (Mommsen and Aldenhoff, 1993: 1–3). In recognition of Weber's contributions to the agrarian question, Freiburg University offered him a full professorship. This may not seem remarkable, except that at age 29 Weber was rather young for such an appointment. Moreover, he had been trained in law and the chair that they offered him was in national economics (Mommsen, 1974a: 25). But, the university recognized his recent achievements and it recognized the probability of future successes. Weber may not have been successful in all respects regarding the agrarian crisis; but, he was highly successful in bringing about significant changes to the ways in which scholars and politicians approached the agrarian issues. Like many Germans, Weber acknowledged that laissez-faire economics were ill-suited to Germany, but he also recognized that the governmental interference was also failing. Furthermore, he knew that the scholarly guidance from the educated elites was not helping. As Lawrence Scaff pointed out, Weber was one of the few scholars who could write convincingly on both the scholarly and the political aspects of these questions. Scaff suggested that Weber provided a "new analytical language" to investigate the agrarian problems. Finally, he observed that Weber delineated the political and scientific limits of any investigations into them (Scaff, 1989: 23). Critics may be inclined to offer two objections to an examination of Weber and the agrarian questions: these are early, if not immature, works, and they are of interest only to historians. These possible objections are without much merit. Weber may have been young at the time and his discussions of the agrarian questions may be rooted in historical contexts; however, as Dirk Kaesler has observed, only by understanding Weber's agrarian studies can one sufficiently appreciate Weber's Inaugural Lecture at Freiburg (Kaesler, 1998: 74). I would add that only by understanding those studies can one comprehend "The Protestant Ethic and the Spirit of Capitalism" (Adair-Toteff, 2015). The agrarian studies are also important because it was during this time that Weber first formulated some of his scholarly methods and developed his political convictions. The scientific and political foundations that he developed in the 1890s continued to dominate his thinking until the end of his life, and they continue to fascinate us today.

The choice to limit this discussion to the years 1892 and 1902 was not arbitrary. The beginning year was easily identified by virtue of Weber starting to work on the agrarian crisis. It is also the year that Wolfgang Mommsen and Rita Aldenhoff used in their valuable introduction to the volume devoted to the "Landarbeiterfrage" in the *Max Weber Gesamtausgabe* (Mommsen and Aldenhoff, 1993: 1). The ending year is not so easily identifiable. On the one hand, most scholars know that Weber had a breakdown in 1898; whether that was caused by his fight with his father and his father's subsequent death is beside the point here. What is, is that some scholars believe that Weber was so incapacitated that he could not work. While there is some truth to this, Weber was able occasionally to work, both by counseling students and former students and by publishing prefatory remarks to a number of his students' writings (Kaesler, 1998: 274–5). Finally, Weber marked his return to better (but never again good) health in 1903 by writing "Roscher und Knies und die logischen Probleme der historischen Nationalökonomie." This lengthy essay was followed by further methodological ones and then, of course, by "The Protestant Ethic and the Spirit of Capitalism."

The Prussian Agrarian Crisis and the Verein für Socialpolitik

We tend to think of German unification occurring in 1990, just after the fall of the Berlin Wall. What we do not tend to think about is that Germany is a relatively new nation, dating back to 1871. One can think of the time between 1866 and 1879 as an "incubation period," that is, the time leading up to the founding of the German Reich in January 1871 and the successive years in which new laws were introduced, new political battles were fought and a new order instituted (Wehler, 1980: 14). To put this into another and more concrete perspective, the Reich did not exist when Max Weber was born in April 1864. In 1871 he was six years old, and in 1879, he was a fifteen-year-old reading

Cicero's letters and Treitschke's history of nineteenth-century Germany (see Weber, 1936: 25–9). When he was twenty-four, he wrote his dissertation, and in 1894 he was twenty-nine when he was appointed professor at Freiburg; in contrast, the German Reich was only twenty-two years old. In light of this, it is not too much of an exaggeration to say that Weber and the Reich "grew up together."

Prior to 1871 Germany was not a nation, but was a collection of numerous principalities. While many of these principalities were rather small, a few like Bavaria (Bayern) were large. The largest and most important of all was Prussia ("*Preußen*"). And, the most important person in Germany was the arch-Prussian, military genius, the Junker Bismarck. Thomas Nipperdey began the second volume of his history of Germany with the words: "In the beginning was Bismarck." ("Am Anfang war Bismarck") (Nipperdey, 1998b: 34, 11). Nipperdey was not intending to be flippant; he was simply stating the fact that Bismarck was responsible for Germany. It was Bismarck who had defeated the French, annexed five northern areas and ensured that Austria would never again be the great power that it had been. It was Bismarck, the Prussian reactionary, who determined that Germany would become a great power, and it was he who ensured the founding of modern Germany. The next task after unification that Bismarck faced was how to modernize Germany (Nipperdey, 1998b: 359). If Germany was to compete on the world stage, then its economy would need to shed its feudal chains and move into the industrial age. Unfortunately, the group that had the most power to ensure this transition was the same group which was most resistant to it – the Junkers.

The Junkers were the dominant social, political and economic class in certain regions of Prussia. Although Heinrich von Treitschke is best known for his massive five-volume history of Germany in the nineteenth century (although it ends in 1848), he wrote a smaller but very informative work about the Prussian Order. It is primarily a history, but in it he details the principles and the characteristics that the Prussians possessed and still possess. Treitschke opines that the Prussian Order was so successful and so respected for so long because the Prussians were hard-working, militaristic,and authoritarian (Treitschke, 1908: 51, 85; Puhle, 1980: 17). They also believed in freedom, but this freedom was not anarchy, because they lived by "rules, laws, and customs" ("*Regeln, Gesetze und Gewohnheiten*") (Treitschke, 1908: 85, 96, 130). They were bureaucratic, disciplined and professional, and they were interested in modernization (Puhle, 1980: 19, 22, 24–5). They were also very paternalistic, traditional and conservative (31–3). Unfortunately, many of these characteristics that made the Junkers so powerful also led to their downfall. Their domination lasted for centuries, but by the early part of the nineteenth century, they were beginning to lose some of their power (Schissler, 1980, 89). Their hold on power was lost through a number of factors: these included the Napoleonic war, the freeing of the German peasants and the beginnings of the industrialization in Germany. But, some scholars maintained that the Junkers overcame the problems with the first two and that the agricultural problem reached its high point in the 1850s and 1860s (105). Our concern here is with the particular agricultural problems that the Junkers faced, that is, the agrarian crisis.

There had been problems with agriculture prior to 1890. That had prompted investigations in 1848/1849 and again in 1872/1873 (Riesebrodt, 1984a: 13). However, the problems were more than offset by the technical improvements in agricultural machinery and by the introduction of better farming practices (Wehler, 1980: 20–4). As a result, much of Germany remained an agricultural nation (Nipperdey, 1998a: 192). By 1914 it had been transformed into a major industrial country, but the process of industrialization occurred primarily in the North and the West. In contrast, the South and especially the East continued to remain primarily agricultural. Agricultural practices also varied depending on regions; most of the Northern and Western farms were primarily family businesses, but some were larger and had paid employees. In contrast, the dominate type of farming in the East was the large plantation-like farming estate ("*Rittergut*") owned by the Junkers. The Junker "Rittergut" tended to have peasants who worked the land in exchange for housing, some food and some land that they could work for themselves (Kaeger, 1890: 94). This type of labor arrangement had continued successfully for centuries, but by the end of the nineteenth century it no longer functioned well. Instead, it was becoming an acute agrarian crisis.

In his 1898 article for the *Handwörterbuch der Staatswissenschaften* Johannes Conrad defined an agrarian crisis as one in which certain circumstances can arise to make the agricultural use of the land unprofitable. He believed that there were a number of factors that were making the Junker "Rittergut" no longer viable. One was the fact that there was a world-wide recession during the late 1889s and early 1890s. A second cause was the falling of prices for the agricultural products. A third was the rising price of feed and other necessary goods and the rise in taxes. A fourth included the lack of credit, the decreasing number and worth of the farms in the area and the increasing indebtedness of the Junker (Conrad 1898: 106–7, 115; see also Riesebrodt 1984a: 3–4). The fifth, and perhaps the biggest problem, was the lack of a sufficient workforce. Too many people in the East-Elbian regions moved away; some went to the western parts of Germany and to the cities, while others immigrated, especially to the United States (Riesebrodt, 1984a: 5). There had been successive waves of emigrations, but during the one that lasted from 1880 to 1893 almost 1.8 million people left (Bade, 1980: 273). Of these, almost 40 per cent came from the East Elbian regions of West Prussia, Pommerania and Posen. This massive emigration from these regions left the Junkers with a severe short-age of agricultural workers. Faced with economic ruin, the landowners reluc-tantly hired people from eastern regions. These people were not German, but were primarily Polish (with some Russians). Not only were they willing to work but they were willing to work for far less than the Germans (292–3). The only possible way to counteract both the shortage of workers and the influx of non-Germans was to have the state encourage what was called "inner colonization." This was the process by which the government would encourage Germans to either stay on those lands or to have others move there from other parts of Germany. The state established a commission that was intended to buy up some of the larger Polish properties, subdivide them, and then sell that at a discount to Germans. This was specifically designed to fos-ter "inner colonization." One of the leading authorities on agrarian politics, Adolf Buchenberger, contrasted "inner colonization" with the older type of colonization by insisting that it did not colonize "leaderless lands" ("*herrenlose Länder*") (Buchenberger, 1892: 529). In another work Buchenberger explains that "inner colonization" was the attempt by the state to solve the problem of the lack of workers by facilitating the movement of Germans from the West to the East. This "settlement politics" was accomplished by erecting political and social barriers for the people from the East and by using economic incentives to encourage the Germans to settle in those areas (Buchenberger, 1899: 72–3). In particular, farmers and workers were pushed to colonize those lands. "Inner colonization" had two goals: to limit the number of people moving to the cities and overseas and to bring more people into the area to help to minimize the labor shortages (Riesebrodt, 1984a: 8–9). This notion of "inner colonization" was discussed by many groups, but it appears that it was a special topic of discussion by members of the Verein für Socialpolitik.

The Verein für Socialpolitik was expressly formed in 1872 in order to address the pressing social questions affecting Germany. It had a dual purpose: to provide scientific and scholarly research on various economic problems and to encourage well-thought out answers to these problems (Krüger, 1988: 98; Aldenhoff-Hübinger, 2010: 638). Specifically, the Verein was formed in order to counteract the dominant theory regarding social and economic problems, that of "Manchester Liberalism." In a letter to Gustav Schmoller, Adolf Wagner wrote that he envisioned founding a society that would free Germany from the "tyranny of Manchesterism" (Boese, 1939: 2; Krüger, 1988: 100). In his opening speech to the first meeting of the Verein für Socialpolitik, Schmoller described the "Manchester doctrine" as believing in the principle of noninter-ference by the state and in the promotion of the "egoism of the individual" (Boese, 1939: 6, 15). One of the other founding members, Lujo Brentano, called Schmoller's speech "masterful," and he especially praised Schmoller's purpose for the Verein: The state and all of society should work together in order to ensure that the working class could also enjoy the "highest goods of culture, education, and well-being" (Brentano, 1931: 78–9; see also Plessen, 1975: 121). But, the Verein was not only for the well-being of the working class; it was designed to defend the workers against the increasing misuse and even abuse by the industrial capitalists (Conrad, E., 1906: 2–3). However, the Verein für Socialpolitik stood not only against Manchester liberalism but it also stood against the radical theory of Marxism (Plessen, 1975: 9, 116; Krüger, 1988: 98; Demm, 1988: 119). Marxism would lead to anarchy and the destruction of Germany. Thus, the Verein für Socialpolitik was intended to help develop social reforms which would order all social relations and would lead to a healthy society (Conrad, E., 1906: 3). This was to be the leadership from above, and the guiding figures were primarily professors. These included Gustav Schmoller, Adolf Wagner, Lujo Brentano, Georg Knapp, Wilhelm Roscher and August Meitzen. Because of their socialist leanings these professors were often referred to as the "*Kathedersozialisten*" ("Socialists of the Lectern"). The main focus of the Verein für Socialpolitik was on the increasing plight of the industrial workers, but the association's members also fully understood that there continued to be a major problem with the agrarian laborers. The Verein was involved in investigations regarding rural workers in the 1880s (Boese, 1939: 56, 60). The death of Kaiser Wilhelm I and the resignation of Bismarck marked a turning point for the Verein because it signaled a change in how the government was going to react to social-political and economical problems (Plessen, 1975: 42). The Verein für Socialpolitik believed that it was the proper association to investigate the agrarian crisis and to write scholarly reports. The reports were then to be used as the basis for directing how the government should intervene in order to correct the situation.

Weber's Scholarly Studies and His Political Conclusions, 1892–1895

Bismarck may have unified Germany, but in the minds of some people he had "broken its back." What they meant was that Bismarck was too dominating a leader, and he was too unwilling or too unable to allow others to share in governing. As a result, when he was removed from his position Germany was left practically leaderless. The leaders who were appointed in his place were too weak and/or too indecisive to act. Furthermore, the years immediately after Bismarck's dismissal were especially troublesome in Germany (Wehler, 1980: 69–70). The Verein was aware of the increasing economic problems, and it was particularly concerned about the growing problems in the East (Riesebrodt, 1984a: 2–3). That is why the association devoted the next several years to investigating the various economic difficulties confronting the German agrarian workers. The main impetus was from Max Sering. Sering had just replaced Gustav Schmoller as the professor of "national economics" at the "*Landwirtschaftliche Hochschule.*" In September 1890 he proposed that the Verein focus its attention on the problems plaguing the agricultural regions in Germany and to report back. This was not only to be a statistical analysis but it was also to be a report that drew conclusions. The executive committee agreed, and people were selected (Riesebrodt, 1984b: 18–19). The first questionnaires were sent out in 1891 with the expectation that the results could be produced by 1892 (Kaesler, 1998: 73).

The investigations into the agrarian worker problems are found in the three volumes of the *Schriften des Vereins für Socialpolitik.* A total of three volumes were published in 1892 under the title *Verhältnisse der Landarbeiter in Deutschland.* A fourth volume appeared later that dealt specifically with the issue of "inner colonization." The first volume focused on the Northwest and the Southwest and included an appendix on the statistics for the German agrarian laborer. The authors were Karl Kaerger, a H. Losch and a H. Grohmann. The total number of pages was 456 (*Schriften des Vereins für Socialpolitik,* 1892a). The second volume treated most of the remaining parts of Western Germany and included three parts: one by Friedrich Grossmann, one by Otto Auhagen and one by Kuno Frankenstein. This was a much larger volume of 765 pages; Frankenstein's alone was almost 400 pages (*Schriften des Vereins für Socialpolitik,* 1892: 243–440). These statistics are important if only because of the contrast with the volume done by Max Weber. This was the third volume, and in it Weber examined all of the areas east of the Elbe River. It was larger than the other two and at over 800 pages was twice the size of Frankenstein's contribution. Three things make Weber's contribution even more remarkable: First, Weber was assigned the most politically and most scholarly difficult area – the area east of the Elbe (Weber, 1993: 157). Second, Weber was not yet a professor and he had not made much of a name for himself. And third, he was trained in law and not in the area of agrarian issues. The question may be raised: Why was Max Weber chosen and for such a difficult task?

Max Weber had been a member of the Verein für Socialpolitik since 1890, yet he seemed content to remain mostly in the background. Martin Riesebrodt offers a plausible explanation of why Weber was asked: It was because of Weber's contact with the "*Staatswissenschaftlich-statistischen*" seminar. This was taught by two important members of the executive committee of the Verein: Gustav Schmoller and August Meitzen (Riesebrodt, 1984b: 23). Riesebrodt adds that Weber was in close contact with Max Sering, one of the initiators of the questionnaire and the author of the volume on "inner colonization" (23). The connection with August Meitzen seems the most important because, not only was he a member of the executive committee and was widely regarded as perhaps the expert on emigration he was also Weber's major professor and he oversaw Weber's "*Habilitationschrift*" on Roman agrarian history. In his introduction to that volume Jürgen Deininger emphasizes Meitzen's importance both on the subject of migration and to Weber personally (Deininger, 1986a: 13–9, 27–9, 48–50). Weber repaid his mentor both by dedicating the work to Meitzen and by referring to him in it (Weber, 1986: 92, 100, 282, 345). Weber was encouraged and supported by Meitzen, and he adapted Meitzen's methodology to the agrarian problems (Aldenhoff-Hübinger, 2010: 641). A second reason why Weber was likely chosen was that he had personal experience with that area of Prussia, especially around Posen. During his military service, he was stationed there twice: in Posen during an eight-week period during July through August 1888 and then outside of Posen in Schrimm during June and July 1891 (Deininger, 1986b: 59; Weber, 1936: 302–8, 330–6). It was from Schrimm that Weber wrote to his brother Alfred about spending much of his free time there correcting his *Habilitationschrift* for Meitzen (Weber, 1936: 336). The other time he seems to have spent either in performing his military service or in seeing the area firsthand. Given Weber's penchant for keen observation, it is likely that his time spent in the area east of the Elbe served him well; both in doing his questionnaire for the Verein and in interpreting and understanding its results.

According to Marianne Weber, Weber had just finished his *Habilitationschrift* when he immediately plunged into his agrarian studies (Weber, 1926: 136). Weber did not have much time to complete his work, and he indicated that he had been rushed. Weber explained that the speed demanded accounted for the large number of typographical errors (Weber, 1984: 56–9). Perhaps it was because of his newness to this task, or perhaps it was because the work of his predecessors was so good, that Weber occasionally referred to the previous investigators. Thus, he notes the importance of Lengerke's writings from 1849 and that by von der Goltz from 1874. However, Weber highlights the fact that he departs from their methods by his offering an even more substantial investigation into the special type of worker who is found in that region (62, 66). This is not to say that Weber did not anticipate objections to his study. He noted that his study is rather one-sided because it reflects the landowners' points of view and not those of the agrarian workers. Furthermore, he allows that the results gathered from his study may appear to be "relative and subjective," but that should not be taken to mean that they are "scholarly and practically" worthless (64–5). Rather, these results offer a rather good glimpse of the "agrarian working conditions" ("*Agrarverhältnisse*"). This term "*Agrarverhältnisse*" is resistant to translation. Scaff translates "*Verhältnis*" as "relation," and there is much to be said for this (Scaff, 1989: 24). The term tends to mean "relation," and Weber used the term in this sense over the course of a number of years. However, Weber was not just interested in labor *relations* or, in labor *relationships*, but in labor *conditions*. The point is that Weber's concern was all-encompassing – he was focused not just on the working conditions, but on the workers' entire lives. That included all of their legal, economic and social conditions. This is especially the case regarding his study of the East Elbian regions – his primary focus was to set out and to understand the agrarian laborer's working and living *conditions*. He lists many of these at the conclusion of his "Preliminary Remarks": "work time, over time and work on Sunday, female and child labor" as well as "old age care and invalid care," and the "general conditions of the labor market" (Weber, 1984: 67).

Weber distinguishes between two different types of laborers. The first are the *"Deputanten,"* that is, the unmarried men who work in the fields and the stables as well as the unmarried women who work in the landowner's house. These workers are housed, fed and paid by the landowner and are contractually bound to work the entire year. Weber notes that their working conditions do not differ significantly from the men and women who work in the towns and cities. The second are the *"Instleute"* and these are the people who are found particularly in the Eastern regions. Like the *Deputanten*, the *Instleute* live in the housing that the landowners provide and they mostly have the same working conditions. They also have some land and are given some feed for their livestock. However, there are several differences between the two types of worker. One was that the *Deputanten* have individual contracts, whereas the *Instleute* had contracts which bound them to two or three others. A second difference was that the *Deputanten* were paid with a stable year's payment, while the *Instleute* were paid with a daily wage (71, 75). A final difference was that the *Deputanten* had a common interest with the landowner in high grain prices, in contrast to the *Instleute* who had an interest in lower prices because they had to pay for the grain. For much of the rest of his introductory remarks, Weber shows his legal training; he wrote about that the *Instleute* lacked a legal contract in the "modern sense" and that their lives were rather precarious (79, 81).

The main portion of Weber's investigations is divided into seven sections, each devoted to a region in that area. While the main bulk of his investigations is devoted to the issue of wages, he is also concerned with other issues. Following Meitzen, Weber also stresses the importance of the soil conditions and he notes how the quality varies from area to area (67, 131, 418, 495, 593–5, 809–10). The majority of the study is rather dry; it is filled with tables about the different regions and their workers. This is not surprising, because after all, it is a statistical study. Weber's investigation showed that during the summer the workers averaged over 12 hours a day and even during the winter they still put in over eight hours. During the summer the worker typically began work at five and ended at eight with a two-hour midday break. The work tended to be back breaking, and there were no days for rest and recuperation. Weber also found that the worker's labor situation was rather precarious. The agrarian worker did not have a legally binding labor contract, so there was no means for him to ensure that his employer would be living up to his end of the deal. In conjunction with this Weber found that there was a continuing problem with importing workers from Poland and Russia because both were able and willing to work for much less.

Weber offers a few surprises in his conclusion: while some critics may not believe that this study is worthwhile, he vigorously defends it. He admits that there is one essential gap in the study, and that concerns the honesty of the answers to the questionnaires (887). He also admits that he did not pursue a complete legal analysis of the agrarian workers, but he insists that was intentional. He does point to some difficulties – that the large estates are pre-dominately patriarchal and that tradition and history tended to determine the area's future. He also admits that it is difficult to determine how much the soil quality determines the life of the *Instleute* (892–4). He ends by suggesting that a complete economic and social-political appraisal of the material cannot be given here; similarly, there cannot be the expectation of an answer to the question of what "happens now," and especially to the question of what "should happen" (918–9). Nonetheless, he insists that the traditional privileges of the Junkers have been allowed to continue for too long and now the German culture in the East is in existential danger (926–7). This is the tragic position of the East and the future of the German culture depends on how the agrarian crisis can be resolved (928).

The results of the investigations were scheduled to be discussed at the 1892 meeting of the *Verein für Socialpolitik*. It was intended to be held in the Fall in Posen, but the outbreak of cholera prompted the organizers to recon-sider. The members initially decided to postpone the meeting until March, and in February 1893, they decided to hold it later in Berlin. The meeting occurred on March 20 and 21 and was one of the "'highpoints" in the history of the Verein. It served for decades as a model for future meetings because of the importance of the speeches and the high quality of the discussions (Boese, 1939: 66–7). Much of this was directly or indirectly a result of Max Weber's work.

On 17 December 1892, the *Verein für Sociapolitik* published Weber's study, and it immediately drew considerable praise. The leading authority on Germany's agrarian problems, Georg Friedrich Knapp, singled it out for praise. Along with Weber, Knapp was to give one of the two main speeches, but he offered to step aside and allow Weber to have the honor to be the single speaker. Schmoller declined Knapp's offer, but in March when Knapp did speak, he complimented Weber for his work and insisted that it made all of the previous knowledge about the subject outdated and because of Weber "we must begin to learn again" (Weber, 1993: 159–62, 165).

When it came time for Weber to speak, he complimented Knapp and noted how much the younger generation owed him. But, Weber was not afraid to contradict or to expand upon what the "old master" had said. He allowed that despite the fact that the study was scholarly, it was "highly political," and he acknowledged that he was going to confront the practical questions of what has happened, was can happen, and what should happen (167). His first observation was on the worker's emigration – they emigrated across the "great water" or they moved to the towns and cities. They especially moved to the areas of increasing industrialization. All of this was, in Weber's opinion, "destructive" because it meant the continual worsening of the workers' conditions in the East (171–5). It was destructive also because it meant the increasing Polonization of those areas, and he counted the large agricultural estates of the Prussian East as the "most dangerous enemy of our nationality" because they were the "greatest Polonizers" (177–9).

Weber's second observation was about the workers' conditions and whether the state should try to help them. For Weber, this is a matter of cultural survival if not a "struggle to survive" ("*Kampf um's Dasein*") (181–3). Weber repeatedly warns of the danger to Germany's culture and its economic interests, and he insists that it is not only possible but good that the state employs its power to prevent the de-Germanization of the area. He concludes by saying that if an enemy appeared at the eastern border and threatened war, there would be no doubt that everyone would rally around the flag. Weber insists that the danger in this case is no less and that Germany must do what it can to defend itself and its future (191, 194, 196).

Weber's study for the Verein für Socialpolitik was not the only agrarian study that Weber undertook. In conjunction with his friend Paul Göhre, Weber produced a slightly shorter but no less important study for the Evangelisch-soziale Kongress, and he did this at approximately the same time that he was working on the larger study for the Verein für Socialpolitik (72). In his first article on the study Weber shows the contrasts between the "ideal" notion of the agrarian laborer and his actual living situation (77, 83). In his opinion, the actual living and working conditions were deplorable and they needed to be addressed. Weber believes that the state has some obligation to the agrarian workers to do that. He closes his speech by saying enough of the questions and confesses that his explanation was too long. He insists that it is pointless to try to determine who is "innocent" and who is "guilty" for these conditions; what everyone needs to do is to recognize that the developing tendencies need to be dealt with (89–90, 93, 100, 104). These are all political points that Weber began to take up in numerous speeches that he gave and papers that he wrote between 1894 and 1897.

Weber and Some Political Consequences, 1894–1897

The Evangelisch-soziale Kongress was formed in 1891, and one of its leading figures was Paul Göhre. He was a trained Protestant theologian, but he was very concerned about the working conditions in Germany's industries. For three months during 1891, Göhre worked incognito in factories, and he published his observations about his experiences. He was attacked by many conservatives, but he was staunchly defended by Weber (Aldenhoff, 1988: 291–2). Weber shared Göhre's concerns about Germany's workers, although at this time he focused on agricultural workers. The fifth conference of the Evangelisch-soziale Kongress occurred in May 1994, and Weber and Göhre both spoke on the agrarian laborers' problems. Göhre spoke first, and he warned that unless drastic measures were taken, German workers would leave the lands in the East and they would be replaced by foreign workers (Weber, 1993: 310). Weber spoke immediately after Göhre and indicated his agreement with him. However, Weber spoke more about how these working conditions were leading to class struggles. The older patriarchal arrangement was dead and something new was needed to replace it (325). Unfortunately, the working conditions were worsening and the people were leaving the land for the city and for overseas. They long for freedom, and they believe that they will find it there (323). For those who remain, there seems to be only one option, and that is for them to engage in class struggle (327, 329–31). Weber was even more realistic than Göhre and others who have an infinite longing for human happiness; he rejected the idealistic view point and insisted that he pursued social policy *not* in order to create human happiness (339, 341). Weber would repeat many of these same points throughout his entire life.

The same year Weber published a paper entitled "*Entwicklungstendenzen in der Lage der ostelbischen Landarbeiter.*" As the title makes clear, his interest is in the developing tendencies of the position of the East Elbian farm laborer, that is, about the future (424). There are actually two versions of this article. The first one appeared in the *Archiv für soziale Gesetzgebung und Statistik,* and it seems to be aimed primarily at specialists, while the second one was published in Hans Delbrück's *Preußische Jahrbücher* and is more of a general and political exposition. Taken together, they offer an intriguing view of Weber's early political judgments.

Weber begins as he tends to do by mounting a defense of his thesis. He agrees with some of his critics that the peculiarities of the East make drawing conclusions problematic, and he notes that the necessarily fragmentary character of the Verein's study seems to underscore the subjectivity of the conclusions. However, he insists that it was a worthwhile study, and the results are beneficial if they are taken as heuristic approaches to the issue of the developmental tendencies of the region (369). In his opinion, the results of the study should not be viewed simply as indications of the life of the workers; rather, they are intimately bound up with the economic destiny of that part of Germany. Far from merely being an economic matter, this is socially and politically important (370–1).

Weber stresses that the Prussian landowner was not an ordinary employer; he did not possess huge amounts of capital nor did he have a businessman's outlook. Instead, he was both traditional and patriarchal, and he was a political autocrat; one who combined "naïve brutality with human friendship" (374, 426–9, 431). He was not bound by legal conventions as much as by the notions of tradition and honor (379, 443). However, the traditions that bound the worker to the area were being broken by the lure of money from the cities. On the one hand, when the German workers moved away, the landowner was faced with the shortage of workers. But, on the other hand, he found that he was able to save money by hiring Polish workers. Not only did they accept lower wages but the landowner no longer had to provide housing and land for them (447). In Weber's opinion this "solution" was misleading. First, he believed that those who attempted to restore Prussian agriculture were wrong because they were seemingly oblivious to the pressures of the world economy and that they were holding to a picture of the traditional economy that was outdated and fictitious (394). Second, the Prussian landowners also seemed oblivious to the lure of not only material rewards for the emigrating German workers but also the promise of more personal freedom (399). However, Weber's biggest objection to the Prussian landowners' approach to their economic problems was that it ignored the great danger of "Polonization" and the resulting reduction in the level of culture (416, 420–1, 448). This is not only a danger to that specific area of Eastern Germany but is a danger to Germany itself. This was also the fundamental point of his inaugural lecture that he gave at Freiburg in 1895.

Max Weber's "*Antrittsrede*" may not be the most famous speech that he ever gave, but it is certainly his most contentious one (Agevall, 2004: 157–60). It was, as Wolfgang Mommsen has suggested, a mixture of scientific and political thinking coupled with a "confessional expression of unusual radicalness and sharpness" ("*konfessionsartigen Aussagen von ungewöhnlicher Radikalität und Schärfe.*") (Mommsen, 1974a: 25). It was also, as Mommsen has argued a highly political speech. Mommsen contended that it was "the most significant document" of Weber's political thinking, at least until the outbreak of the First World War. It has also been mostly ignored, and for some valid and some not so valid reasons. First, while its topic may seem to be straight forward, it is not. That is why Rita Aldenhoff-Hübinger has pointed out that it is subject to least three different types of interpretation: political, practical philosophical and methodological (Aldenhoff-Hübinger, 2004: 145). Second, it does not appear to fit well with the dominant view that Weber was not that important a figure until he became a sociologist. According to this view everything that he wrote before his breakdown is insignificant. This view has been discredited by J. M. Barbalet. In "Weber's Inaugural Lecture and its Place in his Sociology," Barbalet argues that Weber's lecture "is an absolutely necessary key to the proper appreciation of Weber's subsequent work." (Barbarlet, 2001: 148). Third, the lecture's "dry introduction" would have been intelligible to his audience, but to most of today's readers its facts and notions are unknown. Fourth, people have objected to it because of "its strident nationalism" with one scholar calling it "notorious" (see Barbalet, 2001: 149). Weber himself seemed to be aware of this; while he later regarded his "*Der Nationalstaat und die Volkswirtschaftspolitik*" as a bit juvenile, he was very proud of it at the time. He was proud of it because of the hostility and arguments that it generated, and because he said things in it that needed to be said (Weber, 1993: 543–4). Barbalet himself is concerned not just with the lecture, but in showing how it paves the way for the "Protestant Ethic." In contrast, my concern here is with showing how it is the political culmination of Weber's agrarian studies (see Bergstraesser, 1957: 209). To bolster this view, Mommsen further maintained that this speech is the "fruit of his brilliant analysis" of the East Elbian workers, and on the basis of his studies, Weber points to the severe political consequences for Germany (Mommsen, 1974b: 38; see also Bergstraesser, 1957: 212).

Weber's speech can be broken into two sections. The first section is the scholarly part, while the second is the more political part. It is a speech in which Weber often blurs the line between facts and values, an issue that Weber later warned against but acknowledged that is hard to keep separate. Weber begins by saying that he has promised far more than what he can accomplish within this speech and then asks his audience to please follow him to the flat land of the East Elbian region (Weber, 1993: 545). His focus is that area where there is an unusually important difference between the economic and social conditions of existence (545). As with his earlier writings and speeches he notes the poor land and the sinking prices, and he points to the social differentiation. Mostly, however, he draws his audience's attention to the plight of the German agrarian worker and how he is forced to leave the land and is replaced by the cheaper Polish immigrant laborer (546–51). Weber's concern is not just with the economic differences; he is also concerned with the cultural differences, and he notes how the conflict between the German Protestants and the Polish Catholics is reminiscent of the recent "*Kulturkampf*" (550–1). This was not a minor issue for Weber; rather, it was one of his key issues in the years before his breakdown (Torp, 1998: 32, 69; Konno, 2004: 27).

In Weber's opinion, the social and economic practices of the Junkers were rooted in the past and their unwillingness or inability to adapt to the changing circumstances of the modern economy were problematic not only for them but for Germany (Torp, 1998: 64–5). He points to the patriarchal practices of the ruling Junkers and how the feudal traditions are leading them into an "economic struggle to the death" (Weber, 1993: 553). Given the severity of the problem, Weber says that he and his listeners must give up the naïve idealism of their youth and confront this problem realistically. He says that each person is involuntarily confronted with the question: "What can and should be done?" (552–5). He cautions against seeking justice and he warns against the illusion of believing in "peace and happiness." Instead, he insists that Germany is engaged in an economic struggle for power and in an "eternal struggle" for existence (558–66). Weber knows that his listeners do not have much regard for the Prussians, and he says that he "knows well that the name of the Junker sounds unfriendly in southern German ears" ("*Ich weiß es wohl, daß der Name Junker süddeutschen Ohren unfreundlich klingt*" (566). And, he recognizes that some may find that he himself is speaking "Prussian" when he says something positive about them. He reminds them that even today many Junkers have much influence and power and that they continue to have the ear of the monarch. They have often used their influence, not for personal gain but for history and for the sake of the state. For over a quarter century, Germany was guided by the "last and greatest of the Junkers" (Bismarck). He gave Germany its political unity, and against massive resistance, he slowly developed its economic structure. He and the Junkers have done their work, but they now find themselves in an economic death struggle (573). Again, this is not merely a problem for the Junkers and that region; it is a massive problem for all of Germany and for every German. The agrarian crisis was a major problem, but it was part of an even larger one that is best encapsulated in the question: "Who is able and willing to lead Germany?"

Weber acknowledges that there are some people who believe that they could lead Germany but that he is convinced that they are naïve; his question is who has "political maturity" ("*politische Reife*"? (565). The Junkers' time is past; and the upper class is not ready. The same is true for the middle class; Weber announces that he regards himself as a member of the middle class and he shares with others the same perspectives and ideals, but he admits that the middle class does not possess the political maturity to lead Germany. Weber has some hope for the working class, but politically it is immature (570). Only someone who is politically mature can lead Germany, and by mature

Weber means someone who can look past the illusion of human happiness and ignore the false belief in world peace. Germany needs someone who is conscious of "our responsibility *for history*" and is willing to do the "sober work of German politics" (572–4).

Heidelberg and an Infirm Epilogue, 1898–1902

At Berlin in 1894 Weber gave a course on agrarian problems, but it was not until he moved to Freiburg that the agrarian economic and political issues moved to the forefront of his work (Aldenhoff-Hübinger, 2008: 5). However, at Freiburg he was more occupied with giving courses on economics. Accordingly, of the 11 courses that he gave, only one was specifically devoted to agrarian politics. Weber moved to Heidelberg in 1897, and of the seven courses that he gave there, two were on agrarian politics (Weber, 2008: 511–2).

Weber's lectures on agrarian politics were both historical and political. They also embodied his previous legal background and his new discipline of economics. Weber notes that the purpose of agriculture is to produce food and that it is grown on lands. This might seem to be self-evident, but then Weber clarifies that there are a number of factors which influence agricultural profitability: not only the type of soil and the area's climate but also the type and intensity of labor needed to work the soil in a particular region (198–9). He also notes that farming may be traditional, but it is being forced to change; not only is there the increasing use of chemicals and machinery but that the cities and industrial areas are becoming more attractive to workers because of increasing wages there (260–2, 382, 386). In contrast, in the East wages are stagnating, the "Rittergut" is becoming even less profitable, which means even greater depression of wages (264–5). In addition, the "Rittergut" is capital intensive but the owners are finding it increasingly more difficult to obtain loans. In order to counteract the labor flight and to help secure financial help, the state must intervene (275, 287).

Weber made these scholarly and political points during his lectures in 1897 and 1898, but around the middle of 1898, he suffered a severe break-down. He began the agrarian politics course in 1899, but he could not continue. Marianne wrote that Weber would begin his lectures only to suffer a relapse (Weber, 1926: 250, 259). He tried several times to convince the Baden authorities to let him resign his position but was rebuffed. It was not until 1903 that the officials finally accepted his resignation. He continued to be listed as a faculty member but without a faculty chair and without a faculty voice. During the years that he was ill, he published practically nothing. Between 1898 and 1900 he published a few pieces that combined totaled 15 pages; and the slightly revised version of his "*Agrarverhältnisse im Altertum*" also appeared in 1898. He published nothing in 1901, and one short book review appeared in 1902 (Kaesler, 1998: 274–5). During these years Weber kept to himself; he did not speak at all in public, and he rarely received guests. There were some exceptions and these were often his former students. Marianne recounts how Weber's former student Leo Wegener appeared and spoke in such moving terms about his teacher (Weber, 1926: 257). It was during this time that Weber still managed to advise a few students, and Wegener was one. In 1903 Wegener published *Der Wirtschaftliche Kampf der Deutschen mit den Polen um die Provinz Posen: Eine Studie*, and as the title indicates, it was written under Weber's considerable influence. In his preface Wegener twice cites Weber, first to acknowledge that he was the impetus for the study and second to note that whoever has the opportunity to study with Weber will always remain in his debt (Wegener, 1903: v–vi). Martin Offenbacher was another such student, and in his *Konfession und Soziale Schichtung. Eine Studie über die Wirtschaftliche Lage der Katholiken und Protestanten in Baden*, he also acknowledges Max Weber (Offenbacher, 1900: ii). Whereas Wegener examined the economic clashes between the German Protestants and the Polish Catholics in Poland, Offenbacher concentrated on the economic differences between the Catholics and the Protestants in Baden, Germany. This study was published as one of the volumes from the *"Volkswirtschaftliche Abhandlungen der Badischen Hochschulen"* under the editorship of Carl Johannes Fuchs, Gerhard von Schulz-Gävernitz and Max Weber. It was Offenbacher's study that provided Weber with many of his statistical claims that are found in the early pages of the *Protestant Ethic and the Spirit of Capitalism* (Weber, 1904: 1–11). It was Offenbacher who provided all of the statistical origins and much of the intellectual impetus for Weber to write the *Protestant Ethic* (Adair-Toteff, 2015).

Concluding Remarks

Wolfgang Schluchter has suggested that when Weber recovered sufficiently to return to work he was still concerned with agrarian issues (Weber 2009: 5/6; 2000: 121–2). Weber did indeed write a major work on agrarian statistical and social-political observations in Prussia (*"Agrarstatistische und sozialpolitische Betrachtungen zur Fideikommißfrage in Preußen"*) as well as the speech on rural communities that he gave at the St. Louis World Exhibition in 1904 (Weber, 1998). However, Weber was increasingly focused on the problems with Germany's process of industrialization and the role that capitalism played in it. Even before his breakdown, Weber was concerned with this – in his remarks to Karl Oldenburg's lecture "On Germany as Industrial State" (*"Über Deutschland als Industriestaat"*), he made it clear that he objected to the claim that Germany was a unified agrarian country.

Instead, Weber insisted that it was split between the eastern agricultural regions and the western industrializing ones. He also insisted that those who continued to look to the East were bound to the past and were engaged in an agrarian "Idyll." The movement toward industrialization should not, and cannot, be stopped (Weber, 1993: 631, 635–6). It is a dangerous illusion to believe otherwise, because this is the "struggle for existence" ("*Kampf um Dasein*") and one that will only become increasingly difficult. Weber notes that there are optimists and then there are pessimists. He does not count himself among the former, but as a member of the latter, he recognizes that there are enormous risks in Germany's economic expansion. But, as a realist Weber believes that these risks must be taken and that it is the inherent destiny of Germany to do so (639–40).

A year after he gave his "*Antrittsrede*," Weber gave a related one which then appeared in the May edition of the journal *Die Wahrheit*. It is "*Die sozialen Gründe des Untergangs der antiken Kultur*," and in it he draws upon his early work on the Romans. This speech is not historical but is a contemporary warning: the Roman Empire was not defeated by enemies but it succumbed to internal divisions and social strife (Weber, 2006: 101). Weber makes the comparison by his references to the "Iron Chancellor" ("*eisernen Kanzler*," meaning Bismarck) and the Junkers (99–101). If Germany is to avoid a similar fate, it must realistically confront its own internal problems. The agrarian crisis was one critical problem and solving it was crucial to Germany's fate. Weber's writings on the agrarian crisis serve not only as a warning about a long-forgotten problem but contain eternal truths about the nature of politics.

References

Adair-Toteff, Christopher. 2015. "Statistical Origins of the 'Protestant Ethic.'" *Journal of Classical Sociology*. 15, no. 1: 58–72.

Agevall, Ola. 2004. "Science, Values, and the Empirical Argument in Max Weber's Inaugural Address." *Max Weber Studies* 4, no. 2: 157–77.

Aldenhoff, Rita. 1988. "Max Weber und der Evangelisch-soziale Kongreß." In Mommsen and Schwentker 1988. 285–95.

Aldenhoff-Hübinger, Rita. 2004. "Max Weber's Inaugural Address of 1895 in the Context of the Contemporary Debates in Political Economy." *Max Weber Studies* 4. no. 2: 143–56.

———2008. "Einleitung." In Weber 2008. 1–48.

———2010. "Landwirtschaftswissenschaften von der Gründung bis 1945." In *Geschichte der Universität Unter den Linden. 1810–2010. Transformation der Wissensordnung*. Edited by Heinz-Elmar Tenorth in collaboration with Volker Hess and Dieter Hoffmann. 627–50. Berlin: Akademie Verlag.

My thanks to Rita Aldenhoff-Hübinger for her careful reading of my chapter and for her helpful comments on it.

Bade, Klaus J. 1980. "Politik und Ökonomie der Ausländerbeschäftigung im Preußen Osten 1885–1914. Die Internationalisierung des Arbeitsmarkts im 'Ramen der preußischen Abwehrpolitik.'" In Puhle and Wehler 1980. 273–99.

Barbalet, J. M. 2001. "Weber's Inaugural Lecture and its Place in his Sociology." *Journal of Classical Sociology* 1, no. 2: 147–70.

Bergstraesser, Arnold. 1957. "Max Webers Antrittsvorlesung in zeitgeschichtlicher Perspektive." *Vierteljahrshefte für Zeitgeschichte* 3. Heft/Juli: 209–19.

Boese, Franz. 1939. *Geschichte des Vereins für Sozialpolitik. 1872–1932.* Berlin: Duncker & Humblot.

Brentano, Lujo. 1897. *Agrarpolitik. Ein Lehrbuch.* Stuttgart: Verlag von der J.G. Cotta'schen Buchhandlung. Nachfolger.

———1931. *Mein Leben im Kampf um soziale Entwicklung Deutschlands.* Jena: Eugen Diederichs Verlag.

Buchenberger, Adolf. 1892. *Agrarwesen und Agrarpolitik.* Leipzig: C.F. Winter'sche Verlagshandlung. *Lehr- und handbuch der politischen Oekonomie.* Dritte Hauptabteilung: Practische Volkswirthschaftslehre.

———1899. *Grundzüge der deutschen Agrarpolitik.* Berlin: Verlagsbuchhandlung Paul Parey. Second Edition.

Conrad, Else. 1906. *Der Verein für Sozialpolitik und seine Wirksamkeit auf dem Gebiet der gewerblichen Arbeiterfrage.* Jena: Verlag von Gustav Fischer.

Conrad, Johannes. 1898a. "Agrarkrisis." In Conrad *et al.* 1898. Erster Band. 106–20.

———1898b. "Agrarpolitik." In Conrad *et al.* 1898. Erster band. 120–5.

Conrad, J., Elster, L., Lexis, W., Loening, E. Editors. 1898–1901. *Handwörterbuch der Staatswissenschaften.* Jena: Verlag von Gustav Fischer. Second, wholly revised edition.

Deininger, Jürgen. 1986a. "Einleitung." In Weber 1986. 1–54.

———1986b. "Editorischer Bericht." In Weber 1986. 55–89.

Demm, Eberhard. 1988. "Max und Alfred Weber im Verein für Sozialpolitik." In Mommsen and Schwentker 1988. 119–36.

Kaesler, Dirk. 1998. *Max Weber. Eine Einführung in Leben, Werk und Wirkung.* Frankfurt: Campus Books.

Kaerger, Karl. 1890. *Die Sachsengängerei. Auf Grund persönlicher Ermittelungen und statistischer Erhebung dargestellt.* Berlin: Verlag von Paul Paley.

Knapp, Georg. 1891. *Landarbeiter in Knechtschaft und Freiheit. Vier Vorträge.* Leipzig: Duncker & Humblot.

Konno, Hajime. 2004. *Max Weber und die polnische Frage (1892–1920).* Baden-Baden: Nomos Verlagsgesellschaft.

Krüger, Dieter. 1988. "Max Weber und die 'Jüngeren' im Verein für Sozialpolitik." In Mommsen und Schwentker 1988. 98–118.

Mommsen, Wolfgang J. 1974a. "Ein Liberaler in der Grenzsituation." In Wolfgang J. Mommsen, *Gesellschaft, Politik und Geschichte.* 21–43. Frankfurt am Main: Suhrkamp.

———1974b. *Max Weber und die Deutsche Politik. 1890–1920.* Tübingen: J. C. B. Mohr (Paul Siebeck). 2., revised and expanded Edition.

Mommsen, Wolfgang J. Mommsen and Aldenhoff, Rita. 1993. "Einleitung." Weber 1993. 1–68.

Mommsen, Wolfgang J. and Schwentker, W. Editors. 1988. *Max Weber und seine Zeitgenossen.* Göttingen: Vandenhoeck & Ruprecht.

Nipperdey, Thomas. 1998a. *Deutsche Geschichte. 1866–1918. Band I: Arbeitswelt und Bürgergeist.* München: Verlag C. H. Beck.

————1998b. *Deutsche Geschichte. 1866–1918. Band II: Machtstaat vor der Demokratie.* München: Verlag C. H. Beck.

Offenbacher, Martin. 1900. *Konfession und Sozial Schichtung. Eine Studie über die wirtschaftliche Lage der Katholiken und Protestanten in Baden.* Tübingen und Leipzig: Verlag von J. C. B. Mohr (Paul Siebeck).

Puhle, Hans-Jürgen. 1980. "Preußen: Entwicklung und Fehlentwicklung." In Puhle and Wehler 1980. 11–42.

Puhle, Hans-Jürgen and Wehler, Hans Ulrich. Editors. 1980. *Preußen im Rückblick.* Göttingen: Vandenhoeck & Ruprecht in Göttingen.

Plessen, Marie-Louise. 1975. *Die Wirksamkeit des Vereins für Socialpolitik von 1872–1890. Studien zum Katheder- und Staatssozialismus.* Berlin: Duncker & Humblot.

Riesebrodt, Martin. 1984a. "Einleitung." In Weber 1984. 1–17.

————1984b. "Editorischer Bericht." In Weber 1984. 18–33.

————1985. "Von Patriarchalismus zum Kapitalismus. Max Webers Analyse der Transformation der ostelbischen Agrarverhältnisse im Kontext zeitgenössischer Theorien." In *Kölner Zeitschrift für Soziologie und Sozialpsychologie.* 546–67.

Scaff, Lawrence. 1989[1984]. "Weber before Weberian Sociology." In Tribe 1989a. 15–41.

Schissler, Hanna. 1980. "Die Junker. Zur Sozialgeschichte und historische Bedeutung der agrarischen Eliten in Preußen." In Puhle and Wehler 1980. 89–122.

Schluchter, Wolfgang. 2000. "Wirtschaft, Staat und Sozialpolitik. Max Weber als Sozialpolitiker." In Wolfgang Schluchter. *Individualismus, Verantwortungsethik und Vielfalt.* Göttingen: Velbrück Wissenschaft Weilerwist 2000. 118–38.

————2009. *Wirtschaft und Gesellschaft. Entstehungsgeschichte und Dokumente.* Presented and edited by Wolfgang Schluchter. Tübingen: J. C. B. Mohr (Paul Siebeck). *Max Weber Gesamtausgabe.* I/24.

Schoenberg, Gustav. 1896. *Handbuch der Politischen Oekonomie. Volkswirtschaftslehre. In Zwei Bänden.* Tübingen: Verlag von H. Laupp'schen Buchhandlung. Fourth Edition. Volume Two. First half-volume.

Schriften des Vereins für Socialpolitik. 1892a. *Die Verhältnisse der Landarbeiter in Deutschland.* Leipzig: Verlag von Duncker & Humblot. Band 53.

————1892b. *Die Verhältnisse der Landarbeiter in Deutschland.* Zweiter Band. Leipzig: Verlag von Duncker & Humblot. Band 54.

Torp, Cornelius. 1998. *Max Weber und die preußischen Junker.* Tübingen: J. C. B. Mohr (Paul Siebeck).

Treitschke, Heinrich von. 1908. [1862]. "Das deutsche Ordensland Preußen." In Heinrich von Treitschke *Ausgewählte Schriften.* Leipzig: Verlag von S. Hirzel. Volume one, fourth edition. 48–135.

Tribe, Keith. 1981. *Marxism and the Agrarian Question. German Social Democracy and the Peasantry 1890–1907.* Vol. 1. Atlantic Highlands, NJ: Humanities Press.

Tribe, Keith. Editor. 1989a. *Reading Weber.* London: Routledge.

————1989b. "Introduction." In Tribe 1989a. 1–14.

————1989c. "Prussian Agriculture – German Politics. Max Weber 1892-7." In Tribe 1989a. 85–130.

Von der Goltz, Theodor Freiherr. 1893. *Die ländliche Arbeiterklasse und der preußische Staat.* Jena: Verlag von Gustav Fischer.

————1896. "Landwirtschaft." In Schoenberg 1896. 1–140.

————1898. "Agrargeschichte (Neuzeit)." In Conrad *et al.* 1898. Erster Band. 88–106.

Weber, Marianne. 1926. *Max Weber. Ein Lebensbild.* Tübingen: Verlag von J. C. B. Mohr (Paul Siebeck).

Weber, Marianne, editor. 1936. *Max Weber. Jugendbriefe.* Tübingen: Verlag von J. C. B. Mohr (Paul Siebeck).

Weber, Max. 1898. "Agrargeschichte (Altertum)." In Conrad *et al.* 1898. Erster Band. 57–85.

———1904. "Die protestantische Ethik und der 'Geist' des Kapitalismus." *Archiv für Sozialwissenschaft und Sozialpolitik.* Band XX. 1–54.

———1984. *Die Lage der Landarbeiter im ostelbischen Deutschland. 1892.* Edited by Martin Riesebrodt. Tübingen: J. C. B. Mohr (Paul Siebeck). *Max Weber Gesamtausgabe.* I/3.

———1986. *Die römische Agrargeschichte in ihrer Bedeutung für das Staats- und Privatrecht. 1891.* Edited by Jürgen Deininger. Tübingen: J. C. B. Mohr (Paul Siebeck). *Max Weber Gesamtausgabe* I/2.

———1993. *Landarbeiterfrage, Nationalstaat und Volkswirtschaftspolitik. Schriften und Reden 1892–1899.* Edited by Wolfgang J. Mommsen in collaboration with Rita Aldenhoff. Tübingen: J. C. B. Mohr (Paul Siebeck). *Max Weber Gesamtausgabe.* I/4.

———1998. *Wirtschaft, Staat und Sozialpolitik. Schriften und Reden 1900–1912.* Edited by Wolfgang Schluchter in collaboration with Peter Kurth and Birgitt Morgenbrod. Tübingen: J. C. B. Mohr (Paul Siebeck). *Max Weber Gesamtausgabe.* I/8.

———2006. *Zur Sozial- und Wirtschaftsgeschichte des Altertum. Schriften und Reden 1893–1908.* Edited by Jürgen Deininger. Tübingen: J. C. B. Mohr (Paul Siebeck). *Max Weber Gesamtausgabe.* I/6.

———2008. *Agrarrecht, Agrargeschichte, Agrarpolitik. Vorlesungen 1894–1899.* Edited by Rita Aldenhoff-Hübinger. Tübingen: J. C. B. Mohr (Paul Siebeck). *Max Weber Gesamtausgabe.* III/5.

———2009. *Arbeiterfrage und Arbeiterbewegung. Vorlesungen 1895–1898.* Edited by Rita Aldenhoff-Hübinger in collaboration with Silke Fehlemann. Tübingen: J. C. B. Mohr (Paul Siebeck). *Max Weber Gesamtausgabe.* III/4.

Wegener, Leo. 1903. *Der Wirtschaftliche Kampf der Deutschen mit den Polen um die Provinz Posen: Eine Studie.* Posen: Verlag von Joseph Jolowicz.

Wehler, Hans-Ulrich. 1980. *Das Deutsche Kaiserreich 1871–1918.* Göttingen: Vandenhoeck & Ruprecht. 4., revised and bibliographically enlarged.

Chapter 4

CHARISMA AND THE SPIRIT OF CAPITALISM

David Norman Smith

Max Weber famously called charisma "the specifically creative revolutionary force of history."[1] The implication, well understood by many commentators, is that social orders, whether inherited from tradition or rationally legislated, can be undone and remade only by charismatic movements. A corollary of this premise is that credit for social ruptures – revolutionary breaks from the petrified past – belongs uniquely to charisma, which (in "pure" form) Weber calls anti-economic, antinomian, and irrational.

Yet Weber also called modern capitalism "the most fateful force in our modern life."[2] This capitalism, Weber said, is quintessentially rational, calculating and economic – in short, the precise opposite of charisma. Yet modern capitalism has also been the single most transformative force in history. Rational calculation and "forever renewed" profit-making enterprise have revolutionized society root and branch, from the most humdrum precincts of daily life to the political stratosphere. So the question arises: Is *capitalism* now the decisive revolutionary force in society? That is: Can we now credit an *anti-charismatic* force with power that charisma itself lacks?

I will argue that this conclusion, however intuitively plausible, is ultimately misleading. In fact, according to Weber, the rise and spirit of capitalism owe much to the phenomena of charisma. But we can only fully appreciate that point if we grasp that Weber's notions of charisma and capitalism are counter-intuitively subtle and complex. Traditional readings of Weber define charisma as simply a personality trait – a kind of magnetism that wins authority for born leaders – while capitalism is viewed as a calculating quest for profit, pursued *ad infinitum* by ever wealthier capitalists. More closely inspected, however,

---

1   Weber, *Economy and Society* ([1922] 1978), p. 1117. Hereafter, *Economy and Society* will be cited as *E&S*.
2   Weber (1920a), p. 17.

Weber's writings tell a different and less obvious story.[3] Ascetic sectarian discipline, manifest in the "charisma of disciples," has been much more central to
the success of modern capitalism than any form of personal authority, and the
"capitalist spirit" has dissipated rather than grown as capitalists have amassed
greater wealth and personal autonomy.

"Discipleship," viewed in this light, is more fundamental to contemporary
capitalism than leadership. And the spirit of capitalism, Weber says, is found
more typically in "middle-class" circles than among big capitalists.

The larger significance of these heterodox claims was not, for Weber, simply historical. He devoted much of the final decade of his life to inquiry into
the interplay of economic ethics, charisma, sectarian religiosity and the capitalist spirit in China and India – realms where capitalism was still in its infancy.
Would "Occidental" modern capitalism assume worldwide dimensions? The
answer to that question depended largely on what happened in Asia, and
Max Weber was among the first to pose and explore that question. Here, as
elsewhere, his inquiry pivoted around the entwined categories of capitalism,
asceticism, sectarianism and charisma. My goal in what follows is to sketch the
broad outlines of Weber's thinking in this arena.

Fire and Water

Are charisma and capitalism radical opposites? Is charismatic capitalism
adventurist and self-indulgent, while authentic capitalism is precisely the
opposite – prudent and selfless? Weber lent credence to this conclusion in his
rare remarks on charismatic entrepreneurs – almost all of whom he portrays
as robber capitalists driven by the "accursed hunger for gold" (Virgil's *auri sacra
fames*) rather than by the rational profit motive. Charismatic figures of this
kind lead their followers into plunder-seeking gambles that may enrich them
but deflect energy and capital away from the continuous rational enterprise of
genuine capitalism.

Weber held a decidedly low opinion of charismatic buccaneering. The
charismatic quest for profit by any means is neither modern nor revolutionary
but, rather, anachronistic – an irrational pseudo-capitalism, of which Weber
specifies many kinds: adventure capitalism, robber capitalism, monopoly and
political capitalism, etc. In many of his texts, including, perhaps most notably, "*Politik als Beruf*," Weber criticized the venal profit mongering of political bosses and their vote-getting machines. This was political capitalism at
its worst, oriented not to service but to spoils – the kind of patronage politics
which, today, would be called crony capitalism, in precisely Weber's spirit.

3   For full details on the secondary literature, see Smith (2013).

Weber's remarks on charismatic enterprise in the economic realm per se are rare, but they are very similar in content. In *Economy and Society*, for example, shortly after calling charisma revolutionary, Weber inveighed against the feck-lessness of the "charismatic capitalist" Henry Villard, who today would be called a corporate raider – again, in exactly Weber's spirit.[4]

Villard, who was friendly with Weber's family, engineered the hostile take-over of the Northern Pacific Railroad in 1881. This was, and remains, a legendary feat in the annals of corporate raiding because Villard lever-aged the take-over by inducing wealthy friends to invest secretly in a "blind pool" – that is, to trust him, entirely on faith, to invest in an undisclosed venture which, he assured them, would reward them amply. At first this trust seemed to have been justified. Soon after capturing the railroad and stepping up the pace of work,[5] Villard was able to celebrate the comple-tion of the transcontinental route from Minneapolis to Seattle by hosting an extravaganza that brought in luminaries (including Max Weber Sr.) from all corners of Europe. Just months later, however, the enterprise collapsed financially, undone, in part, by a sudden fall in its stock prices (which Villard blamed on market manipulation by his archrival, the notorious railroad baron Jay Gould). Unmoved by Villard's fall, Weber brusquely dismissed his supporters – whose fortunes had soared and fallen so abruptly – as a mere *Beutegefolgschaft*, a "booty following."[6] Their undoing was wholly predictable and undeserving of sympathy, since they had entrusted their millions to a gambler. What blind faith wrought, reality sundered. Charismatic swash-buckling was clearly no way to run a business.[7]

It might seem, in this light, that charisma can inspire only sterile *pseudo*-capitalism. Another possibility, suggested by more recent history, is that charisma is a specifically *anti*-capitalist force. The iconic charismatic move-ments of the twentieth century were all anti-capitalist, whether revolutionary (Russia, China, Cuba, Vietnam, Cambodia, Korea) or reactionary (Germany, Italy). Rational calculation and routinized capital accumulation were never the founding aims of such movements, even if, under postrevolutionary pres-sures, they ultimately pursued economic growth by more-or-less conventional means. Weber, meanwhile, gave additional credibility to the idea that cha-risma is typically anti-capitalist when, near the end of his life, he added Kurt

4   See Weber (2005), p. 484.
5   Many of these workers were immigrant Chinese laborers whose on-the-job mortality rate was extremely high. Villard also linked the Northern Pacific to some of the earliest experiments in industrial farming, which were known as "bonanza farms."
6   In *E&S* this phrase is translated "spoils-oriented following." But it could be translated just as well, if not better, by the colloquial phrase "gravy train."
7   On Villard, see Fuchs, 1991; Villard, 1988; and Buss, 1976.

Eisner's name to his evolving list of illustrative charismatic figures.[8] Eisner, who led the revolutionary socialist movement that overthrew the Wittelsbach monarchy in Bavaria in late 1918, was scorned by Weber as a self-deluded, irresponsible *littérateur*, "who is overwhelmed by his own demagogic success."[9] So this too calls into question the idea that capitalism and charisma may have elective affinities. In our society, charismatic movements appear to spring, not from the quest to accumulate capital by prudential private enterprise but rather from ideological opposition to private enterprise. The charismatic spirit thus appears to stand *against* the spirit of capitalism.

Charismatic movements also seem increasingly utopian, as they beat their wings against the ramparts of a triumphant capitalism. As Weber wrote, in the famous closing pages of *The Protestant Ethic and the Spirit of Capitalism*: "The Puritans *wanted* to be men of the calling – we, on the other hand, *must be*. For when asceticism left the monastic cells to enter working life [and] dominate worldly morality, it helped build the mighty cosmos of the modern economic order … Today this mighty cosmos determines, with overwhelming coercive force, the style of life *not only* of those directly involved in business but of every individual who is born into this mechanism, and may well continue to do so until the day the last ton of fossil fuel has been consumed."[10] The charismatic enemy of capitalism now figures as a latter-day Icarus, soaring too close to the sun. Even the most formidable anti-capitalist movements have shipwrecked. The reactionary movements were defeated, and the revolutionary movements fell back to earth, pulled down into capital's gravitational field. It is ironic but enormously telling that Germany and China, of all countries, now figure as the world's beacons of rational, profit-driven industry.[11]

8 Weber drafted several lists of typical charismatic figures. In "The Economic Ethics of the World Religions" – the essay that prefaced his studies of India, China, and Palestine – he lists the following illustrative figures: "The magical sorcerer, the prophet, the leader of hunting and booty expeditions, the warrior chieftain, the so-called 'Caesarist' ruler, and, under certain conditions, the personal head of a party are such types of rulers for their disciples, followings, enlisted troops, parties, et cetera." (Weber, 1916a), pp. 295–96.

9 *E&S*, p. 242. This was the second of Weber's two lists in *E&S*. The first, written quite a bit earlier, included Byzantine and Scandinavian berserks, the folk heroes Cuchulain and Achilles, epileptoid magicians and "the head of the Mormons," whose Holy Book was probably a "rank swindle" (p. 1112). In another text, which also appears in *E&S*, Weber returned to many of these figures – berserks, shamans, magicians and "Joseph Smith, the founder of Mormonism, who may have been a very sophisticated swindler" – while adding only Kurt Eisner (p. 242).

10 This passage, which I have lightly emended, is taken from Weber ([1904–05] (2002), pp. 120–21.

11 See Smith (2015).

Charisma, in other words, now seems like a distinctly fragile "revolutionary" force – because capitalism is greater and sturdier. Atavistic charismatic movements tried their strength against capitalism and failed. Charismatic revivals obviously remain a lurking possibility, especially in times of economic disturbance; but today, money is the power that makes the world go 'round. The mighty cosmos of the modern economic order seems invulnerable to charismatic challenge.

Or so it seems. In the pages that follow, I will argue that this outlook is one-sided. To start with, Weber's notion of charisma was far more nuanced and unconventional than casual readers might imagine. And, crucially for our purposes, he credited a very specific form of charisma with a major role in triggering and sustaining capitalism, not only in the past, but (potentially) in the present and future as well.

Capitalism is now "globalizing" at an unparalleled rate. In many places, crony capitalism and Villard-like speculation are more typical than modern capitalism, and profit hunger is more common than ascetic discipline. In other words, by Weber's standards, capitalism is growing, but increasingly, without the benefit of the capitalist spirit. Is that tenable? Can capitalism successfully extend and sustain itself with only avarice as its engine?

The Globalization of Charisma

The crux of Weber's thesis about the capitalist spirit – which he introduced in *"Die protestantische Ethik und der 'Geist' des Kapitalismus"* in 1904–1905 – is that, while greed is common in every age and culture, modern capitalism is anchored not in greed but in a sense of obligation to amass capital by ceaseless rational enterprise; the goal of such enterprise is reinvestment, not enjoyment. This goal is so far removed from what Virgil called the "accursed hunger for gold" that it *"may* even be identical with the restraint, or at least a rational tempering, of this irrational impulse".[12]

Rational, dispassionate accumulation of this kind hinges on the *sublimation* of avarice into service. Modern capitalists feel an obligation to their capital. Embracing an ethic of economic stewardship, they feel obliged to render their capital infinite and immortal, and they regard covetousness as sacrilege. The accumulation of capital is a sacred vocation, pursued for its own sake – not for the satisfaction of merely personal goals. Egoistic or eudaemonistic striving for paltry creaturely goals is blasphemy. Only selfless ascetic service to God is conscionable.

12 Weber [1920b] 1958, p. 17.

The Protestant Ethic and the Spirit of Capitalism (hereafter *PESC*) is easily Weber's most celebrated and controversial work. Since "charisma" is his most cele- brated and controversial category, it would be surprising if *PESC* neglected it altogether. And, in fact, the term *charisma* does appear in two key passages. But these passages have been overlooked in the secondary literature, and their aim and content is not what readers of this literature would normally expect. Commentators have often reduced charisma to a one-dimensional stereotype – which they wrongly credit to Weber. *Charisma* in this perspective is treated as a personality trait, an effectively hypnotic power of persuasion. Individuals with this trait are viewed as leaders *ex natura* whose power over unresisting masses is assured by their magnetism. I have argued against this perspective elsewhere, both as an interpretation of Weber and as a reading of sociopolitical real- ity; I have also argued that this misreading reflects the persisting influence of the New Testament theology of charisma, which, filtered through Rudolph Sohm's *Kirchenrecht* (1892), reappeared in thinly secularized form in theories of mass society and has often been mistaken for Weber's sociology of authority.[13]

Sohm, echoing Paul's letters, held that the Christian community is bound together by divine gifts of grace, which emanate from the Holy Spirit and assume many reciprocal forms. In Paul's theology, which was the starting point for Sohm and countless others, the ancient Greek word χάρισμα was given the meaning sacred "gift of grace." Paul and his successors, from Irenaeus and Tertullian to Ritschl and Weinel, held that the faithful enjoy a spectrum of gifts, the *charismata,* which are conferred upon them as individuals by the Holy Spirit. This doctrine was orthodox for two millennia and was defended by myriad expositors, including many who, under the influence of Catholicism, held that institutions, too, can enjoy the blessings of charisma.[14] Sohm, on the

---

13 See Smith (2013, 2011, 1998 and 1992).

14 Countless theologians have expounded on charisma over the centuries, including Ritschl, Baur and myriad others; see, as just one example, Engelmann (1848). Among Weber's contemporaries, key figures include Gloël (1888), Sohm (1892) and Lauterburg (1898). Many intellectual historians, oddly, have alleged that Weber coined the term or inherited it from a meager tradition. In fact, the opposite is true, and to such an extent that, for example, a Google Books search for χάρισμα produces, "about 39,800" hits, across many centuries. Even many eccentric variant terms appear frequently, includ- ing, strikingly, early modern theology in which the letter "s" is spelled "f." *Charifma, Charifmata, Charifmatum* and *Charismatum* appear over 70,000 times in early modern texts (by, e.g., François Hallier, Christian de Wulf, Francisco de Torres, Guilielmus van Est, David Calderwood, Isaac Habert and Johann Heideggerus) and in editions of ancient works by Tertullian, Chrysostom and others. *Karifma, Karifmata, Charifmatibuf, Charifmatibus, Charifmatibus charifmata,* and *Charifmatibus charismata* appear, between them, many hundreds of times. *Charifmatifche* appeared as recently as Baur's *Theologische Studien und Kritiken* (1838). Useful modern sources on the theological and literary ancestry of the

contrary, in the spirit of evangelical Lutheranism, insisted that individuals, and only individuals, can possess *charismata*.

Weber admired the force and incisiveness of Sohm's argument, but he said that Sohm's analysis fell short of sociological generality because he restricted his attention, and the notion of charisma, to Christianity. Weber's concern was not the theology of charisma but charismatic *authority* – a phenomenon that appears in countless cultures, which springs not from divine powers but from *belief* in divine powers. Charisma per se (like *mana, maga,* and *orenda* in Melanesian, Zoroastrian, Iroquois and other cultures) exists only in the eye of the beholder. Anyone can claim to possess the kinds of exotic powers that Weber calls "charismatic." But only those whose claims are "recognized" – that is, endorsed by a following – are charismatic in Weber's sense.

In *Economy and Society*, and in the essays on "The Economic Ethics of the World Religions," drawing upon examples from mythology and ethnology as well as history, Weber sought to explain many kinds of "charismatic" faith and followership. Sorcerers, prophets, gurus and many others have claimed powers denied to ordinary mortals. How they win followers – why "the masses in need" acclaim such figures – Weber sought to grasp as fully as possible. That entailed an ever-ramifying awareness of the enormously diverse factors that cause people in different traditions and contexts to seek supernatural aid or solace. Sohm had limited his attention to Christendom; Weber expanded his field of vision to include charismatic phenomena in cultures the world over.

The net result of this generalizing effort was that Weber investigated a wide range of "charismas," not a single ideal-type. He sought, in effect, to explain not just "charisma" but the plenitude, the plurality, of real-world *charismata* – not "gifts of grace" but *claims* to transcendental gifts that win mass followings. Sociologically, the specific character of these claims matters considerably, since salvationist crusades, for example, differ greatly from gnostic world-rejecting cults – and Weber wants to understand difference as well as similarity. But he emphasizes that all such movements, however much they may differ in other respects, are fueled by mass public faith in the transcendent powers of individuals.

Did capitalism arise on the basis of such a movement?

The "Spirit" of Capitalism ... and Charisma?

A syllogism appears relevant here: If, in fact, the overthrow of exclusive Catholic hegemony in Europe by the Protestant Reformation was a religious

---

Charisma-Begriffe include Warfield (1918), Grau (1946), Sterrett (1947), Leclerq (1948), Pollet (1955), Franzmann (1972), Kydd (1984), MacLachlan (1993) and Harrison (2003).

revolution, and if, in fact, the overthrow of the old order by capitalism was a socioeconomic revolution, then charisma should have figured significantly in those revolutions – assuming, that is, that charisma actually *does* play an indispensable role in toppling old laws and traditions.

But what does "charisma" mean in this context? Personal magnetism? *Mana, maga, orenda?* Gift of grace? Posing the issue in this way puts the conceptual issue in a stark light. If Weber did indeed see charisma as an electrifying, irresistible force of personal leadership – as so many social scientists have alleged – then specific individuals should loom large in Weber's account of the origin and historical effects of the Protestant ethic. Calvin and above all Luther – whose idea of the "worldly calling" *(innerweltliche Beruf)* was the springboard, Weber said, for both Protestantism and the capitalist spirit – would seem destined to play this part. Yet Weber says very little about either of them. Did he simply miss their charisma?

Luther, in particular, might seem to be the very archetype of a charismatic revolutionary. He broke from Catholic rituals and doctrines with prophetic flair ("Here I stand, I can do no other"), and his catalytic role in precipitating the Protestant Reformation is undeniable. From the earliest days of his career as a dissenter and schismatic, Luther was consistently portrayed as a model *Charismatiker*. Boldly risking the fate of his martyred predecessor, Jan Hus, who had been burned at the stake a century before, Luther was credited with a suitably prophylactic charisma – incombustibility – as early as 1521.[15] This became a defining feature of his enduring popular legend. He was also often depicted as a latter-day Moses, leading believers into "the light of the crucified Christ"; in the company of a dove, representing the Holy Spirit; as a prophet and miracle-worker. His first biographer avowed his divine mission, and many historians have since affirmed his world-changing "greatness." A recent historian writes, typically, that Luther's "charismatic authority for the evangelical movement ... finds no parallel in the Protestant movement of his or any other day."[16] Yet Weber himself called attention to just one aspect of Luther's activity – his doctrine of divinely "called" labor. Why? I see two principal reasons.

To start with, Luther bore only a very modest resemblance to Weber's archetype of a revolutionary prophet. Luther was an economic traditionalist who urged his followers to redouble their commitment to routinized daily pursuits, and when the German peasantry revolted against the princely authorities, Luther sided with the authorities, fiercely and fanatically. In short, Luther was neither ascetic, anti-economic nor world rejecting.

15 Scribner (1986), p. 39.
16 Brady (2009), p. 264.

Second, and perhaps even more fundamentally, Luther was not the founder of a sect. Sects, for Weber, are exclusive bodies of religious virtuosi who reject the company of less rigorous believers and dispute merely formal or organizational claims to authority. By these criteria Luther was more like a church father than a sect founder. He was not a friend to doctrinal or cultic rigorism, and he discouraged what he saw as excessive flights of enthusiasm. It was thus not a volte-face when Lutheranism won official recognition as the state church in several realms. It was for this reason, as well, that the impetus given to the capitalist spirit by Luther's doctrine of the calling was credited by Weber largely to Protestant groupuscles outside the Lutheran orbit – above all to the Puritan sects, especially those of Pietist or Baptist origin.

This is where charisma enters the picture in *PESC*. Though the word appears only late in the argument, and *en passant*, Weber's thinking here remained central to his work for the rest of his career. Briefly, he advanced several overlapping premises: that the capitalist spirit is ignited and sustained, above all, by sectarian religiosity; that sectarian religiosity pivots around the ideal of charismatic discipleship (not, as many have supposed, leadership) and consequently has a democratic tendency; and that the entrepreneurial petty bourgeoisie is the primary historical bearer of the capitalist spirit, not the big bourgeoisie.

In other words, the capitalist spirit flourishes best when religious sects and striving entrepreneurs take center stage. That spirit fades, descending into utilitarian self-seeking, when authoritarian churches and capitalist plutocrats take their place.

These points first took shape in the latter half of *PESC*, in Weber's analysis of ascetic Protestantism. Much of what he says there about Calvinism and Baptism is fundamental to his overall perspective. I will return to aspects of that analysis later. But just as relevant for our purposes is what Weber says about the Moravian Brotherhood, an ambitious and eclectic Pietist group which exerted considerable influence in the decades preceding the Industrial Revolution. The Moravians exemplified charisma in two forms that Weber found particularly salient: the "charisma of disciples" and the "charisma of apostolic poverty."

Charisma and Discipleship

In this instance, too, it would be easy to imagine that authentically "Weberian" analysis would revolve around an exceptional leader, and the Moravians were, in fact, led by an outstanding figure, Nikolaus Ludwig von Zinzendorf. A wealthy aristocrat of the Holy Roman Empire, Zinzendorf – known universally as Count Zinzendorf – was remarkable by any standard, and he had a keen sense of his divine calling. In 1741, just months before he traveled to Pennsylvania to help consolidate the Moravian mission to the colonies, he made this very clear.

> I am destined by the Lord to proclaim the message of the death and blood of Jesus, not with human ingenuity but with divine power. … This was my vocation long before I knew anything of the Moravian Brethren, and though I am and shall remain connected with the Moravian Brethren, … I cannot … confine myself to *one* denomination; for *the whole world is the Lord's, and all souls are His* … I know I shall meet opposition … but the message of the crucified Jesus is divine power, and whatsoever opposes it, will be confounded.[17]

That the Moravians saw Zinzendorf similarly is apparent in a 1747 painting by Johann Valentin Haidt, the leading Moravian artist,[18] who portrayed the Count (illumined in the gilded light of the Holy Spirit, which beams upon him from a floating image of Christ's side wound) preaching to a thronging multitude of Moravian converts from many lands (among them Persians, Armenians, Iroquois and Huron) and diverse social conditions, including African slaves from the Carolinas and the Danish West Indies.

Zinzendorf's orthodox Calvinist and Lutheran enemies and sectarian rivals were equally insistent that his inspiration was Satanic. He was assailed, in Pennsylvania, as "the beast of Revelation," a "false prophet," the leader of a band of "devils" and "locusts" "from the bottomless pit."[19] A council of Lutheran theologians in Amsterdam called his eminence among the Brethren "anti-Christlike,"[20] and others deplored the unbridled sensuality of Moravian worship, which caused them, a famous theologian wrote, "to confuse the excitement of natural feeling with the work of the Holy Spirit."[21]

17 Reichel (1888), pp. 93–94, lightly emended. Much of the discussion of the Moravians in the following pages is a revision – in some cases amplified, but more often condensed – of a section of Smith (2013).
18 This painting appears in Fogelman (2007), p. 111. The artist portrayed many of the same individuals (who were actual Moravian converts, many of whom were deceased) in his famous painting of Christ and the "First Fruits." The theology here revolves around Zinzendorf's conviction that, since Christ is the center of Creation, the Holy Spirit must have originated within him, and was only "released" at His death through the stigmata. My thanks to Dan Krier for alerting me to Fogelman's work.
19 Reichel (1888), p. 130. Many of these charges were published by the Pietist "Separatist" Christopher Saur in his Germantown newspaper, the *Hoch-Deutsch Pennsylvanische Geschichts-Schreiber.*
20 They also complained that Zinzendorf mistranslated the New Testament. See Fogelman (2007), p. 146.
21 This is Fogelman's paraphrase (2007, p. 141) of a comment by Bogatzky, author of the famed *Golden Treasury.*

Later commentary, though often secular, remained quite extravagant. The philosopher Herder called Zinzendorf "a conqueror who had few equals"; for Ludwig Feuerbach, he was "Luther reborn."[22] Yet Zinzendorf, like Luther, was personally marginal in Weber's account of Puritanism and capitalism. When, late in *PESC*, Weber turned his attention to Moravian charisma – the very first time he ever mentioned charisma and Puritanism in the same breath – his focus was not leadership but discipleship. What caught Weber's eye was not Zinzendorf's personal authority (which, as we will see, was quite modest) but rather what the contemporary critic Siegmund Baumgarten called the Moravians' "childish obedience to the 'community'."[23]

The Moravians were, in fact, deeply committed to communal life and fellowship – and they hoped to extend this fellowship universally by missionary work. Sohm considered this their greatest virtue and contribution. Pietism in general deserved thanks, he wrote, for its "mighty warning" and "wake-up call" *(Weckruf)* to the sleepy world of orthodoxy, and it was the particular "glory of Pietism" to set the Protestant missionary movement in motion[24] – to send the Reformation beyond Europe. The latter was, in fact, the specific achievement of the Moravians. Spurred by a powerful desire to share their vision of the gospel, they reached out to aristocrats and artisans, capitalists and laborers, slaves and free peoples. Their vision was universalistic and ecumenical, born of a "philadelphian" aspiration to unite Christians of theologically varied traditions on the shared ground of "heartfelt" *(Herzlich)* faith in core evangelical principles. And they held that the Holy Spirit's gifts of grace were available even to non-Christians, in some contexts at least.

The Moravians were the first Protestant missionaries, and they inspired not only Sohm but John Wesley and the Methodists.[25] Originating when, in 1722, Zinzendorf granted sanctuary on his estate to Moravian religious dissidents, the Brethren overcame internal divisions and constituted themselves as a confessional body in 1727, with Zinzendorf as their patron and leader. Initially based in their home community of Herrnhut, they soon branched out. Early missionary outposts were established as early as 1731, and, before long, in a great many places: the Danish West Indies, Greenland, Surinam, Jamaica, the Gold Coast, Algeria, Russia, Norway, Switzerland, The Netherlands, England, Ireland, Wales, Georgia, Pennsylvania, New Jersey, New York, Maryland and North Carolina.[26] Wesley's Methodists soon followed suit and on a very wide

---

22 But, Feuerbach added, as "an imperial count," not "a miner's son"; see Smith, 2013.
23 Cited by Fogelman (2007), pp. 143–44.
24 Sohm (1898), p. 164.
25 Wesley, the founder of Methodism, was profoundly influenced by Zinzendorf.
26 Moravian missions were established in each of these places during Zinzendorf's lifetime. See Engel (2011) and Sensbach (1998) for full details.

scale, but the Moravians were the first in the field. Their efforts had lasting consequences for the global extension of Protestantism.

The Moravians and the Methodists shared something else as well. They were, Weber said, the first Protestants to win workers to the cause of *Berufsarbeit* – that is, to "called" labor. These facts about the Brethren – their evangelism across frontiers, and across class lines – inspired Weber's two references to charisma in *PESC*. The Moravians' "decisive value," he said, was their dual commitment to evangelism and to *Berufsarbeit*. These, in turn, were two sides of the same coin, since evangelism drew the Brethren inexorably to worldly asceticism, as they methodically pursued mundane tasks for the greater good of the missionary enterprise. Ultimately, they forged not only a missionary empire but a global enterprise.[27]

This success could have made the Brethren into Calvinist-style "bourgeois-capitalists," but their ethic was contradictory. The Moravians did not become "businessmen" in the narrow sense, Weber said, because they advocated a pre-bourgeois, quasi-Franciscan asceticism which pivoted around "glorification of the charisma of apostolic *poverty*."[28]

In this, Weber's first reference to charisma, we see no mention of personal magnetism. Weber's claim is that, inspired by the example of the first apostles, the Brethren viewed themselves as "disciples" who owed their status to an "election of grace" (*Gnadenwahl*). They were, they believed, spirit-endowed, gifted with grace – in a word, charismatic.[29] But they were spiritual subjects, not rulers. Although they were God's elect, they had been chosen for service and poverty, not power and wealth.[30]

This outlook bred a form of specifically *working-class* asceticism. The Brethren were loyal not only to Christ but to limitless discipline, above all in the field of called labor. According to Weber this was a turning point for worldly asceticism. For the capitalist, sure of grace and eager for profit, it could seem merely lucky that "religious asceticism furnished him … with sober, conscientious, and uncommonly able workers who clung to their work as their God-given purpose."[31] But viewed "from the *other* side, that of the

---

27 Weber (1905), p. 54.
28 One translator, Parsons, omitted "charisma" from the phrase *"Glorifizierung des Charisma der apostolischen Besitzlosigkeit."* See Weber ([1920c] 1958].
29 Charisma was familiar in the Moravian vocabulary, as we will see below.
30 This led them to partially restore the Catholic *consilia evangelica* – which, as Weber explained later ([1919] 1946), p. 124, is "a special ethic for those endowed with the charisma of a holy life."
31 Compare the parallel passage in Weber (1927), p. 367, where he writes that the rise of the *Beruf* concept "gave to the modern entrepreneur a fabulously clear conscience – and also industrious workers; he gave to his employees as the wages of their ascetic devotion

workers," the picture is different. From this vantage point, "we see glorified, e.g., in the Zinzendorfian species of Pietism, the worker who is faithful to his calling *(Berufstreuen)* and who strives not for gain but rather to emulate the apostles, and who is thus endowed, like them, with the charisma of discipleship *(Jüngerschaft)*."[32]

This, in short, is the charisma of the ascetic worker.[33] Though the disciples are "glorified" by their loyalty to their calling, their glory lies in following orders, not in giving them.

Discipleship and Discipline

The specific form in which "charisma" entered Weber's discourse was thus a kind of charisma from below. *Disciples* were the center of attention, not apostles; *masses*, not masters. How sharply these two approaches differ emerges when we delve further into Moravian praxis. It might be thought that, where there are charismatic disciples, there must be charismatic masters. But that is far from the case here. Zinzendorf's personal role is plain. He was the Moravians' patron and guiding light. But even he was, in a deeper sense, a disciple. The significance of this point emerges from a passage by Zinzendorf in 1737 that Weber quotes to explain discipleship.

Discipleship, Zinzendorf says, requires the imitation of Christ, who "could have known joy" but instead "endured agony and the shame of humiliation." Disciples are hence "the sort of men" who find their bliss in being "humble, despised, reviled"; they care only for service to God; they have nothing or give everything away, and they work as badly paid laborers, "not for the sake of the wage," but rather to fulfill a divine calling *(Berufs)*.[34] An equally archetypal statement appeared in the Brotherly Agreement of 1754:

> We do not ... regard ourselves as men-servants or maid-servants, who serve some men for the sake of a wage, ... but we are here as Brothers and Sisters,

to the calling and of co-operating in his ruthless exploitation of them through capitalism the prospect of eternal salvation ..."

32 Weber (1905), p. 105. For the full original text of this and other key passages, with commentary, see Smith (2013).

33 Weber says the virtues bred by Pietism are those of the patriarchal employer and the *"berufstreue* clerk, worker, and cottage laborer," not the "hard legalism" of bourgeois Calvinist enterprise (1905), p. 56.

34 Zinzendorf ([1737] 1748), pp. 326–27. The opening line, with the archaic spelling *Jüngerschafft*, precedes the passage cited by Weber (1905), p. 54, n. 109, which he drew from Plitt (1869), p. 445.

who owe themselves to the Savior and for whom it is, indeed, a token of grace that they may do all for His sake.[35]

Disciples, that is, serve men – but only as proxies for Christ.[36] They labor ceaselessly and selflessly, not to glorify an autocrat, but to evangelize for the Lord.

About the Brethren's devotion to ascetic labor there can be no doubt: "One does not only work in order to live," Zinzendorf wrote, "but one lives for the sake of one's work, and if there is no more work to do one suffers or goes to sleep."[37] That this was not hyperbole is shown by his profile of the *Herrnhuter* workday: five hours for sleep, three hours for nourishment, and the remainder for labor.[38] Work, for the Brethren, was quite literally worship. In 1758, an elder explained that any activity undertaken in Jesus's name is "for us a liturgy."[39] Work was blessed because Jesus, the "dear carpenter in Nazareth," had labored with his hands. Love feasts celebrated the "blessing of labor" when new tasks were begun. The celebrants rejoiced that Christ "gives a thousand joys to our work."[40]

A résumé of this view was given by Zinzendorf's adjutant August Spangenberg, who wrote that the disciples in the new "General Oeconomy" in Bethlehem, Pennsylvania, "mix the Savior and His blood into their harrowing, mowing, washing, spinning, in short, into everything. The cattle yard becomes a temple of grace."[41] The elect of God *worked*, and nothing, it seemed, was beneath them.

The Sacred Lottery

What, then, was above them? The answer to this question revolves around two practices that gave Moravian discipleship a unique profile: the election of

---

35 This text is not cited by Weber. See Gollin (1967), p. 142; translation lightly emended.
36 Since Christ could not be the *legal* owner, the Brotherly Agreement of 1754 clarifies: "We all belong to the Savior, ... and what we have ... all belongs to Him, and He shall dispose of it as he pleases. Our worthy Brother David Nitschmann, whom we love and honor as a father among us, is, in the eyes of the world, for the sake of good order, recognized as the Proprietor of Bethlehem." Gollin (1967), p. 140
37 Weber (1905), p. 81, n. 19. Gollin cites this line too (1967), pp. 17 and 143.
38 See Gollin (1967), p. 144. Erbe says this was borne out in practice, and that the single men built their barrack by moonlight to conserve their regular workday (1929), p. 90, cited by Atwood (1995), p. 198, n. 48.
39 Atwood (1995), p. 198, n. 46.
40 Atwood (1995), p. 199. Moravian hymns made this point vividly. "Sew and wash with fervor, and the Savior's grace ... will gladden you forever." Gollin (1967), p. 144, translation lightly emended.
41 Gollin (1967), p. 145.

Christ as "Chief Elder" and what the Count called the *"Lossache"* – the business of decision-making by sacred lot *(Los)*. These practices were both intended to give Christ direct authority, unmediated by Zinzendorf or anything merely creaturely. The result was that the lot, not Zinzendorf, was the fount of many critical decisions. Grace "from above" came directly from Christ. It was a gift enjoyed, not by the mighty, but by lowly disciples in the cattle yard.

Zinzendorf was keenly aware of the notion of charismatic authority, which, in a sermon in 1748, he called "the charisma of wise rulership" *(Charisma der Regiments-Klugheit)*. But he disavowed such charisma for himself, saying that, since he was steeped in matters of discipleship *(Jüngerschafts-Materieren)*, he left worldly affairs to others.[42]

For Weber, entrusting their destiny to the lot was one of the Brethren's defining choices. It gave Moravian piety a highly "antirational, feeling-laden" quality,[43] which the Synod of 1764 expressly justified on the ground that Christ's perfect insight infinitely surpassed "even the most carefully weighed thoughts of his workers and servants"; Zinzendorf, in turn, credited the Holy Spirit with "anointing" the lot.[44]

Ultimately, with respect to the sacred lottery, "the most pressing area of concern, within and without" the Brethren, was the issue of obedience. Outsiders attacked the Moravians for "absolute obedience" to the lot's decisions.[45] This was a flat rejection of discipleship; not everyone glorified submission so ardently, or accepted the premise that Christ could intervene directly in communal life. But another feature of the *Lossache* loomed equally large for the Brethren themselves – namely, the fact that reliance on the lot also had an anti-authoritarian tendency, since it deprived Zinzendorf and the senior Brethren of decision-making authority in many spheres. For the Moravians, *"actual power and authority* was in the hands of the slaughtered Lamb."[46]

The Brethren were absolutely pledged to obedience – but not to *human* authority. They symbolized this fact, in many of their meetings and services, by placing an empty chair, representing Christ, at the head of the table.[47] And they entrusted the physical handling of the lot to blindfolded children.

In 1741, the Brethren concluded that preeminence was "too much for a Mortal man," and so, as one of them recalled in 1754, "we asked our Savior

42 Zinzendorf (1748), p. 353. He said this in London, seeking support for the Brethren's colonial missions.
43 Moravian anti-rationalism was, Weber said (1905), p. 52, exceptional even among Pietists.
44 Sommer (2000), pp. 96, 91.
45 Sommer (2000), pp. 90, 93.
46 Kinkel (1990), p. 76; emphasis mine.
47 Kinkel (1990), p. 76, fn. 102.

whether he himself would fill this place, to which he consented" – by lot.[48] Even before this the lot had been widely used – in the appointment of ministers and officeholders (including chief elders); in the consecration of bishops; in fundamental areas of policy; and in the assignment of overseas missionaries, including the initial delegation to the West Indies.[49] According to the Synod of 1869, the adoption of the lot coincided with the founding of the Brethren.[50] In some periods, it was used so often "that it becomes virtually impossible to compile any statistics on its use."[51]

Zinzendorf, in 1743, called devotion to the lot "a charisma of the Brethren," which "belongs among the miraculous powers (*Wunderkräfte*) of His Church."[52] His point in saying this was to affirm that the whole body of disciples – what he called "discipledom" – enjoys charisma jointly.[53] The charisma of discipleship was thus not personal; it was entirely communal, a gift to the Moravians as a body. And they rejected merely mortal authority of every kind. The Synod of 1864, for example, decried rule by spellbinding leaders: "We are a people that stands under the immediate rule of our Head and Lord Jesus Christ," for whom it would be "pathetic" to allow the mortal will of the majority to reign, as in those councils of old where "whoever was most persuasive *(Suade)* won over the majority and did what he wished."[54] Zindendorf "rejected every ... religious thought that suggested some form of fusing, or merging, of the human with the divine as wicked pride."[55] He took pains to deny any overlap between the human and the divine. This led him to reject miracles altogether. "Doing miracles does not belong at all to the essence of a Christian; it does not belong at all to the Gospel." It is simply wrong to confuse "faith in miracles with

48 Gollin (1967), p. 42. Christ's election occurred at the London Synod of 1741. His reign was extended to Bethlehem in 1748.
49 Kinkel (1990), p. 70; Gollin (1967), pp. 52 and 238. Sociologically, the lot was well suited to serve a missionary network that could be centralized only to a very modest extent.
50 Sommer (2000), p. 87.
51 Gollin (1967), p. 237, n. 11.
52 Zinzendorf, cited by Hahn & Reichel (1977, p. 246), from an archival source: *"Die Lossache ist ein Charisma der Gemeine und gehört unter die Wunderkräfte in seiner Kirche."* He adds that this gift of grace is not only a sacred power, but a sacred danger, which should be handled, like fire, with caution.
53 See, e.g., Zinzendorf on the *"Geist des Jüngerthums"* in a 1739 text cited by Plitt (1869), p. 446.
54 This statement is reprinted by Meyer (2003), pp. 257, 260; I've lightly emended the translation.
55 Kinkel (1990), p. 147. Kinkel adds: "Since humans were construed as utterly dependent on God's gracious initiative and activity ... Zinzendorf wanted to exclude every idea which even implied the possibility of human initiative or effort being effective in gaining knowledge of God."

saving faith." While God occasionally grants individuals supernatural powers, even "extraordinary men" who figure as prophets are only God's instruments. Any prophet who forgets this, who exalts himself personally, is merely vainglorious. "If his prophetic office and gift lead him into pride, and he uses them to make himself shine out among mankind," "even if he spoke with the tongues of angels, yet he would be nothing more than a ringing bell."[56]

Discipleship is even further removed from divinity in this tradition by the conviction that Christ is utterly human. God, who is infinitely beyond human comprehension, sacrificed his divinity altogether to make himself known in the entirely human form of Jesus. Many core features of Moravianism required this premise. They saw Christ as God manifest in a state of self-negation, who showed his love for humanity by becoming wholly human – and wholly humble. They insisted that Jesus was not only creaturely but lowly: a menial laborer, who suffered agony, doubt, and death. Discipleship, as the *imitatio Christi*, was the embrace of the lowest humanity, not the highest divinity. The "glory" of the disciples was that the Holy Spirit had granted them the capacity to discern Christ intuitively. They adored Christ not with the head but with the heart, in an entirely *herzlich* way. The relatively few other charismata they claimed (e.g., what Zinzendorf called the *"Sing-Charisma"*)[57] often derived from this foundational gift, since singing, they held, was the best way to experience and communicate *herzlich* feeling.

It is worth recalling, finally, that the Brethren were far from revolutionary. They took pains to assure the authorities that they were meekly submissive. Unlike the incendiary Anabaptists, who had advanced a far more radical theology of discipleship two centuries before, the Moravians were Luther-like in their eagerness to submit. Zinzendorf stressed that the Moravians were "sheep" whose commitment to "passive obedience," even under conditions of despotism, could not be overstated.[58] Similarly, the 1864 Synod reiterated this pledge of subjection and the wish to avoid "irritating" the mighty: "He who Himself submitted and was crucified in shame is our Head, and we dwell in His Kingdom, ... a kingdom of the cross, whose principles are based in subjection."[59]

The Moravians were Christ's disciples, in other words, in the most self-effacing sense. They claimed neither divinity nor worldly leadership but rather

56 Zinzendorf ([1746] 1973), pp. 44–45.
57 Zinzendorf (1758), p. 1. He was reluctant to use hymnals, for fear that "the charisma of singing from memory would be lost." Eyerly (2010, p. 206.
58 Zinzenforf ([1746] 1973, Discourse 20), p. 265.
59 Meyer (2003), p. 258; the same line appears on p. 261 in German.

the Holy Spirit's gift of heartfelt submission – that is, the power of *consent*, not command.

The Sectarian Moment

It would seem, then, that charisma did contribute to the spirit and unfolding of modern capitalism. But the revolutionary effects that Weber credited to charisma in this context were due not to mesmerizing leaders but rather to Puritan sects that internalized an ethic of discipleship and ethically rationalized labor. The Moravians were a paradigmatic sect of this kind. Called to labor in the Lord's vineyard, they carried the gospel of this calling around the world – and even to Benjamin Franklin's doorstep.

Franklin came to know Zinzendorf well in the half-decade before the publication of his manifesto of the capitalist spirit, "Advice to Young Tradesmen" (1748). He was present as a witness when Zinzendorf met with high Pennsylvania officials in 1742 to renounce his noble titles;[60] he interviewed Zinzendorf shortly after the Count's arrival in Pennsylvania; he published Zinzendorf's replies to the envenomed charges of his rivals in the pages of the *Pennsylvania Gazette*; and he published many Moravian sermons and disputations, along with the proceedings of the seven ecumenical synods that Zinzendorf convened during his stay in Pennsylvania. He called Spangenberg "my very much respected friend."[61]

None of this implies, of course, that Franklin had the Moravians in mind when, in his inimitable way, he distilled the worldly asceticism of called labor into proverbial form. But the Moravians were plainly an archetypal sect of the kind that Weber had in mind at the precise moment when – courtesy of publicists like Benjamin Franklin – the capitalist spirit was attaining a kind of routinized preeminence. And what Franklin preached, the Moravians practiced.

---

60 He asked, in the spirit of colonial democracy, to be called "Brother Lewis" or "Pastor Thurnstein."

61 Fogleman (2007), pp. 74, 195; Reichel (1888), p. 130. Works by Zinzendorf published by Franklin include: *Anmerkungen Thurnstein* 1742 (BHZ A 158) *The Remarks, Which the Author of the Compendious Extract, etc. in the Preface to His Book, Has Friendly Desired of the Rev. of Thurnstein, for the Time Pastor of the Lutheran Congregation of J.C. in Philadelphia* (Philadelphia: B. Franklin, 1742). A "Unity Synod" of evangelical German sects met seven times during Zinzendorf's stay in America. Reports of these meetings, together with documentation, were published by Franklin. The title of the first report is *Authentische Relation von dem Anlass, Fortgang und Schlusse Der am 1sten und 2ten Januarii Anno 1741/2 In Germantown gehaltenen Versammlung Einiger Arbeiter derer meisten Christlichen Religionen und Vieler vor sich selbst Gott-dienenden Christen-Menschen in Pennsylvania* (Philadelphia: Gedruckt und zu haben bey Benj. Franklin).

They committed themselves to the infinite accumulation of saved souls and dollars, putting their vocation to the test with limitless faith and devotion.

Soon after finishing *PESC,* Weber traveled to the United States, where, just outside Philadelphia, he attended a Quaker service at Haverford College. He was intrigued by the Quakers' purist, sectarian conviction that "he alone should speak who was moved by the spirit." In deepest silence, without a minister to steer them, they "wait for the spirit to take possession of one of them." But "unfortunately and against my hopes, the spirit did not take hold of the plainly and beautifully costumed old lady ... whose charisma was so highly praised."[62] This passage appears in the 1920 revision of an essay that Weber first published in 1906, recounting his American travels, which served as a pendant to *PESC* – and therein hangs a tale. In the original essay, " 'Kirchen' und 'Sekten' in Nordamerika," Weber analyzed sectarianism with his customary brilliance – but without a single direct reference to charisma.[63] In striking contrast, in the ultimate version of the same essay – which he now called "Die protestantische Sekten und der Geist des Kapitalismus" – Weber put charisma front and center.[64] What had changed?

A clue to the progress of Weber's thinking can be found in the 1920 revision of *PESC*. Here, though he altered very little from the main text of the original version, he did add four essential passages on the *Entzauberung der Welt* – that is, the "demagicalization" or "disenchantment" of the world, which Weber now identifies as a central requisite for the success of the capitalist spirit.[65] This theme was a relatively late but crucial extension of his thinking on this subject. As late as 1910, in his superb and voluminous "anticritical" rejoinders

62 Weber ([1920f] 1946), pp. 317–18. Instead a "brave librarian" ultimately broke the silence. This same event is recorded in Marianne Weber's biography of Max Weber, in an extract from one of his letters ([1926] 1975, pp. 288–89), but without the reference to charisma. Marianne adds that Weber spent time in the Haverford College library "for his study of the spirit of capitalism."

63 Weber published this essay in two forms within three months, first in the *Frankfurter Zeitung* in April and then, in expanded form, in *Die Christliche Welt* in June. See Weber, 1906a & 1906b. In one passage, Weber refers in passing to "the naïve rustic notion" that the priest, "thanks to special gifts of grace," has the capacity for stronger faith than his congregation. (The otherwise excellent English translation in Weber ([1904–05] 2002) omits the word "naïve.") But this is an incidental point, not analytically central to his thinking about the spirit of capitalism.

64 The term *charisma* is used seven times, and very prominently, in the conclusion that Weber added in 1920 (which overlaps in important ways, as well, with the section "Sect, Church, and Democracy" in *E&S*, pp. 1204–10). These additions make the "Sects" essay one of Weber's most enlightening brief contributions on sectarianism and discipleship.

65 These additions comprise nearly a third of all the new text added to the body of the 1920 edition. See, for details, Kalberg's notes in Weber ([1920d] 2009).

to Rachfahl, Weber emphasized the decidedly sectarian and petty bourgeois character of the spirit of capitalism. He rejected altogether the notion that plutocratic self-aggrandizement is "capitalist" in spirit; it is, rather, "Nietzschean," triumphalist, adventurist.[66] In substance, this point closely resembles what he would later say, in *Economy and Society*, about Henry Villard. But at this stage Weber had not yet woven the idea of charisma into the fiber of his critique of capitalism. Only glancing mentions of charisma had appeared in his writings thus far. The same was true with respect to the themes of magic and "demagicalization." But that would soon change, and decisively. In the outpouring of notes and articles that came after 1910 – above all, in the entwined multivolume projects now known as *The Economic Ethics of the World Religions* and *Economy and Society* – both magic and charisma would become central to Weber's thinking on the character, and fate, of the capitalist spirit.

In these writings, a sharp distinction between magical charisma and the ethical rationalization of the world took center stage. Magical charisma, in many forms (Confucian, Hindu and Catholic, among others), was now portrayed as antithetical to capitalism. Weber did not say, in so many words, that capitalism has an elective affinity for ethical charisma of a contrasting, specifically sectarian kind. But that, I think, is the clear implication of his emerging line of argument.

Sectarian fellowship, energized by transcendental commitments, spurs a powerful drive to remake the world ethically – to subordinate the everyday social order to divine ethical commandments. This is what Weber meant by the "ethical rationalization" of the world. This was a "rationalization" pursued by zealously supernaturalist sects whose members claimed the charisma of discipleship. It was as disciples that they embraced the gifts of discipline, and it was this discipline that enabled them to hew to the straight and narrow of called, ascetic labor. Only such labor could impose sacred order on a refractory world. And that – the divine call to sanctify the sinful world – was their "calling." To heed this call, the disciples had to labor with charismatic discipline, the discipline unique to sects. Only that would allow them to straighten the crooked timber of humanity.

Charisma vs. Charisma

Almost all of Weber's writings after 1910 illustrate the development of this perspective. But for present purposes, I will restrict my attention to the very first of the monographic essays written as sequels to *PESC* under the general heading *The Economic Ethics of the World Religions* – "*Der Konfuzianismus*,"

66 See Weber, 1910a & 1910b.

which is known to English-speaking readers under the title *The Religions of China*. This massive study was first published in serial form in 1916, but it had been written several years earlier. It marks a major advance in Weber's thinking about magic, charisma and capitalism, and it concludes with an eye-opening comparison of Confucianism and Puritanism. We learn, in effect, that modern capitalism requires not only the world's demagicalization but, equally, its ethicization. Only one form of charisma can be hegemonic in any given society, and only ethical charisma is compatible with capitalism. Hence, for capitalism to arise and thrive, magical charisma must be overthrown and ethical charisma installed in its place. Sectarian discipleship is the force that drives this revolution.

With respect to China, in particular, Weber's thinking reflected a deep concern for the fate of capitalism globally. He held that, by the early twentieth century, capitalism had been possible in China for many centuries and that it remained a very definite possibility. But Chinese cultural history had not yet opened a path for the capitalist spirit, and, unless that were to happen, Chinese capitalism was likely to remain stillborn. The essential problem was twofold – namely, that Confucianism in China had been simultaneously *too rational* and *too magical* to spark a salvation-oriented yet worldly economic ethic of the kind that had galvanized capitalism in the West. Confucian rationalism is modest and prudent, oriented to the attainment of everyday goals. Confucians adapt to reality and exploit the opportunities they encounter; they do not seek to reorder the world to conform to sacred ideals of transcendental provenance. And the Confucian orientation to magic is equally pragmatic. Magic is regarded as just another way to attain worldly utilitarian outcomes. Supra-mundane concerns – the afterlife, eternal damnation and salvation, atonement for sin – are foreign to the Confucian mentality.

Culture, however, is not fate. Under the right conditions, China, too, is capable of the kind of Puritan rationalism that creates conditions of possibility for the capitalist spirit. This had been shown quite recently by the massive, convulsive Taiping Rebellion (1850–1864), which had deployed powerfully anti-magical, ethically transcendental tendencies against Confucianism and the Chinese empire. This rebellion was only prevented from transporting China into the age of ascetic *Berufsethik*, Weber said, by British force of arms.

In short, Chinese capitalism remains a possibility, but only if the capitalist spirit ripens; and that, in turn, requires the emergence of a rational religious ethic that would strive to subordinate everyday life to divine goals. Hitherto the main barrier to such a religious rationalism in China, Weber says, has been the hegemony of magical charisma, which has taken two basic forms: imperial office charisma, which Weber regards as magical charisma on a grand, routinized scale; and the tangled undergrowth of plebeian Taoist and Buddhist magic, which the imperial Confucian elite tolerated as long as it did not generate heretical sects. The most dangerous heresy, as exemplified by the Taiping Rebellion, was sectarian-charismatic prophecy with an ascetic bent, which threatened to undo Confucianism altogether and provoke a radical religious rationalization of society. In other words, the capitalist spirit was blocked in China by magical charisma and yet had the potential to arise on the ground of sectarian prophetic charisma.[67]

So what we find, then, is not a simple opposition between capitalism and charisma but rather diverse forms of charisma which are associated with diverse forms of capitalism. Villard's claim to a kind of buccaneer charisma, for example, was neither religious nor ascetic but rather amoral and opportunist – a charismatic claim that was tailor-made for untethered adventure capitalism. By contrast, the prophetic claims of the early Puritan sects and their latter-day secular counterparts have very distinct affinities for modern capitalism and for the corresponding ethical-methodical rationalization of daily life.

"Entzauberung der Welt"

Weber did not think that cultural inertia was an insuperable obstacle to sectarianism and capitalism in China. As he wrote, on the penultimate page of *Der Konfuzianismus*, "The Chinese in all likelihood would be quite capable, probably more so than the Japanese, of assimilating capitalism, which has technically and economically been fully developed in the modern culture area. It is obviously not a question of deeming the Chinese naturally 'ungifted' for the demands of capitalism."[68] In fact, in antiquity, China had more closely resembled Occidental culture than it did subsequently: "In the traits relevant for us, the further back one goes in history the more similar the Chinese and

---

67 This argument is not simply a *résumé* of the argument in *PESC* but is rather a crucial new contribution, since the very notion of magic was given a distinctively new emphasis when it was imported into the revised 1920 text. Had Weber integrated the language of magical charisma into the revised text at this juncture, the otherwise latent presence of the notion of charisma would have been much more visible.
68 Weber ([1916g] 1964), p. 248. Here, and afterwards, I will often emend the standard translations, without always indicating this. In this passage, to illustrate that point, the emended translation corresponds to the original text, which reads as follows: "Der Chinese würde, aller Voraussicht nach, ebenso fähig, vermutlich noch fähiger sein als der Japaner, sich den technisch und ökonomisch im neuzeitlichen Kulturgebiet zur Vollentwicklung gelangten Kapitalismus anzueignen. Es ist offenbar gar nicht daran zu denken, daß er für dessen Anforderungen etwa von Natur aus 'nicht begabt' wäre."

Chinese culture appear to what is found in the Occident." Most of the characteristics of ancient China, including "the beginnings of capitalist development in the Period of the Warring States, … are more closely related to Occidental phenomena than are the traits of Confucian China" (p. 231).

The absence of the kind of political capitalism that arose in Greco-Roman antiquity – which Weber credits to the tranquility of the long-pacified Chinese empire – does not explain the absence of "purely economically-oriented capitalism." In fact, objectively, China enjoyed propitious conditions for the rise of capitalism, including the absence of many feudal impediments of the European kind. Yet China never crossed the threshold into modern capitalism. Why? At this juncture Weber points, in part, to the influence of the practical Confucian worldview. Chinese "attitudes," he agrees, were "co-determined by political and economic destinies."

> Yet, in view of their autonomous laws, one can hardly fail to ascribe to these attitudes effects strongly counteractive to capitalist development (p. 249).

What were these attitudes? What aspects of the Chinese worldview blocked modern capitalism? The answer, Weber says, lies in the difference between Confucianism and Puritanism, to which he devotes the entire final chapter of his monograph. Confucian and Puritan rationalism, he says, are "polar opposites" (p. 238), and they are distinguishable by "two primary yardsticks" *(Maßstäbe)*: "One is the degree to which the religion has divested itself of *magic*;" "the other is the degree to which it has systematically unified the relation between God and the world and therewith its own ethical relationship to the world." These criteria are plainly linked. In the West, Weber says, "Puritanism came to consider all magic as *devilish*. Only [transcendental] ethical rationalism was defined as religiously valuable, that is, conduct according to God's commandment" (p. 227). This conviction required accepting, and enforcing, Godly ways *against* the ways of the world. A society like Confucian China, in which magic remained dominant, was very different. Chinese rationalism was worldly in the most classical sense, finding its *point d'honneur* in cultivated adaptation to the everyday world. Imperial China was thus inhospitable to forces that sought to remake the world along divinely ordained ethical lines. In order to follow such an ethic, China would have had to undergo *Entzauberung* – sacrificing magical charisma to the claims of an ethically charismatic deity and movement.

It was an innovation for Weber to posit this twofold distinction. Until this point he had not yet fully established the idea that demagicalization is vital to Puritanism, and indeed, to all ethically rationalized religion. But here he is very definite – and he later imported this point directly into *PESC*. In *Der*

Konfuzianismus, he had written that "the most characteristic forms" of ascetic Protestantism "liquidated magic almost totally."[69]

> In principle, magic was eradicated even in the sublimated form of sacraments and symbols, to such a great extent that the strict Puritan had the corpses of loved ones buried informally, without any 'superstition' – which meant, in effect: burying all trust in magical manipulations. Only thus was the demagicalization of the world [*Entzauberung der* Welt] carried through completely, in all its consequences.[70]

When, in the 1920 edition of *PESC,* Weber mentions *Entzauberung* for the first time, he sounds a similar note: "Every great religious-historical process of the *demagicalization* of the world, which ... repudiated all *magical* means in the quest for salvation as superstition and sacrilege, found here its culmination. The authentic Puritan rejected even hints of [idolatrous] ceremony at the grave, burying those closest to him without song or sound, without the least 'superstition,' to avoid reposing trust in magical-sacramental forms of the attainment of salvation."[71]

The authentic Confucian, by contrast, regarded magic as a normal means of attaining worldly security and serenity. Confucian practicality was balanced, Weber says, by "a boundless and good-natured credulity towards even the most fantastic magical swindle (*Schwindel*)."[72] Even the most sophisticated forms of Confucianism never transcended a "purely magical religiosity," which, Weber said, was evident on all sides – in the high status of ancestor worship, "which was equally fundamental for official and popular religiosity"; in the many surviving forms of the old "animist compulsion of spirits," which included myriad officially tolerated Taoist magical "therapies," including hydromancy, geomancy, meteoromancy, and chronomancy; and, above all, in the exalted yet vulnerable standing of "the emperor who, by personal

---

69 Weber ([1916g] 1964), p. 226, translation emended. The original of this passage (Weber 1916c, p. 372) reads as follows: "*Seine am meisten charakteristischen Ausprägung haben der Magie am vollständigsten den Garaus gemacht.*"

70 Weber adds a significant caveat here: "That did not, however, mean freedom from what we would today reckon 'superstition.' Witch trials also flourished in New England."

71 This is the Parsons rendering (Weber, 1920c), p. 105, which I have extensively emended as per Käsler (2013), p. 146.

72 Weber ([1916g] 1964), p. 231. Although "the educated Confucian adhered to magical conceptions with an admixture of skepticism ... the mass of the Chinese, whose way of life was influenced by Confucianism, lived in these conceptions with unbroken faith." And even "high Chinese officials ... did not hesitate to be edified by the stupidest miracle" (p. 229).

qualification, was responsible for the good conduct of the spirits and the ...
rain and good harvest weather."[73]

Magic's Empire

It was in connection with "charismatic and pontifical" Chinese kingship
that Weber gave one of his first general accounts of the notion of charismatic authority. This account owes much to *fin de siècle* ethnology, especially
Marett's notion of "pre-animist" religion, and closely resembles the discussion in the "Sociology of Religion" section of *Economy and Society*, which
was written in the same phase. "The emperor had to prove his charismatic
authority, which had been tempered by hereditary successorship. Charisma
was always an extraordinary force *(maga, orenda)* and was revealed in sorcery
and heroism."[74]

The extraordinary, in this original sense, was also magical: "At first heroic
strength was considered quite as much a magical quality as 'magical force'
in the narrower sense, for instance, rainmaking, magical healing, or extraordinary craftsmanship." This charismatic quality could also be irretrievably
lost: "Charisma seemed to be guaranteed only so long as it was confirmed by
recurrent miracles."[75] Charisma was thus mercurial as well as magical. Magic
was trusted only as long as it seemed to *work*.

It was from magical charisma of this kind, Weber said, that dynastic charisma arose in China. For many reasons, including the challenge of managing
the unpredictable rivers, imperial authority was infused from the start with
magical hopes and duties. Rain gods had to be entreated, river demons had to
be appeased. "Secular and spiritual authority were united in [the emperor's]
hand, the spiritual strongly predominating." It was the emperor's mandate
"to prove his *magische Charisma* through military successes or at least [stability].

---

73 Weber ([1916g] 1964), pp. 229, 227.
74 Weber ([1916g] 1964), p.30.
75 All of the citations in the next three paragraphs can be found in Weber ([1916g] 1964),
    pp. 29–33. And cf. n. 58, pp. 260–61: "It is impossible to distinguish strictly between
    'charm' and non-charm in the world of pre-animist and animist ideas. Even plowing,
    or any other ordinary act which was a means to an end, was 'magic' in the sense of
    taking into service specific 'forces' (later on 'spirits'). Here only sociological distinctions
    can be made." The possession of extraordinary qualities differentiated the state of
    ecstasy from that of workaday life, the professional magician from ordinary people.
    'Extraordinariness,' then, was rationalistically transformed into the 'supernatural.' The
    artistic craftsman who produced the paraments of the Temple of Yahwe was possessed
    of the *'ruach'* of Yahwe, just as the medicine man was possessed of the force which
    qualified him for his accomplishments."

Above all, he had to secure good harvest weather and guarantee the peaceful internal order of the realm."[76]

What prevailed, in other words, was a kind of magical patrimonialism, in which the Chinese emperor served as ritual principal for the people as a whole, seeking to assure their welfare by charismatic means.[77] He "ruled in the old genuine sense of charismatic authority. He had to prove himself as the 'Son of Heaven' and as the Lord mandated by Heaven insofar as the people fared well under him. If he failed, … if the rivers broke the dikes, or if rain did not fall despite his sacrifices, it was evidence … that he did not have the charismatic qualities demanded by Heaven. In such cases the emperor did public penance for his sins, as happened even in recent times."[78] So great was his magically based authority, so great were the hopes reposed in him, that he ruled even over gods: "The emperor granted recognition to proven deities as objects of worship; he bestowed title and rank upon them and occasionally demoted them again."

> Only proven charisma legitimized a spirit. And while the emperor, to be sure, was held responsible for misfortune, the god was also disgraced … As late as 1455, an emperor gave the spirit of Tasi mountain a public tongue-lashing.[79]

Still, despite his preeminence, the emperor remained the head of the state bureaucracy, and, as such, he was an officeholder himself. He shared his *magische Charisma* with the whole of his bureaucracy: "Officialdom, the pillar of public order and the state, was held to partake of charisma too … All unrest and disorder in his bailiwick – whether social or cosmic-meteorological

---

76 Correct imperial conduct, which originally had a purely ritual significance, acquired the patina of "virtue." The emperor was "the old rainmaker of magical religion translated into ethics." Right conduct was his moral duty, a charismatic ritualism, which ensured peace and prosperity; dereliction of duty would comprise ritual malfeasance, with magical harm and disturbed peace as the consequence.

77 Weber (1916g), p. 39, "The emperor, as supreme pontifex, had ritual privileges which enabled him alone to offer the highest sacrifices."

78 Weber cites an instance in 1832, where "rain soon followed" the emperor's expiatory self-criticism. Hence apologetic self-criticism is a ritual too, a kind of sacrifice of honor, a just confession of a prior failure of justice. "If this was of no avail, the emperor had to expect abdication; in the past, it probably meant self-sacrifice." Weber (1916g), n. 63, pp. 261–62.

79 In (1916g), n. 57, p. 260, Weber gives instances reported by the *Peking Gazette*: On July 13, 1874, a motion was made to "grant recognition to the miraculous power of a temple of the Dragon God in Honan." On April 4, 1883, officials "requested the promotion of a canonized deceased mandarin of the river area, since his spirit was seen hovering over the water."

in nature – demonstrated that the official was not in the good grace of the spirits. Without questioning the reasons, he had to retire from office."

This, plainly, was a monumental form of office charisma – which Weber says grows naturally out of the magical charisma of kings. And office charisma is jealous of rivals. In the Chinese case, this jealously blocked the rise of church and sect alike. The empire assumed the all the main functions of a church in typically "Caesaropapist" fashion, and heterodox sects were suppressed, either by "fire and sword" or by indoctrination.[80] "The 'sacred edict' of 1672 ... expressly ordered the rejection of false doctrines." The motive for this kind of heresy hunting and repression was less theology than power: "Imperial office charisma ... tolerated powers with an independent authority of grace ... as little as" did the Catholic Church. Indulgence was shown to many forms of popular mysticism, but unlicensed sects were forbidden, especially if they were led by mystagogues who claimed divine status, preached heavenly salvation, or cloistered their disciples away from the world.[81]

Ideologically, the authorities rejected prophecies of heavenly salvation on rationalistic grounds, accusing prophets and prophetic sects of "defrauding the people ... for there [is] no compensation in the beyond." But what ultimately proved decisive was the fact that such prophecies "meant contempt for the worldly charisma of the Confucian state office." Soul healing was permitted through ancestor worship, but earthly salvation (rainmaking, repelling barbarians, etc.) was the monopoly of the imperial dynasty and bureaucracy.[82] "Hence any belief in redemption and any striving for sacramental grace threatened not only piety toward the ancestors but the prestige of the administration." Renouncing the traditional ancestor cult was an affront to the most important civic virtue, piety, on which "depended discipline in the hierarchy of office and obedience of subjects. A religiosity which emancipated [the subjects] from believing in the all-decisive power of

---

80 All citations in this and the next two paragraphs are taken from Weber (1916g), pp. 214–18.

81 The rulers tolerated plebeian religiosity as long as it remained within the pale of ancestor worship and Confucian orthodoxy. This tolerance helped them "tame the masses." Taoism in particular was acceptable because it revolved around sorcerers who did not found principled sects but provided magical assistance to individuals *qua* individuals; and Chinese Buddhism was palatable because, unlike its Indian progenitor, it too remained basically magical and nonsectarian. But whenever seeds of hierocracy appeared, whenever sects grew up around priests, the inquisitorial state intervened. Sects, in principle, were "odious" to the empire, since they broke with venerable principles to affirm their own.

82 Ancestor worship, plainly, reinforces imperial interest as the guarantee of dynastic charisma.

imperial charisma and the eternal order of pious relations was unbearable in principle."

This reliance on magical charisma, official and unofficial, gave a powerful impetus to Chinese traditionalism, since, "from magic, there followed the inviolability of tradition as the proven magical means" of ensuring tranquility. Puritanism, in contrast, was ethically anti-traditional, since God's ordinances were meant to reconstitute the world from within: Since there was an absolute conflict "between a transcendent God and a carnally wicked, ethically irrational world," the Puritan affirmed the "absolute unholiness of tradition and the truly eternal task of ethically and rationally subduing ... the given world."[83] Chinese rationalism pursued a kind of ethical entente, in which friction with society was reduced "to an absolute minimum." Puritanism, in contrast, found itself in acute tension with the stubbornly eudaemonistic "irrationalities" of everyday life."[84] The abyss dividing these rival forms of rationalism was "unbridgeable," and China, as a consequence, remained "magicalized" and acquisitive in the traditional manner rather than demagicalized and capitalist in the modern sense.

Geist of Capitalism or Profit Motive?

China was, then, remote from capitalism precisely to the extent that it depended upon (and defended) the routinized magic of imperial office charisma. Weber is well aware that this claim could seem paradoxical, since, in some ways, Chinese culture seemed to revolve around "money and money affairs ... to an extent seldom found elsewhere." The Chinese were endowed with "an almost incredible virtuosity in thrift," a "self-sufficient frugality of unexampled intensity," a "calculating mentality." China had long had many favorable preconditions for unhindered commerce: a pacified, unified empire; free rather than enslaved or enserfed labor; and substantial religious tolerance. "Peace existed, and a far-reaching freedom of commodity trade, movement, occupational choice and methods of production. There was no tabooing whatsoever of the shopkeeper spirit." And yet, despite all this – despite many

---

83 Citations in this paragraph and the note below are taken from Weber (1916g), in this order: pp. 240, 227, 241, 237, 235. All translations are lightly emended.

84 Whereas "all communal action" in China "remained engulfed in and conditioned by the purely personal, above all, by kinship relations," it has been "the great achievement of ethical religions, above all the ethical and ascetic sects of Puritanism, to shatter the fetters of sib [kinship]. These religions established a higher community of faith and a common ethical life in opposition to the community of blood."

centuries of far-flung trade, along the Silk Road and elsewhere – modern capitalism remained alien in China:

> In this typical land of profiteering, one may well see that by themselves neither 'acquisitiveness,' nor high and even exclusive concern for wealth, nor utilitarian 'rationalism' have any connection as yet with modern capitalism.[85]

In some ways, China was even farther than ancient Phoenicia, Greece and Rome "from the 'spirit' of modern capitalism." "Confucian mentality, deifying 'wealth,' [was] akin to the worldliness" of such Renaissance notables as Leon Battista Alberti, whose counsel of prudential estate management and tempered eudaemonism was mistaken by many writers (most famously, Werner Sombart) for an early expression of the capitalist spirit. Chinese businesses, like Alberti, were prudent and pragmatic, but they did not work methodically to accumulate capital indefinitely through ever-renewed productive investment.[86] "Such conceptions have remained alien to China."[87]

Here, yet again, self-seeking reliance on magic precluded ethically rational self-denial. For the Chinese entrepreneur, "success and failure in business did not signify a state of grace but rather the attainment of *magically and ritually significant merit or offense*."[88] Wealth was pursued for its own sake, by any means, including magic, and the quest for wealth was seen, therefore, as a test of magical charisma. For the Puritan, in contrast, "economic success was not an ultimate goal or end in itself," and magic was proscribed, for ethical as well as rational reasons, as a tool of amoral self-love; it served greed, and thus stood in the way of the selfless rationalization of the world.[89]

---

85 Weber [1916g] 1964, p. 243.
86 "The Puritan was taught to suppress the petty acquisitiveness which destroys all rational, methodical enterprise – an acquisitiveness which distinguishes the character of the Chinese shopkeeper." Even such "a Johnny come lately [*Epigone*] as Benjamin Franklin" would, like "the consistent Pietist," practice a kind of daily bookkeeping to tally the balance of virtue and vice. "The Bible was cherished as a sort of book of statutes and a managerial doctrine." (Weber [1916g]), pp. 244, 246
87 These citations appear in Weber (1916g), on pp. 242, 230, 242, 237. Alberti and Fugger, who are both mentioned here, were memorably discussed in *PESC*. Alberti, in particular, is the focal point of note 12 in Chapter 2, which is unquestionably the most important addition Weber made to *PESC* in 1919–1920. Weber takes pains in this note to say exactly what he was, and was not, attempting to accomplish in *PESC*.
88 Weber (1916g), p. 243; italics mine, translation emended.
89 Puritan enterprise did, of course, yield profits, but it did so inadvertently, as a side effect of the quest for salvation, not "the profit motive." Chinese enterprise was unashamedly profit motivated – and yet, *for that very reason*, did not embody the modern capitalist spirit.

The Puritan's *capacity* to exalt God's will, and to remake the world in self-sacrificing obedience to His call, was plainly a gift of grace – and this gift was ethical, not magical. Capitalists and "pious workers" alike were graced with a steady and unwavering resolve; they acquired a specifically ethical unity of "personality" from the single-mindedness of their commitment to sober, practical action to impose divine order on the world. Weber offers one of his clearest and most complete brief statements of this Puritan ethic and its worldly consequences in the closing pages of his contrast between Confucianism and Puritanism:

> Radical concentration on God-willed purposes; the relentless practical rationalism of the ascetic ethic; a methodical, matter-of-fact conception of enterprise management; disdain for illegal, political, colonial, robber and monopoly capitalism, which relied on the favor of princes and men as opposed to the sober, strict legality and harnessed rational energy of everyday enterprise; the rational calculation of the technically best way, of practical solidity and expediency, instead of the old-style artisans' traditionalist joy in inherited skills or their products' beauty– all of these are "ethical" qualities indispensable to the specifically modern capitalist entrepreneur and to the pious worker's specific will-to-work [*Arbeitswilligkeit*] – this relentlessly, religiously systematized utilitarianism, in which rational asceticism takes on the distinctive form of living "in" yet not "of" the world, helped to produce superior rational aptitudes and with them the "spirit" of vocational man [*Berufsmenschentums*].[90]

The latter, the sense of a divine yet worldly calling, was "ultimately meaningless to world-adapted Confucianism, for which life-direction [*Lebensführung*] was rational but driven, unlike Puritanism, from without rather than within. The contrast can teach us that mere sobriety and thriftiness united with 'acquisitiveness' [*Erwerbstrieb*] and esteem for riches are still remote from the 'capitalist spirit,' in the sense specific to the vocational man [*Berufsmenschentums*] of the modern economy."[91]

In other words, modern capitalism is legal-rational, yet fueled by "God-ordained" purposes. These purposes comprise a "calling," which is always, above and beyond all particulars, a call to "concentrate," with tunnel vision, on rationalizing the world in line with God's ordinances, a call to self-denying yet also self-relying conduct. The Puritan capitalist is thus also in a sense a "pious worker" who works "with a will" – God's will. Asceticism in this context means the sacrifice of personal enjoyment as well as personal *Lebensführung*.

90 Weber (1916g), p. 243.
91 Weber (1916g), p. 247, radically modified as per the original (1916c, p. 384).

The goal is to rationalize the world functionally rather than aesthetically; in a utilitarian spirit, so that the divine will can be implemented *efficiently*; impersonally, with ascetic rejection of the satisfactions of artisanal creativity and self-realizing labor.

The "personality" thus formed, it would seem, harbors impersonality at its core; hence, the proverbial coldness (of, e.g., Calvinism) which Weber so memorably documents.

Ascetic Protestantism thus requires the sacrifice of artisanal self-realization and, in general, disalienated labor, which is the ethical side of what Weber calls traditionalism. That was why peasants and former peasants in early modern Europe were so obdurately resistant to the Puritan work ethic, and that was why Methodism, the "Puritanism of the workers," was so important to the diffusion of asceticism across class lines, beyond the bourgeoisie.[92] Personal self-direction is replaced by God's bureaucratically specified will. God here figures as the Taylorist employer writ large, the boss who specifies to the last detail what "pious workers" (capitalists included) must do – and these pious workers are never off duty. So sleep, too (*á la* Franklin) is business, not pleasure, the restoration of waking energy harnessed to serve only as labor power. Taylorism, seen in this light, amounts to "reading God's mind," which is a *duty* for the pious employer, since it is God Himself who wills "the one best way."[93] God, in short, monopolizes the legitimate use of will, and the ethically rational Puritan regards God as *his* boss, as the ultimate Captain of Industry. We find, in this worldview, a "mighty enthusiasm." "Both the Puritan and the Confucian were rational men. But the rational sobriety of the Puritan was founded in a mighty enthusiasm which the Confucian completely lacked."[94] This enthusiasm entailed not only rejection of the sinful world but "eagerness to master the world" – that is, to reject traditional society not by fleeing it, but by remaking it. God was to become Lord over all things worldly. This impelled a quest for *innerweltliche Herrschaft* through called labor, and every calling was, in its own way, a demand to impose and surrender to God's will, to integrate

---

92 When the Moravians, who greatly influenced the Methodists, first worked among the Mohicans in North America, they ran into a stone wall of traditionalism: the Mohicans, it was said, often "sit and laugh at them, as being good for Nothing else but to plow and fatigue themselves with hard Labour; while *they* enjoy the satisfaction of stretching themselves on the Ground, and sleeping as much as they please, and have no other Trouble but now and then to chase the Deer, which is often attended with Pleasure rather than Pain." (Wheeler, p. 84) But the Moravians persisted, and ultimately, by modeling their principles – by showing that they were not too proud to labor in the most humble ways – they won a small number of Mohican converts.

93 Weber (1916g), p. 247.

94 Weber (1916g), p. 247.

sacrifice into everyday life. "Nothing clashed more with the Confucian ideal of gentility than the idea of a 'calling.' The 'princely' man . . . was not a tool of a god. But the [ascetic] Christian . . . wanted to be nothing more than a tool of his God; in this he sought his dignity. Since this is what he wished to be, he was a useful instrument for rationally transforming and mastering the world."[95]

The Confucian ethic was not money-averse. It was, in fact, highly compatible with the profit motive, understood in the traditionalist sense. Yet the Puritans, who scorned self-seeking and viewed money as a base temptation, unintentionally gave money, as capital, a world-transforming power. This power was decidedly not, Weber tells us, a product of magical charisma. Capitalism thrives on *Entzauberung*, and China was steeped in magic.

What, then, of other varieties of charisma? If charisma in *magische* form is an obstacle to capitalism, is charisma in some other form a stimulus to capitalism?

The Underwhelming Magic of "Personal Charisma"

In the secondary literature, "personal charisma," the charisma of the leader, is typically treated as the principal catalyst of epochal historical change – and the rise of capitalism certainly qualifies on that score. But Weber, in his most extended discussion of the intersection of capitalism and charismatic figures, puts matters in a different light. The context is Hindu India, in the twentieth century and earlier. Here, too, Weber finds "boundless acquisitive greed . . . in matters great and small."[96] India is also the heartland of personal charisma. Yet the great charismatic figures – gurus, mystagogues, and even prophets of salvation – have not transcended greed. In fact, rather than undermining the *auri sacra fames*, rather than stimulating rational investment or breaking with magic, the "living gods" of India traded on their charisma – to acquire fortunes, which they achieved as sellers of magical services.

What the Indian masses wanted, above all else, was magical assistance;[97] what the "Guru-Demagogues" wanted, and most needed, was "mass

---

95 Weber (1916g), p. 248. How little Weber loves the "hysteria" of this mighty enthusiasm: China was marked, he writes by "the absence of hysteria-producing, asceticist religious practices"; "frenzy and orgiastic 'obsession' were divested of the charismatic value attaching to sacredness and were only considered symptomatic of demonic rule" (p. 232).

96 Weber ([1916–17] 1967, p. 337; 1916–17, p. 808.

97 Only intellectual strata in India worry about salvation, the masses barely know the meaning of the word – they want magic, and improved rebirth chances; these are the values "for which they did and do strive" (Weber [1916–17, 1967), p. 326. What the aliterary lay strata wanted above all else was grace – "primarily magical grace for the here and now, and only secondarily grace for the future, for rebirth and the hereafter" (p. 254).

patronage." To win public favor, the gurus claimed *magische* charisma on a grand scale. They offered magical help in return for veneration – and pay. The result was an enriched charismatic stratum, not a modern bourgeoisie: "Wealth and especially money enjoy an almost extravagant esteem" in Hindu folk culture, but rather than driving "rational wealth accumulation and capital valorization, Hinduism created irrational accumulation chances for magicians and soul shepherds and benefices for mystagogues and ritually- or soteriologically-oriented intellectual strata."[98]

In the early Indian kingdoms, private magical enterprise had been blocked by the office-charismatic claims of the royal bureaucracy. But conquests – Islamic, and later, English – unsettled royal charisma and cleared a path for the private magic of the gurus. "It was initially the foreign domination of Islam that shattered the political power of the exalted Hindu castes, which gave the development of *Guru*-power free rein, allowing it to grow to *grotesken* heights."[99] Subsequently, by further weakening the traditional hierarchies, and by opening the floodgates to markets and mercantilism, English capitalism created additional wealth-chances for the gurus among the commercial classes. A clientele for magical services grew up among the "petty bourgeois and proletaroid masses," and this, alongside "the increasing wealth of bourgeois strata in the cities, raised the acquisition chances for guru demagoguery [*Guru-Demagogie*]."[100] English capitalism thus spurred Indian *wealth magic*. "Just as English rule gradually promoted capitalistic development – by creating entirely new sources of wealth accumulation and economic ascent – so [the shift from traditional caste hierarchy to *Guru*-power was promoted."[101] Now, instead of Brahmans, "it is the *guru* of the plebeian sect who is ardently and truly hailed as a god."[102] Gurus who became mystagogues (magicians with organized followings) saw the chance to routinize their acquisition chances by forming "sects" which were, in effect, magical service emporia. Since these grouplets were never integrated into a single institutional framework,[103] there

---

98 Weber (1916–17), p. 798. Where Weber wrote "*Kapitalverwertung*," the standard translation ([1916–17] 1967, p. 328) reads: "evaluation of capital."

99 Weber ([1916–17] 1967), pp. 324–25; Weber (1916–17), p. 794.

100 Weber ([1916–17] 1967), p. 323; Weber (1916–17), p. 792.

101 Weber (1916–17), p. 792.

102 Weber (1916–17), pp. 792–93

103 Weber stresses that it was, in contrast, the great achievement of Catholicism to subordinate the sects to a single universal church (to place them "under rigid official discipline"). So tendencies to "human deification" were unrestrained in India. In China, office charisma *precluded* sectarian zeal and mysticism. In Christendom, sects were *included* in the Church, and subordinated thereby to "the *rational office*-character [*rationale Amts*-Charakter] of the administration, which was distinctive and decisive

were a great many such mystagogues, serving innumerable clients. "This … offered the masses the incarnate *living* savior, the helper-in-need, confessor, magical therapist, and above all, object of worship … All sect founders were deified [*vergöttlicht*] and their successors became and are objects of worship."[104]

This, plainly, is "personal charisma" raised to a supremely high level, that of "hagiolatry and indeed a hagiolatry of *living saviors*." These saviors were not merely "leaders" in the ordinary sense but were "incarnate gods" who were endowed with magical gifts of grace – and, like deities, they often served as "magical grace donors" (*Gnadenspender*) as well. In their "devotion [*Hingabe*] to a 'living savior'," the sect revealed "the unbrokenness of magic in general [and, indeed,] the unbrokenness of charisma in its oldest manifestation: as a purely magical power."[105] Yet despite their ultra-charismatic status, despite their occasionally "absolute" authority, these soul shepherds were *not revolutionaries*. The only "salvation" they offered was *private*, promised to each member of the sect *as an individual*.[106] Instead of striving for the political or ethical rationalization of society, the Guru-Demagogues sought enrichment by the sale of magical services: spells against "erotic or economic competitors"; spells to get rich, force debt payments, or win legal cases; and more.

Many of these spells, directed to "functional gods and demons," took the "gross form of *coercive* magic"; other spells assumed the form of *persuasive* magic.[107] Much of this was "spiritual," of course, only in the very crude sense that it was oriented to the spirit world, and even those sects that inclined

over and against the personal or inherited charisma (*persönlichen oder Erbcharisma*) of the gurus." Note that Weber refers to sect heads in Christendom as gurus! But they were gurus who were tamed, not given free rein, and note, as well, that the alienability of personal charisma was blocked by the principle of succession *via ordination*.

104 Weber ([1916–17] 1967), p. 319; Weber (1916–17), p. 787.

105 Weber ([1916–17] 1967), p. 335. The translator renders "*Hingabe*" very oddly as "gift," and *Ungebrochenheit* as "impregnability."

106 The mystagogue is the magician who converts his clientele into a flock, a magical following, but his promise is still "the salvation of individuals qua individuals." Weber ([1916f] 1946), p. 272.

107 I would argue, with this distinction in mind, that the authority of the gurus was far less absolute than it may now appear. Except in those rare cases when they actually enjoyed "unconditional obedience" (*unbedingte Obedienz*), they resembled "gods" of the classically magical kind, whose favor could be *coerced* by the fetishistic ritual of *payment*. In fact, when magic services first became available for purchase, payment itself became the fetishistic act par excellence. All magical services were thereby reduced to a common metric, since the first step in the coercion of a God was mediated through payment to a magician, whose artisan-like skills (spells) were devoted, in varied form, to the unmediated coercion or persuasion of the god. Payment to

toward more refined, inwardly driven worship were still primarily magical in their ultimate outlooks.[108] "With such means the great mass of aliterary and even literary Asiatics sought to master everyday life." In this way, Weber emphasizes, "the "supremely anti-rational world of universal magic also affected daily economic life, and from this, there is no path to rational worldly life-regulation."[109]

> "No community dominated by inner powers of this sort" – "religious anthropo-latry," coercive and persuasive magic, etc. – "could unfold from within itself the 'spirit of capitalism.'"[110]

Indian mass religiosity in general, and guru worship in particular, was suffused with acquisitiveness, but this was, Weber emphasizes, "an 'acquisitive drive' pursued with every artifice, including the universal artifice: magical trial-and-error. It was lacking in precisely that which proved decisive for Occidental economy: the refraction [*Brechung*] and rational objectification [*Versachlichung*] of the drive-character of acquisitive striving and its integration into a system of rational inner-worldly ethic of conduct, like that [of] the 'inner-worldly asceticism' of Protestantism."[111] The only 'this-worldly asceticism' asked by the *guru* was the sacrifice of *payment*: "As the peasant was to the landlord, so the layman was to the [mystagogue as patron]: ... ultimately, mere sources of tribute."[112] In other words, the *gurus'* followers were not, for them, souls to be saved but rather business clients, mere sources of profit.

the magician thus became a kind of magic spell itself, a universal spell that evokes *particular spells.*

108 In some Vishnuite circles, especially among Chaitanya's followers, an emotional form of *bhakti* devotion became central to redeemer-worship; this may have arisen as a sense of erotic kinship to the savior, but, if so, it was later rationalized into sublimated yet still magical form. Weber compares this to Zinzendorf's pietism ([1916–17] 1967), p. 308. Cp. *E&S*, pp. page 537–38, where Zinzendorf's "emotional piety" is cited as one of the classic instances of the sublimation of orgiastic ecstasy.

109 Weber (1916–17), p. 807.

110 Weber ([1916–17] 1967), p. 325; Weber (1916–17), p. 795. Indeed, so strong was this ulterior magical charisma that today, though "capitalistic interests have penetrated Indian society so deeply that they can no longer be eliminated," many observers still believed that, if the thin overlay of English culture were removed, all the old "feudal robber romanticism" of the Indian past would again break forth.

111 Weber ([1916–17] 1967), pp. 337; Weber (1916–17), p. 808. *Versachlichung*, that is, objectification, is here translated as "immersion"; *Eingliederung*, that is, integration, appears here as "accompaniments."

112 Weber ([1916f] 1946), p. 289. Weber refers specifically here to Buddhist mystagogues and the eighteenth-century Jain reformer, Acharya Bhikshu.

Hinduism in this form was thus "exactly the reverse" of "a this-worldly, methodical rationalization of the life-regulation of the masses."[113] Only rare and "now-disappearing" cases of worldly ethical rigor had arisen, most notably in a community inspired by Madhava Vidyaranya, abbot of Sringeri, in the fourteenth century. For Madhava, "man has to create his own holiness ... Yoga and all the [rituals of] intellectual soteriologies are meaningless; God dispenses his grace for correct conduct." On the basis of this teaching, Weber adds, "the path was cleared for an ethic of active, inner-worldly conduct in the Occidental sense." Yet even here, the "absolute authority" of the *gurus*, and their will to commerce, enabled the acquisitive drive to keep the spirit of capitalism at bay. "Indeed," it was precisely in this school that "the charisma of the qualified *guru*, as a personal quality of the possessor, is ... elevated to its highest point" – "and," Weber adds, "treated as an alienable or purchasable property."[114] In other words: even at this "highest point" of personal charisma, *Guru*-power did not spur revolutionary change, and, in fact, by embracing avarice and magic, specifically prevented an otherwise rigorist ethical sect from advancing toward modern capitalism. So commercial was the culture that the private charisma of the *guru* was itself deemed to be private property.[115]

This descent of Hindu mystagogy into avarice and magic was not simply an obstacle to capitalism; it was also a clear indication of the underlying weakness of even the most exalted and charismatic personal authority when mass traditionalism remains robust. Even though capitalism was already infiltrating Indian society through English rule, Hindu religiosity did not allow charismatic *Guru*-power to enter the path of ethical rationalization; personal enrichment was acceptable, but a *Guru*-powered modern capitalism was beyond the pale.

Weber explains the wider implications of this point in his preface to the Confucianism and Hinduism studies. Often, he writes, prophets and other religious virtuosos trim their sails to follow their "followers": they feel themselves "compelled to adjust their demands to the possibilities of the

---

113 Weber ([1916–17] 1967), p. 328; Weber (1916–17), p. 798. Weber makes a similar point vis-à-vis Mahayana Buddhism: "A rational inner-worldly conduct was not to be established on the basis of this philosophically distinguished, spiritualistic soteriology. ... For obedience to the superhuman miraculously qualified *boddisattvas* and magic was, of course, the dominant trait. Magical therapy, apotropaic and magical homeopathic ecstasy, idolatry and hagiolatry, the whole host of deities, angels and demons made their entrance." Weber ([1916–17] 1967), p. 255.

114 Weber ([1916–17] 1967), pp. 317–18; Weber (1916–17), pp. 785–86.

115 Quite often, Weber says, "economically, ... the guru's diocese [*Guru-Sprengel*] was regarded as the guru's personal property, which was not only –most typically – inherited [*vererbt*], but also alienated [*veräussert*] like the 'jajmani' of the artisans," i.e., payment of service-caste artisans by upper-caste patrons. Weber ([1916–17] 1967), pp. 320; Weber (1916–17), p.788.

religiosity of everyday life in order to gain and to maintain ideal and material mass-patronage."[116] They trade their ethical and religious authority over the community for "a magical anthropolatry; the virtuoso is directly worshipped as a saint, or at least laymen buy his blessing and his magical powers as a means of winning mundane success or religious salvation." In these instances, virtuosos are worshipped precisely to the extent that they adapt themselves to mass religiosity rather than working to ethically rationalize and revolutionize society, or to effect mass *metanoia*. Accepting veneration in this way means yielding to magic and hence surrendering claims to a higher charisma – *exploiting* rather than *expelling* magic. In Asia in particular, "the virtuosos allowed the masses to remain stuck in magical tradition" – and as a result, their influence "has been infinitely smaller than [in cases, like Puritan Europe,] where religion has undertaken ethically and generally to rationalize everyday life."[117]

In contrasting cases, to retain their charismatic influence, virtuosos must break from law and tradition to revolutionize society ethically. In such cases, they must enlist a mass base of charismatic disciples who are willing to fight – and, if necessary, die – for a radical *salto mortale*.

Weber says that, in the recent past, a movement of this kind arose in China, in the form of the Taiping Rebellion. A brief consideration of that rebellion will set the stage for a final discussion, in which I argue that the very notion of the worldly calling is charismatic in a sense that Weber implied but did not theorize, and that, in fact, the ethical rationalization of the world is typically achieved by radical sects (which, Weber says, are by no means always small).

The *Taiping* Rebellion and Revolutionary Charisma

Weber is often accused of the Eurocentric view that ethical rationalization and modern capitalism could arise only in the West. It is at least a small irony, therefore, that one of the very few modern movements which he credited with ethically revolutionary rigor was the Taiping Rebellion in nineteenth-century China – and Weber was very clear about the ethnic implications of this claim. "It was not an insuperable 'natural disposition' [*natürliche Anlage*] that hindered the Chinese from producing religious forms akin to those of the Occident. In recent times this has been proved by the striking success of Hong Xiuquan's iconoclastic and anti-magical prophecy of the *T'ien Wang* ('Heavenly King'), the *Taiping T'ien Kuo* (Heavenly Kingdom of Peace) ...

116 Weber (1916f), p. 288.
117 Weber (1916f), p. 289.

To our knowledge it was by far the mightiest … politico-ethical rebellion against the Confucian administration and ethic which China has ever experienced."[118] Many millions of peasants were drawn into the rebellion, and millions died in a bitter struggle which, Weber says, could have succeeded, if England had not taken up arms to oppose it.

The Taiping prophet himself, who was purportedly "a severely epileptic and ecstatic man," was thus a classically charismatic figure of the epileptoid, visionary type. He also "radically and puritanically rebuked every belief in spirits, magic, and idolatry." In this he "perhaps [revealed] the influence of Protestant missions and the Bible," an influence that was evident in many spheres. In 1847, after an ecstatic vision, Hong studied for two months with a Baptist missionary from Tennessee, Issachar Jacob Roberts. He opposed Catholicism but was "friendly … toward Jewry and Protestant Christianity."[119] The New Testament and Genesis were included in his holy canon, and, "among the customs and symbols of the sect" were a water bath, "a kind of tea eucharist," and variations on the Lord's Prayer and the Decalogue. The Taiping rebels accepted Christmas, repentance, prayer, holy matrimony and Sabbath services with Bible reading, sermons and hymns. Their ethic was "half mystic-ecstatic and half ascetic" – and entirely anti-traditionalist. They prohibited opium, alcohol, tobacco, foot binding, braids and – in a sharp blow to Confucianism – "sacrifices at the tombs of the dead" and "traffic in offices." Perhaps most importantly for our purposes, Hong Xiuquan's claim to prophetic charisma was expressly Pauline in character, resting on a vision of himself "as Christ's 'younger brother' *upon whom the Holy Spirit rested.*"[120]

The opportunity this presented for the ethical rationalization of the world, and quite possibly for the emergence of a uniquely Chinese form of capitalism, "was incomparably greater" than that offered by the direct influence of the West.[121] Taiping asceticism "was unsurpassed anywhere else in China, and the fetters of magic and idolatry were broken as well – and this too was

118 Weber (1916g), p. 219, translation emended.
119 Weber (1916g), p. 221. This iconoclasm was overtly anti-Catholic: "There was profound horror of the veneration of saints and images and, especially of the cult of the Mother of God" (p. 220). It is hence not surprising that, while "Protestant missionaries of the Dissenting and of the Low Church repeatedly held services in Taiping prayer halls," Anglicans and Catholics were aloof and unsympathetic.
120 Weber (1916g), pp. 219–20, italics mine. Since he wasn't Christ's equal, he denied that he himself was holy in quite the same sense; and he added, as well, that Christ was junior to God the Father.
121 Weber (1916g), pp. 222–23. Weber contrasts the ethical resolve and asceticism of the Taipings to the merely magical charisma of the "League of Righteous Energy," that is, the Boxers.

unknown elsewhere in China. A benign, personal and universal god, emancipated from national barriers, was embraced. ... Granted, one can hardly say what developmental path this religion might have taken in the event of victory." But it was both the result of a genuine revolution and "inwardly fairly close to Christianity."[122] Its ethic revealed, besides an impulse to *Entzauberung*, a nascent sense of calling á la Luther: Traditional trust in fate "was fused with an ethic of virtue in one's calling [*Berufstugend*] – a fusion made in the spirit of the New Testament."[123]

It was, ultimately, only the enmity of the preeminent capitalist power which prevented the militarily superior Taipings from taking power and, perhaps, constructing their own form of capitalism. "For political and mercantile reasons, Lord Palmerston's government saw fit to prevent this church-state from gaining the upper hand and especially to prevent the treaty harbor of Shanghai from falling into its hands. With the aid of Gordon and the fleet the Taiping power was broken."[124] The charismatic revolution was thus defeated. But the analytic question remains: What kind of movement was this? What kind of charisma did it embody?

It would be easy to imagine that Hong was himself the primary catalyst of the rebellion, and of course, like others in similar contexts, he played an igniting role which should not be gainsaid. But in this instance, the charismatic 'leader' was often far removed from the seat of struggle and command: "Given to visionary ecstasies and a seraglio existence, the *T'ien Wang* ... secluded himself for years in the palace."[125] He was an emblem, an object of worship, an inspiration– and yet, the revolution itself was powered by the solidarity of the Taiping faithful, who were mainly hard-pressed peasants. The Taiping protostate, the governing body at the heart of the rebellion, was intended to be "an ascetic warrior commonwealth," mixing "booty communism" with "acosmic love of the early Christian sort."[126] In true sectarian spirit, á la Donatism and

---

122 Weber (1916g), p. 222.
123 Weber (1916g), pp. 221. Taiping "moral 'correctness' replaced the ritual correctness of the Confucian."
124 Weber (1916g), p. 222.
125 Weber (1916g), p. 222. A hidden or "tarrying" savior is a familiar figure in prophetic religion. As Weber explains elsewhere, "the savior" can be either "a purely constructed figure," as in late Zoroastrianism, or an actual historical figure, "legitimized through miracles and visions" who is thereby "transformed by the popular imagination into a euhemerist demi-god." ([1916f] 1946, p. 273) Many charismatic claimants have understood, further, that by strategically absenting themselves from public sight, they increase their own mystery. On this ground, it is at least possible that the near invisibility of the secluded "Heavenly King" increased his uncanniness and holiness in the eyes of his followers.
126 Weber (1916g), p. 221.

the Anabaptists, the rebels held that "officials were to be selected according to religious charisma and proven moral worth," not bureaucratic expediency. Military discipline was "puritanically strict" – and it was, in fact, precisely this discipline, essentially religious in character, that made the Taiping armies superior to their imperial counterparts.[127] Taiping fighters saw themselves as part of a commonwealth of called warriors, whose aims were not this-worldly or magical but rather ethically rational, moored in acosmic love communism. The charismatic founder was the trigger, but the rebellion itself was the work of his vast sect of called disciples. The disciples fought, in many instances, while the apostle remained in absentia.

Ascetic Charisma

In the "*Zwischenbetrachtung*," the essay that connects his studies of China and India, Weber makes an essential but neglected point – namely, that "magical presuppositions" inhere not only in mysticism but in *asceticism*. Even ethically rational asceticism, that is, despite its ultimate commitment to *Entzauberung*, is magical in origin: "at the threshold of its appearance, asceticism showed its Janus-face: on the one hand, abnegation of the world, and on the other, mastery of the world by virtue of the magical powers obtained by abnegation."[128] Asceticism thus originated as a kind of magical ritualism – as a form of *inner sacrifice*, a burnt offering of pleasures and wishes, which ascetics ingrained into their daily lives as a way to win (and often, prove) magical strength.

This suggests a possibility that leads us a step beyond Weber – but does not, I think, conflict with his underlying premises. Where, given the magical origins of asceticism, does the will to *Entzauberung* originate? Quite possibly, I would argue, in a different, "higher" form of magic. Ascetic service to the will of a jealous god is not instrumental, not coercive or persuasive; but its *goal* (salvation, the afterlife) has the flavor of magic; and its *form* (meticulous, 'methodical' observance of the one best way to rationalize the world) has the flavor of ritual. The key difference is that, in this higher form, asceticism attempts not simply to manipulate magical charisma but to *monopolize* its legitimate use. That could explain, in part, why the earliest Puritans so ardently rejected the competition of office charisma, and why they sought, in general, to purge the world of less universal and less rational magics. What they opposed was not magic per se, since even ethically rational asceticism was tinged with magic; what they opposed was sacrilegious, personal magic, which sought to put God under the opportunistic spell of *coercion* or *persuasion*. The sacrifices

127 Weber (1916g), p. 221.
128 Weber (1916h), p. 327; cp. the original, Weber (1916d).

they made as virtuosos were calculated to achieve salvation by *obedience*, which, since it was "unconditional" (*unbedingte*), was obviously also a form of magical self-abnegation, beyond the reach of ordinary mortals. Unconditional ascetics displayed an uncanny "discipline" that qualified them (in every sense) to be charismatic *disciples*; and discipleship entails, besides service to the divine, cooperation with fellow virtuosos in a shared enterprise. "When religious virtuosos [unite] into active asceticist sects, they attain two aims: the radical disenchantment of the world and the complete blockage of world-rejection as a path to salvation."[129]

Shared worldly enterprise, pursued with an ascetic rigor debarred to the majority, is the hallmark of sectarian virtuosity. Rigorous ascetic labor, in turn, is regarded as proof of a special kind of magical charisma which is so universal, monopolistic, and transcendental, so radically supra-mundane, that it attacks every mundane form of magic – and even the very *principle* of mundane magic. Only sect comrades enjoy the higher charisma which, in "rationalizing" fashion, conceals its own ulterior magicality by debunking every *rival* charismatic claim. Weber said that Sebastian Franck, who was a kind of Puritan himself, had "hit upon the key characteristic of this type of religion when he saw the significance of the Reformation in the fact that now every Christian had to be a monk all his life."[130] The Protestant sect was a 'priesthood of believers.' The consequence was that, in effect, Protestant sects claimed a charisma that was *specific to the office of the priestly believer.* Every believer was a kind of officeholder in the faith community, ordained by baptism; so charisma was *universal among believers,* not restricted to a narrow circle of formally ordained priests. This is why Luther and others so forcefully rejected the Catholic dual morality of *præcepta* and *consilia,* which imposed higher standards on the Church elite than on ordinary believers. *Every* believer in a Protestant sect was called to perform an "office," a mission, for the greater good of the community and the greater glory of God. *All* believers were called, not only those anointed by an institution that dispensed grace. And since, ultimately, only *this* form of office charisma – the charisma of the ordained disciple – was neither self-serving nor demonic, every competing office charisma, like every rival magic, had to be disenfranchised utterly.

The starting point for ascetic Protestantism lies in the concept of the "calling," which Weber traces to late medieval and early modern translations of the New Testament – by Wyclif and, above all, by Luther: "...in the concept of 'calling' is expressed that central dogma of all Protestant denominations which rejects the Catholic division of Christian moral commands into

---

129 Weber ([1916f] 1946), p. 290.
130 Weber ([1920c] 1958), p. 121; cf. n. 10, p. 220.

'*præcepta*' and '*consilia*' and affirms, as the *only* means of living a life pleasing to God, not the overcoming of inner-worldly morality through the pursuit of monastic asceticism, but the fulfillment of inner-worldly duties that arise from the one's station in life. This, then, becomes one's calling."[131] This is a very familiar Weberian formulation – and yet, it embodies a paradox. Martin Luther, the inspiration for ascetic Protestant sectarianism, was neither an ascetic nor a sectarian, and his notion of *Beruf*, while marking a fresh epoch in thought, was so equivocal and ambiguous that it was ultimately of only "dubious relevance"[132] to the idea of the calling that became the "central dogma of all Protestant denominations."

Christiane Frey has said that Weber's genealogy of the notion of the calling only "really becomes comprehensible" when he advances beyond Luther to ascetic Protestantism per se.[133] It is true that Weber's account of this genealogy, which he relegated to a long note, is exceptionally tangled. But I contend that this account is coherent from the start and that it implies a perspective on charisma and the capitalist spirit that transcends Weber's overt argument.

Very briefly: Weber says that the interpretation of the calling as the fulfillment of this-worldly duties sprang from the Bible, but that we owe this meaning to "the spirit of the translators, not ... the spirit of the original."[134] Although Luther used the German word *Beruf* to translate the Greek word κλῆσις (*klê sis*), Weber says flatly that "Greek has no word with an ethical coloring that corresponds at all to the German word."[135] In other words, κλῆσις evidently means something quite different in the Greek New Testament, where it appears mainly in Paul's letters, than *Beruf* does in Luther's *Neue Testament*. "The new meaning of the word corresponded to a new *idea* – a product of the Reformation."[136] But Weber quickly undermines this claim by assigning a meaning to Luther's *Beruf* which closely resembles the meaning he imputes to Paul's κλῆσις. Is this a paradox? Is Weber reading Luther, or Paul, through a glass darkly? Does this matter for our account of charisma and capitalism?

To properly explore these questions, we need to glance at the main text in which Paul uses the term κλῆσις.[137] This is Romans 11:29, where he

131 Weber ([1904–05] 2002), p. 28.
132 Weber ([1904–05] 2002), p. 33.
133 Frey (2008), p. 45.
134 Weber ([1904–05] 2002), p. 28.
135 Weber ([1920c] 1958), p. 52, translation emended.
136 Weber ([1904–05] 2002), p. 28.
137 He uses variants of the word in several other passages.

writes: "ἀμεταμέλητα γὰρ τὰ χαρίσματα καὶ ἡ κλῆσις τοῦ Θεοῦ" – "irrevocable indeed are the gifts and the calling of God." Here Luther renders κλῆσις as *Berufung*. In a related passage, 1 Corinthians 7:20, he uses *Beruf* and *berufen* to render Paul's phrase "*ἐν τῇ κλήσει ᾗ ἐκλήθη*" – "*en tē klḗsei* [*Beruf*] *hē eklḗthē* [*berufen*]*.*" Paul's point here, and in related passages, is that believers should remain in the stations to which God has called them, until the apocalypse, which draws near. Their duty is to answer God's call to eternal salvation, and to tarry, in the meantime, "in the callings to which they have been called." Weber finds, in Luther's rendering of these lines, the seeds of the modern idea of the calling. And yet he also contends that Luther is guilty of reading the concept of *Beruf* anachronistically.

The apparent contradiction here stems from Weber's antithesis between the modern notion of the calling, which he says is "purely secular" (*rein weltliche*) and the Biblical term, which he says is "purely religious." He says the Old Testament defended a strictly traditionalist, anti-chrematistic outlook, while the main textual instances of the "Pauline 'κλῆσις,'" in the sense of God's calling to eternal salvation, [which appear in] 1 Cor. 1:26, Ephesians 1:18, 4:1 [and elsewhere], "all ... relate to the *purely* religious concept of the calling which comes from God by means of the gospel preached by the apostle. The term '*κλῆσις*' has nothing whatever to do with secular 'callings' in today's sense."[138] He says that Luther laid the foundation for the secular concept – and yet, in practically the same breath, he says that Luther's original intent with respect to the interpretation of κλῆσις was, like Paul's, apocalyptic, and that, over time, he became increasingly invested in a traditionalist account in which individual steadfastness in the calling was regarded as a minutely prescribed divine imperative. At no point did Luther endorse asceticism, nor was his ethic ever oriented to the rationalization of the world. He wanted believers to embrace their "callings" meekly and piously, without excessive zeal.

It would be easy to conclude that Weber was not altogether consistent in this account. That is, I think, fair. If Luther was a proto-secularist, his thinking could hardly be of "dubious relevance" to the secularism he inspired. But there is a deeper point here. Luther can be understood as a contradictory figure, whose notion of the calling was Janus-faced. He defended both a Pauline *Berufstheologie* and, simultaneously, an embryonic *Berufsethik* with secularizing tendencies. He represented a transitional moment, when religious apocalypticism could uneasily coexist with an emergent secularity. Ultimately secularization triumphed, but Luther represented a time of unstable balance.

Another way of looking at this transition is to say that Paul's concept of κλῆσις was, above all, *charismatic*. The "calling," which comes from God,

138 Weber ([1920c] 1958), p. 55.

and the "gift of grace," which emanates from the Holy Spirit, belong to the same spiritual continuum. Both are granted to Christians by persons of the Trinity, and both *oblige* their recipients as much as they privilege them. In his paradigmatic line in Romans 11:29, Paul pairs *klê̄sis* with *charisma* very directly: "Irrevocable indeed are the gifts [*charismata*] and the calling [*klēsis*] of God." New Testament believers were infused with a divine spirit which was, at once, a *call* to salvation and the gift of saving grace that enabled them to *answer* the call. Weber hinted at something like this in his opening words on the genealogy of the calling: "It is unmistakable that the German *word 'Beruf,'* and even more clearly the English word 'calling,' carry at least *some* religious connotations – namely, those of a *task* set by *God*."[139] Luther may have begun a secularizing trend, but the religious connotations of his thinking were still evident. So, too, the parallel between κλῆσις [*klê̄sis*], "a task set by God," and χάρισμα [*charisma*], the gift that entails a divine mission, was equally plain.

Charisma, in Weber's sociology, is a gift that is also a mandate. "When the idea of God had already been established," he writes, "'...heroes' and 'magicians',," who must "prove their charisma to their adherents, ... practiced their arts ... by virtue of the divine mission inherent in their talents." The *Charismatiker* "seizes the task for which he is destined and demands that others obey and follow him by virtue of his mission."[140] God's call, in other words, is a mandate for the entire charismatic community. This mandate can come to the community either indirectly, through the medium of a leader, or directly from God. Both modes of transmission are common and, in many instances, the expression of God's will, and call, is direct. It is not by chance that the early Christian community was known as the *ecclesia*, the 'community of the called.' Paul's term for the calling, κλῆσις [*klê̄sis*], is embedded in the very word ἐκκλησία. Charismatic discipleship is the shared embrace of God's mandate as well as His gift. The mission, the call to service, is the corollary of the divine gift – a mission that disciples accept collectively.[141]

The collective side of the tie binding God to His disciples is important to keep in mind. Mass psychologists and social behaviorists have often focused first, and exclusively, on the charismatic claims of prophets and other virtuosos. But no one is charismatic alone. No divine mission can be carried out by a solitary hero. Prophets, in general, *prophesy* –they share their message with an audience, and their only hope of fulfilling their mandate is to win the *support* of this audience.

139 Weber ([1904–05] 2002), p. 28.
140 *E&S*, p. 1112.
141 Accepting the mission is a kind of recompense, in the form of service, for God's favor. The plainly clientelistic mentality of this worldview, however, is raised above utilitarian quid pro quo ethics when it acquires an ethically colored quality in the form of a devout sense of moral obligation.

That is why Weber termed prophets of the mission "emissary" prophets – they ventriloquize God's words to a public that comprises His true ultimate audience. Only when others *join* the prophet – who is, in effect, the first disciple – can the divine mandate be heeded with a chance of success, *collectively*. Prophets, like leaders of all kinds, enjoy authority and the hope of success only to the extent that they win followings. That is why the ancient Israelite prophets are, for Weber, such poor examples of charismatic authority – few prophets of any kind have ever been less immediately authoritative in the eyes of their peers.[142]

The semantic shift in the *Berufsbegriffe*, which Wyclif and Luther began but did not complete, marks a social shift as well. The divine *charismata* and callings of the early Christian ἐκκλησία were eschatological, signs of the coming apocalypse. These gifts and tasks not only foretold the new Jerusalem but they *prepared* the faithful for the struggle and triumph to come. They amounted, then, to a kind of spiritual warrior charisma, equipping the faithful to prevail over the ultimate adversary. This warrior charisma was magically apocalyptic, and, in the time remaining before the apocalypse, the everyday *charismata* in Corinth, Rome and elsewhere were often immediately magical.[143] Luther's original vision was more than a little eschatological as well.[144] But the shift that ensued after his incomplete turn to the modern *Beruf* concept marked a radical departure from magic and apocalypticism altogether – the *Entzauberung* of the calling. In ascetic Protestant form, *Beruf* now acquired an ethical-rational dimension. The Puritan was called not to ecstatic worship or apocalyptic battle, but to self-denying labor to bring the world into conformity with God's will.

This, I contend, is a shift from a *magically* charismatic to an *ethically* charismatic notion of the calling. Charisma is not foreign to this shift, nor is it foreign to the economic ethic that arose alongside the modern notion of the calling. There is, in fact, a Greek word with the ethical coloration of the word *Beruf* – and that word is χάρισμα, in precisely the sense of Weber's notion of *ethical* charisma. The spirit of capitalism was infused from the start with an economic ethic in which a demagicalized form of charisma played an essential part. The "ethical rationalization" of capitalist society was thus wholly as irrational as Weber always insisted, but the irrationality was not simply the antinomian urge to accumulate capital infinitely, without regard for the satisfaction or frustration

142 This is a central point in Weber (1918–19) and was echoed by Marianne Weber in her memoir ([1926] 1975, pp. 593–94).

143 Weber's admired colleague, the liberal theologian Hermann Gunkel, devoted his first book ([1888] 2008) to a sustained exploration of whether the Pauline notion of the *charismata* could be demagicalized.

144 Luther translated 'κλῆσις' as *Beruf*, Weber said ([1920c] 1958, p. 57], only in the spirit of "the eschatological exhortation that everyone should remain in their present condition" until the world ends and they are lifted to heaven.

of real human needs. This irrationality also took the form of a charismatic claim to a divine gift, and call, to impose God's will on a refractory humanity.

Weber recognized, of course, that the spirit of capitalism had evolved since Puritan days. In his own time, capitalism had become plutocratic and swollen with hubris; the higher bourgeoisie was now entirely utilitarian and self-serving. Nor was he optimistic about the prospect of a return to the earlier, ethically charismatic spirit which only the petty bourgeoisie and upwardly mobile workers (in America, the "middle classes") now represented. The spirit of sectarian discipleship was now most visible among the socialists who strove to ethically rationalize society along post-capitalist lines.

What would come next? Weber doubted that socialist democracy was attainable. Otherwise, he suspended judgment. He feared that an archaic, ethically irrational, anti-modern movement could usher in a "polar night of icy darkness" in which democracy in every form would be defeated. He hoped that bourgeois democracy would remain a bulwark against resurgent barbarism. To render that bulwark as strong as possible, engaged scholars had to probe capitalism, and the spirit of capitalism, as searchingly as possible. That task, his own secular calling, led Weber to study the preconditions for an ethically defensible and sustainable global capitalism. Whether, in fact, capitalism could survive without charisma remained an open question.

References

Atwood, Craig. 1995. *Blood, Sex, and Death: Life and Liturgy in Zinzendorf's Bethlehem.* Princeton Theological Seminary, Doctoral Dissertation.

———1999. "The Mother of God's People." *Church History*, 68 (4), December: 886–909.

Brady, Thomas A. 2009. *German Histories in the Age of Reformations, 1400–1650.* Cambridge and New York: Cambridge University Press.

Buss, Dietrich G. 1976. *Henry Villard: A Study of Transatlantic Investment and Interests, 1870–1895.* The Claremont Graduate University, Doctoral Dissertation.

Davis, Isabel. 2012. "Calling: Langland, Gower, and Chaucer on Saint Paul." *Studies in the Age of Chaucer*, 34: 53–97.

Egert, Eugene. 1973. *The Holy Spirit in German Literature until the End of the Twelfth Century.* The Hague, Paris: Mouton.

Engel, Katherine Carté. 2011. *Religion and Profit: Moravians in Early America.* Philadelphia: University of Pennsylvania Press.

Engelmann, Johann Baptist. 1848. *Von den Charismen im Allegemeinen un von dem Sprachen-Charisma im Besnoderen; oder historisch-exegetisch Abhandlung über 1 Kor. 12–14.* Regensberg: G. Joseph Manz.

Erbe, Hellmuth. 1929. *Bethelehem, Pa. Eine kommunistische Herrnhuter Kolonie des 18. Jahrhunderts.* Stuttgart: Ausland u. Heimat, 1929.

Eyerly, Sarah J. 2010. *"Der Wille Gottes."* in *Self, Community, World*, pp. 201–227, edited by Heikki Lempa and Paul Peucker. Bethlehem: Lehigh University Press.

Fogelman, Aaron Spencer. 2007. *Jesus Is Female: Moravians and the Challenge of Radical Religion in Early America*. Philadelphia: University of Pennsylvania Press.

Forell, George W. 1973. "Preface" to Nicholaus Zinzendorf, *Nine Public Lectures on Important Subjects in Religion*. Iowa City: University of Iowa Press.

Franzmann, John William. 1972. *The Early Development of the Greek Concept of Charis*. Doctoral dissertation, University of Wisconsin.

Frey, Christiane. 2008. "κλῆσις /Beruf: Luther, Weber, Agamben." *New German Critique*, 105, Fall: 35–56.

Fuchs, Thomas. 1991. *Henry Villard: A Citizen of Two Worlds*. University of Oregon, Doctoral Dissertation.

Gloël, Johannes. 1888. *Der Heilige Geist in der Heislverkündigung des Paulus: eine biblisch-theologische Untersuchung*. Halle: Max Niemeyer.

Gollin, Gillian Lindt. 1967. *Moravians in Two Worlds*. New York and London: Columbia University Press.

Grau, Friedrich. 1946. *Der neutestamentliche Begriff* charisma, *seine Geschichte und seine Theologie*. University of Tübingen, Doctoral Dissertation.

Gunkel, Hermann. (1888) 2008. *The Influence of the Holy Spirit: The Popular View of the Apostolic Age and the Teaching of the Apostle Paul*, translated by Roy A. Harrisville. Minneapolis, MN: Augsburg Fortress.

Hahn, Hans-Christoph and Hellmut Reichel, eds. 1977. *Zinzendorf und die Herrnhuter Brüder*. Hamburg: Friedrich Wittig.

Harrison, James R. 2003. *Paul's Language of Grace in its Graeco-Roman Context*. Tübingen: Mohr Siebeck.

Käsler, Dirk. 1988. *Max Weber: An Introduction to His Life and Work*, translated by Philippa Hurd. Chicago: The University of Chicago Press.

Käsler, Dirk, ed. 2013. *Max Weber: Die protestantische Ethik und der Geist des Kapitalismus*. Vollständige Ausgabe, 4. Aufl. Munich: Beck.

Kinkel, Gary Steven. 1990. *Our Dear Mother the Spirit: An Investigation of Count Zinzendorf's Theology and Praxis*. Lanham, MD & New York: University Press of America.

Kydd, Ronald. 1984. *Charismatic Gifts in the Early Church*. Peabody, MA: Hendrickson.

Lauterburg, Moritz. 1898. *Der Begriff des Charisma und seine Bedeutung für die praktische Theologie*. Gütersloh: Bertelsmann.

Leclercq, Henri. 1948. "Charismes," in *Dictionnaire d'Archeologie chrétienne et de Liturgie*, pp. 579–98, Vol. 3. Paris: Librairie Letouzey et Ané.

Luther, Martin. 1869. *Das Neue Testament unsers Herrn und Heilandes Jesu Christi, nach der deutschen Uebersetzung*. Köln: Verlag von Wilh. Haffel.

MacLachlan, Bonnie. 1993. *The Age of Grace: Charis in Early Greek Poetry*. Princeton, NJ: Princeton University Press.

Meyer, Dietrich. 2003. "The Moravian Church as a Theocracy," in *The Distinctiveness of Moravian Culture*, pp. 255–262, edited by Peter Vogt. Nazareth, PA: Moravian Historical Society.

Moffatt, James. 1932. *Grace in the New Testament*. New York: Ray Long & Richard R. Smith.

Moussy, Claude. 1966. *Gratia et sa famille*. Paris: PUF.

Plitt, Hermann. 1869–1874. *Zinzendorfs Theologie*, Vols. 1–3. Gotha: Friedrich Andreas Berthes.

Pollet, J. V. M. 1955. "Les charismes," in *Initiation théologique*, 2nd edition, Vol. 3, pp. 1081–1108. Paris: Les Éditions du Cerf.

Reichel, Levin Theodore. 1888. *The Early History of the Church of the United Brethren (Unitas Fratrum) Commonly Called Moravians in North America, A. D. 1734–1748*. Nazareth, PA: Moravian Historical Society.

Robeck, Cecil M, Jr. 1992. *Prophecy in Carthage: Perpetua, Tertullian, and Cyprian*. Cleveland, OH: The Pilgrim Press.

Scribner, R. W. 1986. "Incombustible Luther: The Image of the Reformer in Early Modern Germany," *Past and Present*, 110, February: 38–68

Scully, Samuel Edward. 1973. *Philia and Charis in Euripidean Tragedy*. University of Toronto, Doctoral Dissertation.

Sensbach, Jon F. 1998. *A Separate Canaan: The Making of an Afro-Moravian World in North Carolina, 1763–1840*. Chapel Hill & London: University of North Carolina.

Smith, David N. 1992. "The Beloved Dictator: Adorno, Horkheimer, and the Critique of Domination," *Current Perspectives in Social Theory*, 11: 195–230.

———1998. "Faith, Reason, and Charisma: Rudolf Sohm, Max Weber, and the Theology of Grace," *Sociological Inquiry*, 68 (1): 32–60.

———2011. "Charisma and Critique: Critical Theory, Authority, and the Birth of Political Theology." pp. 33–56 in *Current Perspectives in Social Theory*, 29.

———2013. "Charisma Disenchanted: Max Weber and His Critics." Pp. 3–74 in *Current Perspectives in Social Theory*, 31.

———2015. "Profit Maxims: Capitalism and the Common Sense of Time and Money." pp. 29–74 in *Current Perspectives in Social Theory*, 33.

Sohm, Rudolph. (1892) 1970. *Kirchenrecht*, Bd. 1: *Die geschichtlichen Grundlagen*. Berlin: Duncker und Humblot.

———1898. *Kirchengeschichte im Grundriss*, eleventh edition. Leipzig: Verlag von E. Ungleich.

Sommer, Elisabeth W. 2000. *Serving Two Masters: Moravian Brethren in Germany and North Carolina, 1727–1801*. Lexington: The University Press of Kentucky.

Sterrett, T. N. 1947. *New Testament Charismata*. Dallas Theological Seminary, Doctoral Dissertation.

Villard, Katharine Neilley. 1988. *Villard: The Years of Fortune*. University of Arkansas, Doctoral Dissertation. ProQuest, UMI Dissertations Publishing.

Vos, Geerhardus. 1972. *The Pauline Eschatology*. Grand Rapids, MI: Eerdmans.

Warfield, Benjamin B. 1918. Chapter 1/Lecture 1, "The Cessation of the Charismata," in *Counterfeit Miracles*, pp. 1–32 & 233–247. New York: C. Scribner's Sons.

Weber, Marianne. [1926] 1975. *Max Weber: A Biography*, translated by Harry Zohn. New York: John Wiley & Sons.

Weber, Max. 1904–05. "Die protestantische Ethik und der 'Geist' des Kapitalismus," in *Archiv für Sozialwissenschaft und Sozialpolitik*, 20 Bd. (Heft 1): 1–54.

———1905. "Die protestantische Ethik und der 'Geist' des Kapitalismus, II. Die Berufsidee des asketischen Protestantismus," in *Archiv für Sozialwissenschaft und Sozialpolitik*, 21 Bd. (Heft 1): 1–110.

———[1904–05] 2002. *The Protestant Ethic and the 'Spirit' of Capitalism and Other Writings*, edited and translated by Peter Baehr and Gordon C. Wells. New York & London: Penguin.

———1906a. "'Kirchen' und 'Sekten'," *Frankfurter Zeitung*, 50 (102), April 13 and April 15.

———1906b. "'Kirchen' und 'Sekten' in Nordamerika. Eine kirchen- und sozialpolitische Skizze," in *Die Christliche Welt*, 20, June 14, Nr. 24, pp. 558–62, and Nr. 25, June 21, pp. 577–583.

————(1906/1920) 1946. "The Protestant Sects and the Spirit of Capitalism," in *From Max Weber*, pp. 302–322, edited and translated by Hans H. Gerth and C. Wright Mills. New York: Oxford University Press.

————1910a. "Antikritisches zum 'Geist' des Kapitalismus," *Archiv für Sozialwissenschaft und Sozialpolitik*, 30: 176–202. Available in Weber ([1904–05] 2002), under the title: "Rebuttal of the Critique of the 'Spirit' of Capitalism," pp. 244–281.

————1910b. "Antikritisches Schlusswort zum 'Geist des Kapitalismus'," *Archiv für Sozialwissenschaft und Sozialpolitik*, 31: 554–99. Available in Weber ([1904–05] 2002) under the title: "A Final Rebuttal of Rachfahl's Critique of the 'Spirit of Capitalism'," pp. 282–340.

————1916a. "Die Wirtschaftsethik der Weltreligionen: Religionssoziologische Skizzen: Einleitung," *Archiv für Sozialwissenschaft und Sozialpolitik*, 41 Bd. (Heft 1): 1–30. Available in English, in Weber [(1916f) 1946], under the misleading title: "Social Psychology of the World Religions."

————1916b. "Die Wirtschaftsethik der Weltreligionen: Religionssoziologische Skizzen: Der Konfuzianismus I, II," *Archiv für Sozialwissenschaft und Sozialpolitik*, 41 Bd. (Heft 1): 30–87.

————1916c. Die Wirtschaftsethik der Weltreligionen. (Zweiter Artikel.) Der Konfuzianismus III, IV," *Archiv für Sozialwissenschaft und Sozialpolitik*, 41 Bd. (Heft 2): 335–386.

————1916d. "Die Wirtschaftsethik der Weltreligionen: Zwischenbetrachtung: Theorie der Stufen und Richtungen religiöser Weltablehnung," *Archiv für Sozialwissenschaft und Sozialpolitik*, 41 Bd. (Heft 2): 387–421. Available in English, in Weber [(1916h) 1946], under the title: "Religious Rejections of the World and Their Direction."

————1916e. "Die Wirtschaftsethik der Weltreligionen: Hinduismus und Buddhismus I," *Archiv für Sozialwissenschaft und Sozialpolitik*, 41 Bd. (Heft 3): 613–744.

————[1916f] 1946. "The Social Psychology of the World Religions," in *From Max Weber*, pp. 267–301, edited and translated by Hans H. Gerth and C. Wright Mills. New York: Oxford University Press.

————[1916g] 1964. *The Religion of China*. Glencoe, IL: The Free Press.

————[1916h] 1946. "Religious Rejections of the World and Their Direction," in *From Max Weber*, pp. 323–359, edited and translated by Hans H. Gerth and C. Wright Mills. New York: Oxford University Press.

————1916–1917. "Die Wirtschaftsethik der Weltreligionen: Hinduismus und Buddhismus II," *Archiv für Sozialwissenschaft und Sozialpolitik*, 42 Bd. Heft 2), pp. 345–461, and 42 Bd. (Heft 3): 687–814.

————[1916–17] 1967. *The Religion of India*. Glencoe, IL: The Free Press.

————1917–18. "Die Wirtschaftsethik der Weltreligionen: Das antike Judentum I: Die israelitische Eidgenossenschaft und Jahwe," in *Archiv für Sozialwissenschaft und Sozialpolitik*, 44 Bd. (Heft 1): 52–138; 44 Bd. (Heft 2): 349–443; 44 Bd. (Heft 3): 601–626.

————1918–19. "Die Wirtschaftsethik der Weltreligionen: Das antike Judentum I: Die israelitische Eidgenossenschaft und Jahwe (Schluß)" and "II: Die Entstehung des jüdischen Pariavolkes," in *Archiv für Sozialwissenschaft und Sozialpolitik*, 46 Bd. (Heft 1): 40–113; 46 Bd. (Heft 2): 311–366; 46 Bd. (Heft 3): 541–604.

————(1917–19) 1952. *Ancient Judaism*. Glencoe, IL: The Free Press.

————1919. "Politik als Beruf," in *Geistige Arbeit als Beruf: Vier Vorträge vor dem Freistudentischen Bund. Zweiter Vortrage*. Munich and Leipzig: Duncker & Humblot.

————(1919) 1948. "Politics as a Vocation," in *From Max Weber*, pp. 77–128, edited and translated by Hans H. Gerth and C. Wright Mills. New York: Oxford University Press.

————1920. *Gesammelte Aufsätze zur Religionssoziologie*, Bd. I. Tübingen: Verlag von J. C. B. Mohr (Paul Siebeck).

————1920a. "Vorbermerkung," in *Gesammelte Aufsätze zur Religionssoziologie*, pp. 1–16, Bd. I. Tübingen: Verlag von J. C. B. Mohr (Paul Siebeck).

————1920b. "Die protestantische Ethik und der Geist des Kapitalismus," in *Gesammelte Aufsätze zur Religionssoziologie*, pp. 17–206, Bd. I. Tübingen: Verlag von J. C. B. Mohr (Paul Siebeck).

————[1920b] 1958. *The Protestant Ethic and the Spirit of Capitalism*, translated by Talcott Parsons. New York: Scribners.

————[1920b] 2009. *The Protestant Ethic and the Spirit of Capitalism with Other Writings on the Rise of the West*, translated by Stephen Kalberg. New York and Oxford: Oxford University Press.

————1920c. "Die protestantische Sekten und der Geist des Kapitalismus," in *Gesammelte Aufsätze zur Religionssoziologie*, pp. 207–236, Bd. I. Tübingen: Verlag von J. C. B. Mohr (Paul Siebeck).

————1922. *Wirtschaft und Gesellschaft*. Tübingen: Mohr-Siebeck.

————[1922] 1978. *Economy and Society*. Berkeley, Los Angeles and London: University of California Press.

————1922. *Wirtschaft und Gesellschaft*. Tübingen: Mohr-Siebeck.

————1927. *General Economic History*. New York: Greenberg.

————1946. *From Max Weber*, edited and translated by Hans H. Gerth and C. Wright Mills. New York: Oxford University Press.

————2005. *Gesamtausgabe: Die Wirtschaft und die gesellschaftlichen Ordnungen und Mächte. Nachlass. Schriften und Reden. Wirtschaft und Gesellschaft. Herrschaft*, Bd. 22. Tübingen: Mohr Siebeck.

————2009. *Wirtschaft und Gesellschaft: Entstehungsgeschichte und Dokumente: Gesamtausgabe*, Abt. 1, *Schriften und Reden*; Bd. 24, edited by Wolfgang Schluchter. Tübingen: J.C.B. Mohr.

Wheeler, Rachel. 2008. *To Live Upon Hope: Mohicans and Missionaries in the Eighteenth-Century Northeast*. Ithaca: Cornell University Press.

Zinzendorf, Nicholaus Ludwig. 1748. *Ein und zwanzig Discurse über die Augspurgische Confession*. Bethlehem, PA: Moravian Publication.

————[1746] 1973. *Nine Public Lectures on Important Subjects in Religion*. Iowa City: University of Iowa Press.

————1758. *Sammlung Einiger von dem Ordinario Fratrum während seines Ausenthalts in der Deutschen Gemeinen von Anno 1775 bis 1757 gehaltenen Kinder-Reden*. Barby: Seminario Theologico.

————[1737] 1741. "Antwort auf eine Anfrage in den Franckfurt Gelehrten Zeitungen, Anno. 1737," in *Büdingische Sammlung: Eineiger in die Kirchen-historie*, III. Büdingen: Joh. Chr. Stöhr.

Chapter 5

MAX WEBER'S SOCIOLOGY OF CIVILIZATIONS: A PRELIMINARY INVESTIGATION INTO ITS MAJOR METHODOLOGICAL CONCEPTS

Stephen Kalberg

Until the 1960s, the reception in sociology of Max Weber's works in the United States was located largely along three axes. First, his "Protestant ethic thesis" (1930) became the subject of a heated debate, one that endures to this day. It anchored the wide interest throughout the discipline in the sociology of religion and grounded the casting of Weber as an "idealist." Second, a series of his concepts, all of which were formulated in precise and convincing terms, were welcomed into the young discipline: status groups, bureaucracy, power, authority, and charisma. This took place after the publication of a broad-ranging and highly successful reader (see Weber 1946a) and the translation by Talcott Parsons (1947) of Part I of Weber's massive analytical treatise, *Economy and Society* (1968; *E&S*) (see Zaret 1980). Third, seeking to constitute itself as a rigorous science, the discipline widely adopted Weber's definitions of "objectivity" and "value neutrality" (Weber 1949).

The reception of his works after 1970 underwent a severe transformation. In the spirit of the times, his definitions of "power" and "domination" (*Herrschaft*) permeated sociology more thoroughly, as did his critique of the bureaucracy and bureaucratization. Far more widely than earlier, he became understood as a non-Marxist theorist of inequality and conflict (Bendix 1962, 1977; Bendix and Roth 1971; Collins 1968, 1975, 1981). This reading of Weber reached its pinnacle in the late 70s and early 80s after the fading of a short-lived enchantment with Karl Marx and various neo-Marxist approaches.

Perhaps it was the intensity of the "conflict Weber" reception in these decades that explains the neglect among American sociologists of a reception in Germany that introduced a "new" Weber. In the studies by Tenbruck (1975) and Schluchter (1979, 1981), a heretofore largely neglected theme pervasive throughout Weber's works drove a wide-ranging discussion. These authors and others (see Riesebrodt 1980; Winckelmann 1980; Seyfarth and Sprondel 1981; Hennis 1983, 1987a, 1987b; Habermas 1984) emphasized his comparative thrust – namely, his long-standing attempts to define the uniqueness of "Western rationalism" and his sweeping investigations into the multiple causes behind the particular pathway followed in the West into the modern epoch. Indeed, some claimed here to have discovered Weber's "major theme" (Tenbruck 1975). His large volumes on China (1951), India (1958) and ancient Judaism (1952); his pivotal "Social Psychology of the World Religions" (1946c) and "Religious Rejections of the World" essays (1946b); and the full comparative breadth of *E&S* were now called to the forefront.[1]

Unfortunately, and although this new debate constituted a giant step away from both the "concepts" and "conflict" receptions, it failed to take the next "logical" step: the ways in which Weber's comparative and empirical investigations offer a *systematic* sociology of civilizations resting upon rigorous modes of analysis were never addressed. Indeed, Weber's comparative-historical methodology has only rarely been explored to this day (Salomon 1935; Gerth 1946; Roth 1971a, 1971b, 1971c, 1976; Warner 1970, 1972, 1973; Bendix 1977; Fulbrook 1978; Smelser 1976; Collins 1981; Molloy 1980; Kalberg 1994, 2017). In the meantime the scrutiny of Weber's vast writings in the United States, as well as worldwide, has fragmented into innumerable streams.

In a preliminary manner, this chapter seeks to outline the basic research strategies, procedures, and presuppositions – the practiced comparative methodology – found throughout Weber's empirical oeuvre. Together with the concepts associated with them, they can serve, it is here argued, as foundational components that underpin and sustain a *Weberian sociology of civilizations* empowered to capture systematically the contours and developmental directions of these large-scale entities. Central to this wide-ranging comparative methodology are:

Weber's opposition to organicism;
His notion of subjective meaning;
His broad multi-causality;
His embedding of patterned action in contexts of patterned action;

1   Perhaps Benjamin Nelson was the single proponent of this "large theme" reception on American shores (1974, 1981; see also Kalberg, 1979, 1980). Interestingly, the broad attention to Georg Simmel and Norbert Elias in England, Holland, and Germany in the 80s also found few echoes on the American landscape. For a recent discussion of the reception of Weber in the United States, see Scaff (2014) and chapter 7 in this volume.

His tight linking of the past with the present; and

His emphasis upon the ways in which "social carriers" and the *caput mortuum* concept link the past with the present.

Of course, these aspects of Weber's mode of analysis also are basic *throughout* his empirical investigations. This study contends that, if highlighted and aligned, they can be seen to articulate the methodological foundation for his rigorous approach to the study of civilizations. It maintains further that, when synthesized, the components of Weber's comparative methodology articulate an analytic range greater than that offered by others writing today on civilizations.[2] Only a brief discussion of each element can be provided.

Weber's Opposition to Organicism

Let us commence with a review of the manner in which Weber's sociology opposes fundamentally the assumption of societal unity characteristic of the many organic holism approaches indebted to Comte, Durkheim, Radcliffe-Brown and Parsons. His sociology rests upon diverse *patterns, or regularities, of meaningful action* rather than upon "society":

> There can be observed, within the realm of social action, actual empirical regularities; that is, courses of action that are repeated by the actor or (possibly also: simultaneously) occur among numerous actors because the subjective *meaning* is typically *meant* to be the same. Sociological investigation is concerned with these *typical* modes of action. (1968, 29 [emphasis original; translation altered]; see also pp. 19–21, 311; 1949, 67)

These regularities are captured by Weber's major heuristic construct: the ideal type.[3] That which to him is all-important becomes manifest in this empirically based conceptual tool: the "meaning clusters" dominant in groups.[4]

Importantly to him, rather than falling into alignment relationships such that an internally unified "system" is constituted, groups frequently stand variously in relationships of alliance *and* of antagonism. Domination, conflict and

---

2 Although these pivotal features demarcate major aspects of Weber's mode of analysis, a claim of "comprehensiveness" cannot be offered here. Justification of such a claim would require discussions far beyond the parameters possible in a short article. Hence, this investigation must be comprehended as a *preliminary* study. See Kalberg, forthcoming.

3 On its formation and usage, see Kalberg 1994, 81–91; Albrow 1990; Burger 1976.

4 The "subjective meaning complex" implied by each ideal type answers the question of why it is meaningful to actors to conduct themselves in a specific situation in a specific manner. See Weber 1968, 8–18.

the exercise of power often play large roles as groups shift perpetually. The patterned action located in certain groups may flow in directions opposed to those in other groups, according to Weber, even to such a degree that severe antagonisms not amenable to negotiation and compromise may remain in place over longer periods.

Thus, all presuppositions regarding the "firm and closed" boundaries of "society" remain incompatible with Weber's sociology. The extent to which "unity" exists, as well as "polarization," formulates to him a research agenda only. Moreover, as opposed to organic perspectives, groups in Weber's sociology are never empowered to integrate persons fully. Instead, a tension – empirically of varying degree – always exists between the orientations of persons to particular subjective meanings and to particular groups, and to the "socializing" influence of groups to which they belong (see later).

The prominence in Weber's sociology of an array of societal domains (*gesellschaftliche Sphären*) also testifies to its opposition to all organic holism schools. He stresses in *E&S* the potential of each major arena – the religion, law, economy, domination, status groups and universal organizations (the family and clan) spheres – for causal autonomy and opposes all perspectives that perceive a principled integration of all domains into an overarching "society" (2011b, 97). Indeed, his foundational focus upon a pluralism of arenas and their multiplicities of ideal types further testifies to his basic view: every "society's" empirical reality is constituted both from arrays of peaceful alliances and innumerable conflicts and shifting tensions.

Weber's emphasis upon patterned action and its *diverse* interactions, as well as upon domain-specific developments, also leads his sociology away from organic holism's frequent reference to global dichotomies (e.g., *Gemeinschaft / Gesellschaft,* traditional/modern, particular/universal), broad axioms regarding a society's degree of consensus or conflict and general law postulates. Unlike his empirically based ideal types, the high level of abstraction of these concepts fails to capture historical specificity and complexity.

In sum, patterns of subjective meaning-complexes, as captured by ideal types, comprise the foundational level of analysis in Weber's empirical investigations. His attempt to explain the varying routes and directions taken by civilizations – and, not least, the unique pathway taken by Western civilization – rejects organic holism in favor of ideal types and *E&S*'s broad-ranging analytic of societal domains. Whether "rationalization," "disenchantment," or "universalization" processes occur remain to him always open, empirical and multi-causal conundra to be investigated rather than linear, "general evolutionary" or "advance of progress" processes. Historical cycles are also rejected (see Weber 1976, 357). He would have stood opposed as well to a major holism assumption propounded by Parsonsian Modernization theory: increasing "societal differentiation" will call forth disorder and chaos if overarching and integrative "value-generalization" processes are absent (Parsons 1971, 1977). Finally, Weber confines from the outset all global classifications of civilizations (such as primitive, archaic, historical and modern) to the level of heuristic aids, for he contends that they are useful only as research tools. They fail to capture adequately that which he seeks to define precisely: each civilization's unique-ness and particular development. Weber's stress upon the subjective meaning of action aligns closely with his opposition to organic holism.

The Centrality of Subjective Meaning

Rather than referring "to an objectively 'correct' meaning or one which is 'true' in some metaphysical sense" (1968, 4), Weber's sociology is concerned with the investigation of "subjective meaning-complexes." Through interpre-tive understanding (*verstehen*) and in-depth research, Weberian sociologists seek to "recapture" the ways in which subjective meaning motivates persons in demarcated groups in specific and patterned ways. These researchers do so by reconstructing, to the greatest degree possible, the variety of *contexts* of action in reference to which these patterns of action occur. They then seek *to under-stand* the manner in which actors within their respective groups-based milieux endow their situations with subjective meaning and act accordingly. On the basis of thorough and unbiased empirical research, motives *can* be compre-hended by social scientists, indeed even patterns of meaning in long past and geographically distant civilizations, Weber contends.

In perhaps his best known example, Weber sought to clarify in *The Protestant Ethic and the Spirit of* Capitalism (2011b; *PE*) the ways in which the seventeenth-century Puritan endowed specific action with subjective meaning. To a certain extent this "inner-worldly ascetic" baffled Weber.[5] From the point of view of a "natural" attitude toward life that takes delight in diverse worldly pleasures, the Puritan's strict asceticism could only be seen as strange. The enjoyment of eat-ing, drinking, and relaxation was denied to the faithful; in addition, the single activities deserving of their energies – regular and systematic labor in a calling and a concerted search for wealth and profit – connoted sheer drudgery and pain. Even the cultivation of friendship and intimacy was prohibited to this believer; both comprise threats to one's exclusive allegiance to God. Hence, if examined from the perspective of all "enjoyment of life," the actions of the ascetic devout must be judged as "irrational" (2011b, 80, 92–94, 98, 130–31).

---

5   Inner-worldly implies to Weber that the action *this* believer perceives as relevant to
    personal salvation is action *in* the world rather than separate from the world (as is the
    "other-worldly" action of the monk secluded in a monastery).

However, a methodology that seeks to "interpretively understand" subjective meaning can never uphold this conclusion. Nor can it refer to "strange" as the final explanation. Instead, Weber insists that the actions of Puritans, if their meaning-complex is reconstructed through rigorous research and analysis, will be recognized as subjectively meaningful. Through the careful study of diaries, sermons, autobiographies, and other documents, he aimed to reconstruct the faith of the devout and to comprehend the "psychological premiums" (*psychologische Prämien*) their all-important salvation quest placed upon certain endeavors. Although seemingly odd, the *meaningfulness* of the believer's action would then become plausible and understandable to the social scientist.

Weber emphasized repeatedly that such cross-cultural and cross-epochal explorations must be acknowledged as complex and even precarious. "We moderns" can scarcely imagine the intensity of the Puritan's devotion and focus upon the question of personal salvation nor "*how* large a significance those components of our consciousness rooted in religious beliefs have actually had upon culture [...] and the organization of life" (2011b, 178). Written in 1904 and 1905, *PE* comprises Weber's most powerful demonstration of how a variety of motives by Puritan, Catholic, and Lutheran believers influences activity in different ways.

This orientation to subjective meaning also guided his many further empirical investigations. In his three-volume series, *The Economic Ethics of the World Religions*, for example, Weber explored the origins of the beliefs and actions typical, among others, of Confucians, Daoists, Hindus, Buddhists and Jews. Even the extreme withdrawal from the world of Buddhist mystics can be *understood as meaningful* if placed within the framework of *their* perception of the transcendental realm (as dominated by an immanent and impersonal Being rather than an anthropomorphic and omnipotent Deity), definition of the goal of salvation (to escape from the endless wheel of reincarnation) and view of the appropriate means toward its attainment (through contemplation and the "silencing of the soul" that alone allows immersion into the impersonal All-One). Why, Weber queried further, for example, was scholarship meaningful to the Confucian literati? And why were the commandments of an anthropomorphic God meaningful to the Old Testament prophets?

This central emphasis upon subjective meaning and its empirical context implies the rejection of a major axiom central to Marxism, neo-Marxism, organicism and structuralism: external structures should constitute the major subject of sociological investigation. For Weber, a principled disjunction always remains between "external forms" – classes, status groups and organizations, for example – and the subjective motivations of individuals. It may exist to such an extent that an entire range of motives can be found among persons who otherwise orient their action to a single class, status group, or organization (see 1968, 29–38).

For example, the search for and legitimation of domination can be anchored in affectual motives (an emotional surrender to the ruler), traditional orientations (to customs and conventions), means-end rational calculations (conformity to conventions or obedience to laws for reasons of expediency) and orientations to values (the belief in loyalty and duty and in the domination as just) – or a combination of all of these action-orientations (see 1968, 31).[6] As is obvious if the functioning of structurally identical bureaucracies is compared cross-culturally, a "bureaucratic ethos" motivates functionaries to varying degrees. Similarly, whether a civil servant within a bureaucracy fulfills tasks motivated by values, means-end rational calculations, or a respect for an accustomed way of doing things remains, for Weber, a question for empirical investigation (1968, 30–31) – one answered in different ways despite the formally similar features of this organization. He contends that even the extremely firm organizational structure of the religious sect will not determine the subjective meaning of the devout.[7]

The evaluation of the subjective meaning of persons in groups stands at the foundation of his sociology of civilizations as well as his sociology generally. The motives "behind" observed action vary widely across groups, epochs and civilizations, Weber is convinced. Hence, a methodology anchored in subjective meaning and interpretive understanding proves indispensable. The particular action *meaningful to persons in groups* here moves to center stage; researchers can now investigate "the other" on its *own* terms. Intensely debated among Weber's colleagues, his abandonment of a fixed structural point of reference implied to him a clear conclusion: viable empirical explorations that seek to reveal and define manifestations of subjective meaning in the civilizations of the East and West, as well as in the past and the present, *can* be conducted.

In essence, Weber's sociology of civilizations defines and utilizes a methodology that pushes aside Western-centric assumptions and advocates an understanding "from within" – once in-depth research has been conducted – even of groups radically different from those familiar to Western scholars. His

6   Weber's conviction that the diverse sources of legitimation constitute the central issue
     in respect to domination, rather than the sheer "external form" of a domination orga-
     nization, stands at the foundation of his interest in the subject of domination (see, for
     example, 1968, 952–54, 1068–69, 1104–9). "For what motives do people obey com-
     mands," he queries.
7   "Viewed externally, numerous Hinduist religious communities appear to be 'sects'
     just as do many religious communities in the West. The sacred values, however, and
     the manner in which values were mediated, pointed in radically opposed directions"
     (Weber 1946c, 292; translation altered).

empirically rooted sociology of subjective meaning had the effect of a) banishing the set of "universal standards" commonly utilized by his era's social scientists to evaluate other cultures and b) of delegitimizing Western triumphalism. However distant and "odd" at first glance, the subjective meaning of persons in groups must be investigated in terms of its *own* dynamics, Weber maintains. Only then will the internal workings of civilizations be comprehended.

Multi-causality I: "No Resting Place"

A critical presupposition throughout his sociology of civilizations concerns causality: only reference to a broad array of causes will explain the origins of patterned action. Innumerable clusters of regular action develop into groups in Weber's sociology, which may then become strong "carriers" of patterned action (see later).[8] A succinct examination of this aspect of his methodology constitutes the task of this section.

Power and the search to legitimate action as "valid" have been omnipresent causes of new patterned action throughout history, Weber holds (see 1968, 30–38). Pivotal for him as well are, for example, technological innovations, significant historical events, economic and political interests and ideas (see Kalberg 1994, 68–78). And, by the sheer force of their personalities, great charismatic leaders can mobilize large populations on behalf of their missions and introduce new regularities of action. Religious and secular value constellations may also, even if never enunciated by an extraordinary and heroic figure, ground new and influential directions to patterned action.

Indeed, values *may* be powerful enough to deflect or even curtail patterns of social action placed into motion by political and economic interests, Weber contends, especially if a cohesive stratum, organization, or class congeals as their carrier. Once established, religious beliefs may have a strong impact upon economic and political development, he maintains, and even shape an epoch's legitimating principles and world view. To him, "the content of religious ideas. ... carry purely within themselves an autonomous momentum, lawful capacity and coercive power" (2011b, 390 [n. 96]).

A causal analysis that focuses alone on economic interests will remain blind to the manner in which, for example, the authority of tradition in China, once strengthened by magical forces and Confucianism, thwarted for centuries the pursuit of economic interests (see 1951, 227–9). The "development of an organized life oriented systematically," Weber argues, "toward *economic*

---

8 Values, traditions, means-end, and affectual action *must*, according to Weber, acquire bounded groups as their carriers – or they remain devoid of causal efficacy and societal impact (see later).

activity has confronted broad-ranging internal resistance" wherever "magical and religious forces have inhibited the unfolding of this organized life" (2011a, 246). Finally, the sheer weight of immovable tradition may effectively oppose all innovative patterns of action, regardless of their sources and even if supported by charismatic personalities.

Weber frequently calls attention to religious doctrines and salvation paths. Each may independently influence the practical conduct of believers: "The Indian doctrine of Kharma, the Calvinist belief in predestination, the Lutheran justification through faith, and the Catholic doctrine of sacrament" (1946c, 286–87). And: "Religious rationalization has its own dynamics, which economic conditions merely channel; above all, it is linked to the emergence of priestly education" (1968, 1179). However, Weber emphasizes also the opposite line of causality–yet nonetheless then stresses a further reversal:

> The nature of the desired sacred values has been strongly influenced by the nature of the external interest-situation and the corresponding way of life of the ruling strata and thus by the social stratification itself. But the reverse also holds: wherever the whole way of life has been methodically rationalized, its direction has been profoundly determined by the ultimate values toward which this rationalization has been oriented. (1946c, 286–87; translation altered; see pp. 268–70, 286, 290)

However, Weber again emphasizes that the reverse occurs regularly: the content and shape of a value configuration may be strongly influenced by political and economic interests (see 1946c, 267–69; 1968, 341).[9] Interests, whether political, status-oriented or economic, always motivate people, he contends. Capitalism's unfolding was surely influenced, and particularly at decisive points, by the economic interests of pivotal groups and their pursuit of sheer power. Weber stresses that the "economic form," whether manifest as guild-based capitalism, the putting-out system or mercantilism, has always been important and must never be omitted from causal analyses of modern capitalism's origin and expansion (see 1927).

Nonetheless, a broad spectrum of causes outside the inexhaustible sway of interests always exists, as these passages also indicate. Furthermore, Weber repeatedly discovers tensions and conflicts across patterns of action and across and within groups, as well as fissions and fusions – which then cause further shifts and realignments. Values and interests merge and diverge in the most

---

9   "The religiously determined way of life is itself profoundly influenced by economic and political factors operating within given geographical, political, social and national boundaries" (1946c, 268).

complex ways. New regularities of social action are placed into motion with newfound coalitions. New carrier groups crystallize, yet they often remain unstable and fragile. As noted, even structurally identical organizations – the capitalist firm, the bureaucracy and even sects – do not carry the same sets of values by virtue of this similarity (1946c, 292).

The crucial role of the analytic framework presented in Weber's *E&S* – domains and domain-specific ideal types – now becomes apparent. Furthermore, by designating in *E&S* *multiple* sphere-specific ideal types as endowed with potential causal status, he proclaims that a *broad pluralism* of patterned action must remain prominent in *every* causal analysis. In effect, this procedure – reference to an *array* of societal domains and domain-specific ideal types – both acknowledges, for example, cultural forces in a principled fashion *and* offers a safeguard mechanism against an elevation by researchers of a single factor – or a few factors – to positions of general causal priority. Weber argues that a causal analysis of enduring economic organizations and forms of domination, for example, must include reference not only to power and national interests but also to the values and traditions that offer backdrop legitimation to these "structures" (see 1968, 31–36, 212–16, 952–54).

All attempts to locate a "resting point" – a single causal force – must be seen as a futile endeavor (1946c, 268; 1968, 341). As Weber repeats on various occasions, "no significant generalizations can be made" and no "general formula" will establish a causally "prior" or "dominant" pattern of social action (1968, 341, 577, 1179; 2011b, 178–79). The sources of patterned action are extremely pluralistic; he insists: "We would lose ourselves in these discussions if we tried to demonstrate these dependencies in all their singularities" (1946c, 268). Further attention to his "societal domains" will illuminate his broad multi-causality.

Multi-causality II: Societal Domains

E&S offers a wide-ranging examination of patterned social action in a vast variety of contexts. While addressing questions and dilemmas specific to the domains of law, religion, the economy, domination, universal organizations (the family and clan) and status groups, Weber inventories how meaningful action *may* crystallize and become regular as a consequence of diverse "internal" (values and ideas) and "external" (political and economic interests) configurations. That is, to him, regular action in each sphere may become uprooted from its "natural," reactive flow and become endowed with a distinctly *meaningful* aspect vis-à-vis patterned action in every other sphere (see 1968, 4–18). Weber maintains that persons are "placed into various life-spheres, each of which is governed by different laws" (2005, 267; see 1946b, 323–24).

Each domain indicates to the researcher *probable* empirical orientations – and even likely patterns – for social action. Hypotheses can be formed. Furthermore, although *analytically* distinct in terms of dilemmas, themes, problems, and sets of questions, these spheres may empirically overlap and intertwine in some epochs and regions to such a degree that their boundaries are scarcely visible; in other epochs and regions they develop more "autonomously" – yet even in these empirical cases the arenas seldom unfold at the same tempo or in a parallel manner (see 2011b, 97). Weber's discussion of these domains in *E&S* assists conceptualization of how some can be seen to cast their influence broadly.

He offers many illustrations. His examination of domination, for example, evaluates the extent to which "developmental chances" of a type of action are subject to "economic, political or any other external determinants." However, it also assesses the degree to which the types of domination follow "an 'autonomous' logic inherent in their technical structure" (1968, 578, 654–55, 1002). Weber is especially cognizant of how an empirical attribution of *legitimacy* to domination by persons in demarcated groups endows – with a greater likelihood – this realm with an independent profile. The *power* of the Brahmins in classical India, for example, did not alone account for the caste system's endurance and opposition to the development of a "citizenry" endowed with equal rights. Rather, the widespread *belief* that the Brahmins legitimately possessed prestige and authority proved also pivotal (1958, 90–91, 113–14, 127–29; see earlier).

In sum, *E&S*'s various societal domains constitute an array of constructs. In combination, they contribute strongly to Weber's broad multi-causality. Comprised of constellations of ideal types, each arena signifies an indigenous dilemma.[10] Each sphere can be seen to be "co-determined by other than economic cases" (1968, 341; see p. 935).[11]

These brief examples must suffice to demonstrate that the broad multi-causality at the core of Weber's sociology is anchored in ideal types and societal domains. Moreover, their significance never derives from their location either in an overarching entity – a "society" – or within diffuse, evolutionary or differentiation historical trends. Rather, for him, they always remain deeply *embedded in constellations* of regular action-orientations. We must turn now to just this theme: the centrality of *contexts* in Weber's sociology of civilizations.

---

10 Weber's title (rather than that given posthumously by his wife) for E&S was *The Economy and the Societal Orders and Powers.* This title captures his multi-causality.

11 For more in-depth discussion of Weber on this theme, see Kalberg 1994, 50–78; 2011, 341–43.

Multi-causality III: The Embeddedness of Social Action in Contexts of Social Action and Weber's *Verstehende* Sociology

Weber's stress upon a multiplicity of causes for patterned action introduces great complexity. Indeed, he discovers not only multiple interactions at the foundation of all new regularities of action but also dynamic – or conjunctural – interactions. The multi-causal ways in which patterned action, amid contexts of patterned action, crystallizes and becomes *embedded in* new contexts of regular action are emphasized. As noted, even the movement of history by great charismatic personalities occurs in Weber's sociology within contexts of patterned social action (see Kalberg 1994, 50–78).

His comparative texts offer many examples of his context-oriented analysis of the origins and expansion of regular action. Albeit briefly, we must here call direct attention to this foundational element in his systematic study of civilizations. Cognizance of this component a) assists understanding of its complexity in regard to issues of causality and b) facilitates the Weberian sociologist's quest interpretively to understand the social action of persons in groups far and wide.

Weber's comparative investigations attend profoundly to the contexts of social action. To him, whether patterned action – for example, toward a charismatic ruler, the salvation path of inner-worldly asceticism, an historical event or a particular type of law or economy – proves causally significant depends not simply upon the firmness of its boundaries, power or the influence of a carrier group. Pivotal also is the manner in which *constellations* of patterned action interact: Each *milieu* of regular action places a particular imprint upon new and ongoing regular action. Its substance is influenced, as well as its impact.

Hence, Weber's case analyses abjure a focus upon the action-orientations themselves or the fact of their appearance. Instead, the multiple patterns of action in reference to which they become manifest remain decisive if new regular action is to arise, expand, and attain sociological significance. Groups are always "located" in a multitude of groups, which form a setting. A civilization's religion-based "economic ethos," for example, must be investigated in reference not only to doctrines and religious organizations but also in respect to laws, the family, economic "forms," political organizations and types of domination.

Weber is convinced that a *complex* interaction of multiple action patterns – and the alteration of each as a consequence – characterizes empirical reality. He attends continuously to the diverse ways in which arrays of action become juxtaposed and congeal into unique patterns. A given effect in principle results not only from a multiplicity of action-orientations but also from their variable ordering. To him: "The totality of *all* the conditions [… must] 'act jointly' (*zusammenwirken*) in a certain way and in no other if the concrete effect and no other is to be allowed to appear" (1949a, 187; translation altered; emphasis original). Thus, Weber seeks to integrate "the 'particular fact' […] as a real causal factor into a real, hence concrete context" (1949a, 135; see also 1975, 197). Interaction in a "correct" dynamic must occur if the causes of patterned action are to be explained at the level of adequate causality. Far from linear, this interaction fuses patterns of action heretofore unconnected and calls forth qualitatively new causal impulses of varying capacities. Conjunctural inter-actions are also acknowledged; they may significantly strengthen or weaken regular action – *and* call forth fully unforeseen regularities of action.

In sum, on the basis of his conceptualization of "societies" as lacking organic unity and as instead comprised from endlessly intermingling, conflict-ing and jockeying patterns of action, Weber maintains that *interactive* influences are very often effective causes. Particular attention must be paid to the ways in which precisely the dynamic interaction of *multiple* patterns of action places an independent causal thrust into motion. Only such a complex and cause-oriented methodology that *emphasizes* multi-causality *and* conjunctural interac-tions can capture, he argues, both the intricate and perpetual interweavings of – and the inexorable tensions between – values, conventions, customs, laws, economic and political interests, power and domination.[12]

Weber's comparative-historical texts repeatedly pose a specific question: In light of the embeddedness of action in contexts of patterned action, "what social action is *possible?*" In a demarcated milieu in which action takes place in reference to, for example, constellations of regular action oriented to the economy, religion, law, domination, status and universal organizations arenas, what subjective meaning carried by further patterns of action *can* arise? Even the influence of mighty missionary prophets depended upon the existence of a "certain minimum of intellectual culture" (1968, 486). What regulari-ties of social action, Weber queries, will likely become predominant if, for example, bureaucratic organizations saturate a particular civilization, includ-ing the political arena? His sociology of civilizations is pervaded by attempts to discover the parameters within which specific patterns of action appear. He is convinced that systematic comparative research will offer clarity and insight in respect even to the question of whether a competing set of values *can* be introduced into – and expand in – a specific civilization.

12 The above points, as well as the remaining discussion in this section, are indebted to the
     more in-depth analysis in Kalberg (1994, 30–46, 98–101, 168–76). Weber's contextual
     and conjunctural methodology is examined there in far greater detail. It is applied in
     reconstructions of his analyses of the rise of the caste system in India, monotheism in
     ancient Israel and Confucianism in ancient China (see Kalberg 2012, 145–92).

Ideal types prove central to this focus upon contexts. As discussed, they identify the patterned meaningful action that delineates groups. In doing so, they assist conceptualization of both the possibilities for new regularities of action to arise and probabilities for them to become sociologically significant. That is, some constellations of ideal types demarcate contexts that allow, utilize and even intensively cultivate certain new patterned action, while others tend to circumscribe and exclude them (see Kalberg 1994, 39–46, 98–102, 168–76). Moreover, regularities of action never spread across civilizations in uniform ways, according to Weber, for they constantly confront new constellations of patterned action carried by groups of varying cohesion and power. Each influences the congealing of action and its impact, indeed even in a unique fashion.

The orientation of action to, for example, missionary prophecy found fertile ground in ancient Israel, yet its revolutionary power confronted firm barriers in ancient India, China and Egypt (see Weber 1968, 418–19, 447–50). Similarly, configurations of regular action prepared the way for a petty bourgeoisie to form and become powerful in the medieval West; a different constellation of patterned action in India and China erected clear obstacles to such an expansive development of this class in these civilizations (see, e.g., 1968, 508). "And why then," Weber queries, "did capitalist interests not call forth [a] stratum [of professionally trained] jurists and [rational] law in China or India," as they had in the West (2011a, 245)? Likewise, whether the market economy spreads depends in part upon whether a legal context – in the form of a measure of guaranteed contractual freedom and a broad legal authorization of transactions – for its expansion has become stable, or whether laws exclusively delimit "a person's non-economic relations and privileges with regard to other persons" (1968, 668).[13] And what arrays of patterned action and groups assisted the rise of different types of legal education?

The effects of legal training are bound to be different where it is in the hands of *honoratiores* whose relations with legal practice are professional …. The existence of such a special class of honoratiores is, generally speaking, possible only where

13 The entire passage illuminates Weber's position: "There exists, of course, an intimate connection between the expansion of the market and the expanding measure of contractual freedom or, in other words, the scope of arrangements which are guaranteed as within the total legal order of those rules which authorize such transactional dispositions. In an economy where self-sufficiency prevails and exchange is lacking, the function of the law will naturally be otherwise: it will mainly define and delimit a person's non-economic relations and privileges with regard to other persons in accordance not with economic considerations but with the person's origin, education, or social status" (Weber 1968, 668).

legal practice is not sacredly dominated and legal practice has not yet become too involved with the needs of urban commerce. (1968, 793)

Likewise, the expansion of new techniques related to a type of law occurs, according to Weber, when "economic situations" prove amenable:

The specific type of techniques used in a legal system [...] are of far greater significance for the likelihood that a certain legal institution will be invented in its context than is ordinarily believed. Economic situations do not automatically give birth to new legal forms; they merely provide the opportunity for the actual spread of a legal technique if it is invented. (1968, 687)

Moreover, while the status of the entrepreneur and businessman in Antiquity and the Middle Ages was alike quite low, Weber stresses that the reasons for this evaluation varied according to social context: it resulted in the ancient world from the contempt of a leisure class of rentiers for traders and tradesmen, while it originated in the Middle Ages from criticism of commercial relations by the Catholic Church – for these interactions could not be regulated by ethical norms (1976, 66–67; 1946b, 331; 1968, 353, 583–88, 709). The multiple ways in which, depending upon whether a facilitating milieu exists, arrays of patterned action juxtapose and crystallize into groups – and unique configurations of powerful groups – repeatedly constitutes his concern.[14]

Weber's pivotal notion of interpretive understanding also powerfully serves to define his sociology of civilizations as awarding high priority to the contexts of action within which patterned action appears and expands. To him, the *location* of subjective meaning within configurations of regular action is indispensable for its understanding. Again, his societal domains and domain-specific ideal types serve as heuristic orientational mechanisms that facilitate the contextual location of action – if only because, in charting an immense spectrum of subjectively meaningful action, they thereby facilitate an understanding of broad arrays of empirical action as plausible, meaningful, and causal. Indeed, as noted, Weber's adherence to a methodology of interpretive understanding *assists* sociologists to recognize action heretofore perceived as "irrational" as in fact, once located contextually, "rational."

Finally, his orientation to the interpretive understanding of action points in a further manner to the centrality in his sociology of civilizations of an embedding of action contextually: it assists, and even challenges, sociologists to become aware of the uniqueness of their own era. He laments the widespread

14 For further examples that demonstrate the centrality of social contexts for Weber, see Kalberg 1994, 38–46, 168–92.

tendency in the social sciences to define the modern epoch as unchained from a sacred and feudal past. To the extent that this occurs, a greater likelihood exists that interpretations of the past will take place by reference to the radically different assumptions of the present. Asserting time and again that "we moderns" can barely comprehend the actual character of major questions and dilemmas in past epochs, Weber fears that present-day presuppositions will be unknowingly *imposed* upon the past (see earlier).

Only if social scientists today are assisted in their efforts to comprehend, through interpretive understanding, social action *in its indigenous contexts* can the full promise of Weber's sociology of civilizations be realized. Researchers will then become more aware, he is convinced, of the great diversity of ways in which individuals in different epochs and civilizations act subjectively meaningfully. In effect, by calling attention to action as meaningful that otherwise might be belittled or dismissed, *E&S*'s vast analytic of societal spheres and sphere-specific ideal types *expands* the capacity of a social science methodology to assist *understanding* of the subjective meaningfulness of action – even action taking place in radically different civilizations. By locating patterned action in distinct civilizations in contexts of patterned action, its meaningfulness within this setting becomes understandable. An enhancement of the sociologist's horizon and cross-cultural comprehension thereby occurs.

Weber's cognizance of regular action's embeddedness, as well as its contextual, constellational, and conjunctural interactions, accounts for his warnings in strong terms against all diffusion theories. He admonishes as well against all inter-civilizational and inter-epochal analogies (see 1976, 39–43, 341; Kalberg 1994, 83). Although they often appear plausible, similarities "are all too easily deceptive," and such analogies "are highly unreliable for the most part, indeed are often an obstacle to clarity and understanding" (Weber 1976, 39–40; see 1968, 18–28). Instead, he stresses that each civilization's "rationalism" comprises a "characteristic individuality": each implies a unique configuration of social action and a distinguishing dynamic. And each is empowered to shape new action-orientations in a singular fashion to varying degrees. This axiom stands as a cornerstone component in the systematic methodology that grounds Weber's sociology of civilizations.

Multi-causality IV: The Tight Linking of the Past with the Present

As discussed, multiple and complex constellations of patterned action and innumerable groups, as captured by ideal types, are omnipresent in Weber's sociology of civilizations. His emphasis upon the multi-causal and contextual origins of empirically based regular action and groups anchors the close interweaving in his sociology of the past with the present. Given facilitating contexts of groups, the influence of some groups may even penetrate deeply into a subsequent epoch. To Weber, "that which has been handed down from the past becomes everywhere the immediate precursor of that taken in the present as valid" (1968, 29). Even the abrupt appearance of "the new" – even the "supernatural" power of charisma – never fully ruptures ties to the past (1968, 577; 1946c, 273). Even the monumental transformations called forth by industrialization failed to sweep away the past. To him, viable legacies (*Ueberbleibsel, Ueberreste, Vermächtnisse*) live on.

His orientation in *E&S* to societal domains and ideal types stands at the foundation not only of this treatise's dynamic and contextual approach to causality but also of its capacity to analyze the many subtle ways in which the past interlocks with the present. As noted, he contends that the various societal spheres are endowed with a potentially independent capacity; they may develop at times in a nonparallel manner and at their own pace. And, in documenting patterns of meaningful action, each ideal type implies the possibility of an autonomous sustaining element – indeed, one that *may* cast its influence even beyond its epoch of origin. The dichotomy frequently proclaimed by commentators as capturing Weber's "view of history" – his contrast of the stable and routine character of tradition to the revolutionary character of charisma – fails to render the complex relationship in his sociology between the past and the present.

The vast variety of patterns of action articulated in *E&S*, their "open" interaction, and their variable degree of closure all lead in the direction of a single conclusion: the past interweaves tightly with the present. Regularities of action in some groups can be recognized as becoming firm, even to the extent of developing in terms of indigenous problematics and penetrating deeply into subsequent eras. The anti-organistic "view of society" (see earlier) that flows out of this systematic opus – as constructed from numerous causally effective, competing and reciprocally interacting patterns of action as manifest in groups – easily acknowledges the "survival" of some regularities of action from the past and their significant influence, as legacies, upon patterns of action in the present. Even in the face of large-scale structural transformations, such as bureaucratization, urbanization and secularization, Weber's empirically based concepts and procedures are empowered to take cognizance of the diverse, multiple and substantive ways in which the past perpetually influences the present.

His conceptualization of the causes of patterned action and group formation as contextual, widely pluralistic and "open," and his insistence that societal domains may develop empirically in a nonparallel manner along their "own" pathways and at their own speeds, leads him also to reject evolutionary theories (1976, 366). All depictions of history as following linear lines and as pursuing an inevitable "progressive" course stand opposed to his foundational tenets. Switchbacks, reversals, paradox, unforeseen coalitions and unexpected consequences characterize Weber's studies rather than a collapsing of regular action and groups into "necessary," directed and predictable historical developments. To him, some patterns of action always "survive" from the past and exercise a significant influence upon patterns of action in the present; legacies are central (see Kalberg 1994, 159–64; 2012, 65–72). Furthermore, although rationalization, disenchantment and bureaucratization pathways can be conceptualized by Weber's concepts and procedures, his entire sociology stresses that the *empirical* unfolding of these sweeping "processes" depends upon singular concatenations of hosts of patterned action, as well as the crystallization of facilitating contexts of regular action.[15]

Weber often charts legacies from the religious domain. In the United States, central values in Protestant asceticism – disciplined and routine work in a profession, the regular giving to charity organizations, the perpetual formation by persons of goals, the orientation to the future and the unending attempts to "master" the world's challenges (*Weltbeherrschung*), an optimism regarding the capacity to shape personal destinies, and a strong intolerance of "evil" – remain integral in American life today despite the fact that most who uphold these values remain unaware of their intimate linkage to a religious heritage (1968, 1187). Moreover, the "direct democratic administration" by the congregation, as it took place in the Protestant sects in the United States, left a legacy crucial for the establishment of democratic forms of government, as did the unwillingness of sect members to bestow a halo of reverence upon secular authority (see Weber, 2005, 277–90; see Kalberg 2012, 68–72; 2014).[16]

Weber's attention to legacies runs throughout his writings. Brief mention here, albeit in perfunctory fashion, of a few examples will serve to highlight the ways in which long-range legacies pervade his sociology of civilizations.[17]

15 The author has identified two distinct modes of diachronic interaction, each of which charts the manner in which past patterned social action influences present regular action, reappear throughout Weber's texts in general: "legacy" and "antecedent condition" interactions. This detailed discussion, which can be found in Kalberg (1994, 158–67; 2011, 343–44), cannot be repeated here.

16 As it concerns their influence upon the formation of the American political culture, seventeenth-century Puritanism's long-term legacies have been examined at Kalberg 2014. This volume particularly emphasizes the ways in which American civic associations can be viewed as direct legacies of the Puritan sect. The American civic sphere is here understood as a secularized and weakened version of the Puritan's ethical community.

17 These examples are largely from Kalberg 1994, 160–61. For further illustrations, see pp. 162–68; see also Kalberg 2017 and Kalberg Forthcoming. Weber's related concept – "antecedent conditions" – cannot be investigated here (see Kalberg 1994, 158–64).

The Old Testament scriptural prophets "cast their shadows through the millennia into the present" (1952, 334). For example, the legalistic ethic of Jewish law "was absorbed by the Puritan ethic and thus put into the context of modern bourgeois economic morality" (1968, 1204).

The "rational traditions of Roman law" influenced not only Canon law (1968, 828), but also modern formal law (1968, 843–55), and Canon law "became [...] one of the guides for secular law on the road to rationality" (1968, 829).

Feudalism's high sense of dignity rooted in personal honor and the basic attitudes of knighthood survived and influenced, in later epochs, the Western *ministerales*, the English gentleman ideal, and even the ideal of the Puritan gentleman. For all these strata, "feudal knighthood was the original, specifically medieval center of orientation" (1968, 1068–1069).

Ancient "political feudalism" in China cast a broad shadow, crucially assisting the development of the status ethic of Confucianism in the classical and post-classical eras (1951, 46).

A "sober practical rationalism" from Roman times, in casting the framework for the dogmatic ethical systematization of belief, constituted "the most important legacy of Rome to the Christian Church" (1968, 554–55).

The Protestant ethic of the seventeenth century influenced the birth of the spirit of capitalism in the eighteenth century (2011b).

The religious congregation in the Western Middle Ages established a singular cultural orientation toward universal values that assisted the spread of confraternization across heretofore hostile groups and, hence, the unfolding of guilds in the medieval cities and the growth of trade (1968, 1243–50).

The "unique organization of the Catholic Church as a rational institution" – its organs of rational law-making (the councils, the dioceses, the Curia, and the papal powers) – became "one of the guides for secular law on the road to rationality" (1968, 792; see also p. 828).

The opposition of ancient Judaism and ancient Christianity to magic and a pluralism of gods facilitated, in the cities of the medieval West, the fraternization of different ethnic groups heretofore in possession of indigenous gods and exclusionary magical practices (1952, 124, 131, 134, 224).

The patrimonial bureaucracy, natural law, and the Catholic Church's hierocracy left legacies that supported the unfolding of the modern bureaucracy (1968, 866-75, 1028-30).

Western feudal domination's notion of "contract" formulated a legacy that fused with a variety of developments to facilitate the rise of the modern state (1968, 1078-89).

Ancient Judaism's severe formulation of the believer's submission to God established a precedent for Calvin's Predestination doctrine (1968, 486).

Such innumerable examples that indicate the influence of legacies from the past upon the present appear throughout Weber's comparative studies. The presentist orientations of all functionalist modes of analysis stand in this respect in strict opposition to his works. To him, the past always penetrates deeply into the present, even interlocking with its core contours and, to some extent, molding them. Patterned action, ideal types, and societal domains, once juxtaposed with a broad-ranging multi-causal methodology and a rigorous orientation to social contexts, articulate a uniquely Weberian "view of history" – one that perpetually and tightly interweaves the past with the present.

This central aspect of the methodology at the foundation of Weber's sociology of civilizations will be more clearly demonstrated by two brief discussions: first, of social carriers and, second, of the caput mortuum mode of linking the past with the present.

Social carriers and the caput mortuum linkages of the past with the present

In addition to identifying the multiple causes at the origins of patterned action and the formation of groups, as well as emphasizing that new patterns of action become firm only in reference to a context of groups, Weber examines in his comparative texts also the manner in which some groups become strong social carriers of patterned action and even develop a degree of "autonomy." To him, values, traditions and interests have congealed in all civilizations; however, only social action supported by influential carriers have become sociologically significant and left an imprint. Status groups, classes and a variety of organizations (*Verbände*) serve as the most significant bearers of action in Weber's texts.

Salient to him is not only the internal cohesiveness of groups but also their possession of a degree of power or authority. Only then will the patterned action they carry successfully oppose the patterned action carried by other groups. Indeed, power and authority play important roles in his many discussions of the congealing of regular action and its acquisition of carriers capable of initiating and sustaining historical developments. History constitutes an incessantly moving terrain, Weber contends. Patterned action may fade and then later, owing to an alteration of *contexts*, acquire carriers and become reinvigorated in groups. If powerful carriers appear and form coalitions of groups – whether, for example, those oriented to a religious doctrine, a type of law or domination, social honor, the accumulation of profit and goods, a salvation path or a universal organization – patterned action may even cast its influence beyond the era of its formation.

Even the values-based, world view "tracks" at the foundation of a civilization may, if strong carrier groups crystallize on their behalf, cast their imprint across centuries. For example, Weber insists that the existence of cohesive groups of persons *oriented* to religion and religious organizations (churches, sects, synagogues, etc.), whether priests, monks, ministers, theologians or lay groups, constitutes an important factor if religious world views are to crystallize, unfold into coherent sets of values binding upon the devout and uproot social action effectively from its common orientation to mundane interests, means-end rational calculations, conventions and customs (see, e.g., 1946c, 269–70). As he notes: "Unless the concept 'autonomy' is to lack all precision, its definition presupposes the existence of a bounded group of persons which, though membership may fluctuate, is determinable" (1968, 699; translation altered).

In some civilizations, a great continuity of social carriers across epochs has been characteristic. The patrimonial bureaucracy and literati stratum in China, for example, remained the central carriers of Confucianism for more than 2,000 years. In India, the Brahmins carried Hinduism for more than a millennium. In Japan, "the greatest weight in social affairs was carried by a stratum of professional warriors [...] Practical life situations were governed by a code of chivalry and education for knighthood" (1958, 275). Puritanism, the major carrier of the Protestant ethic in the United States, illustrates how patterned social action, according to Weber, changes its carrier status group or organization. In doing so, it survived into a subsequent epoch, influencing it substantively. How did this take place?

Weber argues in *The Protestant Ethic* (2011b) that ethical *values* of *religious* origin had "migrated" from their original carriers – ascetic Protestant churches and sects – to a further carrier organization: the family. Even as significant secularization occurred, these values remained prominent in early socialization: children were taught to hold in high esteem, for example, individual achievement, self-reliance, ascetic personal habits, methodical work, and hard competition. As young adults, they were socialized to oppose worldly authority, avoid all ostentatious display, and distrust the state (see 2011b, 158–78). These values, even as they gradually lost their explicitly religious dimension became firmly anchored in the family. They were taught in intimate, personal relationships to children (see Kalberg 2014, 47–58).

In other words, they were cultivated further – or *carried* – by this organization as binding ethical values and hence continued to influence social action. In this way, patterned action originally cultivated in ascetic Protestant sects and churches endured in a later epoch and long after these organizations had become, as carriers, weaker. Weber refers to this alteration as a caput mortuum transformation: in this case patterned action with origins in the distant past, when it acquires strong carrier groups, survives into subsequent epochs in altered form.

The clusters of values that comprised the Protestant ethic endured in utilitarian manifestations, Weber further maintains. As he notes, once sincerely upheld by the faithful and endowed with legitimacy by religion-oriented values in the seventeenth and eighteenth centuries, today "the idea of an 'obligation to search for and then accept a vocational calling' [...] wanders around in our lives as the ghost of past religious beliefs" (2011b, 177). To him, "victorious capitalism, [...] ever since it came to rest on a mechanical foundation, no longer needs asceticism as a supporting pillar" (2011b, 177; see 1968, 575). Indeed, "in the saddle," modern capitalism "is capable, without any otherworldly reward, of coercing a willingness to work" [18] (2011b, 394, n. 122), and "the pursuit of gain, in the United States, where it has become most completely unchained and stripped of its religious-ethical meaning, [...] tends to be associated with purely competitive passions" (2011b, 177). Examples of such caput mortuum linkages of the past with the present can be found throughout Weber's sociology of civilizations (see, e.g., 1968, 1150, 1154, 1187; 2011b, 93–94; 1927, 313–14).[19]

Conclusion

Taken together, central features of Weber's comparative methodology comprise a rigorous foundation for his systematic sociology of civilizations. They emphasize that these large-scale entities cannot be comprehended without thorough study of their multiple "complexes" of subjective meaning, that patterns of action – *and* their embeddedness in contexts of regular action – must be recognized, that regular action embedded in the past endures into – and formulates contexts for – patterns of action influential in the present and that an evaluation of the *strength* of cohesive social carriers must occur in a systematic fashion.

In light of his orientation to innumerable ideal types and the manner in which they assist conceptualization of moving coalitions and conflicts, as well as his acknowledgment of a *series* of societal domains, Weber's opposition to all organic holism schools is evident (see earlier). Rather than a collapsing of

---

18 Or, as Weber also notes in *PE*: "As the religious roots of an idea died out, a utilitarian tone then surreptitiously shoved itself under the idea and carried it further" (2011b, 174).

19 For a more detailed discussion of social carriers, see Kalberg 1994, 58–62.

patterned action into a unity of harmony and homeostasis or a directed and predictable stream, switchbacks and reversals are ubiquitous in his sociology of civilizations, as are unforeseen alliances, conflicts and consequences. His methodology is also attentive to paradox and irony.

As noted, Weber's foundational stress upon patterned action's boundaries and location contextually in multiple groups steers his analysis of civilizations away from global themes, such as evolution, value-generalization and social differentiation. He rejects for the same reasons all general statements and theories that investigate civilizations by reference to either a progressive or cyclical unfolding of ideas, values or interests on the one hand or expanding diffusion processes on the other hand. As discussed, cross-epochal and cross-civilizational analogies and parallels are likewise rejected, for they also fail to grasp the unique and complex embeddedness of groups.

Moreover, analogies and parallels inadequately acknowledge that unforeseen consequences and "fateful events" play a significant part, as Weber's foundational methodology recognizes, in the common fission and fusion of groups. Rather than either progressive steps or occasional radical change, he views history as a polychromatic net of shifting groups engaged continuously in both antagonistic and coalescing interactions – and even kaleidoscopic interweaving and splintering. Unique configurations perpetually crystallize, albeit at varying speeds, in this dynamic tapestry. And routinization and decline *may* occur. Conversely, a sustained development in a particular civilization, despite regular setbacks, toward "rationalization" and "bureaucratization" *can* take place. However, all of these developments occur alone as a consequence of identifiable and conducive arrays of *empirical* groups and their facilitating concatenations. And according to Weber, concerted social change may involve "progress" only in respect to technological innovations and the unfolding of a single societal arena.

His approach to the study of civilizations must be viewed as grounded in a combination of research procedures and strategies clearly distinct from those of all who have endeavored in the recent past to investigate and compare these large-scale entities. Many scholars today neglect modes of analysis pivotal to Weber's methodology, such as an orientation to subjective meaning (see Huntington 1996; Parsons 1971, 1977; Wallerstein 1980, 1984, 1989; Fukuyama 2006; Pomeranz 2000). Others ground their analyses in presuppositions rejected by Weber, such as organic holism and vague, nonempirical constructs (see Parsons). Still others oppose his embedding of patterned action in deep contexts of patterned action (see Huntington, Fukuyama and Parsons). A variety of theorists reject Weber's attention to social carriers and his tight linkage of the past and the present. His multiple research strategies and procedures, when taken together, constitute a unique and complex contribution to the sociology of civilizations. His methodology is singularly well-equipped to investigate civilizations in a rigorous manner.

Despite the sustained orientation here to the unusual scope and systematic character of the mode of analysis at the foundation of Weber's sociology of civilizations, it must be stressed again that this study can claim only preliminary status. Above all, a) Weber's forceful attention in his sociology of civilizations to model-building, which includes arrays of elective affinity, developmental ("rationalization") and "mixed types" models from *E&S* (see Kalberg 1994, 102–42), and b) his analysis of the "variable intensity" of action (see Kalberg 1994, 62–68), has been omitted. Both require attention. The addition of these components will further reveal the expansive range of Weber's sociology of civilizations and its unusual capacity to offer profound guidance and direction to civilizations researchers. It will also demarcate his methodology unequivocally from all purely narrative (see Braudel 1992a, 1992b; McNeill 1992; Tilly 2008; Tilly and Wood 2012) and geographical (see Diamond 1999) schools.

Finally, and despite its preliminary status, this short investigation has moved beyond the "concepts" and "conflicts" receptions of Weber. It has sought to demonstrate that a systematic sociology of civilizations deeply anchored in major components of his *verstehende* procedures can contribute insights and a methodology useful today for the demarcation of the contours of civilizations, for the understanding of the development of civilizations and for the comprehension of cross-civilizational interactions, whether more acrimonious or more harmonious.

References

Albrow, Martin. 1990. *Max Weber's Construction of Social Theory*. New York: St. Martin's Press.

———1962. *Max Weber: An Intellectual Portrait*. New York: Doubleday Anchor.

———1977. *Nation-Building and Citizenship*, enlarged ed. Berkeley: The University of California Press.

Bendix, Reinhard. and Guenther Roth. 1971. *Scholarship and Partisanship*. Berkeley: The University of California Press.

Burger, Thomas. 1976. *Max Weber's Theory of Concept Formation*. Notre Dame, IN: Notre Dame University Press.

Braudel, Ferdinand. 1992a. *Civilization and Capitalism*. New York: Harper & Row.

———1992b. *The Wheels of Commerce*. Baltimore, MD: Johns Hopkins University Press.

Collins, Randall. 1968. "A Comparative Approach to Political Sociology." in *State and Society*, pp. 42–68, ed. Reinhard Bendix. Berkeley: The University of California Press.

———1975. *Conflict Sociology*. New York: Academic Press.

———1981. "Weber's Last Theory of Capitalism: A Systematization." *American Sociological Review* 10, no. 6: 925–42.

Diamond, Jared. 1999. *Guns, Germans and Steel*. New York: W.W. Norton.

Fukuyama, Francis. 2006. *The End of History*. New York: HarperCollins.

Fulbrook, Mary. 1978. "Max Weber's 'Interpretive Sociology': A Comparison of Conception and Practice." *British Journal of Sociology* 29, no. 1: 71–82.

Gerth, Hans. 1946. "Introduction," in *From Max Weber*, pp. 3–74, ed. H.H. Gerth and C. Wright Mills. New York: Oxford.

Habermas, Juergen. 1984. *Theorie des kommunikativen Handeln*. Suhrkamp: Frankfurt.

Hennis, Wilhelm. 1983. "Max Weber's 'Central Question.'" *Economy and Society* 12, no.2: 136–80.

———1987a. *Max Weber: Essays in Reconstruction*. London: Allen & Unwin.

———1987b. "Personality and Life Orders: Max Weber's Theme," in *Max Weber, Rationality and Modernity*, pp. 52–74, ed. Sam Whimster and Scott Lash. London: Allen & Unwin.

Huntington, Samuel. 1996. *The Clash of Civilizations*. New York: Simon and Schuster

Kalberg. 1979. "The Search for Thematic Orientations in a Fragmented Oeuvre: the Discussion of Max Weber in Recent German Sociological Literature." *Sociology* 13, no. 1: 127–39.

———1980. "Max Weber's Types of Rationality:" *The American Journal of Sociology* 85, no. 3: 1145–79.

———1994. *Max Weber's Comparative-Historical Sociology*. Chicago: The University of Chicago Press.

———2011. "Max Weber," in *The Wiley-Blackwell Companion to Major Social Theorists*, pp. 305–72, edited by George Ritzer and Jeffrey Stepnisky. Malden, MA: Wiley-Blackwell

———2012. *Max Weber's Comparative-Historical Sociology Today: Major Themes, Modes of Analysis, and Applications*. London: Routledge.

———2014. *Searching for the Spirit of American Democracy: Max Weber on a Unique Political Culture, Past, Present, and Future*. London: Routledge

———2017. *The Social Thought of Max Weber*. Los Angeles: Sage.

———Forthcoming. *Max Weber's Sociology of Civilizations*.

McNeill, William. 1992. *The Rise of the West*. Chicago: University of Chicago Press.

Molloy, Stephen. 1980. "Max Weber and the Religions of China." *The British Journal of Sociology* 31, no. 3: 377–400.

Nelson, Benjamin. 1974. "Max Weber's 'Author's Introduction' (1920): a Master Clue to HIs Main Aims." *Sociological Inquiry* 44, no. 4: 269–78.

———1981. *On the Roads to Modernity*, ed. Toby E. Huff. Totowa, NJ: Rowman & Littlefield.

Parsons, Talcott. 1971. *The System of Modern Societies*. Englewood Cliffs, NJ: Prentice-Hall.

———1977. *The Evolution of Societies*. Englewood Cliffs, NJ: Prentice-Hall.

Pomeranz, Kenneth. 2000. *The Great Divergence: China, Europe and the Making of the Modern World Economy*. New York: W.W. Norton.

Riesebrodt, Martin. 1980. "Ideen, Interessen, Rationalisierung." *Koelner Zeitschrift fuer Soziologie und Sozialpsychologie* 32, no. 1: 111–29.

Roth, Guenther. 1971a. "The Genesis of the Typological Approach," in *Scholarship and Partisanship*, pp. 253–65, edited by Reinhard Bendix and Guenther Roth. Berkeley: University of California Press.

———1971b. "Sociological Typology and Historical Explanation," in *Scholarship and Partisanship*, pp. 109–28, edited by Reinhard Bendix and Guenther Roth. Berkeley: University of California Press.

———1971c. "Max Weber's Comparative Approach and Historical Typology," in *Comparative Methods in Sociology*, pp. 75–93, edited by Ivan Vallier. Berkeley: University of California Press.

————1976. "History and Sociology in the Works of Max Weber." *The British Jounal of Sociology* 27, no. 3: 306–18.

Salomon, Albert. 1935. "Max Weber's Sociology." *Social Research* 2, no. 3: 368–84.

Scaff, Lawrence. 2014. *Weber and the Weberians.* London: Palgrave Macmillan.

Schluchter, Wolfgang. 1979 [1976]. "The Paradox of Rationalization," in *Max Weber's Vision of History*, pp. 11–64, edited by Guenther Roth and Schluchter. Berkeley: University of California Press.

————1981. *The Rise of Western Rationalism.* Berkeley: University of California Press.

Seyfarth, Constans and Walter M. Sprondel, eds. 1981. *Die Dynamik der gesellschaftlichen Rationalisierung.* Stuttgart: Enke Verlag.

Smelser, Neil. 1976. *Comparative Methods in the Social Sciences.* Englewood Cliffs, NJ: Prentice-Hall.

Tenbruck, F. H. 1975. "Das Werk Max Webers." *Koelner Zeitschrift fuer Soziologie und Sozialpsychologie* 27, no. 3: 663–702 ["The Problem of Thematic Unity in the Works of Max Weber." *The British Journal of Sociology* 31, no. 3 (1980): 316–51].

Tilly, Charles. 2008. *Contentious Performances.* New York: Wiley-Blackwell.

————and Lesley J. Wood. 2012. *Social Movements.* New York: Russell Sage.

Wallerstein, Immanuel. 1980. *The Modern World System II.* New York: Academic Press.

————1984. *The Politics of the World Economy.* Cambridge: Cambridge University Press.

————1989. *The Modern World System III.* New York: Academic Press.

Warner, Stephen. 1970. "The Role of Religious Ideas and the Use of Models in Max Weber's Comparative Studies of Non-Capitalist Societies." *Journal of Economic History* 30, no. 1: 74–99.

————1972. *The Methodology of Max Weber's Comparative Studies.* Unpublished Dissertation. The University of California at Berkeley.

————1973. "Max Weber's Sociology of Nonwestern Religions," in *Protestantism, Capitalism, and Social Science: the Weber Thesis Controversy*, pp. 32–52, edited by Robert W. Green. Lexington, MA: D.C. Heath & Co.

Weber, Max. 1927. *General Economic History.* New York: Free Press.

————1946a. *From Max Weber: Essays in Sociology (FMW).* Edited and translated by H.H. Gerth and C. Wright Mills. New York: Oxford.

Weber, Max. 1946b. "Religious Rejections of the World," in *FMW,* pp. 323–59.

————1946c. "The Social Psychology of the World Religions," in *FMW,* pp. 267–301.

————1947. *The Theory of Social and Economic Organization.* Translated by Talcott Parsons. New York: The Free Press.

————1949a. "Critical Studies in the Logic of the Cultural Sciences." in *The Methodology of the Social Sciences,* pp. 113–88, edited and translated by Edward A. Shils and Henry A. Finch. New York: Free Press.

————1949b. "'Objectivity' in Social Science and Social Policy," in *The Methodology of the Social Sciences,* pp. 50–112, edited and translated by Edward A. Shils and Henry A. Finch. New York: Free Press.

————1951. *The Religion of China.* Edited and translated by Hans H. Gerth. New York: The Free Press.

————1952. *Ancient Judaism.* Edited and translated by Hans H. Gerth and Don Martindale. New York: Free Press.

————1958. *The Religion of India.* Edited and translated by Hans H. Gerth and Don Martindale. New York: The Free Press.

————1968. *Economy and Society.* Edited by Guenther Roth and Claus Wittich. New York: Bedminster Press.

————1975. *Roscher and Knies.* Translated by Guy Oakes. New York: The Free Press.

————1976. *The Agrarian Sociology of Ancient Civilizations.* Translated by R.I. Frank. London: NLB.

————2005. *Max Weber: Readings and Commentary on Modernity.* Edited by Stephen Kalberg. New York: Wiley-Blackwell.

————2011a. "Prefatory Remarks." in Max Weber, *The Protestant Ethic and the Spirit of Capitalism*, pp. 233–49, translated by Stephen Kalberg. Oxford: Blackwell.

————2011b. *The Protestant Ethic and the Spirit of Capitalism.* Translated by Stephen Kalberg. Oxford: Blackwell.

Winckelmann 1980. "Die Herkunft von Max Webers 'Entzauberungs-Konzeption.'" *Koelner Zeitschrift fuer Soziologie und Sozialpsychologie* 32, no. 1: 12–53.

Zaret, David. 1980. "From Weber to Parsons and Schutz: the Eclipse of History in Modern Social Theory." *American Journal of Sociology* 83, no. 3: 1180–1201.

Chapter 6

WEBER'S FORAY INTO GEOPOLITICS

Stephen P. Turner

Weber was involved in two major political events in his lifetime, and many minor ones. The best known, most consequential and most discussed is the production of the constitution of the Weimar Republic, which Weber contributed to by writing an extensive newspaper article and serving on the constitutional commission. The second was abortive, but on a larger stage. Although his efforts were without immediate consequences, the event itself was the pivotal, stage-setting world political event of the twentieth century: the Versailles peace conference. Weber contributed to this by writing, or contributing to the writing, of the German response to the Entente on the subject of "The Authorship of War," the notorious war-guilt clause of the treaty. But the text has received little discussion, despite the fact that the analysis has some commonalities with the article on the constitution and bears on some great themes: leadership and the issue of the Deutsche Sonderweg (the alternative path of German development). One reason for this neglect is the fact that Weber was only one of the four signatories of this text. It was also controlled to some extent by the German Foreign office and the leader of the German delegation. Nevertheless, much of it is clearly his work, and contains some material that qualifies some of the standard interpretations of his political thinking, and opens a new set of questions about his geopolitical thinking.

The text was presented by the German delegation to Versailles, of which Weber was a member. It was rejected out of hand by the victorious Allies, who had negotiated their own account of the question of responsibility for the war. In what follows, I will give the context for the document, for Weber's involvement, and discuss some of the issues relating to the war and its genesis itself – the subject of the analysis in the text. The topic of the origins of The Great War, as it was then known, has a vast literature. No historical topic has been discussed at such length, by so many historians of so many countries and with such inconclusiveness, so the context given here will be necessarily highly selective. Nevertheless, some of the outstanding historical issues relate directly to Weber's interpretation of the war, and I will touch on at least the major ones here.

There is more to the story of Weber's role in foreign policy, which is also related to this event. Weber wrote on war aims during the war and served on a technical delegation to Vienna to explore issues related to economic integration with Germany.[1] One of his most important writings concerned the need to revise the constitution, which led to his appointment to the committee that wrote the postwar constitution. This indirectly concerned foreign policy. In what follows I will concentrate on the text of the German response, but the complex background to this text needs some explication in order to understand its significance and the way in which it is a characteristic Weberian text.

The Heidelberg Background

The Armistice ended hostilities on November 11, 1918. In a short period of time before the Armistice, the German government had changed, the Kaiser had abdicated, and the last Chancellor of the old regime, who facilitated the transition to parliamentary rule, Prince Max von Baden, resigned and appointed the leader of the Social Democratic party, Friedrich Ebert, as his successor. Germany was proclaimed a republic. The mutiny of sailors who were being ordered to sea for a pointless battle, followed by a full-fledged revolt of sailors at Kiel, who seized power in the city in the name of a soldiers' and workers' council, the proclamation of a Socialist Republic in Bavaria, the demands of Woodrow Wilson for political change as a precondition of negotiations, the collapse of the German army in the field, and a British naval blockade which starved the populace and continued after the Armistice, were among the dramatic events that occurred within a few months.

In the period immediately after the Armistice, Weber had called, in highly emotional terms, for German resistance to the prospect of the loss of Danzig (Gdansk) and wavered between a fatalistic acceptance of the treaty and the hope that its terms would produce a unified will to reject the treaty, which he thought would lead to the dissolution of the state and occupationand that could itself lead to renewed German unity and resistance. This was not as extreme a view as it later appeared: civilian governments as well as military leaders contemplated a levée en masse, or people's war, in defense of the fatherland, partly to forestall a French invasion but also to strengthen the German negotiating position.[2] There was a domestic political choice as well to

---

1	Wolfgang Mommsen, *Max Weber and German Politics 1890–1920*, translated by Michael S. Steinberg (Chicago: University of Chicago Press, [1959] 1984), 255–56.
2	Michael Geyer, "Insurrectionary Warfare: The German Debate about a Levée en Masse in October 1918," *The Journal of Modern History* 73, no. 3 (2001): 459–527 (478).

decide whether the future unity of Germany would be better served by negotiation or by the unifying experience of life under the occupation of foreign
armies. The latter was preferable as a matter of national honor, but it exposed
Germany to the risk of being dismembered into smaller states.

"Politics as a Vocation," the speech he gave in January 1919, included a
reference to Luther's "Here I stand, I can do no other,"[3] and this reflected
his frame of mind, which alternated between fury at those, like Kurt Eisner,
the revolutionary leader who had proclaimed a Bavarian republic, whom he
regarded as betraying the country, and those, like Eric Luddendorf, the military co-dictator at the end of the war, who had failed it. At first Weber had
defended the honor of Luddendorf, with the phrase "A warlord must believe in
his star."[4] These comments, taken out of the very specific context of the period
between the time leading up to the Armistice and before Versailles, have been
used to portray Weber as a rabid nationalist. They were, however, mainstream
opinions at the time. As the reality of defeat became clearer, Weber was to say
that "Ludendorff, the bloody dictator, has carried on a criminal game with our
nation. He and all of his accomplices belong behind bars,"[5] and Weber suggested that, as a matter of honor and to save the honor of the German army,
Luddendorf give himself up to the Americans for trial.

Immediately after the Armistice, the Allied powers began the complex
negotiations over the shape of the postwar world in a major conference at
Versailles. The Armistice had been signed after the publication of Woodrow
Wilson's "Fourteen Points," which included a vision of the postwar "new
world order" – the phrase actually appears in the German response – including the creation of a League of Nations to prevent future wars and an equita-
ble resolution of the issues of the war. The complex negotiations between the
Allies during the first months of this conference over the terms to be offered
Germany were not public. It is important to what follows that the Germans
were unaware of the strong disagreements that had broken out between the
Allies and assumed that positions that were publically available, which represented the American view, were the starting points for a serious negotiation
of peace.

Each side had anticipated peace negotiations for several years: most of the
major powers had committees in place and were working by the end of 1917,
including the Germans, who had two official committees of experts that collected expert reports. The *Arbeitsgemeinschaft für Politik des Rechts* (Working Group

3 Max Weber, "Politics as a Vocation," *From Max Weber: Essays in Sociology*, translated by
   H. H. Gerth and C. Wright Mills (New York: Oxford University Press, [1919] 1946),
   77–128 (127).
4 Mommsen, *Max Weber and German Politics 1890–1920*, 294.
5 Ibid., 295.

for a Policy of Justice), also known as the *Heidelberger Vereinigung*, was formed in Heidelberg as an *unofficial* body in anticipation of German participation in the final peace negotiations. The organization had Max Weber's fingerprints all over it. It first met in Weber's house in February 2 and 4, 1919. The working group was attempting to provide an intellectual framework for the German diplomatic response and to rally public support for that response, in the hope that the Allies would show some respect for German public opinion in the newly Republican state.

The participants were for the most part prominent academics, among them international law professor Albrecht Mendelssohn-Bartholdy; historians Hans Delbrück and Friedrich Meinecke; economist Lujo Brentano; and the historian of religion Ernst Troeltsch and Marianne Weber, both of whom lived in Weber's house and were central to its main social activity, a salon whose meetings included the best and brightest of Heidelberg's intellectual scene. Graf (Count) Max Montgelas was a participant in the Verein; Prince Max von Baden, former Chancellor, whom Weber later tried to persuade to return to political life, was a supporter. Weber's brother Alfred was an active member. The group had several women, including Lina Richter, who was an expert on the effects of the British naval blockade, which continued during the Armistice, and had written an atrocity exposé on the topic.[6] The members of the group had in several cases established their credibility by their public independence from the old regime. Several of them had a record that could commend them to the Allies, for such acts as opposing unrestricted submarine warfare or aiding prisoners of war. Weber was among them: he had publically attacked the Kaiser and was regarded as a dissident.

Weber, in an editorial in the *Frankfurter allgemeine Zeitung*, identified five issues the working group would concentrate on:

> the examination of enemy atrocity propaganda; the objective use of the German material on atrocities committed by the enemy; an expert inquiry into unlawful use of German private property by the enemy; the defense of the right to self-determination, especially on Germany's eastern frontier; and the re-organization of the Army on a democratic basis.[7]

Some of these were themes that had been long-term preoccupations for Weber, especially the Polish question and what he saw as the failure of German propaganda to respond to the successful use of atrocity stories by the Allies.

---

6   Lina Spiess Richter, *Family Life in Germany under the Blockade, Compiled from Reports from Doctors, School Nurses, Children's Judges & Teachers* (London: National Labour Press, 1919).

7   Quoted in Alma Luckau, *The German Delegation at the Paris Peace Conference* (New York: Columbia University Press, 1941), 49.

The question of war-guilt was also a large part of this discussion and had been from the start of the war. Each of the great powers attempted to appear as the victim. France, in particular, was concerned to establish the guilt of Germany and to provide evidence for an interpretation of their ally Russia's general mobilization in response to the Serbian crisis, which made this crucial act appear innocent and defensive.[8] During the war countries had published documents supporting their version of the events leading up to the war. Some of this documentary record was sheer invention, and even more was concealed. The German files were assiduously cleaned of damaging evidence.[9] Montgelas had resigned from the army early in the war to concentrate on the study of the origins of the war. He was an important participant in the publication of exculpatory editions of German diplomatic papers, producing, with Walter Schucking, a huge edition of documents, and publishing a classic: *The Case for the Central Powers*.[10]

Weber himself, during the crucial period between the Armistice and the signing of the Treaty of Versailles, opposed the publication of secret papers by Kurt Eisner. These papers pointed to the guilt of aggressive Prussian militarists and industrialists. Weber claimed that they added nothing to what was already known, and denounced their publication. His thoughts about "guilt" were passionately expressed in his speech to students in January 1919, "Politics as a Vocation":

Instead of searching like old women for the "guilty one" after the war – in a situation in which the structure of society produced the war – everyone with a manly and controlled attitude would tell the enemy, "We lost the war. You have won it. That is now all over. Now let us discuss what conclusions must be drawn according to the *objective* interests that came into play and what is the main thing in view of the responsibility towards the *future* which above all burdens the victor." Anything else is undignified and will become a boomerang. A nation forgives if its interests have been damaged, but no nation forgives if its honor has been offended, especially by a bigoted self-righteousness.[11]

8 C.f. The French Government, *The French Yellow Book of 1914*, translated by *The Times* (London: The Times Publishing Company, 1914).

9 Holger H. Herwig, "Patriotic Self-Censorship in Germany," *The Outbreak of World War I: Causes and Responsibilities* 6th edn. (Boston and New York: Houghton Mifflin Company), 153–59. The process of suppressing documents continued well into the 1960s, when private diaries were still being unearthed. The leader of this effort, which began as early as 1914, Bernard von Bulow, was present at Versailles and much later in touch with the *Heidelberger Vereinigung*.

10 Max Montgelas, *The Case for the Central Powers: An Impeachment of the Versailles Verdict*, translated by Constance Vesey (London: George Allen & Unwin, Ltd., 1925).

11 Max Weber, "Politics as a Vocation," [1919] 1946),118.

Wolfgang Mommsen has suggested that Weber's comments in this speech were prophetic:

> Max Weber was all too right to be concerned that acceptance of the treaty would have devastating effects on the domestic situation and would severely burden the new democratic order. In his famous speech on *"Politik als Beruf"* ("Politics as a Vocation") on January 28, 1919, he predicted that "a polar night of icy darkness and austerity" awaited the Germans; "in ten years, for a variety of reasons, the reaction [will] long since [have] set in." And that, with a slight delay, is exactly what happened.[12]

Some of the reaction, however, was immediate: Eisner was assassinated on February 21, 1919.

In the working group, there was a degree of consensus on how to respond to the question of German guilt. The group called for a "nonpartisan and neutral inquiry commission, to which all archives will be opened and before which all nations will be allowed to speak" which they thought could alone "allocate the share of guilt which every country had in the outbreak of this world conflict and in carrying it on until European civilization has been destroyed."[13] Montgelas expressed the view that Germany had made serious errors at the beginning of the war, by acquiescing to the Austro-Hungarian attack on Serbia, by marching through Belgium and by including unproved assertions in the declaration of war on France. During the first session, he recommended ignoring the problem of the remote causes of the war in order to concentrate on refuting the claim that Germany had been planning the war for years in advance. Montgelas also raised the crucial question of whether mobilization meant war. Russia had mobilized, in a situation where all the general staffs of Europe understood that mobilization was a kind of predeclaration of war, in which the declaration itself would coincide with, or follow, an attack. If so, the German war was a defensive one, as the Germans had claimed all along, because the Russians mobilized against Germany first and refused to halt their mobilization. This implied that the Germans entered the peace negotiations defeated but honorable, not the author of the war, and certainly not the sole author.

Over the next few months, the participants in this group wrote editorials, explained the diplomatic situation as they understood it and attempted to

---

12 Wolfgang Mommsen, "Max Weber and the Peace Treaty of Versailles," translated by Sally E. Robertson, *The Treaty of Versailles: A Reassessment after 75 Years*, ed. Manfred F. Boemeke, Gerald D. Feldman, and Elisabeth Glaser (Cambridge: Cambridge University Press, 1998), 535–46 (546).

13 Luckau, *The German Delegation at the Paris Peace Conference*, 48.

create a consensus. Their public statement contains their statement of their political credentials:

> We have, at a time when Germany was at the height of her political power, fought in our country against a policy which disregarded the rights of other nations. We have in particular condemned the wrong done to Belgium, although our opinions differed as to which form of opposition, in this question as well as in others, could be reconciled with Germany's security during the war.[14]

Their initial statement about what was to be called the authorship of the war was this:

> We do not deny the responsibility of those in power before and during the war, but we believe that all the great powers of Europe, who were at war, are guilty. We are fully conscious of the fact that the imperialistic tensions of world commerce were among the causes of the dangerous situation in July, 1914. But we believe that alertness and a fixed determination in all countries could have prevented the world war. We are therefore convinced that the Allies have no right to pronounce judgment in a case in which they themselves are involved.[15]

In this passage, commercial rivalries are given a central role, but one which implicates all sides. Referring to this cause deflects guilt and distributes it to all the great powers.

The group also addressed itself to the German people, with several aims: to prepare the nation for reform;"to create a state of justice and order within its own frontier so that there will be left to the enemy no pretext to refuse to the German government the right to defend its own just cause"; for a future Germany in which Prussia would have a diminished role and South Germany, "owing to its democratic tradition and its happier solutions of inner controversies," would need to take greater responsibility; and for the reform of the military and the officer class appropriate to a democratic order.[16]

Defending German honor was critical. Much of the discussion dealt with the need to refute Allied atrocity propaganda; the Bryce report on German atrocities that had been published during the war and the reports on German atrocities in Alsace that had appeared after the Armistice; and establishing Allied mistreatment of prisoners and the illegality of the British naval blockade. But it was also an attempt, as Luckau later reported on the basis of

14 Ibid., 47.
15 Ibid.
16 Ibid., 48.

conversations with the participants, to prepare the German people for the loss of Alsace-Lorraine to France and the province of Posen to Poland.[17]

The problem of guilt was entangled with the problem of the origin of the war itself. Montgelas had been obsessed with the problem from an early point in the war. In his own responses, Montgelas sought to confine the issues to the precipitating events of the war rather than this background. Even this immediate context was contestable subject matter, but the key facts were these: the assassination of the Archduke Franz Ferdinand of Austria was performed by Serbian terrorists with what at the time were unprovable but very probable connections with the Serbian state. Austro-Hungary needed, for prestige reasons, to demand something. Under international law they were entitled to some form of retaliation, if indeed the state was involved, as it obviously was, however indirectly, by tolerating and encouraging an atmosphere of hostility. They issued an ultimatum, carefully drafted in light of international law, demanding cooperation in finding the truth about the assassination conspiracy and demanding the arrest of certain probable participants. The Germans supported their ally, but tried to tone down the demands. The Serbs replied with evasions and meaningless concessions, but struck a conciliatory tone. Austro-Hungary mobilized against Serbia, and invaded – catastrophically for themselves, as it turned out. The Russians mobilized against Austro-Hungary in an apparent show of force in support of Serbia. But they also mobilized against Germany in Poland.

There was a clear German case for claiming that the Russian mobilization forced their hand and that the alliance system, in which Austro-Hungary was allied with Germany, and France with Russia, forced them to treat France as an enemy. But the Russians could make a similar argument: the Austro-Hungarian mobilization against Serbia forced them to mobilize against *their* alliance partners. The same logic applied on the Western Front: Germany was forced, by the logic of the alliance system, to defend itself against France. Mobilization was tantamount to an act of war; France was obliged by its treaty obligations to support its ally. As a matter of military strategy, the German actions were a matter of self-preservation: the general staff believed that the German army would be placed at a disadvantage and vulnerable both on the west, to France, and in the east, on the Polish salient. In both cases, the Germans made offers, though ungenerous ones, whose acceptance would have stopped the advance of the armies. The best alternative defense was to attack. The actions they took were "defensive" only in the strategic sense, as they would have been understood by the General staffs of the other European powers. For the ordinary person, they were unjustifiable acts of

---

17 Ibid., 50–51.

aggression, shrouded in lies that fulfilled threats that German officials had made in the past.

Mitteleuropa

At an earlier point in the war, when Germany was winning in the field, the politician who Weber was most closely and personally associated, Friedrich Naumann, published an important book, *Mitteleuropa* (1916),[18] on the political and economic organization of Central Europe.[19] Weber became involved in an officially backed attempt to investigate the prospects for its implementation, though he demurred from some of its ideas. The book looked forward to a conclusion in the form of peace negotiations that assured that Germany would retain and secure its newly won status as a great power. The insistence of the text that this was a defensive war was belied by the offensive goals for a new place for Germany in the world expressed in the book. Indeed, the book became a weapon, as evidence of German hegemonic aims, in the hands of Americans supporting entry into the war.

Naumann understood the geopolitical situation as this: Germany was caught between the great empires of Britain and, closer at hand, Russia, and was unable to defend itself, control its destiny or overcome the threat of having its trade shut down by these rivals. There were three choices, or perhaps, as Naumann pessimistically noted, only two: creating a greater German-dominated area that could control its destiny or enter into a kind of alliance with one side or other that effectively amounted to subordination.[20] Of the two alliance options, Naumann thought, only one was feasible: subordination to the British. This would be culturally destructive. The better option according to Naumann, would have been an alliance with France, but the War of 1871 had produced a level of bitterness that precluded this.

The creation of Mitteleuropa, an alliance and economic union of Central European nations, which would de facto be dominated by Germany, was thus the sole good option. The moment the book was written was the moment at which this possibility seemed to be at hand. After the early successes of German arms in the war, it was not unreasonable, from the German point of view, and on the basis of past European experience of short decisive wars with

18 Friedrich Naumann, *Mittel-Europa* (Berlin: G. Reimer, 1915). English translation, *Central Europe*, translated by Christabel M. Meredith (Westport, CT: Greenwood Press, [1915] 1971).
19 The larger history of this idea is explained in Henry Cord Meyer, *Mitteleuropa in German Thought and Action* (The Hague: Martinus Nijhoff, 1955).
20 Naumann, *Central Europe*, 190.

quick peace conferences, to suppose that a favorable peace settlement might be concluded, perhaps even one including indemnities from the vanquished.[21]

Naumann's basic claim was this: the real issue of the war was whether Mitteleuropa would come into being. The nationalists and Pan-Germans failed to understand this, because they failed to understand the facts of economic life – that Germany on its own was not viable as a world economic "body." On its own, it was simply too small.[22] And the economic issues were closely related to defense issues. The issue of food security alone assured that Germany was not viable as a state: it needed an agricultural component to complement its industrial power.[23] But it was better to keep silent about these aims.

Naumann believed that the future of the world politically and economically was one of trading groups organized as "superstates." Britain, or rather Britain together with the British Empire, was the model.[24] What impressed Naumann, in addition to the fact that the British controlled a huge share of the arable land of the world,[25] was the way in which the colonies contributed to the war effort. The Mitteleuropa solution was designed to mimic these aspects of the British superstate.

> A vital middle Europe needs agrarian territories on its boundaries, and it must make the accession easy and desirable for them. It needs, if possible, an extension of its northern and southern sea-coasts; it needs its share in overseas colonial possessions.[26]

The geopolitical obstacle to this outcome was Russia, the great power that dominated Central Europe. The war was a way of overcoming the earlier history that produced the situation in Central Europe that needed to be rectified, a history in which Russia had functioned as a Gendarme, intervening to settle domestic unrest.

The practical obstacle to a Central European superstate was the problem of nationalities, democracy, the anticipatable obstinance of elements of the population[27] and the practical matter of how to deal with the economic consequences of the loss of tariff protection in a Customs Union. Naumann believed, however, that there was a way forward, though the details were brutal. This was not to be a marriage of mutual benefit, in the usual sense, so much

---

21 Ibid., 158.
22 Ibid., 192.
23 Ibid., 198.
24 Ibid., 204.
25 Ibid., 206.
26 Ibid., 198.
27 Ibid., 70.

as a painful acceptance of the necessity of German domination in the face of the bad alternative of Russian domination. Naumann believed that war debt would have powerful consequences for Central Europe: it would force Austria to be open to consolidation and reform, force Germany to expand its use of government backed cartels, and to permanently extend government control over the economy by monopolizing the food and supply storage that would be required by the new kind of semi-autarchic state that he envisioned.[28] In short, the war produced an opportunity for the kind of political and economic consolidation that Naumann advocated.

The model that Naumann had in mind and continually returned to, for multiple lessons, was Hungary after 1848. The Hungarian Revolution was the most successful democratic liberal revolution in Central Europe. But it was crushed by Russia after struggling against the Hapsburgs, with the result that the liberals were banished. However, the Hungarian state was given special "equal" status within the Empire. This largely empty prize was sufficient to pacify the remaining Hungarians and to preserve Imperial control under the now "dual" monarchy. For Naumann, the lesson was simple: nationalist passions were easily placated by duping, and the illusion of self-governance, of one's "own" king, was sufficient. As a political reality, he said, it is essential to conserve "the dignity of the State itself." So Naumann proposed to involve the state, or at least the legitimating parts of the state, the monarchy and parliament, in a maximal role in approving the superstate arrangements.[29]

The outcome of the Hungarian Revolution was ideal – for Russia. With the investment of only a few thousand troops at the end of the conflict, Russia had underlined its role as the preserver of order in Central Europe and the dominant power, showed the dependence of the Hapsburgs on its support and goodwill, and prevented the emergence of a liberal and therefore ideologically threatening state in the middle of its zone of control. This was the kind of power that Naumann wanted to pass to Germany and to be extended by new arrangements that were technically superior to the sending of troops.

The real aim was a matter of what he called "technical politics" as distinct from questions of dignity.

> Looked at as technical politics, the creation of Mid-Europe in the centralization of certain political activities, that is to say the establishment of fresh central points for the joint working of the whole of the enlarged territory.[30]

28 Ibid., 163.
29 Ibid., 250.
30 Ibid., 250–51.

Centralization implies a loss of sovereignty, and a superstate would produce sharp limits on sovereignty.[31] The legal mechanism would be treaties, but the product of these treaties would be commissions that themselves become "organs."[32] The commissions, located in the same place, would be the kernels of the superstate.[33] There would necessarily be a democratic deficit: these commissions would be run by experts.[34] But the appearance would be concealed by the democratizing that would result from the extension of suffrage that Naumann, like Weber, believed would be the inevitable result of the war.[35]

Weber would certainly have concurred with a point Naumann made about the difference between the organizational capacities of the capitalism of Northern Germany and that of the potential partners within Central Europe. This difference is the source of the core economic problem facing any sort of customs union. The industries of Northern Germany, with their distinctive form of organization and organizational capacity, would overwhelm the local industries and capitalism of the rest of Central Europe. If the tariffs that protected these industries were abolished, the industries would vanish, along with the livelihoods they provided. This was the greatest obstacle to union. The only solution Naumann had was to insist that these industries could be brought up to Northern German standards of organization.

Resistance was inevitable: the Austrians were exemplary of the obstinate character of the peoples of Central and Eastern Europe. A million conversations, as Naumann put it, would be needed.[36] Naumann seems to imply that after these conversations, people will accept the necessity of an alliance with Germany, despite the fact that the Germans, especially the German minorities, are hated.[37] In a telling comment, he observes that "the Austrian has for us on many occasions the same feeling we have for the English world-group economic system, a mixture of envy, respect, and defiance."[38] This meant that the Germans needed to go beyond merely offering "the mutual barter of advantages and disadvantages."[39]

Weber looked in a different direction: he wrote to Naumann about making Germany responsible for the follies of Austria and Hungary.

31 Ibid., 254.
32 Ibid., 257–59.
33 Ibid., 268.
34 Ibid., 269–70.
35 Ibid., 255.
36 Ibid., 70.
37 Ibid., 27.
38 Ibid., 236.
39 Ibid., 237.

I have read your book with the utmost interest ... now when I am *beginning* to have a chance to read something. The book is unexcelled as a propaganda piece for the general *idea* precisely because it ignores certain problems. Of these, the most important is this: "Mittleleuropa" means that *we* shall have to pay for *every* stupidity with our blood – and you know it – that will be committed by the thick-headed policies of the Magyars and the Vienna court. The other side can also say: *every* stupidity of 'his majesty," every "Krüger dispatch," all of German "world policy"; for these, we (the Austrians, etc.) are mercenaries that will have to fight these battles. This is the most difficult aspect of this problem. *Even* in this war for existence, *how* Vienna diplomacy has continued to err! And *what a sense-less* policy we ourselves have carried on since 1895. Can we bind this all together so that each part has the feeling: I can live with these stupidities, since the other one is here suffering with me.[40]

We will see what this "senseless policy" was in the response to the allies. But there was another use to which Weber put the Hungarian model. He was long concerned with Poland, and came to see a Hungarian solution as desirable there: a free Poland under German influence as a part of a system of buffer states between Germany and Russia. The core idea, however, was the same as Naumann's. A German zone of influence which would answer both military questions and resolve the kinds of issues with food security and trade that Naumann had correctly placed at the heart of his analysis.

The image of a world system of superstate entities fit with a traditional politics of balance of power, in which maintaining the balance of power between rivals assured that none of the rivals would be tempted to take advantage of the relative weakness of another rival. Balance meant peace and facilitated diplomatic cooperation by raising the cost of war. The unification of Germany had upset the balance of power, but Bismarck had been careful to avoid provocations. This worked; when he convened a diplomatic conference on Africa, Germany got its share of colonies.

This was Weber's image of international politics: he even spoke of the "law of the 'power pragma' that governs all political history."[41] The point of constructing a superstate was to be able to balance against rivals. But balancing against rivals in the multistate European system was difficult: bilateral

40 Mommsen, *Max Weber and German Politics 1890–1920*, 217 (italics in the original).
41 Max Weber, "Between Two Laws," *Weber: Political Writings*, edited by Peter Lassman and Ronald Speirs (Cambridge: Cambridge University Press, [1916] 1994), 75–79 (78). Reconciling this remarkable passage with Weber's general methodological views is difficult, but not impossible; cf. Stephen Turner and G. O. Mazur, "Morgenthau as a Weberian Methodologist," *European Journal of International Relations* 15, no. 3 (2009): 477–504.

balancing is relatively easy; multilateral balancing requires alliances between great powers, that is to say, states with significant offensive capabilities. The British approach to these alliances was well understood: Tönnies, in his wartime text, lays it out clearly:

> For, if the other powers are so grouped that they maintain among themselves the balance of power or would again find themselves in such a status after a short war, England invariably casts its weight into the scales against its opponent, and by doing so it incites and stirs up wars or lengthens them, in order to humble, weaken and rob its opponents.[42]

In short, the point of the British superstate's policies was to prevent the creation of hegemons in its own backyard. The strategy is captured nicely in a comment by Duff Cooper, during a meeting in the midst of the run up to the Second World War: "The main interest of this country had always been to prevent any one power from obtaining undue predominance in Europe."[43] The British, in short, had a counterhegemonic strategy based on the balance of powers. The Germans had ambitions, but were they hegemonic, or merely a desire for, as the much repeated phrase of the time put it, a place in the sun? What might this place in the sun imply for the rest of Central Europe? And how did Weber himself understand the possibilities? The text of the reply to the Allies at Versailles contains some revealing answers.

The Background to Versailles

Germany sent a massive group of experts and diplomats to Versailles. Much of the expertise was economic, as had been the case for one of the official bodies preparing for the Peace, the *Paxkonferenz*.[44] The issue of war guilt was critical. All four of the persons assigned to the task of writing the official German response came from the *Heidelberger Vereinigung*: Hans Delbrück, Max Graf Montgelas, Max Weber, Albrecht Mendelssohn-Bartholdy. What they found when they arrived was shocking and unexpected. Some legal background is needed to understand the issues here. Customary international law handled

---

42 Ferdinand Tönnies, *Warlike England: As Seen by Herself* (New York: G. W. Dillingham Publishers, 1915), 80–81.

43 John Julius Norwich (ed.), *The Duff Cooper Diaries: 1915–1951* (London: Phoenix, 2006), 260–61.

44 Alma Luckau, "The Official Organization for the Preparation of Peace, the Paxkonferenz," German Preparations for the Treaty, *The German Delegation at the Paris Peace Conference* (New York: Columbia University Press, 1941), 28–41 (28–29).

the problem of the mutual claims of nations after war through the notion of indemnity or reparations:

> For centuries it had been the accepted principle of European civil warfare that the vanquished side should pay to the victors the cost of the war. The same principle is adopted in the legal systems of all countries in litigation between individuals. Costs follow the event. The man who goes to law and fails must pay the cost of the proceedings. With equal reason the country which goes to war and is defeated should be called upon to pay the cost of the hostilities.[45]

This was German practice: indemnities were imposed on France after the 1870–71 war, and in Brest-Litowsk the Germans imposed huge demands. This was a problem for the German side. As Max Weber's brother Alfred pointed out, the German treaty with the revolutionary Russian government, which was extremely harsh and resulted in the loss of a great deal of territory, could be used against any German claim that the treaty to be imposed on them was unjust, though he blamed, as Luckau explains, the "militaristic execution of that treaty more than the conditions themselves."[46]

Prior to this war, however, indemnities had been modest, or relatively modest, because wars were shorter and less destructive, especially of private property. The costs of such a vast and long-running war far exceeded the losers' ability to pay. This was a fact connected to the manner in which the war was fought. The focus of the customary law of war in Europe was the protection of civilians and private and nonmilitary property through adherence to the principle that the conduct of war should involve injury and damage only to the combatants themselves, insofar as possible. Total war, or war involving the destruction of the private productive capacities of the nations at war, was excluded by this principle. One of the many charges against Germany was precisely that it had violated this rule, especially by engaging in unrestricted submarine warfare against passenger ships, and that it engaged in the systematic destruction of wealth in order to end competition. The term "total war," which came to characterize this kind of conflict, was coined by Erich Ludendorff, in his 1919 memoir of the war.[47]

45 F. J. P. Veale, *Advance to Barbarism: How the Reversion to Barbarism in Warfare and War-Trials Menaces Our Future* (Appleton, WI: C. C. Nelson Publishing Co., 1953), 112.
46 Alma Luckau, *The German Delegation at the Paris Peace Conference* (New York: Columbia University Press, 1941), 50. This was also Wilson's view, as he expressed it in a passage that appears after the Fourteen Points in his speech to congress (Delivered in Joint Session, January 8, 1918. http://www.fordham.edu/halsall/mod/1918wilson.html).
47 Erich Ludendorff, *Ludendorff's Own Story, August 1914–November 1918; the Great War from the Siege of Liège to the Signing of the Armistice as Viewed from the Grand Headquarters of the German Army* (New York and London: Harper & Brothers, 1919).

Customary international law avoided the problem by never assigning responsibility for starting wars. The indictment by the Allies was thus a novelty. The "Report of the Allied Commission on the Responsibility of the Authors of the War and on Enforcement of Penalties" sought to determine the "responsibility of the authors of the war," the "facts as to breaches of laws and customs of war," and "the degree of responsibility for these offenses" (clearly implying, what was later made even more clear, responsibility not only for breaches of law but of the peace itself) "attaching to particular members of the enemy forces, including members of the general staffs, and other individuals, however highly placed."[48]

The statement of "The Commission on the Responsibility of the Authors of the War and on Enforcement of Penalties" instituted at the plenary session of the Paris Peace Conference of 25 January 1919, summarizes the issue: "Germany, in agreement with Austria-Hungary, deliberately worked to defeat all the many conciliatory proposals made by the Allies Powers and their repeated efforts to avoid war."[49] This was a contestable judgment and involved a question of intent, but it was supported by the actions of German diplomacy, which had in fact foiled, responded negatively to, or refused, a long series of treaties, initiatives for mediation and attempts at diplomatic resolutions short of war.

The allies' text is a recounting of diplomatic and military acts. It ignores Russia, other than to mention the Czar's note asking the Germans to agree to submitting the issue between Austro-Hungary and Serbia to the Hague Tribunal, a note that was never answered, because the Germans thought it was a ploy to give the Russians more time to prepare for an invasion. There is no mention of the Russian mobilization. The stress is on the invasion of France through Belgium. The statement of the Chancellor in his speech on the 4 August was taken as evidence of German guilt.

Necessity knows no law. Our troops have occupied Luxemburg, and perhaps have already entered Belgian territory. Gentlemen, that is a breach of international law ... We have been obliged to refuse to pay attention to the justifiable

48 Hans Delbrück, Max Graf Montgelas, Max Weber, Albrecht Mendelssohn-Bartholdy, "Observations on the Report of the Commission of the Allied and Associated Governments on the Responsibility of the Authors of the War; Carnegie Endowment for International Peace," *German White Book: Concerning the Responsibility of the Authors of the War* (New York: Oxford University Press, [1919] 1924), 12–29 (12).

49 "Observations on the Report of the Commission of the Allied and Associated Governments on the Responsibility of the Authors of the War; Carnegie Endowment for International Peace," [1919] 1924), 12–29 (21). First World War.com. "Report of Commission to Determine War Guilt, 6 May 1919." http://www.firstworldwar.com/source/commissionwarguilt.htm. (2009) (Accessed 10/12/2013)

protests of Belgium and Luxemburg. The wrong – I speak openly – the wrong
we are thereby committing we will try to make good as soon as our military aims
have been attained. He who is menaced, as we are, and is fighting for his all can
only consider how he is to hack his way through.[50]

The Americans attached a dissent from this report, noting the "novelty" of
the proceedings,[51] distinguishing legal and moral responsibility and objecting
to the attempt to go beyond international law and the law of war to try the
Kaiser.[52] But they also added documents showing German obstruction of a
peaceful solution to the Serbian question.

The German Reply

In spite of the novelty of the charge of "authorship," the Allies report itself
focused entirely on traditional issues of diplomacy and military action. The
German reply responded in kind, up to a point: then the content changes.
There were no rules of argument, and there was no legal structure to rely on.
The starting point, inevitably, was the material on which Montgelas was an
expert, and in one case could testify from his own experience, involving the
intentions behind the various diplomatic and military actions of the German
government prior to the war. The beginning parts of the text provide an
exculpatory account of the reasons for German diplomatic actions immediately prior to the war, and the document as a whole consists almost entirely
of diplomatic documents added as appendices.[53] The larger problem for the
German case was the list of acts that Montgelas wished to exclude: the longer
diplomatic prehistory of the war.

Once we read past the sections dealing with the minutiae of diplomatic
exchange, however, we get an argument, which was the work of Weber, which
deviated drastically from this narrow construction of the issues, and has no
parallels in diplomatic writing. Recognizing the strangeness of the document,
and the extent of its reliance on Weber's ideas, is essential to understanding it. One can get a sense of the distinctiveness of Weber's contribution by

---

50 Alma Luckau, "Report of the Allied Commission on the Responsibility of the Authors
    of the War and on Enforcement of Penalties," *The German Delegation at the Paris Peace
    Conference* (New York: Columbia University Press, 1941), 272–87 (282).

51 Ibid., 284.

52 Ibid., 284–5.

53 The reply, together with the documents, was published as the *German White
    Book: Concerning the Responsibility of the Authors of War*, translated by The Carnegie
    Endowment for International Peace (New York: Oxford University Press, 1924).

contrasting it to the extensive later writings of Montgelas, who made a career of defending the German diplomatic effort.

The initial indicator of Weber's presence in the text is the repeated use of the term "responsibility" to mean the political responsibility of leaders to their own nation. The concept is absent from Montgelas's accounts, but central to Weber's thinking and to the account in the text discussing the German response to Russian mobilization. This was a central element of the immediate events precipitating the war: the German refusal to negotiate, cited in the Allies' statement, set into motion the military conflict. The German reply pins the "real cause of the World War" squarely on Russia:

> For her purposes she therefore utilized her military alliance with France concluded in 1892, and extended in 1912 by a naval convention and further alliances in order to set in motion the "machinery of the Entente," at the moment which seemed favorable, and to drag her friends into the long, premeditated war. Herein lies the real cause of the World War.[54]

The text explains the German response in familiar Weberian language of the political responsibility of leaders:

> In the event of a general Russian mobilization, any German Government which waited on the pretext of an offer of negotiations until that mobilization had been completed would have taken upon itself a fearful responsibility before its own people – a responsibility which nobody could bear. The documents delivered to the enemy Governments prove that so long as Czarism lasted its plans were such as to render it impossible to assume responsibility for such a course.[55]

The model of responsible leadership here is familiar from Weber's contemporary speech on Politics as a Vocation: it is the idea of the statesman bound by the ethics of responsibility.[56]

---

54 Luckau, "Report of the Allied Commission on the Responsibility of the Authors of the War and on Enforcement of Penalties," 297.

55 Ibid., 293.

56 It is this model which is further developed by Weber's follower Hans J. Morgenthau. See Stephen Turner, "Hans J. Morgenthau and the Legacy of Max Weber," *Political Thought and International Relations: Variations on a Realist Theme*, edited by Duncan Bell (Oxford: Oxford University Press, 2009), 63–82; Stephen Turner and Regis Factor, *Max Weber and the Dispute Over Reason and Value: A Study in Philosophy, Ethics, and Politics* (London: Routledge & Kegan Paul, Ltd., 1984); Turner and Mazur, "Morgenthau as a Weberian Methodologist."

The core argument of the text involves a series of counterfactuals.[57] The key premise is methodological:

> In our opinion, the question of the origin of the war can never be settled in principle by the method adopted in the report of the enemy Commission – that is, by the enumeration of single occasions which transformed a chronic state of high political tension into a war. In addition to the utter and astonishing inaccuracy in the presentation of single facts, that is where the fundamental mistake of the entire proceeding lies.[58]

The text suggests an alternative set of questions:

1. Which governments had in the past done most to promote that state of constant menace of war from which Europe suffered for years before the war?
2. Which governments pursued political and economic aims which could only be realized by means of a war?

The answer to both questions was Russia: "Among the great European Powers, there existed at least one, whose policy, pursued systematically for many years before the war, could only be realized by an offensive war, and which therefore worked deliberately towards that end. That power was Russian Czarism."[59] France also had such an interest: The "French Government had never unreservedly relinquished its intention to regain possession of Alsace-Lorraine, that this purpose could be realized only through the instrumentality of war."[60] This was no rhetorical flourish: in the case of Russia, a major goal was breaking out of the treaty limitations that prevented Russian warships from passing through the Dardanelles, locking their southern fleet into the Black Sea. German aid to Turkey held the Russians in check.[61] This was cited by the Allies as an aggressive act and is emblematic of the issue of interpretation: if one treats the

---

57 Counterfactuals were a central research tool for Weber, built into his technical notions of adequate cause and objective possibility. See Stephen Turner and Regis Factor, "Objective Possibility and Adequate Causation in Weber's Methodological Writings," *The Sociological Review*, 29 NS (1981): 5–29; Max Weber, "Critical Studies in the Logic of the Cultural Sciences," *Max Weber: Collected Methodological Writing*, edited by Hans Henrik Bruun and Sam Whimster, translated by H. H. Bruun (London: Routledge, [1906] 2012), 139–184.
58 Luckau, "Report of the Allied Commission on the Responsibility of the Authors of the War and on Enforcement of Penalties," 295.
59 Ibid., 296.
60 Ibid., 297.
61 Cf. Sean McMeekin, *Russian Origins of the First World War* (Cambridge, MA: Harvard University Press, 2011).

Russians as the aggressors, the German response is defensive and a product of necessity; if one treats the Russian actions – and they were the first to mobilize in response to the Austro-Hungarian Serbian conflict, thus expanding the war if only in the form of a threat – as "defensive" or moderate, the German response is at fault, and the Russian mobilization merely a pretext.

The text then turns to the contrast between German motivation and Russian motivation. The argument is the one made by the *Heidelberger Vereinigung*, and reflects Weber's own published views on Bismarck's foreign policy:

> Germany did not desire the World War, although she may have regarded it as a danger which lay within the sphere of practical considerations. For more than forty years the German Government, to use the very words of the report of the Commission, was considered as a "champion of peace." Plans of conquest were worlds removed from the thoughts of the leading German statesmen. In Russia it was otherwise. The realization of the purposes of leading pan-Slavist circles was unattainable without war.[62]

In short, the geopolitical premise of the "Weberian" part of the text was that Germany, unlike other countries, had no goals that required war. Russia and France, in contrast, both had longstanding goals that only a war, and in the case of Russia only a large European war, would enable them to achieve. In the case of Russia, it was access to the Aegean from the Black Sea for its warships. For France, it was the return of Alsace-Lorraine and perhaps even control of the Saar. Montgelas does make this argument. But he does not embed this in a larger account of Germany within the balance of powers in the way that this text does.

This was an argument with difficulties. The idea of Mitteleuropa, which had deep roots before Naumann's book, provided ample motivation for Germany. The creation of a Central European union under German leadership would have been facilitated, even been "unattainable without war": war debts alone, as Naumann pointed out, would have given Germany the power to induce Austro-Hungary to cooperate. But the model of unification was not based, as the Russian one was, on conquest. It was based instead on the Hungarian model of states with formal but largely illusory independence. The pan-Slavist model required the dismemberment of the Austro-Hungarian Empire and the seizure of territory held by it, territory with Slav populations, as well as the dismemberment and defeat of the Ottoman Empire, to control the Dardanelles.

---

62 Luckau, "Report of the Allied Commission on the Responsibility of the Authors of the War and on Enforcement of Penalties," 294.

The analysis proceeds by deploring various actions of the German gov-ernment, but denying that these were the result of war-like intentions. "The former German Government, in our view, committed serious errors, but they are to be found in quite a different quarter from that in which a certain section of public opinion among our enemies seeks them."[63] The error was a funda-mental one: the failure to conclude an alliance with Britain:

> Germany's position in the decade preceding the war was determined by the fact that, in an age which knew as yet no means of preventing war, the country could not honorably avoid the ordeal of arms with an apparently impregnable Czarism without sacrificing not only her pledged faith, but her own national independence. *The sole remedy in those circumstances would have been a firm and binding alliance with England, which would have inspired both parties with confidence, and protected Germany as well as France from any war of aggression.* It has yet to be proved that such an agreement could have been concluded by an English Minister, considering the state of English public opinion during the years immediately preceding the war and in the teeth of those tendencies which we have had to record above. We repeat that we would recognize every demonstrable step taken by an English Government towards this end as meritorious, and any failure of a German Government to seize such an opportunity as a blunder. (Italics added).[64]

The idea of an alliance with Britain was Naumann's Plan B (or perhaps Plan C, as it he would have preferred an alliance with France, which he thought was impossible). It represented subordination, particularly cultural subordina-tion – a theme Weber insisted on in his own wartime writings.[65] And it was opposed, by the German military and diplomatic elites, on the reasonable grounds that such an alliance would put Germany in the position of being Britain's army in Europe, and an instrument of British policy. But in the text of the German reply to the Allies the cultural issue is transformed:

> We consider it to be Germany's great misfortune – due partly to fate, but partly to faults in our political leadership – that our inevitable opposition to Czarism brought us also into opposition, and finally into warlike compli-cations, with countries to which we were bound by a strong community of

63 Luckau, "Report of the Allied Commission on the Responsibility of the Authors of War and Enforcement of Penalties," 295.

64 Luckau, "Report of the Allied Commission on the Responsibility of the Authors of the War and on Enforcement of Penalties," 298.

65 See Regis Factor and Stephen Turner, "Weber, the Germans, and Anglo-Saxon Convention," *Max Weber's Political Sociology: A Pessimistic Vision of a Rationalized World*, edited by Ronald M. Glassman and Vatro Murvar. (Westport, CT: Greenwood, 1984), 39–54.

intellectual interests, and with which we are convinced that an understanding was possible.[66]

Germany, in short, belonged with, not in opposition to, what was to become "the West," with which it shared "intellectual interests."

The "faults in our political leadership" were a result of deeper causes: a problematic "political inheritance" and a problematic state structure.

> The real mistakes of German policy lay much further back. The German Chancellor who was in office in 1914 had taken over a political inheritance which either condemned as hopeless, from the very start, his unreservedly honest attempt to relieve the tension of the international situation, or demanded a degree of statesmanship and above all a strength of decision which on the one hand he did not sufficiently possess, and on the other could not make effective within the structure of the German State as it existed at that time. It is a capital error to seek to place moral blame in quarters where in reality nervousness, weakness in face of the noisy demeanor of the above-mentioned small but unscrupulous group, and lack of ability to make quick unequivocal decisions in difficult situations brought about disaster.[67]

"Above all a strength of decision": this is a telling phrase. Historians of the war point as well to the fact that it was difficult to tell who was in charge of German policy. The lack of central authority in the "the structure of the German state" was a cause of the inability of the Chancellor to act to relieve tension, and more generally to pursue a coherent policy, and also to be able to face down "the noisy demeanor" and "reprehensible and irresponsible utterances of a small group of chauvinist writers." This reasoning points to a novel motivation for Weber's own attempts at constitutional reform that strengthened the power of the leader and made it at the same time responsible to democratic public opinion, which the text asserts would never have supported a premeditated war. The "political inheritance" in question was one which encouraged the idea that Germany had to be self-sufficient, an idea central to the notion of Mitteleuropa and to the later Nazi policy of autarky. What is the connection between the idea of autarky and Weber's political thought? I would guess that he would have been tremendously skeptical of any consistent attempt to achieve "autarky," even if the final goal was to protect the German nation. He probably was too conscious of the importance of "world markets" for Germany and its industry and for the availability of affordable food for the populace.

66 Luckau, "Report of the Allied Commission on the Responsibility of the Authors of the War and on Enforcement of Penalties," 297.
67 Ibid., 295.

For Weber, the principal error, the failure to conclude an alliance with Britain, was a product of mistrust, and mistrust was fostered by the press – a favorite Weberian topic. But the text also admits that much of this mistrust was a result of German naval construction.

> For our part, we admit unreservedly that the ultimate extent and the spirit of German naval construction in recent years – not the fact of its accomplishment – might have aroused mistrust in England. As this mutual mistrust was undoubtedly one of the principal causes of the strained situation in Europe, we think it regrettable that no means of removing it was found.[68]

This principal cause was aggravated by Germany's refusals to agree to arms limitations as proposed in 1907: "We should have wished for a different attitude on the part of Germany in connection with The Hague Peace Conference and on the occasion of the statement of German plans for naval construction."[69] But the mistrust went both ways, and fault was on both sides, and especially the press:

> On the other hand, we regret that deep mistrust was fostered in Germany by, well-known and frequently quoted articles in English newspapers, by the agitation carried on by the Northcliffe press and the influence which it commanded, and by acts such as the refusal to codify maritime law in the English House of Lords.[70]

The text adds a curious political observation about the socialist parties, of a kind also not found in texts like Montgelas's.

> On the other hand, before the war the views of the French parties under the leadership of Jaurès, and those of the German Socialists and middle-class Democrats were extraordinarily closely akin.[71]

Neither was in support of a war of aggression. The text considers a counterfactual possibility, and explains why it did not occur.

> Any exertion by those parties of their influence in favor of a peaceful compromise with Germany was, however, prevented by the fact that France was bound by her close alliance to the policy of Russian Czarism.[72]

---

68 Ibid., 298.
69 Ibid., 298.
70 Ibid., 298.
71 Ibid., 297.
72 Ibid., 297.

This meant that the responsibility lay with the French diplomats who failed to act to restrain Russia, or acted to encourage war.

> Official documents prove that, on occasions which might have given rise to a conflict between Russia and Germany, the French Government gave no advice of a nature to dissuade Russia in principle from her warlike attitude, but rather often offered counsels calculated to encourage her in maintaining it.[73]

In any case, the treaties with Russia, which the French reaffirmed, meant that "France was bound hand and foot to Czarism."[74]

These arguments are revealing, if not especially novel: they show Weber thinking organizationally about the German political structure, and strategically about the European balance of power, and why Germany failed to find a place in the European balance of power, to its own detriment. But there is a twist. The text of the German reply openly rejects a certain theory, a theory later to be made influential by J. A. Hobson as a theory of imperialism, attributed to its academic source in a work Weber knew well and cited favorably in *The Protestant Ethic*:[75]

> It is also a subject for regret that a theory current in certain circles of all countries – a theory which we regard as completely erroneous – regarding the alleged natural necessity for a commercial war, should have received powerful support from the work of a very capable American writer (Veblen, *Theory of Business Enterprise*, 1904).[76]
>
> Thus the nationalist agitations in the various countries reacted upon each other, intensifying their violence. In view of all this, we must regard it as especially deplorable that the opinion combated by us, to wit, that the war was prepared and waged on the part of England as a means of overthrowing a troublesome competitor, will probably be established for all time in German public opinion by the conditions of peace at present laid before us.[77]

This is a strange passage for a number of reasons. Citations to academic theorists are simply not found elsewhere in the documents used at Versailles. It

---

73 Ibid., 297.
74 Ibid.
75 Max Weber, *The Protestant Ethic and the Spirit of Capitalism*, translated by Talcott Parsons (New York: Charles Scribner's Sons ([1930] 1958), 258n187, 275n71.
76 Thorstein Veblen, *The Theory of Business Enterprise* (New Brunswick, NJ: Transaction Publishers, 1904).
77 Luckau, "Report of the Allied Commission on the Responsibility of the Authors of the War and on Enforcement of Penalties," 298.

conflicts with Weber's own statements in earlier periods.[78] Moreover, it contradicts the *Heidelberger Vereinigung* statement, which, as noted, made a point of "the fact that the imperialistic tensions of world commerce were among the causes of the dangerous situation in July, 1914." What are we to make of this change?

Acknowledging the role of commercial rivalry was simply inconsistent with the main narrative: the claim that Germany had no aims that could only be accomplished by war. The argument of *Mitteleuropa* was an economic one, which proposed a German surrogate in Central Europe for the Colonies of Britain and France. This reasoning supplied a motive of the same type as those of Russia and France: the kind of unification envisioned by Naumann could not be accomplished without war. Mitteleuropa depended on a larger war; this is why Naumann had claimed that the war was about whether Mitteleuropa would be born. Moreover, as the authors of the text well-knew, commercial rivalry and the need to protect and project German economic interests in the larger world were central to the arguments for massive German naval construction, which the text acknowledges as a major cause of distrust.

The Veblen reference also points to an irony. Veblen had written two important books on the war, during the war. The first, *Imperial Germany and the Industrial Revolution*,[79] was the source of what would later be known as the theory of the German Sonderweg or alternative path of development. As Veblen put it, Germany received modern technology ready-made, without the cultural consequences produced by the long use of it. Germany was "unexampled among the western nations both as regards the abruptness, thoroughness, and amplitude of its appropriation of this technology, and as regards the archaism of its cultural furniture at the date of its appropriation."[80]

Weber himself had written against the Prussian aristocracy: it was a concern throughout his career.[81] The *Heidelberger Vereinigung* had alluded to the

---

78 In 1898 Weber wrote that

after a period of seeming peaceful competition, it is now completely certain that the trade expansion of all civilized countries (*bürgerlich organisierte Kulturvolker*) reaches the point where only power will decide the share of individual nations in the economic domination of the world and thus determine the standard of living of their population and especially of their working class. (Quoted and translated in Guether Roth, "Max Weber's Articles on German Agriculture and Industry in the Encyclopedia Americana (1906/1907) and Their Political Context," *Max Weber Studies* 1, no. 4 (2006): 183–205 (187)).

79 Thorstein Veblen, *Imperial Germany and the Industrial Revolution* (New York: Macmillan, 1915).

80 Veblen, *Imperial Germany and the Industrial Revolution*, 86.

81 Max Weber, "Suffrage and Democracy in Germany," *Weber: Political Writings*, edited by Peter Lassman and Ronald Speirs (Cambridge: Cambridge University Press, [1916] 1994), 80–129 (114–120).

weight of the Prussian tradition by noting the future importance of South German democratic traditions. Nevertheless, the text of the German reply, written by non-Prussians, contained no mention of Prussian militarism or the Prussian aristocracy. The omission contrasted to Clemenceau's remarks in his short and brutal reply to the German text: "For many years the rulers of Germany, true to Prussian tradition, strove for a position of dominance in Europe."[82] Why was Prussian militarism not mentioned? There are perhaps three reasons. The first is that the overriding concern of both Weber and the German delegation was German unity: it was one thing to expound on the errors of past leaders; the Prussian aristocracy was still a force that needed to be integrated into a future Germany. The second was that to indict this class for its belligerence would have simply confirmed the Allies in their belief that Germany was a rogue nation and the true author of the war. The third is that Weber and Germans generally shared in the notions of honor of this class. Their aggressiveness in the peace conference, which led to harsher terms, was largely a result of their attempts to preserve national honor by arguments against war guilt.

The concept of "honor" – *Ehre* – plays a large role in German culture, and was central to German behavior at Versailles. The English observers of the war crimes trials mandated by the Versailles treaty to be run in the German courts were surprised that the major penalties for abuse of prisoners were for crimes against honor, insults rather than physical abuse or malfeasance.[83] They noted that the category did not even exist in English law. Veblen regarded it as part of the retrograde feudal overlay of German society. Veblen's other wartime book, *An Inquiry into the Nature of Peace*, is scathing on the subject of honor, this "spiritual capital," as he called it.[84] Veblen regarded honor as a euphemism associated with dueling rather than honesty, and national honor as a convenient "stimulus to warlike enterprise."[85] Weber dismissed the hand-wringing of his compatriots in the face of defeat in similar terms: "We lost the match, you won it." Weber's opinion, as Mommsen put it, was that "It was cowardly and dishonorable to complain ... It was necessary to bear the consequences manfully and *silently*."[86] But Weber, unlike Veblen, wanted to see Germany as a normal country rather than a country on an alternative path of development,

82 Alma Luckau, "Allied Reply to the German Counterproposals," *The German Delegation at the Paris Peace Conference* (New York: Columbia University Press, 1941), 411–72 (411).

83 Cf. Claude Mullins, *The Leipzig Trials: An Account of the War Criminals' Trials and Study of German Mentality* (London: Witherby, 1921).

84 Thorstein Veblen, *An Inquiry into the Nature of Peace and the Terms of Its Perpetuation* (New York: B. W. Huebsch, 1919), 27.

85 Veblen, *An Inquiry into the Nature of Peace*, 27.

86 Mommsen, *Max Weber and German Politics 1890–1920*, 294.

as a country cursed by its proximity to aggressive Czarism, which did what any country would have done in response to Russian mobilization. But he was himself trapped in the notion of honor: he wanted this acknowledged in order to preserve German honor.

There is a further irony. Weber's own scholarly writings had taken up the problems of national interest, honor, and the driving forces of international politics and imperialism, notably in a section of *Economy and Society*. What he says there is much closer to Veblen with respect to the nature of international relations. Weber notes that "Empire formation does not always follow the routes of export trade, although nowadays we are inclined to see things in this imperialist way. As a rule, the "continental" imperialism – Russian and American – just like the "overseas imperialism" of the British and of those modeled after it, follow the tracks of previously existing capitalist interests, especially in foreign areas that are politically weak. And of course, at least for the formation of great overseas dominions of the past-in the overseas empires of Athens, Carthage, and Rome – export trade played its decisive part."[87]

He offers a corrective to this, but it is a very partial one, by arguing that other economic interests played a role in the imperialism of the ancient world, of "at least equal and often of far greater importance than were commercial profits: ground rents, farmed-out taxes, office fees, and similar gains." But he agrees that "in the age of modern capitalism the interest in exporting to foreign territories is dominant."[88] And he argues that economic interests were not always the initial cause of political imperialism:

> The causal nexus has very often been the reverse. Among the empires named above, those which had an administration technically able to establish at least overland means of communication did so for administrative purposes. In principle, this has often been the exclusive purpose, regardless of whether or not the means of communication were advantageous for existing or future trading needs.[89]

The named imperialisms, however, were precapitalist: the Mongols, China, Egypt, Persia, the Carolingian empire, and the Crusades, and even with most of these "the economic importance of trade was not altogether absent"[90] and other economic motives played a role.

87 Max Weber, *Economy and Society: An Outline of Interpretive Sociology* 3 vols, ed. Guenther Roth and Claus Wittich (Berkeley: University of California Press, [1968] 1978), 914.
88 Weber, *Economy and Society*, 914
89 Weber, *Economy and Society*, 913.
90 Weber, *Economy and Society*, 914–15.

Weber also agrees with Veblen as well on the importance of considerations of honor:

> Experience teaches that claims to prestige have always played into the origin of wars. Their part is difficult to gauge; it cannot be determined in general, but it is very obvious. The realm of "honor," which is comparable to the "status order" within a social structure, pertains also to the interrelations of political structures.[91]

These considerations, he also agrees, are an accelerant to war and political irrationality, which work by magnifying political differences:

> by virtue of an unavoidable "dynamic of power," wherever claims to prestige flame up – and this normally results from an acute political danger to peace – they challenge and call forth the competition of all other possible bearers of prestige. The history of the last decade [1900–1910], especially the relations between Germany and France, shows the prominent effect of this irrational element in all political foreign relations.[92]

But Weber uses these arguments to make a point continuous with his Versailles arguments and contrary to the idea of the Deutsche Sonderweg: to suggest that Germany is no different from other countries with respect to these irrationalities. This holds for the motivations for political unification in the service of trade and market efficiencies. In this text he is clear about how the two interact, and the obstacles posed by Russian domination of Poland. Eliminating this domination would have benefitted Germany. It was an interest that could only have been satisfied by war with Russia – an interest in war of precisely the kind that Weber, in his Versailles response, denied that Germany had.

What Does This Tell Us New About Weber?

In one important respect, the Weber of the reply to the Allies is a very different one from the image of the belligerent nationalist that we have inherited. He accepted that the German policies of the post-Bismarck period were catastrophic and that an alliance with Britain was the only way to secure the European balance of power in the face of Czarism. There was precedent for using Germany as the European balancer. Austria had played this role for Britain in the middle of the nineteenth century.[93] One may question whether

---

91 Weber, *Economy and Society*, 911.
92 Weber, *Economy and Society*, 911.
93 Paul W. Schroeder, *The Transformation of European Politics*, 1763–1848. (Oxford: Clarendon Press, 1994), 130–31.

accepting this subordinate role would have been consistent with German honor, however realistic it was. Before German unification, Prussia had resisted this role. But Weber was prescient here as well. His strategic solution to the wicked problem of the place of Germany in Europe was eventually realized in the Cold War, with West Germany as part of the NATO alliance, a nonparticipating and neutralized France, and with the United States playing a large part of the role that the British had formerly played in Europe. But it preserved the peace of Europe and eventually led to the goal that Weber sought: a unified Germany with set of friendly buffer states between Germany and Russia.

Weber's ideas about strong leadership, which were only partially realized in the Weimar constitution, also look different in the light of this text. The contrast that underlies the text is between diplomats and military leaders and the public: a public that would never have accepted premeditated war and diplomats and military leaders who would. This is a primitive version of the Democratic Peace hypothesis. The importance he attached to the idea is reflected in his comments on the relations between the French and German socialist parties. The public would have been empowered by a popularly elected president with real authority to override the bureaucracy, including the diplomats and military leaders. This was his original constitutional design. Whether a functioning constitution of this sort would have prevented the rise of Hitler is an open question. Veblen's point about the use of honor, combined with Weber's own prediction about the reaction to the dishonor of Versailles, suggest that a politician who used the popular sense of honor to promote war would override the innate pacifism of a democratic public. This is precisely what occurred.

Chapter 7

MAX WEBER IN THE UNITED STATES

Lawrence A. Scaff

Max Weber represents an unusual and instructive example of a thinker who in his own time was relatively unknown, but who in our era has become internationally prominent. Today his work is widely cited not simply in the human sciences and halls of academia but also in the arena of public discourse.[1] The change seems remarkable. How did it come about? What explains this kind of recognition, and what is the basis for Weber's present reputation? Under what conditions did it become possible for us to speak about a distinctive kind of intellectual commitment associated with Weber's name – a Weberian theory, a Weberian analysis or "paradigm," even a "Weberian Marxism" or an "analytical Weberianism?"[2]

Anyone who has studied Weber's thought closely and knows his writings well will be tempted to answer that the reason lies in the power of the thought alone. We may want to assert that the texts speak for themselves and justify the author's fame. Or we may insist that the questions he raised, the significance of the problems he addressed, and the depth of his insights provide a sufficient rationale for his present-day reputation. But such an answer comes all too

---

1   For typical recent examples referencing the "Protestant Ethic" thesis and "Politics as a Vocation," see Fareed Zakaria, "Capitalism, Not Culture, Drives Economies," and Ezra Klein, "A Remarkable, Historic Period of Change," both in *The Washington Post*, 1 August and 11 November 2012, respectively; Robert J. Shiller, "Why Innovation Is Still Capitalism's Star," *The New York Times*, 18 August 2013; and David Brooks, "The Refiner's Fire," *The New York Times*, 24 February 2014.

2   Characterizations found in Randall Collins, *Weberian Sociological Theory* (Cambridge: Cambridge University Press, 1986); and Gert Albert, Agathe Bienfait, Steffen Sigmund, and Claus Wendt, eds., *Das Weber-Paradigma* (Tübingen: Mohr Siebeck, 2003). The idea of "Weberian Marxism" was introduced by Maurice Merleau-Ponty, *Les aventures de la dialectique* (Paris: Gallimard, 1955); "analytical Weberianism" is used by Edgar Kiser and Justin Baer, "The Bureaucratization of States: Toward an Analytical Weberianism," in *Remaking Modernity: Politics, History, and Sociology*, ed. J. Adams, E. Clemens, and A. Orloff (Durham, NC: Duke University Press, 2005), pp. 225–245.

easily. A more complex and contingent process becomes apparent when we consider the actual historical circumstances, the cultural and political context and the social relationships characterizing the reception of Weber's work.

The most obvious way to answer our questions is to propose a provisional thesis: in order to understand the "Weber phenomenon," we must understand what occurred with Max Weber and his work in the United States starting in the 1920s. The work of translation and interpretation proceeded simultaneously elsewhere, especially in Japan, though also in Mexico.[3] However, considered from an international perspective, the crucial developments relating to the permanent "institutionalization" of the thought took place primarily in key university circles in the United States. The transmission of ideas over long periods of time is surely advanced by institutional mechanisms and pedagogies that survive for generations. The reading and use of Weber's texts was promoted by exactly this kind of long-term institutional support.

However, there is a second alternative approach to an answer, found in the fact that Max Weber traveled to the Unites States, twice, as it were: the second time in spirit with avid readers of his work, but the first time in person with Marianne Weber and colleagues attending the Congress of Arts and Science in St. Louis. The actual North American journey covered nearly three months in 1904, while the reception started twenty years later and lasted for decades, persisting to this day. The actual journey to the New World stirred Weber's imagination and provided substance for his inquiries. It became a turning point in the biography of the work. The subsequent "spiritual" appropriation in the United States consolidated, extended and institutionalized the work in the human sciences; it became the essential condition for Weber's worldwide reputation.

The juxtaposition of the two "journeys" presents an unusual opportunity to inquire how these two moments in the genealogy of Weberian thought – the *Amerikareise* and the subsequent *Rezeptionsgeschichte* – might be related to each other. Can Weber's actual journey to the New World inform us about the later attractions of his thought for American scholars of the interwar and postwar generations? Are there deeper reasons for the work's enduring fascination for the audience in the United States? What is it about the particular historical configuration that encouraged the reconstitution in the United States of Weber as a "classic" of enduring contemporary significance? These kinds of questions can be raised in other national and linguistic contexts as well. In the

3   Wolfgang Schwentker, *Max Weber in Japan. Eine Untersuchung zur Wirkungsgeschichte 1905– 1995* (Tübingen: Mohr Siebeck, 1998); Álvaro Morcillo Laiz, "Aviso a los navegantes. La traducción al español de *Economía y sociedad* de Max Weber," *Estudios sociológicos* 30 (2012), 609–40.

North American case they are potentially consequential because of the genealogy of the discovery and propagation of Weber's work.

Institutionalizing Weber

The structural and organizational conditions for the success of Weber's ideas in the United States are by now reasonably well known. The starting point was the introduction of his texts to the English-speaking world initiated in the 1920s and 1930s in the United States. I have written about these important developments in detail previously.[4] The appropriation and extension of Weber's work occurred essentially in three waves: the first was the translations, analyses and promotional activities of Frank Knight, Talcott Parsons, Edward Shils and C. Wright Mills. The second overlapping series of events supplemented these beginnings with the teachings, writings and translations of the large number of Weimar Era émigrés who fled Nazi Germany and settled in the United States, many reinventing themselves in a new environment as active scholars and teachers. The third extended development was the postwar outpouring of translations and the expansion of interest in new directions, in new locations and with new groups of scholars and intellectuals.

The first wave of scholarship was inaugurated by Frank Knight, the founder of the earliest Chicago school of theoretical economics, who produced the first English translation of Weber's work, the Munich lectures compiled by Hellman and Palyi as *General Economic History* (1927). Knight's lifelong interest in Weber grew out of a fascination with the historical origins of economic systems, particularly modern capitalism. Coming from an evangelical Protestant background, he was especially intrigued by the possible role in economic development played by cultural factors, such as the belief system of a salvation religion. The Munich lectures seemed to Knight to represent Weber's final, most mature reflection on these topics, well worth his skills as a translator. The young Talcott Parsons shared an upbringing and interests similar to Knight's, though his introduction to Weber occurred in very different circumstances. As a graduate student in Heidelberg in 1925, Parsons was suddenly brought into the orbit of Weber's work. He first read the preface and the essays on the "Protestant Ethic and the Spirit of Capitalism" in the first volume of Weber's *Gesammelte Aufsätze zur Religionssoziologie*, finding the narrative so compelling

---

4   Lawrence A. Scaff, "Max Weber's Reception in the United States," in *Das Faszinosum Max Weber. Die Geschichte seiner Geltung*, ed. Karl-Ludwig Ay and Knut Borchard (Konstanz: UVK, 2006), pp. 55–89; and *Max Weber in America* (Princeton, NJ: Princeton University Press, 2011), pp. 197–244. See also the recent study by Joshua Derman, *Max Weber in Politics and Social Thought: From Charisma to Canonization* (Cambridge: Cambridge University Press, 2012).

that he became immersed in the text "as if it were a detective story," he later wrote.[5] The previous year he had studied at the London School of Economics, attending lectures by R. H. Tawney, Morris Ginsberg, L. T. Hobhouse and Bronislaw Malinowski, but without ever hearing Weber's name mentioned, even though Tawney was writing *Religion and the Rise of Capitalism*. Indeed, Tawney avoided mentioning Weber's parallel inquiries until the preface to the second edition of his work.[6] In the Heidelberg milieu, by contrast, Weber's work seemed to be everywhere. Studying with Alfred Weber, Karl Jaspers, and Karl Mannheim (who was teaching a seminar on Weber), Parsons lost little time in choosing a D.Phil. dissertation topic on "capitalism" in recent German scholarship. Not far behind this decision came the proposal to translate a major part of Weber's sociology of religion, eventually reduced to the book appearing as *The Protestant Ethic and the Spirit of Capitalism*. With Marianne Weber's encouragement, support and timely interventions, following three years of labor, the text finally appeared in 1930.

As can be seen in Table 1 (see the Appendix) these two texts translated by Knight and Parsons survived for nearly 20 years as the main public sources in English of knowledge about Weber. But other efforts to recover Weber's work were also underway among small circles of scholars. In this respect the most significant "fugitive" publications emerged at the University of Chicago, where in the 1930s Edward Shils had begun translating numerous Weber texts. His passion for translating Weber focused mainly on selections from the philosophy of science essays collected by Marianne Weber in the *Gesammelte Aufsätze zur Wissenschaftslehre*, including "Science as a Vocation," followed by Chapter One of *Economy and Society*, and "Politics as a Vocation." Like Parsons, Shils was initially compelled to engage with Weber's thought for personal edification and out of a sense of intellectual adventure: "I was overpowered when the perspectives opened up by Weber's concepts brought together things which hitherto had never seemed to me to have any affinity with each other," he wrote retrospectively; "reading Max Weber was literally breathtaking. Sometimes, in the midst of reading him, I had to stand up and walk around for a minute or two until my exhilaration died down."[7] Shils eventually began circulating his work to students and faculty in mimeograph format. He was

5   Talcott Parsons, "The Circumstances of My Encounter with Max Weber," in *Sociological Traditions from Generation to Generation*, ed. Robert K. Merton and Matilda W. Riley (Norwood: Ablex, 1980), p. 39.

6   R. H. Tawney, *Religion and the Rise of Capitalism* (London: Harcourt, Brace & Co., 1937, 2nd ed.); the first edition was published in 1926.

7   Edward A. Shils, "Some Academics, Mainly in Chicago," *The American Scholar* 50 (Spring 1981): 184.

encouraged by Knight, whose Weber seminar – a close reading in the original German of *Wirtschaft und Gesellschaft* – he had attended.

In the hands of Knight and another colleague, the German-born sociologist Louis Wirth, and with Shils's assent, the texts then became important as part of an effort to define, reform and integrate the University of Chicago's social science curriculum. Coming to fruition late in the 1930s and supported by the University's celebrated president and educator, Robert Hutchins, these pedagogical innovations were the first important institutionalization of a selection of Weber's texts and ideas – the classic distinction between class and status, the conception of social action, or the typology of authority (*Herrschaft*). We should emphasize that the introduction of translated Weber texts in the classroom had to do not simply with professorial interests, but with practical pedagogical disputes and requirements. It was the era in the universities when the social sciences were defined and disciplinary boundaries were drawn. In the United States the debates were intense at Chicago and Harvard, and at public institutions like the University of Wisconsin. Knight in particular was concerned not merely with distinctions among disciplines, but also with the project of countering parochial tendencies in scholarship and integrating knowledge across the social sciences. For Knight it was the breadth of coverage, conceptual richness, methodological acumen, and empirical and historical grounding in Weber's work – in a word, its vision – that appealed to him. Its world-historical sweep offered a route to professionalization that could attract broad support, and it carried the promise of having unquestioned intellectual prestige in the battles playing out in the sciences. In the classroom the innovation took a specific form: armed with Shils's translations, instructors at Chicago addressed the pedagogical questions in the social sciences by placing major portions of Weber's dense prose in the hands even of the uninitiated undergraduates. Reinhard Bendix was one of these student novices, and the more senior instructors included David Riesman, Daniel Bell, Morris Janowitz and Milton Singer. This was the kind of educational laboratory in which Weber's ideas began to grow and take root. The collection of mimeographed texts used for these purposes can still be found in the open stacks of the University's Regenstein Library.

The early translation of Weber's work into English was a leap to a new phase in the reception of his ideas. We should remember, however, that there is always a politics and sociology of translation. As with James Strachey's translations of Sigmund Freud, so also with the translations of Weber: they introduced a certain kind of conceptual terminology that has taken on a life of its own, often based on the translators' interests and outlook or on the then current state of scientific discourse. The act of translation is always an act of interpretation, or more strongly, *mis*interpretation – a sometimes subtle distortion of the original, exaggerating some connotations and deeper intuitions while diminishing others. Should *Handeln* mean "action" or "behavior?" Should *Wahlverwandschaften* be "elective affinities" or "correlations?" Should *Herrschaft* translate as "authority," "domination" or "imperative coordination?" The language favored by Parsons and Shils that gained ascendancy tended to emphasize the "behavioral" and "causal" side of Weber's conceptual syntax, downplaying or avoiding altogether the complexities in concepts like *Entzauberung* (disenchantment, demagification) or *Lebensführung* (life-conduct, the way one leads one's life). Numerous debates have been triggered by such choices and their intellectual consequences: criticizing a distorted position, distinguishing the author's actual views from those imposed by the translator, rediscovering an essential but forgotten concept or reconstructing the theory on an alternative textual basis. This interpretative dynamic will be promoted at the very least by changing interests in the sciences and the culture in which intellectual life is embedded.

Considering the scope of Chicago's influence and dispersion of its graduates across academia, it is not surprising that basic knowledge of Weber's work became widely propagated through university social science curricula. But in this respect there was another important source of knowledge and influence as well, stemming from those who emigrated from Germany in the 30s and who began to staff social science departments at numerous other institutions.

The Émigrés' Weber

The recognition of Weber's work and the growth of interest in some of his key concepts, such as "charisma" and "bureaucracy," was significantly affected by the emigration of scholars and intellectuals from Germany after 1933: distinguished scholars like Karl Mannheim and Friedrich von Hayek at the London School of Economics; Franz Neumann and Paul Lazersfeld at Columbia University in New York; and of course the many faculty concentrated at the New School for Social Research in New York. In the United States five universities with prestigious and influential graduate programs became crucial in the 1930s for the development and propagation of knowledge about Weber: Chicago, Harvard, Columbia, the New School and Wisconsin. But during the decade there was also an influx in the United States of numerous widely dispersed émigré scholars on other campuses who knew Weber personally or knew his work well: for example, Paul Honigsheim at Michigan State University; Arthur Salz at Ohio State University; Eric Voegelin at Louisiana State University; Karl Loewenstein at the University of Massachusetts; Carl Landauer at the University of California at Berkeley; and Melchoir Palyi at Southern Illinois University.

Some of the émigrés were especially important for the interpretation, extension and application of Weber's ideas. Alexander von Schelting is one obvious example. Having met Parsons when they were students in Heidelberg, von Schelting later traveled to the United States as a Rockefeller Fellow and renewed their exchange of views. Associated for a time with Howard Becker at Wisconsin, he eventually found a position at Columbia, where he taught a joint Weber seminar with Shils. Von Schelting served importantly as a bridging figure from the Weimar Era methodological focus on Weber's work to the reinterpretation of Weber's methodology and conception of social action. It was the social action "frame of reference" that began to preoccupy Talcott Parsons, and for that purpose von Schelting became Parsons's leading authority: the chapters on Weber in *The Structure of Social Action* bore the imprint of von Schelting's guidance, especially on the critical concept of the "ideal type" and its analytic uses and possible limitations.[8]

Hans Gerth was another émigré scholar who contributed significantly to the transmission and dissemination of Weber's work. In some ways his role was unique. Following a somewhat different path than von Schelting, Gerth had been associated in Germany with Mannheim and members of the Frankfurt Institute for Social Research, such as Theodor Adorno. But in 1937 he found himself in badly diminished circumstances exiled in London with Mannheim. With Parsons's encouragement and Shils's assistance, Gerth finally made his way in 1940 as an "enemy alien" to Howard Becker's sociology department in Madison, Wisconsin. It was a propitious relocation, for the fateful outcome was Gerth's encounter with two ambitious graduate students: C. Wright Mills and Don Martindale. The Gerth and Mills and Gerth and Martindale partnerships became an essential chapter in the narrative of production for some of the most important Weber texts: both the widely used student-friendly reader, *From Max Weber: Essays in Sociology* (1946), and the translations of *Ancient Judaism* and *The Religion of India* that completed Weber's *Collected Essays in the Sociology of Religion*. In addition, the partnership with Mills brought Gerth's disorganized brilliance into a setting where it could be reshaped by Mills's entrepreneurial savvy. Two of the classics of postwar American sociology – Mills's critical take on postwar American life in *White Collar* (1951) and *The Power Elite* (1956) – owed a great deal to lessons learned from Gerth's immersion in Weberian concepts and ways of thinking about society.

At the New School for Social Research many of the émigrés were thoroughly familiar with Weber's work. Emil Lederer had known Weber personally, assisting as a young Heidelberg economist with the publication of the

---

8   Talcott Parsons, *The Structure of Social Action* (New York: Free Press, 1937 [1949].), especially Chapter 16.

Archiv für Sozialwissenschaft und Sozialpolitik. Albert Salomon also was acquainted with Weber in Heidelberg, formulating the tagline of Weber as the "bourgeois Marx" in an early article, a judgment with an impressively long shelf life. But in the New School milieu, his interests took a more systematic turn, and in the first issues of *Social Research* Salomon presented one of the first précis of Weberian thought – a survey of his methodology, politics and sociology – for a general audience.[9] Salomon's broadened view of the work heralded the emergence of a rather different Weber from the professional sociologist and specialized historical economist put forward by American authors. The impression of a shift in focus was strengthened by other scholarship emerging from the New School, such as Alfred Schutz's use of Weber in phenomenology, Arnold Brecht's in political theory or Frieda Wunderlich's in agrarian economics.[10] Subsequently this emergent tradition of wide-ranging, even eclectic approaches to Weber's work was continued by Benjamin Nelson when he arrived at the New School in the 1960s.

The reasons for the turn to Weber among the émigrés had to do with several fundamental issues. There was a sense among these displaced scholars that if one wanted to engage in social research, then one had to come to terms with the figure of Max Weber, widely credited by them with being the "most important thinker" of their times.[11] Furthermore, Weber as the self-described "outsider" took on the function of providing orientation to the experience of displacement and the condition Adorno labeled the "damaged life." The rationale for such an appropriation was to be found in the work itself, since Weber could be read to have confronted the specter of capitalist modernity, writ large in America, with an acceptable cosmopolitan and critical sensibility familiar to a European. But the result of this émigré perspective was then a different kind of Weber, more attuned to the critical problematics of modern life, the unsettled position of the scholar and teacher, and the demanding existence of the "intellectual desperado" (Siegfried Krakauer's pointed characterization

9 Albert Salomon, "Max Weber," *Die Gesellschaft* 3 (1926), 131–53; "Max Weber's Methodology," "Max Weber's Political Ideas," "Max Weber's Sociology," *Social Research* 1 (1934), 147–68, 368–84; 2 (1935), 60–73.

10 Alfred Schutz, "Concept and Theory Formation in the Social Sciences," *Journal of Philosophy* 51 (1954), 257–73; and *Collected Papers, I: The Problem of Social Reality*, ed. M. Natanson (The Hague: Nijhoff, 1962); Arnold Brecht, "The Rise of Relativism in Political and Legal Philosophy," *Social Research* 6 (1939), 392–414; and *Political Theory: The Foundations of Twentieth Century Political Thought* (Princeton, NJ: Princeton University Press, 1959); Frieda Wunderlich, *Farm Labor in Germany 1810–1945* (Princeton, NJ: Princeton University Press, 1961).

11 Peter M. Rutkoff, and William B. Scott, William B., *New School: A History of the New School for Social Research* (New York: Free Press, 1986), p. 201.

of Weber) confronting a world in turmoil. As Franz Neumann formulated the change, in Germany Weber's work had been reduced to its least inspiring dimensions, but it was instead in America under new conditions that it "really came to life" and broke free of superimposed schemes and strictures that tamed its real potential.[12]

At Columbia University émigré scholars like Neumann, Paul Lazarsfeld, Karl Wittfogel, Peter Gay and Theodore Abel also joined in the kinds of discussions emanating from the New School in Lower Manhattan. Neumann thought Weber's appeal for historically and theoretically grounded inquiry, combined with intellectual sobriety, showed the way for the émigré scholar's vocation. The appeal offered a kind of corrective to unhistorical naïveté and crude, theoretically uninformed empiricism. In his early work Abel also sought to bring Weber's ideas into the orbit of American social science.[13] Columbia provided a perfect setting for the cross-fertilization of these émigré perspectives with the work just emerging in the social sciences, encouraged by well-connected scholars like Robert Merton. One result of such convergence was the postwar "Seminar on the State" that began meeting in 1946, attended by Merton, a newly arrived C. Wright Mills, Wittfogel, Gay, Daniel Bell, S. M. Lipset, Richard Hofstadter, and David Truman, among others – a meeting ground for historians, sociologists and political scientists. Minutes of the group's meetings show a striking reliance on some shared central ideas from *Economy and Society*, such as the chapter on bureaucracy, applied in these discussions to the development of the modern state in a variety of circumstances, from the Soviet Union's contemporaneous efforts at economic development to the politics of decolonization in the developing world.[14]

Stemming from these discussions, Merton's *Reader in Bureaucracy* (1952) illustrated one path of development for a new Weberian perspective: no longer interpretation of the work as such, but an application of useful ideas drawn from Weber's texts and extended to novel problems and various research domains. It was this fruitful problem-oriented context in which the ideas could be restated, applied, criticized, elaborated, extended and renewed.

---

12 Franz L. Neumann, "The Social Sciences," in *The Cultural Migration: The European Scholar in America*, ed. Franz L. Neumann *et al.* (Philadelphia: University of Pennsylvania Press, 1953), p. 22.

13 Theodore F. Abel, *Systematic Sociology in Germany* (New York: Columbia University Press, 1929); "The Operation Called *Verstehen*," *American Journal of Sociology* 54 (1948), 211–18.

14 The minutes for 1946–47 are in the Columbia University Seminars Office Archive; see also Ira Katznelson, *Desolation and Enlightenment: Political Knowledge after Total War, Totalitarianism, and the Holocaust* (New York: Columbia University Press, 2003), pp. 121–34.

Elective Affinities

The circumstances and relationships identified so far may be sufficient for identifying the conditions under which Max Weber's work was recovered, appropriated and institutionalized, with a leading role played by universities and intellectual circles in the United States. But my discussion has ignored the possibility of deeper sources of connection internal to the experience of reading an author, referenced in the kinds of enthusiasms recorded in Parsons's and Shils's previously cited autobiographical reflections. In an early essay with the arresting title, "Neither Marx nor Durkheim … perhaps Weber," Edward Tiryakian has proposed that the essential reason for Weber's acceptance in the United States, his "greater heuristic merit" than other social theorists, was that he "had a much greater range of exposure to American society," including the face-to-face encounters during the journey of 1904, and "a profound insider's understanding of ascetic, this-worldly Protestantism."[15] With this assertion Tiryakian has followed Benjamin Nelson's broadened conception of the "Protestant ethic" as referring "to the existential and cultural foundations of any society committed to the mastery of this world through intensive discipline and consensual organization of personal and social orders."[16] Such a foundation spelled out in the categories of "inner-worldly asceticism" has been widely considered an essential characteristic of cultural identity in the United States. Weber's experience as an observer of American life in 1904 is of course in itself not an indication of more perceptive understanding of this cultural formation, nor can it speak to the conditions for a certain kind of affirmative reader response. But we now know much more about the biography of the work as linked to the *Amerikareise*, and we have a much clearer understanding of the horizon of the author's comprehensive vision. In these changed circumstances Tiryakian's insight is worth exploring further.

For the generations of scholars I have mentioned the engagement with Max Weber became to an important degree a matter of appropriating his enthusiasms and spirit as their own. The prehistory of this appropriation has an important and singular source: not only the transformative experience of reading, as essential as that may be for informing and altering one's Weltanschauung, but also the *subject* foremost in Weber's mind in 1904: his well-known controversial cultural-historical investigation of the "Protestant Ethic" and its relationship to the "capitalist spirit."

15 Edward Tiryakian, "Neither Marx nor Durkheim … Perhaps Weber," *American Journal of Sociology* 81 (July 1975), 14–15.
16 Benjamin Nelson, "Weber's Protestant Ethic: Its Origins, Wanderings, and Foreseeable Futures," in *Beyond the Classics: Essays in the Scientific Study of Religion*, ed. C. Glock and P. Hammond. New York: Harper & Row, 1973, p. 83.

Weber used the journey to the United States to observe both sides of this world-historical relationship: on the one hand, numerous expressions of the spiritual life in social communities, educational institutions and religious events, and on the other the ethos, the culture and the everyday expressions of modern capitalism – "the most fateful force of our modern life"[17] – in its most massive and unconstrained forms. The dual theme was never far from his consciousness as he gazed on the social landscape of the New World and absorbed its lessons: a culture filled with "secularized offspring of the old puritan religiosity," as he wrote at the end of his travels, but also a harsh world in which "with almost lightening speed everything that stands in the way of capitalistic culture is being crushed," as he observed about native culture on the Indian Territory frontier.[18] Stated concisely, the problematic of Weber's thinking and writing then reproduced the contradictions of the journey, with the paradoxes of the spiritual and material culture represented in the dynamics of the "Protestant Ethic" text. Weber's American readers could not miss the points of reference: the work conveyed an appreciation of the zeal behind a spiritual quest, but also an analysis of the fervor motivating material conquest. It represented an investigation of themselves and their culture – their hopes, enthusiasms, triumphs, disappointments and failures.

The journey had multiple dimensions to it, becoming essentially a survey of contemporary life in the United States: the cities, most of which Weber saw east of the Mississippi River; capitalism's dynamic and business enterprise; the issues posed by rapid immigration; ethnicity, race, and race relations; the woman question and family life; the native American population and the frontier; questions of educational policy and the universities and colleges; the conditions of agriculture and rural society; industrial workers and the politics of labor; the nature and meaning of American democracy; the quality of public life and the media; and of course religion and spiritual life. For Weber's sociology of religion the experience served as an opportunity to investigate the relationship between religious belief and economic ethics. Sociologically, it became a question of understanding the presence of a relatively high degree of religiosity within a culture in which the effects of market capitalism and the entrepreneurial ethos were on display to an unparalleled extent. Weber often

17 "der schicksalsvollsten Macht unseres modernen Lebens:" in the 1920 "Vorbemerkung" to the *Gesammelte Aufsätze zur Religionssoziologie* (Tübingen: Mohr [Siebeck], 1920), vol. I, p. 4; hereafter cited as *GARS*.

18 The two phrases are from Weber's 1904 letters: 19 November on board the "Hamburg" in New York harbor; and 29 September from Indian Territory. (The unpublished 1904 letters from the United States are in the Nachlass Max Weber, GStA Berlin, Rep. 92, Nr. 6.)

sought to trace the way in which the two forces could persist alongside each other in a dynamic social *modus vivendi*.

One of the most obvious expressions of Weber's restless spirit was his engagement with religious communities, the churches and the sects of the North American experiment. The search for secularized cultural survivals of the old sacred Puritan religiosity became for Weber an absorbing ethnographic puzzle, pursued among other ways most obviously as a participant-observer in nine different denominational events during his travels. Weber memorialized most of these varieties of religious experience in commentaries or brief references in his published work. The fundamental conceptual distinction he introduced between a "church" as a compulsory organization for administering grace and the religious "sect" as a voluntaristic community of qualified believers emerged from these encounters. The participant-observer opportunities also provided points of reference and intellectual inspiration for the second part of "The Protestant Ethic and the Spirit of Capitalism," especially the chapter comparing Calvinism, Pietism, Methodism, and the Baptist sects (including Quakerism) that was completed when he returned home to Heidelberg. These episodes were supplemented and reinforced in numerous other ways, particularly the Webers' visits to universities and colleges from Tuskegee to Harvard, and their observation of settlement houses, voluntary associations, and racial and ethnic communities.

The overall effect of Weber's engagements in the New World emerged in his texts as the groundwork for three narratives that captured the imagination of the American audience. I shall call them the narratives of voluntarism, achievement and redemption.

By the narrative of voluntarism I am referring to the way in which Weber developed his conception of the "sect" and its effects on the individual and society. It was not simply the formal features of the sect that attracted Weber's attention – voluntary membership, congregational supremacy, election of the minister, a religious polity and offices legitimated by popular authority – but more importantly its social consequences and implications for the individual. The sect was essentially the social mechanism for the "testing" and "proof" of a person's character, honesty, trustworthiness, and overall moral standing – a regime of testing the self performed by one's peers. It served as the crucible in which the moral personality of the *Berufsmensch* was formed. A society of sects was voluntaristic in the sense that it emphasized the formation of civil society as a dense web of personal social relationships and voluntary associations. This distinctive view of the social world made sense because Weber considered the sect the original model in America of the voluntary association and public associational life, a distinctive feature of the United States enshrined in American consciousness. It appeared everywhere, from the social practices of the residential college to the clubs promoting the "Americanization" of immigrant youth. The voluntaristic model was the source of the peculiar version of "individualism" and its anti-authoritarian predispositions in the United States. Weber commented on these characteristic formations, both in correspondence and in his published texts. His readers schooled in vocational culture would have had no difficulty absorbing the message. Parsons even chose to cast his first version of Weberian sociology as the *voluntaristic* theory of social action.

The narrative of achievement is woven into the very idea of the "Protestant Ethic" as an historically consequential social formation emphasizing the character-forming and disciplining power of "inner-worldly asceticism." The orientation of active world-mastery and the norms of worldly accomplishment then carry over to the conception of the "capitalist spirit" that Weber found embodied in the figure of Benjamin Franklin, the most American icon imaginable. It mattered little whether the portrait of Franklin was historically accurate, as some critics have maintained. What counted was the sketch of this spiritual type, set forth already with systematic rigor by Franklin himself in his "Autobiography," a book given by Friedrich Kapp to the young Weber, who then as a mature author reproduced the model personality in the pages of the "Protestant Ethic." Mastery of the world presupposed mastery of the self, and when put into practice it entailed the conquest of the New World's primordial wilderness. Nature posed riddles and mysteries that could be solved pragmatically. However, the outcome of a problem-solving, practical orientation was fraught with moral ambiguity: either subduing and despoiling nature for utilitarian purposes, or constructing an "iron cage" of self-inflicted domination, or more hopefully promoting the stewardship and care of nature as a spiritual necessity. Weber's ecological awareness posed the problem in the closing pages of "The Protestant Ethic," as his readers would have noticed.

But the problem had an answer too, found in the didactic counternarrative of redemption, atonement and renewal in "The Protestant Ethic" and the one essay directly about the United States, the 1906 article on "The Protestant Sects and the Spirit of Capitalism."[19] In key passages Weber managed to capture the most fundamental topos of the culture of the United States. The quest for salvation that began as a religiously inspired message became transformed into a secularized cultural theme: the search for the possibility of breaking free from constraints in order to create a better life, to renew the self, to gain a second chance by atoning for moral failures and to find reconciliation with God, humankind and the world. Weber reproduced this alternative cultural narrative in the pages of the "Protestant Ethic," just as he had noted it in the two most potent literary references of the American journey: Gottfried Keller's

19 *GARS* I, pp. 17–236, in the version revised and published in 1920.

"*Romeo und Julia auf dem Dorfe*," and Peter Rosegger's "*Jakob, der Letzte.*" These were literary tales of self-discovery and self-disclosure, and in Rosegger's mythic retelling of the book of *Genesis* a fable of redemption in a reconstituted edenic, harmonious, multi-ethnic human community, located predictably in the New World. This particular vision appeared in Weber's mind during an interlude in the mountains of North Carolina. The literary references in correspondence anticipated the cultural contents of the finished text. Readers could not overlook the point of this narrative. It was the most potent founding myth of the American experience.

When Alexis de Tocqueville wrote the first volume of *Democracy in America* some 70 years before Weber's journey, he called attention to the "habits of the heart," that is, "the whole moral and intellectual state of a people"[20] that characterized the qualities of American life: namely, a unique alignment of spiritual zeal, democratic freedom and practical initiative. In Weber's account of the American experience, these habits have been transformed: it is as if they have now been elaborated in a new way in a probing of the moral and spiritual foundations of a society emerging as the epitome of modern capitalist culture. What Tocqueville saw as a patterned relationship, Weber began to view as a paradoxical linking of spiritual ideals with material ambitions. His work offered something different to the audience in the United States: not merely an account of social forces, but a triad of narratives with didactic overtones and a characterological sketch of well-known figures and recognizable social types.

The Postwar Weber

As the record of translations suggests, it was not until the 1950s in the social science disciplines that the Weberian imprimatur started to become widely circulated. Considering the textual basis for this development, four publications were especially important, as Table 1 indicates: Hans Gerth and C. Wright Mills published their easily accessible reader, including a dramatic and informative biographical sketch, *From Max Weber: Essays in Sociology*. It was the Weber "source book" others had wanted years earlier, now perfectly adapted to classroom use. Delayed by the war, Parsons published a translation of the first four chapters of *Economy and Society*, consulting a short version of the text written by Shils and von Schelting and then revising and expanding work begun by H. M. Henderson at the suggestion of Friedrich von Hayek. This was the only part of *Economy and Society* that Weber had prepared for publication

20 *Democracy in America*, tr. George Lawrence., ed. J. P. Mayer. Garden City, NY: Anchor Books, 1969, p. 287.

shortly before his death in 1920. By giving the chapters the title *The Theory of Social and Economic Organization*, Parsons announced his intention to appropriate Weber for a general theory of society. It was Weber the "theorist" that became Parsons's model. In publishing *The Methodology of the Social Sciences*, Edward Shils (with the assistance of Henry Finch) released for public scrutiny most of his decades-long quest to master Weber's philosophy of science in translation, introducing readers to commentary on the "ideal type" and a concept of "value neutrality" in place of Weber's proposal for "value freedom" (*Wertfreiheit*). Finally, by 1958 different translators had published all of what remained of Weber's writings in the *Gesammelte Aufsätze zur Religionssoziologie*, though Weber's original three volumes were out of sequence and in five different books – a situation that has never been rectified, even though Parsons and others had warned from the beginning about the looming confusion in understanding the structure of Weber's arguments. Regardless of the vicissitudes of partial and piecemeal translations, by 1960 in the Anglophone world a substantial body of Weber's writings were widely and inexpensively available to scholars, teachers, students and the general public.

Over the last 50 years there has been continuous expansion and refinement of the textual basis of the Weberian project, casting a much wider net for those interested in the work, as Table 2 indicates. The growth of interest has led to the publication of far more accurate retranslations of important texts, such as the widely read 1904 essay on "Objective Knowledge" in the social sciences.[21] But burgeoning interest has also encouraged filling major and minor gaps in the textual record. By far the most significant contribution has been the 1968 publication of the complete English translation of *Economy and Society*, compiled and edited by Guenther Roth and Claus Wittich, and incorporating Parsons's earlier text. This is the monumental text that easily captured first place in the International Sociological Association's survey of the most important books of twentieth century sociology. However, a word of caution is in order about the mythic status of this apparent *summa* of Weber's thought. For as scholars have begun to appreciate, *Economy and Society* is not actually Weber's text, but a posthumous editorial reworking of mainly unfinished manuscripts from his desk. Marianne Weber and Melchoir Palyi produced the first version, and Johannes Winckelmann continued with his own edition. Only with the current work of the editors of

---

21 Max Weber, "The 'Objectivity' of Knowledge in Social Science and Social Policy," in *The Essential Weber: A Reader*, ed. Sam Whimster, tr. Keith Tribe (London: Routledge, 2004), pp. 359–404 (translated by Keith Tribe); and in Max Weber, *Collected Methodological Writings*, ed. Hans Henrik Bruun and Sam Whimster, tr. Hans Henrik Bruun (London: Routledge, 2012), pp. 100–38.

the *Max-Weber-Gesamtausgabe* has it become possible to restore the text to its original form and authorial voice, a project that may yet open new doors onto interpretive possibilities.

Recovering, bringing together, and translating the work has yielded some noteworthy surprises: for instance, the presence of a "structural" perspective in a study like *The Agrarian Sociology of Ancient Civilizations*, published by New Left Books, that seemed to some to have affinities with neo-Marxist class analysis, though it actually revealed a vocabulary Weber shared with Marx and many others in German political economy. In addition, the political commentary in Weber's essays on Russia seemed to anticipate subsequent twentieth-century development and revealed an analytic approach to large-scale social change, if not precisely a "theory" of revolution. Or Weber's early writings on the stock and commodity exchanges, previously unknown outside specialist circles, demonstrated a hitherto hidden side of Weber as a political economist concerned with macro-processes, micro-level choices and their relationship in rule-governed markets. It was only recently that even another two Weber texts were retrieved, both on topics in applied political economy, and published originally in English in the *Encyclopedia Americana* for 1906/07.[22]

The effect of these retrievals and innovative interpretations has been a significant reshaping of the Weberian field of inquiry, an extension of the horizon and an expansion of interests into new and uncharted territory. It has become possible to address Weberian themes and approaches in widely dispersed domains of inquiry, from rational choice theory and formal modeling in the social sciences to the contemporary significance of the religion and civilization of Islam.[23] It is partly in response to such wide-ranging and varied applications that the question of the "paradigmatic" standing of Weberian thought has become timely and relevant.

The identification, translation and analysis of Weber's writings starting in the 1950s and especially in the American universities was important not only for the social science disciplines in the English-language world, but because the intellectual capital generated by this activity became the basis for a reintroduction of Weber's work on the European continent. Indeed, the survival of Weber's thought and the growth of Weberian perspectives in America

---

22 Max Weber, *Wirtschaft, Staat und Sozialpolitik. Schriften und Reden 1900–1912. Ergänzungsheft. MWG I:8*, ed. Wolfgang Schluchter (Tübingen: Mohr [Siebeck], 2005; see Guenther Roth, "Max Weber's Articles on German Agriculture and Industry in the *Encyclopedia Americana* (1906/07) and their Political Context," *Max Weber Studies* 6 (2006), 183–205.

23 See Zenonas Norkus, *Max Weber und Rational Choice* (Marburg: Metropolis Verlag, 2001), and Toby E. Huff and Wolfgang Schlucher, eds., *Max Weber and Islam* (New Brunswick: Transaction, 1999).

was the precondition for his return to Germany after 1945. In some cases outside the German-language sphere the use of Weber's thought had proceeded somewhat independently. In France, for example, there were the early contributions of Raymond Aron and Maurice Halbwachs, although little sustained interest was evident until the postwar work of Julien Freund and Pierre Bourdieu.[24] In Japan, by contrast, a questioning of capitalist modernity and religion produced an early and independent intellectual perspective, with Weber's *General Economic History* translated in 1927, the same year as Knight's English translation, and Kajiyama Tsutomu's translation of *The Protestant Ethic and the Spirit of Capitalism* following in 1938. Other scholars, such as the economist Otsuka Hisao, promoted a continuing exploration of Weber's ideas.[25] But it was obviously in Germany that the postwar reintroduction of Weber's work was felt most keenly. Relying in part on the version of Weberian sociology promoted by American scholars like Parsons or Reinhard Bendix, the efforts in Germany to recover the work achieved public notice and some notoriety during the political struggles and academic debates of the 1960s.[26] Of course, Parsons had rechanneled Weber's ideas into the postulates of systems theory and structural functional analysis, while Bendix had purposefully avoided "general theory" in favor of promoting historical sociology with a Weberian accent. These finer distinctions were often lost in the strains of Weber's uncertain homecoming.

However, the contentious decade of the 1960s turned out to be a prelude to the serious incorporation of Weber's work in the scholarship of the 1980s and afterward, evidenced in Germany in the major and quite different contributions of scholars like Wolfgang Mommsen, M. Rainer Lepsius, Jürgen Habermas and Wilhelm Hennis, and in the United States especially by work in comparative historical sociology, political and economic sociology and investigations of state development. In addition, the critique of modernization theory, an approach closely aligned with the Parsonian version of Weber, was helpful in preparing the way for a full-scale reassessment of Weber's social theory. Indeed, while the growth of Weberian perspectives in the United States was the precondition for the work's international importance, it was also the catalyst for the critical reassessment of Weber's

24 Monique Hirshhorn, *Max Weber et la sociologie française* (Paris: Edition L'Harmattan, 1988).
25 Wolfgang Schwentker, *Max Weber in Japan*, and his article, "The Spirit of Modernity: Max Weber *Protestant Ethic* and Japanese Social Sciences," *Journal of Classical Sociology* 5 (2005), 73–92; also Takeshi Ishida, "A Current Japanese Interpretation of Max Weber," *The Developing Economies* 4 (2007), 349–66.
26 Chronicled in Otto Stammer, ed., *Max Weber and Sociology Today*, tr. Kathleen Morris (New York: Harper & Row, 1971 [orig. 1965]).

contribution, its liberation from limiting preconceptions and the emergence of the idea of a distinctive Weberian approach to knowledge about society.

Conclusion

In my retelling, then, in the United States the organizational and institutional features of the reception of Weber's work were supplemented by the cultural forms of identification between text and reader. This combination of historical and social factors – organizational, institutional and cultural – accounts for the rise to prominence of Weber's work in America.

Yet viewed from a distance, the Weberian "genealogy" has followed a remarkable path: from relative local obscurity, followed by a reputation acquired well outside its cultural home for reasons having little to do with authorial intentions, then a surprising return to its point of origin, and finally emergence into the visibility and vicissitudes of worldwide attention. Today Weberian thought has long since ceased to be bounded by national traditions. It has ventured beyond such limiting horizons and into the international arena of the human sciences.

One obvious result of this long and unusual trajectory, starting in the 1920s and extending into our century, has been the articulation of a "classical" canon of social theory with Weber occupying a central place in the pantheon of major thinkers. In the process, furthermore, Weber has become not simply the theorist of social action and the origins of capitalism, but the thinker addressing the world-historical dynamic of rationalization processes. This is a potent invention, for it connects Weber's thought to *the* most consequential problem of modern social and political life: the dissociation of individual action from the social mechanisms of economic, administrative and legal control. With this fateful turn Weberian social theory now belongs to the Western philosophical tradition. It speaks to the most fundamental questions of the human condition. In addressing such questions, it then becomes possible to speak of a distinctive Weberian perspective, approach, theory or even paradigm.

But today Weber's contributions are not confined only within academic specialties and debates. The ideas have migrated into the sphere of public opinion, political comment and cultural interpretation. The problems of the new century have moved on, and Weber's thought with them. The thought has remained timely because of its immersion in questions about the forces shaping our modern world. As long as such questions persist, Weber's ideas and Weberian theory promise to remain a source of fascination and edification.

APPENDIX

Table 1. Max Weber's Work in English Translation: The Main Books and Articles, 1927–1960

Date	Title	Translator/Editor
1927	*General Economic History*	Frank Knight
1930	*The Protestant Ethic and the Spirit of Capitalism* (GARS I, pp. 1–206)	Talcott Parsons
1946	*From Max Weber: Essays in Sociology*	Hans Gerth & C. Wright Mills
1947	*The Theory of Social and Economic Organization* (EaS, part I, chs. 1–4)	A. M. Henderson & Talcott Parsons
1949	*The Methodology of the Social Sciences* (GAW, pp. 146–290, 451–502)	Edward Shils
1951	*The Religion of China: Confucianism and Taoism* (GARS I, pp. 276–536)	Hans Gerth
1952	*Ancient Judaism* (GARS III)	Hans Gerth & Don Martindale
1954	*On Law in Economy and Society* (EaS, ch. 8)	Max Rheinstein & Edward Shils
1958	*The Religion of India* (GARS II)	Hans Gerth & Don Martindale
1958	*The City* (EaS, ch. 16)	Don Martindale & Gertrud Neuwirth
1958	*The Rational and Social Foundations of Music*	Don Martindale, Johannes Riedel & Gertrud Neuwirth

Table 2. Max Weber's Work in English Translation: The Main Books and Articles, 1960–2012

Date	Title	Translator/Editor
1963	*The Sociology of Religion* (from WuG, Part 2)	Ephraim Fischoff
1968	*Max Weber on Charisma and Institution Building*	S. N. Eisenstadt
1968	*Economy and Society* (WuG)	Guenther Roth & Klaus Wittich
1973	*Max Weber on Universities*	Edward Shils
1975	*Roscher and Knies* (GAW, pp. 1–145)	Guy Oakes
1976	*The Agrarian Sociology of Ancient Civilizations* (GASW, pp. 1–311)	R. I. Frank
1977	*Critique of Stammler* (GAW, pp. 291–383)	Guy Oakes
1979	"Developmental Tendencies in the Situation of East Elbian Rural Labourers" (GASW, pp. 470–507)	Keith Tribe
1980	"The National State and Economic Policy" (GPS, pp. 1–25)	Ben Fowkes & Keith Tribe
1981	"Some Categories of Interpretive Sociology" (GAW, pp. 427–74.	Edith Graber
1985	"'Churches' and 'Sects' in North America"	Colin Loader
1994	*Political Writings* (selections from GPS)	Peter Lassman & Ronald Speirs
1995	*The Russian Revolutions*	Gordon Wells & Peter Baehr
1998	"Preliminary Report on a Proposed Survey for a Sociology of the Press" (from GASS)	Keith Tribe
1999	*Essays in Economic Sociology*	Richard Swedberg
2000	"Stock and Commodity Exchanges" (from GASS)	Steven Lestition
2001	*The Protestant Ethic Debate: Max Weber's Replies to His Critics, 1907–1910*	David Chalcraft & Austin Harrington
2001	*The Protestant Ethic and the Spirit of Capitalism*	Stephen Kalberg
2002	*The Protestant Ethic and the 'Spirit' of Capitalism & Other Writings* (the 1904/05 text)	Peter Baehr & Gordon Wells
2002	*The History of Commercial Partnerships in the Middle Ages*	Lutz Kaelber
2002	"Voluntary Associational Life" (from GASS)	Sung Ho Kim
2004	"Introduction to the Economic Ethics of the World Religions" (from GARS I)	Sam Whimster
2004	"The 'Objectivity' of Knowledge in Social Science and Social Policy" (from GAW)	Keith Tribe
2005	"The Relations of the Rural Community to Other Branches of Social Science"	Peter Ghosh
2012	*Collected Methodological Writings* (GAW)	H. H. Bruun & Sam Whimster

Chapter 8

MAX WEBER ON RUSSIA'S LONG ROAD TO MODERNITY

Sven Eliaeson

Max Weber's writings on Russia have not the reputation of being the peak of his scholarship. Nevertheless they are regarded as a still basically true representation of the Russian predicament, with its obstacles for a normal route to modernity, although Weber's characterization of the Russian Revolution as conducted by "a local sect" might appear as an exaggeration even after *die Wende* and the implosion of the Soviet Empire. Seventy years is a short period in history. Weber dealt with Russian affairs both 1905–6 and 1917–18. His main concern was Germany's security policy but he also felt that constitutional issues were crucial. In fact Wilhelmine Germany and Czarist Russia had a common problem of pseudo-constitutionalism and transformation. According to, among others, Wolfgang J. Mommsen, outmoded forms of state were a main cause for the outbreak of World War I, a tragedy out of control, like a downhill rolling snowball, both Germany and Russia as nonrational actors,

Weber's interests were thus both geostrategic and domestic. Germany experienced itself as encircled by enemies. The eastern border was a soft one, due to a lack of ethnic homogeneity (see Weber 1895).

In an ad hoc speech at the Weber centennial in Heidelberg in 1964, Max Horkheimer recalled how disappointed he was over Weber lecturing on the Russian Revolution, without any indications about what he would advise students to do in their search for policy orientation in turbulent days:

Max Weber lectured on the Soviet system. The auditorium was crowded to its doors, but great disappointment followed. Instead of theoretical reflection and analysis, which, not only in posting the problem, but in every single step of thinking would have led to a reasoned structuring of the future, we listened for two or three hours to finely balanced definitions of the Russian system, shrewdly formulated ideal types, by which it was possible to define the Soviet order. It was all so precise, so scientifically exact, so value-free that we all went sadly home. (Here quoted from Uta Gerhardt 2011: 181)

Reactions from students in search of guidance were like this when Weber delivered his *"Politik als Beruf"* in early 1919. In this popular lecture Weber touched upon the Russian situation. Those in search for "total reason" were not satisfied by the Weberian distinction between science and politics. It is not quite clear if Horkheimer listened to this lecture or the one on "Socialism," held both in Vienna and Munich.[1]

Max Weber was keenly interested in conditions in Russia, as primarily shown in his essays on the Russian prerevolution of 1905 published the following year in *Archiv für Sozialwissenschaft und Sozialpolitik*, a journal for which Weber was a contributing editor.[2] January 1905 brought Bloody Sunday in St. Petersburg, which was followed in May by the Japanese victory over the Russian navy at Tsushima – the first time in modern history that a nonwhite people defeated one of the white colonialist peoples.

The year 1905 was a fateful year in general, with mutinies within the Black Sea Fleet (Battleship Potemkin) and uprisings at the Kronstadt naval base.

The tsar had relinquished his absolute power and Russia was moving toward a parliamentary system; a *Duma* was elected and Russia was suddenly, and for the first time, controlled by a government. However, the tsar still retained sufficient power to oppose the proposed constitution drafted by the Duma, and only the prime minister had the right to request an audience with the tsar.

An election was held in April that made the Constitutional Democrats the strongest group in the Duma. This Duma was dissolved in June 1906, and the newly elected Duma did not convene until February 1907. It was dissolved in June of the same year in connection with a "reactionary" coup in

1   It was formerly believed that the "twin lectures" were given in quick succession in Munich during the revolutionary winter of 1918–19. Later research has persuasively shown that "Science as a Vocation" had been delivered by November 1917. "Politics as a Vocation" was meant as popular education rather than an academic lecture in the strict sense; it was moreover not delivered in a lecture hall but in "Vortragssaal der Buchhandlung Steinicke" in München-Schwabing. Weber had been induced to appear, since *Freistudentischer Bund* had otherwise threatened to invite Kurt Eisner, whom Weber despised; he considered Eisner a traitor because he had in correspondence with US President Wilson accepted the idea of Germany as being to blame for the outbreak of war in 1914 – something Weber moreover considered a tactical move intended to wrest Bavaria from the Little Germany created by Bismarck.
2   English version in Max Weber, *The Russian Revolutions*. Translated and edited by Gordon C. Wells and Peter Baehr, Cambridge: Polity, 1995. The volume is an annotated selection of Weber's writings on Russia, both from 1906 and from near the end of World War I.

which Pyotr Stolypin was advisor to Nicholas II. Stolypin was an impressive figure. During his tenure as prime minister, agrarian reforms were instituted that were intended to establish a modern, capitalist system of agriculture, but the reforms never proceeded beyond half measures because the *mir*, the village communities, demonstrated such serious resistance to development and the abandonment of tradition.

Weber began to analyze conditions in Russia during the period between Bloody Sunday and Tsushima. He quickly learned enough Russian to be able to follow the Russian daily papers. There was a reading room in Heidelberg that had Russian newspapers, but Weber also subscribed to several (as documented by his request to have them forwarded to Flanders while there on a recreation trip).

This interest in Russia had a long prehistory. Max Weber had laid the foundations of his scholarly repute and career with his extensive studies resulting in a work of more than 800 pages on farm workers' conditions east of the Elbe. These studies were sponsored by the *Verein für Sozialpolitik* and are reflected in his inaugural address in Freiburg im Breisgau, "The Nation State and Economic Policy," *Freiburger Antrittsrede*.[3]

Weber is usually ascribed a Russophobic attitude, which may be accurate on a geopolitical level. The German border to Poland coincided with the border to Czarist Russia, and the encircled Germany had an interest in making sure this border toward the east did not become too porous. For this reason, Weber recommended stemming the inflow of guest workers: the Polish peasants were, after all, prepared to "eat grass" and outcompete German smallholders in a kind of reverse social Darwinism.[4] The politically and militarily dominant Junker class had a utilitarian interest in cheap seasonal labor and wanted protectionist tariffs against American competition in the grain market, tariffs which would have conflicted with Germany's national interest in modernization. Agricultural policy is a focal point (*Schwerpunkt*) in Weber's scholarly profile. This was expressed at the 1904 World's Fair in St. Louis, Missouri, where Weber appeared before an audience for the first time in eight years and then chose to speak specifically about German agricultural policy from a historical perspective.

3   Published in 1895. *Der Nationalstaat und die Volkswirtschaftspolitik* is included in *GPS* (Gesammelte Politische Schriften). The English version is found in, for instance, Max Weber, *Political Writings*. Edited by Peter Lassman and Donald Speirs, Cambridge: Cambridge University Press, 1994. There are several translations.
4   See Ola Agevall, "Science, Values, and the Empirical Argument in Max Weber's Inaugural Address," in *Max Weber Studies*, Vol. 4:2 (July 2004), a thematic issue dedicated to Weber's relevance as a theorist of politics, edited by Sven Eliaeson and Kari Palonen.

Weber's Russophobia did not result in any lack of Russian students in Heidelberg, who flocked to the university – and to Weber. So it was more a matter of geopolitics than ethnic stereotypes, which may be noteworthy in light of Weber's disdain for Poles – stereotypes instilled in him during military service in Posen/Poznan.

Agricultural policy is important in Weber's analyses of Russia – he emphasizes the obstacles to efficiency that could have smoothed the way for industrialization and modern capitalism. The liberal Russian *zemstvo* movement[5] held out the promise of a Russian transformation to Western modernity. As prime minister, Sergei Witte advocated the rationalization of Russian society. Earlier, as finance minister, he had worked to improve the infrastructure by means including railway construction, most importantly the building of the Trans-Siberian Railway, which was intended to replace the Suez Canal as a transport route.

That no real revolution came about in 1905–6 was to a large degree the result of peasant lethargy; there were no social movements there of the kind found in France in 1789 or Sweden in the 1430s. Witte resigned when he felt he no longer enjoyed the Tsar's confidence. "Even today, Weber's articles about the Russian Revolution of 1905/1906 can help to illustrate the distance between Russia and the West and to understand the – possibly – irreconcilable Russian conflict between traditionalistic rigidity and desperate struggle for modernization, in short, the chances of Russia's transformation to Western modernity."[6] This was written after *die Wende* and the implosion of the Russian Empire in 1991–92. But civil liberty and the rule of law without administrative arbitrariness ("sultanism" is one term Weber uses to designate the opposite of a legal state)[7] was a utopian goal in a Russia characterized by lethargy and illiteracy, where the rural tradition of *obshchina* presented an obstacle

---

5   *Zemstvo* were nongovernmental base organizations at the regional level, which also arranged national assemblies (after 1903, when they had held an assembly in Schwarzwald, near Schaffhausen). The *zemstvo* movement was dominated by liberal/constitutional goals; it had no official sanction and was stymied by schisms in the Kadet party. See *MWG: Abteilung I: Schriften und Reden*, Volume 10; Max Weber, *Zur Russischen Revolution von 1905*, editor W. J. Mommsen in cooperation with Dittmar Dahlmann, Tübingen 1989: 88 ff. Dittmar Dahlmann characterizes the league of *zemstvo* constitutionalists as a lobbying group for large landowners, but the *zemstvos* were also assembled bodies for local management of road construction, social welfare, trade, tax collection, etc.

6   Karl-Ludwig Ay, "On Some Observations of Max Weber," in Sven Eliaeson & Hans Lödén (eds.), *Nordisk säkerhetspolitik inför nya utmaningar* (Nordic security policy in the face of new challenges), Stockholm: Carlssons, 2002: 88.

7   Borrowing from Juan L. Linz and Alfred Stepan, Archie Brown labels the Ceausescu-family rule in Romania from the 1970s "increasingly sultanistic". (*The Rise and Fall of Communism*, London: The Bodley Head, 2009: 543.)

to private ownership and marginalized the kulaks' relationship to ordinary farmers.[8] Farmland was normally not privately owned but was instead held in common by the village, something that did not promote novel initiatives or improvements in operational efficiency. One might, like Weber, talk about a natural, primitive communism that worked against the pride and ambition that private ownership can evoke.[9] In theory, the land allotments could be redistributed on an egalitarian basis every 15 years within the village community, and it was not until the new Russian Land Code of 2001 that farmers could gain full and unrestricted rights, including the right to buy and sell land. The landowning large farmers and estate owners outside the obshchina system were opposed to the small-scale and hidebound smallhold peasants, among whom the kolkhoz system had, so to speak, ready soil – hence the expression "primitive communism."

As a national liberal German patriot, Weber's interest in the geopolitical dimension and the problems and prospects of liberalism in 1905–1906 makes perfect sense. This was connected to Germany's own preparliamentary state of affairs: a complex federal system with no real parliamentarianism and a Kaiser who was absolute monarch of Prussia and inclined to consider himself the same for all of Germany. Outmoded forms of government were a main cause of the outbreak of World War I – as pointed out by Wolfgang Mommsen, one of the editors of the thick volume of *Max Weber Gesamtausgabe (MWG)*, issued in 1989 and containing Weber's writings on the Russian prerevolution. Mommsen further believes that Weber's writings on Russia *after* the October Revolution should be viewed in light of the situation in Germany at the time. Sham democracy prevailed there under Prince Max von Baden as parliamentary chancellor (that is, reporting to the *Reichstag;* before that, the Reichstag's main power had been to decide on finances, but the chancellor had reported to the Kaiser) during the final phase of Wilhelmine rule, even though Germany was an open society with a dawning party system and free media. Weber also discussed the nascent Russian party system and the relationship between church and state, two interests dear to his heart. The Orthodox Church's repudiation of the profane world did not make modernization any easier. The divorce between the Eastern and Western churches of 1054 still has its acknowledged predictive force.

---

8   *Obshchina* refers to peasant communes (cooperative communities) responsible for (re) allocation of land, and collectively responsible for taxes until 1903, as well as for law enforcement.

9   Richard Pipes is the scholar on Russian affairs who has most energetically propounded the significance of private property rights. See, for example, "Max Weber and Russia," in *World Politics*, Vol. 7:3 (1955): 371–401.

Weber's concern with Russia has an interesting sequel. After the war, he was forced to support himself – his mother Helene had invested the family fortune in German war bonds, which became worthless after the war – and was a probationary employee in Vienna, but after a year in that city, he chose to accept an offer at Ludwig Maximilian University in Munich to succeed Lujo Brentano. He had several alternatives to choose among, including Bonn. He had not enjoyed bustling Vienna, where he was forced to jostle with *profanum vulgus* on the streetcars. (In addition, his employer forgot to pay him on time. In Munich, he was also closer to his mistress, Else Jaffé von Richthofen).

Weber's lecture, "Socialism," given to Austrian military officers (later also held in Munich) is an intriguing document – a sort of bouillon cube or distillate of his political analyses.[10] Here, he thoroughly explores *The Communist Manifesto*, which he deems to have certain scholarly qualities (see Jessop 2010). He cautions against a system in which both economic and administrative power are held in a single hand and deems the Russia that had been taken over by a "local sect" a huge experiment. Also telling is a famous argument at the Café Landtmann in Vienna between Weber and Joseph Schumpeter, when Weber became so incensed that he forgot his hat upon his hasty departure, witnessed by a Swiss-Austrian banker Felix Somary, who recounts the incident in his memoirs. Actually, there was cognitively more that united Weber and Schumpeter than divided them – but while "Schumpy" welcomed an interesting, full-scale social experiment, Weber was more civic-minded and inclined toward an ethos of responsibility. One should keep in mind that Weber had lived through the Bavarian Soviet Republic in 1919, was dragged into its aftermath and became a character witness who probably saved the life of Ernst Toller, victor at Dachau, in the vanguard of a hastily assembled army of workers and peasants. The third and final phase of the Bavarian Revolution was dominated by communists (including Eugene Leviné and Ret Marut) and a number of stark raving mad, psychopathic Russian anarchists who instituted, among other things, a curfew for "bourgeois" elements and a court-martial to deal with violations.

Weber died in June 1920 of complications from pneumonia. If we were to apply the Lazarus-approach, "what would Weber say today, if reawakened from the dead ones?" the lecture on "Socialism" is possibly the best source for speculation and counterfactual reasoning.

In connection with the 1917 revolutions, Weber wrote, as noted, about Russia's transition to sham democracy. His perspective focused on the prospects

---

10 "Sozialismus" is included in *GPS* but is also available in English-language anthologies, such as Max Weber, *Political Writings*, Cambridge: Cambridge University Press, 1994; originally published as a pamphlet in Vienna 1918, a lecture given to Austrian officers by invitation of the Hapsburg *Feindepropaganda-Abwehrstelle*.

for a stable peace between Russia and Germany. In the popular outline lecture "Politics as a Vocation" of January 1919, Weber touches upon conditions in Russia. One should remember that immediately after World War I, there was a fear that Bolshevism would prevail, and socialist revolts were by no means unusual. For a time, Bavaria was joined by Hungary and Saxony as Soviet Republics, Finland had experienced a bloody civil war and the Spartacists rose up in Berlin. And the Ruhr region was a hotbed of revolutionary activity. The danger was not averted until the "Miracle at the Vistula" in August 1920 when Pilsudski vanquished a much larger Russian army outside Warsaw (see Davies 2003).

Weber tended to overestimate "soldier's communism," the revolutionary potential of homeward-bound troops, yet underestimate the leaders of the Bolshevik regime, whom he regards as *café literati*, a category he consistently disparaged. The assimilation of soldiers who had served at the front into society is one of Weber's main reasons for advocating the full implementation of democracy in Germany as well, which is best evinced in "Suffrage and Democracy in Germany," perhaps the most important of his political writings during the war, in some competition with "Parliament and Government in Germany under a New Political Order," which Johannes Winckelmann preferred to regard as the draft of a never accomplished Weberian political sociology of the state (see later).

"*Wahlrecht und Demokratie in Deutschland*" was published first as a pamphlet, number 2 of a series, *Der deutsche Volksstaat: Schriften zur inneren Politik. Parlament und Regierung im neugeordneten Deutschland: Zur politischen Kritik des Beamtentums und Parteiwesens* (Munich & Leipzig 1918) based on five articles first published in the liberal *Frankfurter Zeitung* between April and June 1917. According to Weber, the delay was due to the "usual technical difficulties of printing" (quoted from *Political Writings*: 130), most likely a euphemism for difficulties with wartime censorship. Weber's criticism of the Kaiser's dilettantish interventions in politics made these texts controversial. Weber was at times close to being charged with lese majesty. Johannes Winckelmann, co-creator with Bernhard Pfister of the Max Weber Archives in Munich, actually compiled a Max Weber: *Staatssoziologie* based primarily on Weber's more exhaustive wartime articles in *FZ* and published as a supplement to *WuG*. It should be noted that *GPS* can be downloaded for free from Potsdam University. The various issues preserve the original pagination, which makes them more useful for researchers.

After the implosion of the Russian Empire in the early 1990s, the question was asked as to which classics of social science were significant for the understanding of both ongoing and imminent transformation processes. The answers have varied, but Max Weber has been a favorite alongside Talcott

Parsons, Karl Polanyi, Carl Schmitt, Joseph Schumpeter, Gunnar Myrdal, Karl Marx and S. N. Eisenstadt. Randall Collins (1986, esp. chap. 8, "The Future Decline of the Russian Empire") identified the tensions that would lead to the breakdown of the USSR, although he did not manage to predict when it would occur. Considering that several other roads to modernity already exist elsewhere in Europe, it is a reasonable prediction that whichever version Russia chooses, it will be path dependent. But "path dependence" is a truism; all nations are "dinosaurs" controlled by formative historical memories. For more "flesh on bones," see Liah Greenfeld (1992).

There has been an abiding antagonism or tension between history and theory ever since the days of Comte and Ranke. Particularisms and *Sonderwege* imply a nomothetic ideal as a contrast, which seems at once unattainable, perpetually "on the horizon." It may be legitimate to create new taxonomies, today dependent upon globalization having reached qualitatively new levels that have put older modernization theories (e.g., Parsons' and Stein Rokkan's) in mothballs before we have found new instruments.

In the current Russian reception of Weber, focus is primarily on the basis of legitimacy and aspects of the sociology of religion. Russia today is postsecular and the Orthodox Church is playing a key role in the government's legitimization process, a notion that can be supported in many ways, including quantitative media studies. Weber did not develop any ideal type of democratic legitimacy, although he may have considered doing so toward the end of his life.[11] To him, democracy was a subtype of what he called charismatic legitimate rule, which was inherently a nonstable transitional form between traditional legitimacy and the legal-rational legitimacy of modern government. Weber overestimated the role of charisma, but here he still feels refreshingly au courant: Singapore indicates that a calculable legal state is more important than "democracy" (polyarchy and open society).

No dedicated "value rational" democrat, Weber was instead a rational or "functional" democrat, defined more by an ethos of responsibility than by an ethos of conviction. His first priority was to integrate the working class into the German nation and modernize the German polity, to develop Germany from

---

11 This is the same problem Guenther Roth deals with in *The Social Democrats in Imperial Germany* (Totowa, NJ, 1963). I will otherwise refrain here from going any deeper into the widespread controversy that followed Wolfgang Mommsen's famous dissertation on Max Weber and German politics (1959, English translation of the second edition, as *Max Weber and German Politics 1890–1920*, Chicago 1984), regarding Weber's pragmatic "contextual" approach to the appropriate balance between parliamentary power and presidential authority. See also Sven Eliaeson, "Constitutional Caesarism: Weber's Politics in their German Context," in Stephen Turner (ed.), *The Cambridge Companion to Weber*, Cambridge: Cambridge University Press, 2000.

Machtstaat to *Volksstaat*. Accordingly, he advocated the institution of parliamentarianism and full political rights, including for the working class.

There is much to say about the concept of charisma – both its interpretation and operationalization are relatively complex matters, and Weber himself had an ambivalent attitude toward rapture versus reason. He could probably find the prospects for a successful Russian jump start to modernity appealing, provided that this circumvented the rigid bureaucracy of the West, molded by the iron cage of rationality. After all, the functions of charisma include generating meaningful new values. But the irreversible trend of rationalization is the cognitive main tendency in the Weberian view on history. Russia is a country that seems always to have been on the way toward Western modernity (Steiner 2010) – but obviously slowly, and in a way punctuated by savage kicks and starts. Ivan the Terrible, Peter the Great, and Lenin/Stalin are all coworkers in the same long-term project, while liberal-constitutional forces have never really been given the chance.[12]

If one comes across the term neo-Weberianism, there is reason for skepticism: the term does not exist in Weberology. It is hardly wrong as a designation for Michael Mann and Randall Collins, but neither of them have any acknowledged role in Weberology – they are rather typical examples (setting aside their other merits) of the iconographic use of Weber. From a longer time perspective, it is noteworthy that Pitirim Sorokin[13] carried Weber with him in his baggage to the United States and that there may be a line of influence to Parsons, for whom, according to some, Sorokin was the model for his Weber-inspired system construction. Igor S. Kon wrote a widely used textbook in which Weber plays a prominent role.[14] Alexander von Schelting occupied himself a great deal with both Weber and Russia – but as far as I know, not at the same time or combined.[15]

12 In common with Prussia, Tsar Peter's role model was the Swedish Oxenstiernian state bureaucracy, impartial and rational, which has perhaps not been given the attention it deserves. But transferring the Swedish model to the conditions of the peasants was difficult because of translation problems, since the relevant words do not exist in the Russian language. Torkel Jansson writes on the subject in *Rikssprängningen som kom av sig: finsk-svenska gemenskaper efter 1809* (An unsuccessful dismemberment of a realm: Finnish–Swedish relations after 1809), Stockholm: Atlantis, 2009.

13 Pitirim Sorokin is one of the most influential migrants in sociology. His life trajectory is dramatic. Among other things, he was sentenced to death in Russia and put on the "philosophers' ship" in 1921 with intellectuals expelled from the Soviet nation. His background is partly Finnish.

14 Igor S. Kon, *Der Positivismus in der Soziologie: Geschichtlicher Abriss*, Berlin: Akademie Verlag, 1968.

15 Alexander von Schelting, *Max Webers Wissenschaftslehre: das logische Problem der historischen Kulturerkenntnis: die Grenzen der Soziologie des Wissens*, Tübingen 1934, and *Russland und der Westen im russischen Geschichtsdenken der zweiten Hälfte des 19. Jahrhunderts, aus dem Nachlass herausgegeben und bearbeitet von Hans-Joachim Torke*, Wiesbaden: Harrassowitz, 1989.

There are significant parallels between Weber and Lenin when it comes to viewing imperialism as the highest stage of capitalism, although from different value premises. Both apply the British economist Hobson's theories on imperialism and business cycles, and Weber's power realism (in the same tradition as Thomas Hobbes and later Henry Kissinger and Hans Morgenthau) leads him to advocate German participation in the hunt for colonies as an aspect of the European balance of power. In terms of foreign relations, Weber was closer to Hitler than to Bismarck. One should add that Hitler's programs essentially coincided with the principles of most of the major parties in the Weimar Republic; the difference was the brutal means Hitler employed to implement the program.

Weber's work on the Protestant ethic and the spirit of capitalism makes up Part I of his posthumously published *GARS* (*Gesammelte Aufsätze zur Religionssoziologie*) and must be depressing reading for a Russian whose home is east of the famed divide of 1054.[16] Entrepreneurialism and Protestant virtues seemingly have a positive correlation, which is also supported by Estonia's great successes compared to its neighbors, with the laggard of Greece a fine complementary illustration. More recent survey research seems to suggest that the main line of demarcation in attitudes is not between Protestant and other Christian churches, but between Protestantism and Roman Catholicism on one side and Orthodoxy on the other.[17] Karl Schlögel's studies of urban culture point in the same direction. West of the 1054 divide, the center of the village is not the sole province of the church but is shared with the town hall. The virtues of civil society and its institutions are gradually diluted in the porous *Kresy* of Poland. *Magdeburger Stadtrecht* reached Kiev but no further.

One may speak of a delayed reception of Weber everywhere – more delayed in Eastern Europe than in the West. *WuG* was translated at the same time it was deconstructed in *MWG* to its composite parts. The details are rather complex, and I will not go into them here. There is a Weber reception

16 Weber's work on the Protestant ethic and the spirit of capitalism was published first as an essay in two parts in *Archiv* ... 1905 and in a second edition as a book in 1920. It is included as the first section of *GARS (Gesammelte Aufsätze zur Religionssoziologie)*, Weber's main historical-empirical work. His so-called sect essays of 1906 (*"'Kirchen' und 'Sekten'"*), were written under the impression of having visited hillbilly relatives in Mt. Airy, NC, during his long journey in America, were published in two parts in *FZ*. The text is a shortcut to Weber's Calvinist thesis and its routinization (*"Der Puritaner wollte Berufsmensch sein, wir müssen es sein"*). English edition (Max Weber, "Churches and Sects in North America") in the ASA journal *Sociological Theory*, Vol. 3:1 (Spring 1985). Weber's method here can most closely be characterized as participatory observation and the predestination doctrine of the Calvinist thesis becomes very clear.

17 Bernhard Weßels (2010) "Religion and Economic Virtues," in Eliaeson & Georgieva (eds.), *New Europe: Growth to Limits?* Oxford: Bardwell Press, 2010.

also east of the Curzon line, with Davydow and I. S. Kon, but not really at the research frontier.

Weber's long obsession with Russia mainly depends on security policy concerns – but another dimension is that Russia and Germany had similar problems of renovating their forms of state into modernity and full-fledged mass democracy.

Bibliography

Agevall, Ola (2004) "Science, Values, and the Empirical Argument in Max Weber's Inaugural Address," in *Max Weber Studies*, Vol. 4:2 (July 2004).

Ay, Ludwig (2002) "On Some Observations of Max Weber," in Sven Eliaeson & Hans Lödén (eds.): *Nordisk säkerhetspolitik inför nya utmaningar* [*Nordic Security Policy in the Face of New Challenges*], Stockholm: Carlssons.

Breuer, Stefan (1998) "The Concept of Democracy in Weber's Political Sociology," in Ralph Schroeder (ed.): *Max Weber, Democracy, and Modernization*, Basingstoke: Macmillan.

Brown, Archie (2009) *The Rise and Fall of Communism*. London: Bodley head.

Collins, Randall (1986) *Weberian Sociological Theory*. Cambridge: Cambridge University Press.

Davies, Norman (2003 [1972]) *White Eagle, Red Star: The Polish-Soviet War, 1919–20*, London: Macdonald (first ed, this book has many editions).

Davydov, Yuri N & Piama P. Gaidenko (1992) *Russland und der Westen*. Frankfurt/Main 1995 (Heidelberger Max Weber-Vorlesungen 1992).

Eliaeson, Sven (2000) "Constitutional Caesarism: Weber's Politics in their German Context," in Stephen Turner (ed.), *The Cambridge Companion to Weber*, Cambridge: Cambridge University Press.

Gerhardt, Uta (2011) *The Social Thought of Talcott Parsons. Methodology and American Ethos*. Farnham: Ashgate.

Greenfeld, Liah (1992): *Nationalism: Five Roads to Modernity*. Cambridge, MA: Harvard University Press.

Jessop, Bob (2010) "The Communist Manifesto as a Classic Text," in Sven Eliaeson & Nadezhda Georgieva (eds.), *New Europe: Growth to Limits?* Oxford: Bardwell, 199–219.

Kon, Igor S (1968) *Der Positivismus in der Soziologie: geschichtlicher Abriss*. Berlin: Akademie-Verlag.

Lassman, Peter & Speirs, Ronald (eds., 1994) *Max Weber: Political Writings*. Cambridge: Cambridge University Press.

Linz, Juan & Stepan, Alfred (1996) *Problems of Democratic Transition and Consolidation*. Baltimore & London: Johns Hopkins.

Mommsen, Wolfgang J. (1984[1974, 1959]) *Max Weber and German Politics 1890–1920*. Chicago 1984 (English transl of 2nd ed. from 1974. Chicago: University of Chicago Press.

Pipes, Richard (1955) "Max Weber and Russia," in *World Politics*, Vol. 7:3: 371–401.

Roth, Guenther (1963) *The Social Democrats in Imperial Germany*. Totowa, NJ: Bedminster.

von Schelting, Alexander (1934) *Max Webers Wissenschaftslehre: das logische Problem der historischen Kulturerkenntnis: die Grenzen der Soziologie des Wissens*. Tübingen: Mohr.

————(1989) *Russland und der Westen im russischen Geschichtsdenken der zweiten Hälfte des 19 Jahrhunderts, aus dem Nachlass herausgegeben und bearbeitet von Hans-Joachim Torke*. Wiesbaden 1989.

Schlögel, Karl (2003) *Im Raume lesen wir die Zeit: Über Zivilisationsgeschichte und Geopolitik*. Munich & Vienna: Hanser.

Steiner, Helmut (2010) "'Russia in Europe': A Historical and Topical Debate," in Sven Eliaeson & Nadezhda Georgieva (eds.), *New Europe: Growth to Limits?* Oxford: Bardwell Press.

Weber, Max (1995) *The Russian Revolutions.* Translated and edited by Gordon C Wells and Peter Baehr. Cambridge, UK: Polity Press.

Abbreviations of collections from his work:

GARS = Gesammelte Aufsätze zur Religionssoziologie

GAW = Gesammelte Aufsätze zur Wissenschaftslehre

GPS = Gesammelte politische Schriften

MWG = Max Weber Gesamtausgabe.

———(1994 [1895]) "The Nation State and Economic Policy" (*"Der Nationalstaat und die Volkswirtschaftspolitik,"* so-called Freiburger Antrittsrede, in Lassman and Speirs (1994 eds): Cambridge, UK: Cambridge University Press.

———"Socialism," in Lassman & Speirs (eds): 272–303.

———"Suffrage and Democracy in Germany," in Lassman & Speirs (eds): 80–129.

Weßels, Bernhard (2010): "Religion and Economic Virtues," in Eliaeson & Georgieva (eds.), *New Europe: Growth to Limit?* Oxford: Bardwell Press.

Chapter 9

THE RELIGION OF CHINA AND THE PROSPECTS OF CHINESE CAPITALISM

Jack Barbalet

Introduction

Max Weber's *The Religion of China* is a work of remarkable synthesis, effectively summarizing the broad findings of European scholarship on China up to the time it was written. While Weber drew on a large literature it is not always possible to know what his sources are because of frequent inaccurate attribution and inadequate referencing, repeated in the English translation (van der Sprenkel 1954, 275). This situation has been corrected with the modern German edition in which there is a rectified and complete bibliography (Schmidt-Glintzer and Kolonko 1991). Excluding his own texts Weber referred to 159 titles in *The Religion of China*. While not all of these are about China the vast majority of them are, so that the work represents an encyclopedic foray in earlier and contemporary sinology. A long footnote that constitutes a partial bibliographic essay, in which Weber displays an erudite grasp of scholarly commentary and analysis as well as documentary sources, concludes with the following disclaimer:

> I did not have an expert sinologist to cooperate on the text or check it. For that reason the volume is published with misgivings and with the greatest reservation. (Weber 1964, 252)

Nevertheless, it is generally agreed, Weber's discussion remains more or less true to the state of knowledge and historical conventions that run through his sources including a characterization of Confucianism essential for his argument, which shall be addressed in the next section.

Weber's ability to assimilate a vast body of literature, his scrupulous attention to detail and his incessant quest to derive meaning from information leads him to pose important questions concerning Chinese history, society and thought, and the insights he provides in answering them continues to impress his readers, including experienced China scholars. At the same time such scholars cannot fail to notice not only limitations in Weber's sources but also in his own account that is based upon them. The character of Weber's sources and his acceptance of their rendition of Chinese culture are indicated in the following section, which outlines the sinological apprehension of Confucianism as orthodoxy, on which Weber bases the second half of *The Religion of China*. It must be remembered, however, that Weber is concerned not only with what he calls Chinese 'mentality.' *The Religion of China* presents a detailed and often sophisticated outline of political and social institutions, as indicated in the third section of the paper, not always appreciated by commentators on Weber's work. Another aspect of *The Religion of China* not adequately acknowledged is that its discussion of the relationship between values and economic orientation differs in significant ways from its ostensible source in *The Protestant Ethic and the Spirit of Capitalism*, the details of which are set out in the fourth section below.

The purpose of Weber's discussion of Confucianism is to demonstrate its unsuitability for provision of a capitalist spirit, to inculcate a practice of 'calling' ensuring single-minded devotion to this-worldly orientation. It is shown below that Confucianism, while itself not directed to money-making for its own sake, entails self-cultivation practices that did achieve such a purpose when taken up by market actors in Qing China. It has to be added that such actors were not involved in the construction of modern capitalism and the final section of the paper returns to an aspect of Weber's institutional argument to consider how it might contribute to our understanding of why this was so. It is shown that Weber's institutional argument is itself in need of correction. Finally, the conclusion suggests that Weber's view concerning the impossibility of modern capitalism in China was simply premature, and that his method ill-equipped him in understanding why.

Confucianism Revealed

An underlying assumption of Weber's account in *The Religion of China*, and a major tenet of his argument concerning the failure of modern capitalism to develop in China, is the claim that Confucianism constitutes an orthodoxy against which all other creeds are heterodox. It is necessary to describe this representation of Confucianism as an assumption and not a fact because it is in many ways an invention of European sinology and betrays the latter's missionary roots. This is not to doubt the historic figure Kongzi (literally Master Kong), a teacher and political aspirant who lived during the Spring and Autumn period (771–476 BC) of Chinese history. This and the subsequent

Warring States period (476–221 BC) were marked by political upheaval, realignments of political alliance and protean statecraft. A feature of these times was the formation of itinerate colleges of political and military advisers, led by a leading thinker, offering their services to competing states and their princes. Kongzi was one of a number of such thinkers who populated this period of Chinese history.

While Kongzi and Mengzi are relatively unfamiliar names, although known to Weber (1964, 113, 124), their Latin transliterations, 'Confucius' and 'Mencius,' respectively, given by members of the sixteenth-century Jesuit mission to Beijing, are universally familiar. The Jesuit missionaries were also responsible for constructing from broader currents what became known as 'Confucianism' (Jensen 1997). The missionary interest in China has been not only to convert the Chinese to Christianity but also to interpret Chinese traditions in such a manner as to make the Chinese amenable to conversion, finding 'equivalent' Chinese terms for Christian notions and personalities or roles (Wong 2005). According to Jensen (1997, 33):

> For sixteenth-century Chinese, the native entity, Kongzi ... was the object of an imperial cult, the ancient ancestor of a celebrated rhetorical tradition, and a symbol of an honored scholarly fraternity (the *ru*, or 'Confucians') represented by a phalanx of officials who staffed every level of the imperial bureaucracy. But before the eyes of clerics newly arrived from the West he appeared as prophet, holy man and saint.

Although Weber does not relate this history in *The Religion of China*, he effectively enacts it when he claims that the 'canonization of Confucius is the first certain example of a historical figure becoming a subject of worship' (Weber 1964, 174). The context of this remark is a discussion of the 'functional' deities of the 'official Chinese state cult,' but the footnote attached to it provides no source for or elaboration of this unlikely claim but distractingly refers to canonization in the Catholic church (Weber 1964, 290n3). And yet this is an appropriate indicator if it implicitly acknowledges the responsibility of Matteo Ricci, the leader of the sixteenth-century Jesuit mission to Beijing in this 'canonization' rather than that of Chinese officials as Weber implies.

The Jesuit approach, of Christian 'accommodation' with Confucianism, was based on the idea that Confucianism constituted an advanced ethical monotheism which took the form of a natural religion. The European Enlightenment notion of 'natural religion' supposed a pagan morality absent of miracle, revelation or sacrament. The Jesuit construction of Confucianism was highly influential in subsequent European thought, which extolled the virtues of moral Confucian China against corrupt aristocratic Europe, especially in the works of Quesnay, Leibniz and Voltaire (Hudson 1961, 319–25; Zhang 1998, 99–101). While the eighteenth century European vision of China lost its political and popular appeal after the French Revolution as both Europe and China underwent significant transformations that led to a more negative image of China as stagnant and uncivilized (Hudson 1961, 326–28) – an image borrowed by Weber (1964, 55) and explained in terms of bureaucratic ossification (Weber 1964, 60, 151–52) – the missionary and sinological representation of Confucianism persisted into the nineteenth century and beyond. This representation included the idea that Confucianism was originally a native Chinese religion. Weber is both true to this interpretive tradition and also dissents from it. In addition to the supposed canonization of Confucius, he holds that Confucius claimed that the 'order of the world … could not be retained without belief [and therefore] the retention of religious belief was politically even more important than was the concern for food' (Weber 1964, 143). There is no attribution here but the most likely reference is *Analects* Book 12 Chapter 7 in which the belief referred to, according to the Legge translation used by Weber, is not religious but the people's 'faith in their rulers'; this latter cannot 'be dispensed with' even though 'military equipment … [and] food' may be 'part[ed] with' (Legge 1971, 254). In spite of these contortions the sacralization of Confucius and Confucianism undertaken by missionaries from the sixteenth to the nineteenth centuries is not completely accepted by Weber, who goes on to insist that Confucianism is not a religion (Weber 1964, 146, 156). This is largely a consequence of Weber's rejection of the idea of natural religion and his insistence that religion must operate through explicitly God-embracing beliefs and devotional piety.

The earlier Jesuit tendency to set themselves as the true and loyal interpreters of Confucius and Confucianism led to the idea that this tradition of thought constitutes an orthodoxy that is not only opposed to Daoism and Buddhism but that it is 'misunderstood and betrayed' by the revisionist and synthesizing neo-Confucian scholars from the Song dynasty (Zhang 1998, 103). The notion of Confucian orthodoxy is continued by nineteenth- and twentieth-century sinologists (Legge 1880; de Groot 1912) and advocated by Weber, who follows their example. Weber so closely adopts the missionary sinologists' approach that he disregards or is unaware of neo-Confucianism. His insensitivities to developments in Confucian thought has given rise to criticism (Metzger 1977); although others, while acknowledging the fact, see it as methodologically explicable (Schluchter 1989, 112). Weber's wholesale acceptance of the idea that there is throughout imperial Chinese history a Confucian orthodoxy blinds him to the significance of Buddhism after the third century and its transformation of Chinese thought and practices (Gernet 1995; Qi 2014, 105–28), a significance one writer sees as a hidden force of modernization in China (Buss 1985, 84). Weber is oblivious to the periods of Buddhist influence, indeed dominance, where he assumes a continuing and undifferentiated Confucian presence (Collins 1990b, 59) and philosophical hegemony from the eighth century (Weber 1964, 165). With the exception of a brief, inadequate, confused and misleading discussion in a mistitled section of Chapter 7 of *The Religion of China* (Weber 1964, 195–96; see also 217), he has nothing to say about Buddhism in China, sinicized from the third century, and its influence on social organization and economy. The closest he comes to recognition of its significance is to acknowledge 'the profound traces' left by 'popular Buddhism' on the 'workaday life of the masses' (Weber 1964, 234).

The supposed orthodoxy of Confucianism is almost entirely a European projection (Barbalet 2014a, 290–95). Chinese state adoption of Confucianism, unlike European state assertion of Christianity, served internal organizational purposes and did not entail enforced doctrinal adherence of state subjects. It is often noted that during the Han dynasty (206 BC to 220 AD) Confucianism was an 'official ideology' and therefore a state 'orthodoxy' (Balazs 1966, 18–19; Gernet 1996, 159–60). But the application of these English language terms to the Han court requires careful qualification. The regulation of both the court elite and state administration through Confucian humility, docility, submission and seniority-hierarchy as well as inculcation of its doctrines, prescribing elite-group membership, did not preclude alternate currents in the broader society (Balazs 1966, 156–57) nor did it threaten 'the eclectic character of intellectual life at the Han court' (Gernet 1996, 160). Even the imperial civil service examination system, based on recitation of the Confucian classics, was not to establish or maintain orthodoxy but rather to promote a 'way of thought' (Weber 1964, 121) that both preserved privilege and encouraged status group formation (Weber 1964, 46, 86, 117).

Chinese officials during the period that Weber treats were not interested in the beliefs of the religions and movements they opposed. It is only when such forces mobilized against the state, or through their behavior, including expression of strong emotion or particularistic attachment, were seen as constituting a threat to public order, that the state attempted to control them: 'It was not philosophical or theological objection but practical political consideration that was the leading motivation for the traditional antagonism towards heterodoxy' (Yang 1961, 193). Indeed, the imperial state did not legislate for beliefs nor advocate doctrine. In matters of worship Chinese state officials, as Watson (1993, 96) puts it:

> were not concerned with ... mental constructs; what mattered was which deities people chose to worship, not what they believed about them. The state stressed

form rather than content. There was never any attempt to foster a standardized set of beliefs in Chinese religion.

The unity of the Chinese state was achieved not by orthodoxy, as Weber supposes and the sinologists of his day maintained, but orthopraxy – not rightness of belief but of practice. Weber's concern with orthodoxy simply fails to understand the nature of Chinese culture and mentality as based on orthopraxy and its significance for political rule.

Weber found the missionary sinological crystallization of a Chinese orthodox 'mentality' in Confucianism as an ideal device by which to demonstrate his purpose of showing that the cultural basis of modern capitalism is located only in the history of European developments. The missionary contrast of Christianity and Confucianism, their juxtaposition in a common moral universe as distinct but competing ethical discourses, permits Weber's demonstration that Confucianism has a rational dimension but that 'Confucian rationalism meant rational adjustment to the world' (Weber 1964, 248). What is necessary for the development of capitalism, in Weber's (1964, 248) estimation, however, is 'Puritan rationalism [which] meant rational mastery of the world.' This view is parallel to the seventeenth- and eighteenth-century European complaint against the perceived pacifism and lack of martial courage on the part of Confucian China against the standard of the European elevation of military power and glory (Hudson 1961, 320–21). Weber (1964, 114–15, 169) not only notices the difference between Chinese quiescence and European valiance and striving but he insightfully explains it in terms of the unifying and pacifying consequences of China's imperial political structures against the competitiveness and martial conflict between European principalities and states (Weber 1964, 61–62; see also 103). Each formation, he believes, has a commensurate economic dimension, with the European alone leading to market competition and economic rationality.

The Dual Constitution of *The Religion of China*

Weber's discussion of state forms and relations introduces an institutional argument for which he is seldom given sufficient credit. Indeed, Weber's interpreters typically ignore this aspect of *The Religion of China* and almost exclusively focus on the absence of an appropriate religious tradition in explaining China's failure to experience modern capitalism (Giddens 2011, 177–78; Parsons 1968, 541–42, 577; Schluchter 1989, 103–11). Weber's intention, and what unifies the argument of *The Religion of China*, is to demonstrate the uniqueness of the West in its institutions as well as in the patterns of its thought and values. This purpose would be successful in its own terms if Weber were intent on only comparing civilizations, but in attempting to explain the formation of modern capitalism in Europe and its absence in China in terms of religious beliefs and orientations, the institutional argument and the value argument come into a contradictory relationship with each other. Much of the scholarship on *The Religion of China* resolves this contradiction, however, by simply ignoring the institutional argument as providing an alternative framework to the argument concerning religious traditions.

It is not unusual to hear the complaint from writers close to Weber sources that the English title, *The Religion of China*, fails to match the original *Konfuzianismus und Taoismus*, given by Weber to his essays originally published in 1915 and in augmented form in 1920. Weber's translator, Hans Gerth, writing during the rise of the Cold War in 1951 notes that he 'named this volume *The Religion of China* in order to avoid the isms' of the original title (Weber 1964, ix), although the offending suffixes are retained in the subtitle of the translation, *The Religion of China: Confucianism and Taoism*. A point too frequently ignored, however, is that neither the English title nor the original German indicates the important fact that just over half the book is not primarily concerned with Confucianism or Daoism but with the economic, political and social institutions of early China. Indeed, even astute Weber scholars continue to focus primarily on the argument about Chinese 'mentality,' principally Confucianism, and ignore the institutional argument set out in the work or reduce it to an aspect of the argument concerning Confucian values (Kalberg 2012, 145–64). There is thus a neglected aspect of Weber's approach that is key to his discussion of China (Huang 1994) but not confined to it, namely that he entertains an unresolved dichotomy of institutional and religious factors in the post-*Protestant Ethic* accounts of historic formations.

Weber's signature argument, first outlined in *The Protestant Ethic and the Spirit of Capitalism*, concerns the 'elective affinity' between elements of the Protestant creed and capitalist motivation, the 'influence of certain religious ideas,' as he puts it, 'on the development of an economic spirit, or the *ethos* of an economic system' (Weber 1991, 27). This argument underlies the discussion of Confucian and Daoist 'mentality' in *The Religion of China* in so far as it falls short of the capacity – inherit in Protestantism, according to Weber – to promote the capitalistic ethos. But before writing the *Protestant Ethic*, in his talk on 'The Social Causes of the Decline of Ancient Civilization' delivered in 1886 (Weber 2013), in the discussion of his doctoral dissertation, submitted in 1889, on commercial partnerships in the Middle Ages (Weber 2002), and in key parts of later works, including *Economy and Society* (1978), *General Economic History* (1981), as well as *The Religion of China* (1964), Weber also treats institutional not ideational or value factors as independent variables. In attempting to reconcile the institutional and religious arguments coterminous in *General*

Economic History, Collins (1990a, 21, 33) holds that Weber provides an explana-
tory role to religious organizations not doctrine. But a cursory examination
of the relevant sections of the text reveals that this is not correct (see Barbalet
2008, 166–69). The problem remains of unreconciled contrary arguments
concerning the basis of capitalism in *General Economic History* and, as we shall
see, in *The Religion of China.*

The methodological schizophrenia, of institutional reasoning on the one
hand and arguments based on the causal efficacy of mentality and values
on the other – presented together in a single text – is especially clear in *The
Religion of China* because in it Weber develops a negative case of why modern
capitalism did not develop in the Chinese empire. Weber writes that 'bourgeois
industrial capitalism might have developed from the petty capitalist beginnings' in China but for a number of reasons 'mostly related to the structure
of the state' it was prevented from doing so (Weber 1964, 100). After setting
out the details of this position, Weber changes direction and argues instead
that it was the absence of an appropriate religious tradition that prevented the
advent of industrial capitalism in China.

In addition to recognizing the problematic dualism of the unreconciled
institutional and religious arguments in *The Religion of China,* two further
remarks are called for, one relating to the problematic nature of Weber's
institutional argument and the other to a certain coarsening of the religious
argument as it is presented in *The Religion of China,* against the standard of
The Protestant Ethic. First, Weber's discussion of Chinese institutions is conducted in a largely historical narrative that is source to the construction of
a number of important ideal type conceptualizations, especially concerning
variant bureaucratic and state forms. But as a number of commentators have
shown (Collins 1990b, 58–73; Creel 1977; Faure 2013; Hamilton 1984; van
der Sprenkel 1965; Yang 1964), Weber's historical account is seriously flawed,
partly because of the limitations of the sources on which he drew but also
because of some of his own assumptions. The limitations of Weber's sources
will not be gone into here. In discussion below some problems with Weber's
institutional argument will be explored. Before those matter are dealt with it
can be noted how the argument concerning the religious element in the development of modern capitalism is significantly different in *The Religion of China*
from the presentation in *The Protestant Ethic and the Spirit of Capitalism.*

The Religious Argument Simplex

The continuity of Weber's approach is in the endeavor, in his discussion of
the consequences of Confucianism, to explore 'the influence of certain religious ideas,' as he says in *The Protestant Ethic and the Spirit of Capitalism,* 'on the

development of an economic spirit' (Weber 1991, 27). In the *Protestant Ethic* Weber not only distinguishes but separates the ethos of capitalism from the economic system of capitalism. This is not simply in the fact that the historically novel ethic, of earning money 'purely as an end in itself' conjoined with 'the strict avoidance of all spontaneous enjoyment of life' (Weber 1991, 53), may be 'present before the capitalistic order' (Weber 1991, 55). More to the point, in *The Protestant Ethic and the Spirit of Capitalism,* Weber not only regards the advent of the capitalistic ethic as an unintended consequence of the Protestant Reformation (Weber 1991, 90) but he at the same time insists that he has 'no intention whatever of maintaining such a foolish and doctrinaire thesis as that the spirit of capitalism ... could only have arisen as the result of certain effects of the Reformation, or even that capitalism as a system is a creation of the Reformation' (Weber 1991, 91). Yet he seems to abandon this qualification in *The Religion of China* in the detail of his claims that it is 'the lack of a particular mentality' which has 'handicapped' the emergence of 'rational entrepreneurial capitalism' in China (Weber 1964, 104). Indeed, the last chapter of this work is a finely argued and entirely tendentious demonstration that Confucianism is not identical with European reform religions. Of particular interest in this account is an entirely novel idea that the Puritan ethic goes directly to a capitalistic ethos and that the Christian devout is the capitalist entrepreneur (Weber 1964, 243, 247), a position never entertained in *The Protestant Ethic and the Spirit of Capitalism.*

In his original account of the elective affinity of Calvinist asceticism and capitalist entrepreneurial motivation, Weber links the two through the historical development of the practice of 'calling' or 'vocation' associated with this-worldly or mundane commitments and engagements. He says that a person's calling is in their 'fulfilment of the obligations imposed upon [them] by [their] position in the world' and that this 'valuation of the fulfilment of duty in worldly affairs [is] the highest form which the moral activity of the individual could assume' (Weber 1991, 80). In the *Protestant Ethic* Weber indicates that this sense of a calling operates differentially for the Calvinist ascetic and the capitalistic entrepreneur (Weber 1991, 118–9, 69), and elsewhere, in the vocation lectures (Weber 1970a, 1970b), he applies the notion of calling without a prior religious dedication to a vocation, scientific or political (see Barbalet 2008, 46–74). The point to be made here is that in the *Protestant Ethic,* the religious element is in the historical construction of a representation of self as engaged in a vocation, and the capitalistic element is an adaptation of this form to money making. There is no supposition of identity between the religious ethic and the capitalist ethos except in that each of them assumes the form of a mode of self-control in which impulses are overcome and firmly held this-worldly convictions are realized, through a particular 'clarity of vision and ability to act'

(Weber 1991, 69). There is a further element of the argument in the *Protestant Ethic* that is absent from *The Religion of China*.

The link, between the Calvinist this-worldly religious calling and the capitalistic ethos, that Weber postulates in *The Protestant Ethic and the Spirit of Capitalism* as arising from an historical accident, he says has no continuing role in the development and operation of capitalist economies. Weber (1991, 70) writes that in a society dominated by ongoing capitalist activities, any 'relationship between religious beliefs and conduct is generally absent, and where it exists … it tends to be of the negative sort.' He goes on to add that the 'devotion to the calling of money making,' which underpins the spirit of capitalism, 'no longer needs the support of any religious forces' and that any 'attempts of religion to influence economic life' are experienced as 'unjustified interference' (Weber 1991, 72). Weber's understanding in 1905, when the *Protestant Ethic* first appeared, is that 'the capitalism of to-day, which has come to dominate economic life, educates and selects the economic subjects which it needs' and in doing so it draws 'on a way of life common to whole groups of men [and women]' (Weber 1991, 55). But less than a decade later Weber shifts his views about the moral capacity of those imbued with the capitalist ethos to remain true to the requirements of upstanding conduct he ascribes as necessary for the capitalist system.

In *The Religion of China* Weber spells out the 'indispensable ethical qualities of the modern capitalist entrepreneur' (Weber 1964, 247) in a manner that places the religious component firmly within the economic in a manner at odds with the treatment in the *Protestant Ethic*. The relevant ethical qualities are described as including a 'radical concentration on God-ordained purposes' (Weber 1964, 247). In the context this is required for and supports 'a horror of illegal, political, colonial, booty, and monopoly types of capitalism … as against the sober, strictly legal and the harnessed rational energy of routine enterprise' (Weber 1964, 247). No doubt Weber is on one level responding to the profiteering and racketeering of a wartime economy that was gripping Germany as he wrote. Indeed, in the *General Economic History*, originally given as lectures in 1917, is a similar assessment of requirements for capitalism. Weber says that the development of the concept of calling gave to the 'modern entrepreneur' an ability to provide to his workers who were subject to 'ecclesiastical discipline,' by virtue of his employing them, 'the prospect of eternal salvation' (Weber 1981, 367–68). Here is an acknowledgement that while the religious element did not necessarily operate for the capitalist, the effectiveness of his 'ruthless exploitation' of workers he employed was facilitated by their faithful devotion. But Weber's formulation is ironic, pointing to a religiously informed life 'inconceivable to us now, [which] represented a reality quite different from any it has today' (Weber 1981, 368). He continues by noting that the historically earlier mark of 'ethical fitness ... identified with business honour' was achieved through religious acceptance within Protestant communities (Weber 1981, 368). All of this is now eclipsed in the most unfortunate manner, according to Weber: 'Ascetic religiosity has been displaced by a pessimistic though by no means ascetic view of the world ... [in which] private vices may under certain conditions be for the good of the public' (Weber 1981, 369). Weber concludes the *General Economic History* with a pessimism about capitalism which brings together a now impossible requirement of a conjunction of religion and economics for which the *Protestant Ethic* has little space:

> Economic ethics arose against the background of the ascetic ideal; now it has been stripped of its religious import. It was possible for the working class to accept its lot as long as the promise of eternal happiness could be held out to it. When this consolation fell away it was inevitable that those strains and stresses should appear in economic society which since have grown so rapidly. (Weber 1981, 369)

Through exposure to a war economy, with its felonious opportunities for capital and its infelicitous consequences for labour, Weber effectively revises the schema of differential forms of 'vocation' or 'calling', religious and economic, set out in the *Protestant Ethic*. In the *General Economic History*, and slightly earlier in *The Religion of China*, he uncomfortably melds together religious ascetic and capitalist entrepreneur, at least in his narrative of everyday participation if not in his general ideal type of the conditions necessary for modern capitalism (Weber 1981, 276–78), to which we shall return below.

Confucianism Redux

In the 'Confucianism and Puritanism' chapter of *The Religion of China*, Weber requires a more or less direct Protestant religious contribution to capitalism that Confucianism is necessarily unable to provide. This is a departure from the methodology of the *Protestant Ethic*, although not from the moralizing pragmatics of the *General Economic History*, indicated above, in failing to articulate a differentiation in the form and impetus of distinct callings, religious and economic, each of which corresponds to a respectively distinct 'value sphere.' This latter consideration is a matter which Weber discusses with nuanced sensitivity elsewhere (Weber 1970a, 147). The conflation of religious and economic engagements in *The Religion of China* may be a reflection of Weber's broader preoccupations brought by experience of wartime profiteering, as suggested above, but in any event it reduces the value of his discussion here for understanding the prospects of

a Chinese capitalism. Even more apparent is the distortion of his characterization of Confucian ethics. Weber's purpose in attempting to demonstrate the impossibility of capitalism under conditions of Confucian ethical
norms is to show the veracity of his account of Western capitalism and
its historical uniqueness in terms of the singular European Reformation
from the sixteenth century. But his characterization of Confucianism in
this account is a distortion, and it reveals the need for appreciating not the
ethical but the institutional context, which Weber had earlier attempted to
portray in the work but then abandoned.

In addition to Weber's misleading representation of Confucian ethics the
discussion here shall briefly treat the irrelevance of those ethics for consideration of the prospects of capitalism in China. Weber (1964, 235) characterizes
Confucianism as imbibing only 'adjustment' to the 'conditions of the "world"'
so that any man under its influence 'does not constitute a systematic unity but
rather a complex of useful and particular traits.' He goes on to say that the
Confucian way of life:

> could not allow a man an inward aspiration toward a 'unified personality' …
> [because] life remained a series of occurrences. It did not become a whole
> placed methodically under a transcendental goal. (235)

In his pacific acquiescence the Confucian is merely an outcome of circumstances and without any integrity of his own. This is a theme elaborated by
Weber in his chapter on 'The Confucian Life Orientation' in which it is stated
that 'Confucianism means adjustment to the world' (152), that 'equilibrium of
the soul should and could be attained only if man fitted himself into the internally harmonious cosmos' (153) and that 'Confucianism was only interested in
affairs of this world such as it happened to be' (155). All of this, the quiescence
and malleability of the Confucian self, is socially realized in Confucius' dictum
that 'I bow to the majority,' according to Weber (1964, 163). The difficulty
with this assessment is that it cannot be substantiated, and it is not even clear
that Weber fully believes it himself.

Beginning with the last quotation in the above paragraph, Weber infers an
injunction to 'bow to the majority' from a passage from Confucius which he
quotes as 'Where we are three I find my master' (163). There is no attribution,
but this text is close to *Analects* Book 7 Chapter 21 in the Legge translation that
Weber draws upon, which reads:

> The Master said, 'When I walk along with two others, they may serve me as my
> teachers. I will select their good qualities and follow them, and their bad quali-
> ties and avoid them. (Legge 1971, 202)

Weber's bowdlerization of Confucius's statement and meaning may serve his purpose in characterizing Confucianism as pragmatically unprincipled, but the text itself reveals a stable commitment which assumes a firm discernment, uninfluenced by the flow of events, between appropriate and inappropriate behaviour. Learning from others, as Confucius puts it, is decidedly not a matter of passively following the crowd, as Weber would have it. This removes support from the image of the Confucian as a vacillating uncentred individual without an inner core. Indeed, Weber does acknowledge that there are 'all sorts of particularized affinities to be found between Confucianism and the sober rationalism of Puritanism' (Weber 1964, 161).

When considering the 'Central Concept of Propriety' in Confucianism Weber notices the 'self-control, self-observation and reserve' of the Confucian who 'thought of prudently mastering the opportunities of this world through self-control' (156). This brief description indicates an orientation parallel to the idea of a calling in Protestantism that Weber so clearly elaborates in the *Protestant Ethic*. But in *The Religion of China*, the self-control of the Confucian is sharply contrasted with that of the Puritan (236–48). The discussion here is turgid, passionate and frankly loaded against the possibility of a Chinese capitalism because Confucianism is without the theologically driven angst of the Puritan who in his God-given despair must change the world capitalistically, according to Weber, while the Confucian can only adjust to it. In this contrast 'Nothing conflicted more with the Confucian ideal of gentility than the idea of a "vocation" ' (248). Weber achieves this convenient conclusion by making the Puritan ascetic directly into a capitalist entrepreneur, a move that is not part of the original argument in the *Protestant Ethic* (Weber 1991, 68–71) and requires historical conjuring. At the same time he excludes the possibility of the Confucian construction of calling or 'vocation' itself being transposed from an ethical or bureaucratic practice to a commercial practice involving different sets of people and purposes with a consequent rationalization of the secondary non-Confucian arena, much as he had argued in the *Protestant Ethic* when pursuing the 'influence of certain religious ideas on the development of an economic spirit' (Weber 1991, 27). But in *The Religion of China* Weber's articulation of a direct transformation of a community of worshipers into a class of capitalist entrepreneurs collapses the incremental iteration and social relocation of calling treated in *The Protestant Ethic and the Spirit of Capitalism*, a development that actually occurs in China, unnoticed by him. Weber's denial of a Confucian calling analogous to a Protestant calling is supported by his idea that only the Puritan but not the Confucian experiences tension with the world. But this claim results not only from a lapse of investigation on Weber's part but also of imagination. Any system of thought that postulates a condition from which a present experience departs, to its detriment, generates a type of tension analogous to the Puritan experiences of the difference between the heavenly and earthly kingdoms (Yang 1964, xxxvii). Confucius's inspiration and ethic is premised on such a difference between an ideal state of being, from which present conditions have departed.

While Weber does not entertain the possibility and his approach in *The Religion of China* precludes it, the self-discipline of the Confucian calling was in fact applied in the economic arena during the Qing dynasty (1644–1912). During this period a number of handbooks were published and circulated that were based on Confucian principles but directed to the guidance of merchants in pursuit of their pecuniary careers. In drawing on Confucian self-cultivation practices merchants advanced their commercial interests against their spontaneous impulses and distractions from the purposes of profit making. This is similar to the way in which the development of calling among Calvinists and Puritans was borrowed by early entrepreneurs and applied not to congregational rectitude but to enterprise. Whereas Calvinist doctrine and practice 'led to a fearful demand for economic restriction (and political control) rather than the entrepreneurial activity as Weber has described it' (Walzer 1976, 304), the self-restraint and vocational single-mindedness associated with it enhanced pursuit of profit-making when applied to market engagements. Similarly, while Confucian values could not consistently legitimize the profit motive and market activities (Brook 1997, 33–38) the Confucian self-cultivation practices and sense of calling inculcated by them were effectively applied by businessmen who operated outside the institutional range of the Confucian literati (Lufrano 1997). The merchant handbooks of Qing China effectively transferred the traditional Confucian practices of self-cultivation from the institutions of filial piety and bureaucratic administration to the extraneous non-Confucian practices of the market. The 'inner mental attentiveness' (*jing*) central to Confucian self-cultivation in this new context functioned to first dispel or at least manage the external distractions which might lead 'honourable merchants' to errors of judgment in business and, second, to renounce the appeals of 'gambling, whoring and opium smoking' to which 'petty merchants were particularly attracted' (64). The importance of self-control in suppressing such 'natural' impulses in promoting money-making is explicit in these manuals (63–67).

Institutions with Chinese Characteristics

The failure of the Chinese economy at this time to move from a merchant to a modern industrial form cannot be attributed to the absence of a sense of self-control and purpose of money making associated with Weber's idea of calling. Nor can the predominance of Confucian values be entirely held responsible. While it is possible to show that such values existed, it is more difficult to specify how they may inhibit the activities of those who not only fail to share them but also their exponents. As Weber (1964, 85–86) shows, imperial office permitted the accumulation of varying amounts of wealth. Those officials without mercantile background typically entrusted their accumulated funds to merchants who would manage their investments for them (Elvin 1973, 291–92). At the same time, land-holding families and, especially after the seventeenth century, merchant families routinely financed an able son's study for the imperial examination. In this sense, then, any 'sharp dichotomy between "officials" and "merchants,"' according to Elvin (1973, 292), 'is therefore misleading.' Indeed, value impermissibility is itself likely to be either irrelevant for economic activity or, if effective, will counterintuitively have a positive rather than an inhibitory effect. In discussing the negative values regarding enterprise of the Russian aristocracy, which are in many ways similar to those of Chinese mandarins, Gershenkron (1965) shows that the prevailing preindustrial value system did not prevent industrialization and that the research question might be focused not on how values inhibit entrepreneurial activity but on the propensity of values to change and in response to what factors they may do so (Gershenkron 1962, 68). Gershenkron (1965, 68–69) regards entrepreneurs as 'men who by definition ... may not be orientated in their action by any discernible set of values' who experience 'a far-reaching divorce between their actions and the general value system to which they may still adhere.' In this vein it should be remembered, according to Schumpeter (1980: 190), that anti-capitalist values were rampant during the period of capitalist emergence in Europe, a point he incidentally directs against Weber's Protestant Ethic argument and its underlying ideal-type methodology (191).

It is typical of Weber's ambiguity, concerning what he sees as the factors responsible for the failure of China to experience modern industrial capitalism, that he vacillate between Chinese mentality and Chinese institutions as the determining factors. After treating at length Confucian orthodoxy as the basis of China's economic traditionalism, he concludes the second Part of *The Religion of China* with an apparently definitive statement that the Confucian 'mentality' was 'strongly counteractive to capitalist development' because of its 'autonomous laws' (Weber 1964, 249). But immediately preceding this final sentence of the work, Weber says that the mentality which can be characterized by these 'autonomous laws' is in fact 'deeply co-determined by political and economic destinies.' This ambiguity parallels his conclusion of the first Part of the book in which it is claimed that '[r]ational entrepreneurial capitalism ... has been handicapped' in China 'by the lack of a particular mentality' but also 'by the lack of a formally guaranteed law, a rational administration and judiciary, and by the ramifications of a system of prebends' (104). Given that '[b]oth economic and intellectual factors were at work' (55) it is important to consider what Weber has to say about the former as well as the latter.

The Religion of China opens with a discussion of the history of money in China, moves on to an account of the Chinese city and then provides an important discussion of the development of the imperial state organization and the characteristically Chinese bureaucracy, followed by a treatment of the institutions and organization of rural society, which is then followed by a discussion of the sib or patrilineal kinship clan that concludes the first part of the book. The first chapter of the second part is also occupied with a consideration of a particularly Chinese institution, the literati. This extensive treatment of institutions is entirely comparative insofar as Weber interposes the account of Chinese elements with analogous and contrasting cases drawn from the histories of European and ancient civilizations. Weber's account of Chinese institutions has given rise to reflection and criticism of variable illumination and intensity. It is not possible here to review Weber's complete argument and the discussion it has provoked. The following brief account will be confined to his treatment of the sib (although in what follows the term 'clan' will be used) and its relationship to the prospects of capitalist development. This is because Weber is clearly adamant that the clan is an undisputed inhibitor of capitalist organization, and yet it is implicated in the capitalistic revolution that has gripped China since the 1980s.

Weber points out that kinship, through the clan organization, is the source of not only personalized business dealings but local or village administration and civic regulation involving the maintenance of ceremonies, education, credit provision and welfare as well as protection and the maintenance of order. The clan as a corporate entity owned property, the profit from which was distributed to household heads. Weber says that the form of property held by the clan was confined to landed property as the clan was too irrational to engage in capital investment (Weber 1964, 89, 103). Indeed, Weber's assessment of the clan, and the business of Chinese individuals in general, is that the solidarity of relations through kinship meant that there was 'no rational depersonalization of business' so that for 'the economic mentality, the personalist principle was ... a barrier to impersonal rationalization' (85, 236). To this general assessment Weber provides a series of particular instances. Because the clan supported household self-sufficiency, Weber (1964, 90) says, it was responsible for 'delimiting market developments.' Through kinship relations the clan supported its members against discrimination and thus 'thwarted' labour discipline characteristic of 'modern large enterprise' and the 'free market selection of labour' associated with it (95; see also 97). Finally, the kinship clan was inherently opposed to innovation and fiscal innovation in particular 'met with sharp resistance' (95–96).

Historical research since Weber's time has revised many of his empirical claims. Two points in particular relate to those concerning market inhibition and fiscal innovation. The full extent of market development in China was not appreciated by Weber's sources. It is now known that China experienced significant market generated growth from the late Song dynasty (960–1279), which lasted until the beginning of the nineteenth century (Elvin 1973; Pomeranz 2000). Indeed, Elvin provides much evidence concerning the reach of markets in rural China. He writes that '[i]ncreased contact with the market made the Chinese peasantry into a class of adaptable, rational, profit-orientated, petty-entrepreneurs' and that 'in the course of the seventeenth century the number of market towns ... began to multiply at a rate exceeding that of the population increase' (Elvin 1973, 167, 268). It is by no means clear, therefore, that the lineage clan delimited market developments. Indeed, the clan operated as a market actor and, against the assessment Weber provides and his sources urged, there is evidence that innovative financial devises were developed by clan managers. Lineage trusts operated from the beginning of the seventeenth century with an express purpose 'to amass and incorporate business property and protect it from the predations of household division' (Zelin 2009, 627).

The trust was a device for the rational protection of investment folios based on the lineage organization and which overcame its fiscal limitations:

> While lineage trusts themselves remained closed corporations whose membership was determined by birth, trusts behaved like individuals in the market place, buying and selling salt manufacturing shares and developing portfolios that included both wholly owned family firms and shares in a variety of non-kin ventures ... by the Qing [dynasty], the institution of the lineage trust ... had become a popular device for the protection of investable assets. By creating a trust a successful merchant could keep his company intact, allowing each of his sons to succeed not to bits and pieces of the firm, but to equal shares in an undivided pool of assets that could likewise be passed on to their heirs. (Zelin 2009, 627)

Thus the problem of the clan noted by Weber (1964, 82–83), of the dissipation of capital stock through a 'democratic' inheritance regime, was overcome by a rational innovation unnoticed by his sources.

But not only is there a factual problem with Weber's account of Chinese kinship institutions, his interpretation of the family as an inherently traditional form of organization interferes with his appreciation of its role in enhancing economic prospects, not only Chinese. The idea, forcefully stated in *The Religion of China*, that through kinship obligation the family is a source of traditional constraint that inhibits the capitalist ethos of profit making for its own sake, can also be found in *The Protestant Ethic and the Spirit of Capitalism* when Weber writes that Protestant calling generates emotional detachment and depersonalizes family relations and where he presents early modern European entrepreneurs as individuals free of family ties and traditional obligations (Weber 1991, 70, 107–108; see Barbalet 2008, 216–18). And yet the unit of enterprise and the major proximate sources of entrepreneurial attainment in early modern Europe was not the individual entrepreneur free of family responsibility and commitment but individuals who were economically enriched by kinship networks and marital alliances who thereby had immediate access to reputation, credit and uniquely reliable associates (Grassby 2000), a pattern of familial capitalism that reaches to the present day (Church 1993; La Porta, Lopez-de-Silanes, Shleifer 1999; Zeitlin 1974). Weber excludes consideration of these possibilities by hypothesis. In *The Religion of China* he writes that 'the ascetic sects of Protestantism ... established the superior community of faith and a common ethical way of life in opposition to the community of blood, even in a large extent in opposition to the family' (Weber 1964, 237). It is correct to note that while the clan was 'completely preserved' in China, 'in the occidental Middle Ages it was practically extinct' (86). But it was the Catholic Church, not the Protestant faith, that first discouraged adoption, concubinage, marriages without the woman's consent and similar practices that sustain kinship organization, so that by the ninth century in Europe the nuclear family predominated over the joint or extended family (Greif and Tabellini 2010, 137).

Weber's misapprehension of the role of the family in capitalist prospects and his treatment of the particularism of kinship as necessarily opposed to rationality of enterprise has a further, methodological dimension. This is his conflation of formalism and rationalization that derives from his application of the ideal type form. In an important discussion in which the economically rational contribution of lineage to present-day Chinese capitalist development is outlined, Peng (2005) shows that Weber erroneously assumes that formalism necessarily underwrites rationalism and that in fact informal and personalist factors may contribute to rational economic activities (347–49). Clan organization or kinship lineage can function to rationalize and protect property rights, to facilitate transactions and reduce transaction costs and to provide network benefits, including bridging ties (338–39). The general point, that Weber's insistence that the 'personalist principle was ... a barrier to impersonal rationalization' (Weber 1964, 236), has met widespread criticism in the context of his theory of organization. Selznick's pioneering observation that 'individuals have a propensity to resist depersonalization, to spill over the boundaries of their segmentary roles, to participate as *wholes*' led him to appreciate the interplay of 'informal associations' and 'the formal system' through 'unwritten laws' and the corollary that to 'recognize the sociological relevance of formal structures is not, however, to have constructed a theory of organization' (Selznick 1948, 26–28). Organization theorists have continued to point to the noncontradictory and possibly facilitating relations between informal and rational organizational elements, against Weber's insistence on the necessary and exclusive association of only formal and rational elements.

Conclusion

This is not the place to present an argument concerning the development of modern capitalism in China since the post-Mao reforms of the 1980s, led by Deng Xiaoping. But this development, its relationship with the revival of kinship clans (Faure 2006, 73–80), suppressed during the Mao period, the role of *guanxi* networks (Barbalet 2014b) and the party-state in the processes of profit-seeking, marketization and capital formation (Boisot and Child 1996; Lin 2010) raises questions of central concern to the present discussion. One is the extent to which Weber was simply premature in dismissing the possibility of an indigenous Chinese capitalist takeoff and another is the adequacy of his understanding of capitalism at all. Weber's conception of capitalism is largely based on West European and American historical experiences (Weber 1991, 52), up to the late nineteenth and early twentieth centuries; individualistic, competitive, and world-dominant, but prior to the triumph of the corporation which removed the individualistic and competitive elements of markets that Weber (1981, 276) sees as crucial. Indeed, both the emergence of China as a major force of global capitalism and the global financial crisis (GFC) that peeked in 2008 provide evidence for the unsuitability of Weber's ideal type for understanding the nature and trajectory of modern capitalism.

The role of the party-state in initiating capitalism in China and state ownership of substantial productive capital, on the one hand, and the commonplace fraud in accounting practices revealed by the GFC, on the other, in different ways indicate the limitations of assuming 'rational capital accounting' as a necessary feature of capitalism today, if it ever was (Barbalet 2008, 153–58). Weber's second elemental feature of capitalism, indicated in the *General Economic History*, 'freedom of the market,' misunderstands the institutional nature of markets in their subjection to legal, political and conventional or moral constraints (Schultz 2001; Schumpeter 1966, 417–18) and especially the compromise of such 'freedom' by corporations (Wilks 2013). Three of the remaining four conditions of Weber's ideal type conception – 'rational technology,' 'calculable law' and 'free labour' (Weber 1964, 277) – are similarly contingent elements of capitalism circumstantially relevant rather than foundational. Weber's final ideal-type element of capitalism, 'the

226 THE ANTHEM COMPANION TO MAX WEBER

commercialization of economic life,' is abundant in China today and with the exception of a brief period from 1949 to 1978 has been since the Song dynasty from the tenth century.

In *The Religion of China* Weber's argument is directed to the question of why modern capitalism, that is to say industrial capitalism, did not emerge in China. His consideration of the supposed inability of Confucianism to provide an ethic supportive of a capitalist ethos does not properly address this question but relates rather to market or commercial capitalism, which Weber acknowledges in different ways did indeed operate in imperial China. The advent of industrial capitalism since the 1980s, because it operates with 'personalist' social forms both familial and political that Weber dismissed as irrational and therefore noncapitalistic, cannot satisfy Weber's claim that the Chinese 'would be quite capable ... of assimilating capitalism which has technically and economically been fully developed in the modern cultural area' (248). The question of the absence of modern industrialization in imperial China requires consideration of the conditions for application of advanced technology to production. Elvin (1973, 298–99) shows that throughout the Ming and Qing dynasties resourcefulness associated with innovation was present and entrepreneurship was well developed, but there was an absence of technologically driven production in late imperial China for the following reason:

> A rational strategy for peasant and merchant alike tended in the direction not so much of labour-saving machinery as of economizing on resources and fixed capital ... This situation might be described as a 'high-level equilibrium trap'. In the context of a civilization with a strong sense of economic rationality, with an appreciation of invention ... it is probably a sufficient explanation of the retardation of technological advance. (Elvin 1973, 314–15)

The subsequent economic decline of China in the late Qing was no doubt also due to associated institutional factors as well as others that Weber discusses, especially those connected with government capacities.

The weakness of the Qing court, in dealing with foreign debt especially following the Opium Wars of the mid-nineteenth century and China's defeat by Japan in 1895, reflected only the most visible limitation of the imperial regime. Population surplus, that rendered labour-saving innovation and therefore industrialization unnecessary, eventually led to a disruption of both cultivation and commerce. The autonomy of provincial administration seriously undermined the central government's ability to implement any reforms it initiated (see Weber 1964, 47–50). The collapse of the last imperial dynasty with the 1911 Republican Revolution bequeathed these institutional problems to its successors (Bergère 1984). The command economy and population control devised by the Communist Party sufficiently overcame these and associated problems to permit capitalist development from the 1980s. In this sense Weber's dismissal of the prospects of Chinese capitalism was simply premature. That part of Weber's argument which is useful in understanding the institutional limitations on the historic trajectory of modern capitalist development in China is typically ignored or under-emphasized by his readers. Weber's argument concerning the inability of the Chinese mentality to develop a capitalistic orientation, when it is not positively misleading, seems to offer little for an understanding of China's path to the 1980s. But then the purpose of Weber's analysis in *The Religion of China* is to demonstrate the correctness of his arguments concerning the uniqueness of the West and the supposed veracity of his claims concerning the singular power of Protestant asceticism to found modern capitalism. In this endeavour imperial China is simply drawn upon as a negative case.

References

Balazs, Etienne. 1966. *Chinese Civilization and Bureaucracy.* New Haven, CT: Yale University Press.

Barbalet, Jack. 2008. *Weber, Passion and Profits: 'The Protestant Ethic and the Spirit of Capitalism' in Context.* Cambridge: Cambridge University Press.

————2014a. 'Weber's Daoism: A Failure of Orthodoxy.' *Journal of Classical Sociology.* 14(3): 284–301.

————2014b. 'The Structure of *Guanxi*: Resolving Problems of Network Assurance.' *Theory and Society.* 43(1): 51–69.

Bergère, Marie-Claire. 1984. 'On the Historical Origins of Chinese Underdevelopment.' *Theory and Society.* 13(3): 327–37.

Boisot, Max and Child, John. 1996. 'From Fiefs to Clans and Network Capitalism: Explaining China's Emerging Economic Order.' *Administrative Science Quarterly.* 41(4): 600–628.

Brook, Timothy. 1997. 'Profit and Righteousness in Chinese Economic Culture.' In *Culture and Economy: The Shaping of Capitalism in Eastern Asia*, pp. 27–44, edited by Timothy Brook and Hy V. Luong. Ann Arbor: University of Michigan Press.

Buss, Andreas E. 1985. *Max Weber and Asia: Contributions to the Sociology of Development.* Cologne: Arnold-Bergsträsser-Institut. Materialien Zu Entwicklung und Politik.

Church, Roy. 1993. 'The Family Firm in Industrial Capitalism: International Perspectives on Hypothesis and History.' *Business History.* 35(4): 17–43.

Collins, Randall. 1990a. 'Weber's Last Theory of Capitalism.' In his *Weberian Sociological Theory*, pp. 19–44. Cambridge: Cambridge University Press.

————1990b. 'The Weberian Revolution of the High Middle Ages.' In his *Weberian Sociological Theory*, pp. 45–76, Cambridge: Cambridge University Press.

Creel, Herrlee G. 1977. 'The Beginnings of Bureaucracy in China: The Origin of the *Hsien*.' In his *What is Taoism? And Other Studies in Chinese Cultural History.* pp. 121–59. Chicago: University of Chicago Press.

de Groot, Jan Jakob Marie. 1912. *The Religion of the Chinese.* New York: Macmillan.

Elvin, Mark. 1973. *The Patterns of the Chinese Past.* Stanford, CA: Stanford University Press.

Faure, David. 2006. *China and Capitalism: A History of Business Enterprise in Modern China.* Hong Kong: Hong Kong University Press.

————2013. 'Commercial Institutions and Practices in Imperial China as Seen by Weber and in Terms of More Recent Research.' *Taiwan Journal of East Asian Studies,* 10(2): 71–98.

Gernet, Jacques. 1995. *Buddhism in Chinese Society: An Economic History from the Fifth to the Tenth Centuries.* New York: Columbia University Press.

————1996. *A History of Chinese Civilization.* Cambridge: Cambridge University Press.

Gershenkron, Alexander. 1965. 'Social Attitudes, Entrepreneurship, and Economic Development.' In his *Economic Backwardness in Historical Perspective.* pp. 52–71, Cambridge, MA: Harvard University Press.

Giddens, Anthony. 2011. *Capitalism and Modern Social Theory.* Cambridge: Cambridge University Press.

Grassby, Richard. 2000. *Kinship and Capitalism: Marriage, Family and Business in the English-Speaking World, 1580–1740.* Cambridge: Cambridge University Press.

Greif, Avner and Tabellini, Guido. 2010. 'Cultural and Institutional Bifurcation: China and Europe Compared.' *American Economic Review.* 100(2): 135–140.

Hamilton, Gary G. 1984. 'Patriarchalism in Imperial China and Western Europe: A Revision of Weber's Sociology of Domination.' *Theory and Society,* 13(3): 393–425.

Huang, Su-Jen. 1994. 'Max Weber's *The Religion of China*: An Interpretation.' *Journal of the History of the Behavioral Sciences,* 30(1): 3–18.

Hudson, G. F. 1961. *Europe and China: A Survey of their Relations from the Earliest Times to 1800.* Boston: Beacon Press

Jensen, Lionel. 1997. *Manufacturing Confucianism: Chinese Traditions and Universal Civilization.* Durham, NC: Duke University Press.

Kalberg, Stephen. 2012. *Max Weber's Comparative-Historical Sociology Today: Major Themes, Modes of Causal Analysis, and Applications.* London: Ashgate.

La Porta, Rafael, Lopez-de-Silanes, Florencio and Shleifer, Andrei. 1999. 'Corporate Ownership around the World.' *Journal of Finance,* 54(2): 471–517.

Legge, James. 1880. *The Religions of China: Confucianism and Taoism Described and Compared with Christianity.* London: Hodder and Stoughton.

————1971. *Confucius: Confucian Analacts, the Great Learning & the Doctrine of the Mean.* New York: Dover Publications.

Lin, Nan. 2010. 'Capitalism in China: A Centrally Managed Capitalism and Its Future.' *Management and Organization Review,* 7(1): 63–96.

Lufrano, Richard John. 1997. *Honorable Merchants: Commerce and Self-Cultivation in Late Imperial China.* Honolulu: University of Hawai'i Press.

Metzger, Thomas A. 1977. *Escape from Predicament: Neo-Confucianism and China's Evolving Political Culture.* New York: Columbia University Press.

Parsons, Talcott. 1968. *The Structure of Social Action. Volume 2.* New York: Free Press.

Peng, Yusheng. 2005. 'Lineage Networks, Rural Entrepreneurs, and Max Weber.' *Research in the Sociology of Work,* 15: 327–55.

Pomeranz, Kenneth. 2000. *The Great Divergence: China, Europe, and the Making of the Modern World Economy.* Princeton, NJ: Princeton University Press.

Qi, Xiaoying. 2014. *Globalized Knowledge Flows and Chinese Social Theory.* New York: Routledge.

Schluchter, Wolfgang. 1989. *Rationalism, Religion and Domination: A Weberian Perspective.* Berkeley: University of California Press.

Schmidt-Glintzer, Helwig and Kolonko, Petra. (eds). 1991. *Max Weber: Die Wirtschaftsethik der Weltreligionen. Konfuzianismus und Taoismus. Schriften 1915–1920.* Tübingen: J. C. B. Mohr.

Schultz, Walter J. 2001. *The Moral Conditions of Economic Efficiency.* Cambridge: Cambridge University Press.

Schumpeter, Joseph A. 1966. *Capitalism, Socialism and Democracy.* 5th Edition. London: George Allen and Unwin.

———2008. 'Capitalism.' In his *Essays: On Entrepreneurs, Innovations, Business Cycles, and the Evolution of Capitalism*, pp. 189–210, edited by Richard V. Clemence with an Introduction by Richard Swedberg. New Brunswick, NJ: Transaction Books.

Selznick, Philip. 1948. 'Foundations of the Theory of Organization.' *American Sociological Review*, 13(1): 25–35.

van der Sprenkel, Otto B. 1954. 'Chinese Religion.' *British Journal of Sociology*, 5(4): 272–75.

———1965. 'Max Weber on China.' In *Studies in the Philosophy of History: Selected Essays from History and Theory*, pp. 198–220, edited by George H. Nadel. New York: Harper.

Walzer, Michael. 1976. *The Revolution of the Saints: A Study in the Origins of Radical Politics.* New York: Athenium.

Watson, James L. 1993. 'Rites or Beliefs? The Construction of a Unified Culture in Late Imperial China.' In *China's Quest for National Identity*, pp. 80–103, edited by Lowell Dittmer and Samuel S. Kim. Ithaca, NY: Cornell University Press.

Weber, Max. 1964. *The Religion of China: Confucianism and Taoism*, translated and edited by Hans H. Gerth, with an Introduction by C. K. Yang. New York: Free Press.

———1970a. 'Science as a Vocation.' In *From Max Weber: Essays in Sociology*, pp. 129–56, edited by H. H. Gerth and C. Wright Mills. London: Routledge.

———1970b. 'Politics as a Vocation.' In *From Max Weber: Essays in Sociology*, pp. 77–128, edited by H. H. Gerth and C. Wright Mills. London: Routledge.

———1978. *Economy and Society: An Outline of Interpretive Sociology*, edited by Guenther Roth and Claus Wittich. Berkeley: University of California Press.

———1981. *General Economic History*, translated by Frank Knight with a new Introduction by Ira J. Cohen. New Brunswick, NJ: Transaction Books.

———1991. *The Protestant Ethic and the Spirit of Capitalism.* London: HarperCollins.

———2002. *The History of Commercial Partnerships in the Middle Ages*, translated by Lutz Kaelber. Lanham, MD: Rowman & Littlefield.

———2013. 'The Social Causes of the Decline of Ancient Civilizations'. Pp. 387–412 in his *The Agrarian Sociology of Ancient Civilizations*, translated by R.I. Frank. London: Verso.

Wilks, Stephen. 2013. *The Political Power of the Business Corporation.* Cheltenham: Edward Elgar.

Wong, Man-kong. 2005. 'The Use of Sinology in the Nineteenth Century'. Pp. 135–54 in *Colonial Hong Kong and Modern China: Interaction and Reintegration*, edited by Lee Pui Tak. Hong Kong: Hong Kong University Press.

Yang, C. K. 1961. *Religion in Chinese Society.* Berkley: University of California Press.

———1964. 'Introduction'. Pp. xiii–xliii in Max Weber, *The Religion of China: Confucianism and Taoism.* New York: The Free Press.

Zelin, Madeleine. 2009. 'The Firm in Early China'. *Journal of Economic Behavior and Organization.* 71(3): 623–37.

Zeitlin, Maurice. 1974. 'Corporate Ownership and Control: The Large Corporation and the Capitalist Class'. *American Journal of Sociology.* 79(5): 1073–119.

Zhang, Longxi. 1998. *Mighty Opposites: From Dichotomies to Differences in the Comparative Study of China.* Stanford, CA: Stanford University Press.

Chapter 10

POLITICS WITHOUT MAGIC: MAX WEBER IN WEIMAR GERMANY

Joshua Derman

Introduction

Among the terms most often associated with Max Weber's sociology are the German word *Entzauberung* and the famous phrase "*die Entzauberung der Welt*." Anglophone readers have generally come to know them as "disenchantment" and "the disenchantment of the world," thanks to the popularity of Hans Gerth and C. Wright Mills's anthology of translations, *From Max Weber*. There is good reason, however, to think twice about substituting "disenchantment" for *Entzauberung*. When we speak of disenchantment, we typically mean that someone has been freed of illusions and, correspondingly, disappointed with the outcome of a situation (Lehmann 2009, 11–12). Such emotive connotations are not entirely irrelevant in the context of Weber's discussion of *Entzauberung*, but they do imply the kind of scholarly value judgment that he claimed to eschew. A more appropriate translation would be the literal one, "demagification," which has the advantage of acknowledging the religious sources of his interest in the concept. Weber's investigations into the sociology of magic, and its role in the development of world religions, provided the context in which *Entzauberung* first appeared in his writings, namely, in his article "Some Categories of Interpretive Sociology" (1913) and the concurrently written manuscript on "Status Groups, Classes and Religion" for *Economy and Society* (Winckelmann 1980, 15).

Weber understood magic to be a form of "relatively rational behavior" aimed at coercing the spirits of the natural world, primarily for this-worldly and specifically economic benefits (Weber [1922] 1978, 399–403, 422). One of his major sociological interests concerned the ways in which certain religions, most notably ancient Judaism and ascetic Protestantism, had historically divested themselves of magical beliefs and superstitions. These religions posited the existence of an omnipotent God, incapable of being coerced, whose creation of the world precluded the existence of immanent natural spirits. Moreover, they encouraged believers to shun magical practices in favor of rational life conduct in accordance with ethical commandments (Weber [1915] 1946b, 290; [1920] 2009, 107, 135, 137; [1920] 1951, 226–30; [1921] 1952, 4, 219–25, 262, 394, 400; [1922] 1978, 630). Demagification, in this sense, represented an eminently religious process, not a symptom of secularization, though its significance for economic life was considerable. As epitomized in the form of ascetic Protestantism, religious demagification gave lay believers an incentive to seek salvation "primarily through immersion in one's worldly vocation," and thus paved the way for the spirit of modern capitalism (Weber [1922] 1978, 630).

However, there was also an explicitly nonreligious sense in which demagification appeared in Weber's sociological writings. Weber identified a secular trend in the development of Western culture, beginning with Greek philosophy and culminating in the Scientific Revolution, that helped bring about "the demagification of the world" (Weber [1915] 1946a, 350–51; [1919] 2004b, 12–13; [1920] 2009, 107). The scientific demagification of the world meant that individuals had attained "the knowledge or the conviction that [...] principally there are no mysterious, incalculable forces that come into play, but that, on the contrary, we can in principle *control everything by means of calculation*" (Weber [1919] 2004b, 12–13). Few of us possess the firsthand knowledge of physics and electrical engineering necessary to explain what makes a streetcar move. But we do believe that we could in principle explain its locomotion without making recourse to vital spirits or occult forces. Causal reasoning constitutes our primary mode for comprehending the world around us. By divesting the world of spirits and subjecting it to a regime of physical laws, modern science has produced cultural effects analogous to those of religious demagification. Since ascetic Protestantism promoted "the methodical application of science for *practical* purposes" (Weber [1910] 2002, 317), modern applied science could even be considered the causal byproduct of religious demagification. Thus, through the kind of historically self-reversing process familiar to readers of Friedrich Nietzsche's work, demagified religion had set in motion a train of cultural developments that eroded the capacity for religious belief and rendered the world an increasingly meaningless place (Weiß 1991, 16–17; 1992, 137–44; Schluchter 2009). Once natural phenomena could be explained through causal reasoning, there was no longer much point in asking what these processes meant or what value they possessed:

> Wherever rational empirical knowledge has consistently brought about the demagification of the world and its transformation into a causal mechanism, it finally comes into tension with the ethical postulate that holds the world to be a

divinely ordered and thus somehow ethically *meaningful* cosmos. The empirical
view of the world, and particularly the mathematically oriented one, develops a
principled rejection of every approach that asks after the "meaning" of inner-
worldly events. (Weber [1915] 1946a, 350–51)

Weber wrote about demagification in the context of his sociology of
religion and his musings on the meaning of modern scholarship. There he
portrayed his interest as primarily a scholarly one: demagification was a mac-
rohistorical process that he sought to understand without passing judgment
on its desirability. Yet, in his capacity as a political thinker, Weber appeared
to relish playing the role of a demagifier. Though he never discussed the term
Entzauberung in a political context, his political sociology and especially his
polemical writings pursued a strategy that tacitly evoked "the demagification
of the world." In his scholarly analysis of modern politics, Weber searched for
the causal forces that determined policies and devised models to predict the
outcome of political conflicts; when he engaged in political arguments about
current events, he was eager to dismiss the ideological pieties of his opponents,
preferring instead to discuss the interests and power struggles that constituted
their real motivations. In the same way that modern science divested the natural world of entelechies and teleological principles, Weber sought to dispel the
metaphysical claptrap that his opponents employed to disguise the brute realities of political life. "Whoever wants to pursue worldly politics must, above all,
be free of illusions, and acknowledge the inevitable, eternal struggle among
men on earth, as it actually takes place, as a fundamental fact," he counseled
his listeners (Weber [1896] 1988, 29). There were no "mysterious, incalculable
forces" in German politics, he suggested, only the conflicting power interests
of individuals and groups, each struggling to enlarge its scope of influence.
    Some of the most illuminating perspectives on Weber's role as a politi-
cal demagifier can be found in the writings of his German contemporaries.
Weimar intellectuals were well placed to appreciate Weber's approach to
understanding German politics. In the aftermath of the First World War and
the German Revolution, when received values appeared to have lost their binding force, Weber's effort to purge political discourse of ideological detritus was
capable of making a particularly powerful impression. This chapter focuses on
the work of three Weimar intellectuals who admired Weber's scholarship as
well as his politics: the sociologist Albert Salomon, the historian Eckart Kehr
and the philosopher Karl Jaspers. Each believed that Weber had implicitly
enacted the demagification of political life through his writings and personal
activism. While Salomon was the first to interpret Weber in these terms, Kehr
and Jaspers went further and openly endorsed what they understood to be
Weber's contributions to demagification. Kehr and Jaspers can be counted

among the handful of Weimar intellectuals who self-consciously styled themselves as Weber's political disciples. As this chapter will argue, the substance of their identification with Weber's political thought consisted in their attempt to promote demagification through their own intellectual projects.

In his journalism and, less pointedly, in his political sociology, Weber tried to show how political conflicts could be explained by disregarding the noble mantras of their participants and focusing one's attention, instead, on the underlying interests at work. After applying Weber's method to his own historical investigations, Kehr arrived at a conclusion that shocked his colleagues and eventually precipitated a revolution in German historiography: domestic power interests and not geopolitical considerations or foreign machinations, Kehr argued, were to blame for the catastrophic course of Wilhelmine imperialism. Jaspers was equally impressed by Weber's ability to reveal the power constellations underlying contemporary politics. But he was also convinced that Weber, having thoroughly demagified politics, wished to restore to it a sense of dignity and meaning. In his popular work of existential political philosophy, *The Intellectual Situation of the Age*, Jaspers endorsed what he saw as the peculiarly "anthropological" focus of Weber's political activism (Hennis 1987, 46): the fundamental desire to ensure conditions that were conducive for the self-cultivation of human greatness. This, Jaspers believed, was an ideal that could live on, and even acquire greater force, after the totalizing political ideologies and technological aspirations of the early twentieth century had revealed themselves to be inhospitable for authentic selfhood.

The afterlife of Weber's concept of demagification enables us to perceive, as if in microcosm, many of the characteristic features of his early German reception (Derman 2012). Though Weber was hardly a household name in Weimar Germany, his concepts were appropriated by a number of exceptionally innovative thinkers who left a major mark on their disciplines. Their sensitivity to the fact that Weber's polemical interventions complemented and sometimes even overshadowed his scholarly pursuits inclined them to see him as a radical and uncompromising thinker. For these enthusiasts, the demagification of the world was freighted with great normative significance: it represented a way of relating to the modern world that Weber was seen to affirm through his writings and personal interventions. Weimar intellectuals were fascinated by Weber's intellectual affinities to critical thinkers such as Karl Marx, but they also marveled at his refusal to indulge in utopian schemes for Germany's economic or political future. When admirers like Kehr reflected on Weber's relentless attempts to cleanse politics of bogus ideologies, they came to see him as a principled skeptic, a man whose intellectual significance lay principally in his critical and destructive energies. Yet others, like Jaspers, were capable of seeing Weber as a beacon of profound hope and faith in the modern world. That Weber could be seen in such different light by Weimar intellectuals tells us something about the polarizing cultural climate in which they lived. But it also testifies to the inherent tensions and contradictions in Weber's oeuvre, and the challenges attendant in reconciling his scholarship with his political engagements and uncompromising personality.

Politics and Interests

In *The Protestant Ethic and the "Spirit" of Capitalism* (1904/5), Weber assigned a critical role to religious ideas in the development of methodical life conduct and, by implication, in the proliferation of modern forms of capitalist enterprise. However, in subsequent writings he took pains to note that religious attitudes toward life conduct were also determined by the "interest situation" (*Interessenlage*) of the social strata that were most associated with the religion's historical development (Weber [1915] 1946b, 270, 281, 286–87). Weber posited the existence of a special "carrier" stratum for each of the major world religions: literary officials for Confucianism, a hereditary caste of scholars for Hinduism, mendicant monks for Buddhism, crusading warriors for Islam, a bourgeois "pariah people" for ancient Judaism and wandering artisans for early Christianity. Weber explicitly rejected the notion that religious ethics could be interpreted as the "reflection" or "mouthpiece" of a social stratum's class interests (270, 277). But he did insist that "carrier" strata had left an important historical mark on the supreme values or psychological states of holiness endorsed by each world religion (279, 281). Where political officials served as the "carrier" of a world religion, their sense of social duty and respect for rules inclined them to emphasize the importance of ritual observance in religious life. Intellectuals, ever prone to contemplation, tended to gravitate toward mysticism, whereas warriors remained committed to "absolutely worldly interests." Peasants depended on nature for their livelihood and sought magical tools to control it. Merchants and artisans, who busied themselves with economic calculations, displayed a particular affinity for the methodical life conduct demanded by prophetic religions (282–85).

Weber's sociology of religion offered a nuanced account of the relationship between social circumstances and religious ethics. Unlike Karl Marx or Friedrich Nietzsche, who sought to "unmask" religious beliefs as expressions of class interest or *ressentiment*, Weber never questioned the independent social reality of religious experience (Baehr and Gordon 2012, 388–89). Measured against the empathetic analysis of religion in his sociological writings, Weber's brusque treatment of ideology in his political speeches and journalism is all the more striking (Turner 2004, 110). In these latter texts, Weber depicted a world in which principles counted for little and "interest situations" determined nearly everything of importance. The prime example is his most famous piece of political journalism, "Parliament and Government in Germany under a New Political Order," which attempted to advance the case for wartime constitutional reform. Weber directed his ire against the proponents of the "German ideas of 1914," who criticized the alleged materialism and individualism of parliamentary democracy and defended Germany's constitutional monarchy as the apotheosis of a unique national essence (Mommsen 1990, 407–21). Weber tried to discredit his opponents by demonstrating that their professed ideology was fundamentally linked to their interest situation. Those who were most vocal about "the need to pre-serve the 'German spirit' from the stain of 'democracy,'" he argued, were the defenders of "vested interests in the status quo" (Weber [1918] 1994, 161). If not guilty of outright hypocrisy, they were at least "naively plac[ing] themselves at the service of [the] slogans" of the "beneficiaries of existing conditions" (195). Weber aimed to show that the "German ideas of 1914" mattered little to the leading politicians and parties who rejected constitu-tional reform. Their political positions, he argued, were taken primarily out of concern for personal and party interests.

Weber traced the custom of invoking an inviolable German constitutional ethos to Otto von Bismarck, the founding genius of the German state, who cloaked himself in "monarchic sentiment as a cover for his own power inter-ests in the struggle between the political parties" (Weber [1918] 1994, 144). In an attempt to weaken political challengers, Bismarck engineered a con-stitution that severely delimited the powers of parliament. The chief benefi-ciaries of the political system he constructed, following his departure from office in 1890, were government officials and the pro-agrarian Conservative Party, who together availed themselves of the clarion call for "monarchic gov-ernment" to defend their own prerogatives. The outcome was "pure rule by officials," drawn predominantly from the Conservative Party and unchecked in any fundamental way by either the Kaiser or the parliament (173, 189–90, 209). German politics had become dominated by the "*uncontrolled rule by officials* under the banner of pseudo-monarchic slogans" (269).

While Bismarck may have constructed this political system, he was not the only political force responsible for its persistence. Weber believed that the leading German political parties were complicit in their own emasculation: they had come to support the constitutional status quo for fear that parlia-mentarization would erode the entitlements they had managed to wring from Bismarck and his successors. The Catholic Center Party had grown accus-tomed to receiving unofficial office patronage, a privilege which it might no longer receive as a minority party under a parliamentary regime. Elements of the National Liberal Party likewise appreciated their ability to leverage personal connections into positions in the civil service (193–94). "In truth it is assuredly not the 'German spirit' that is committed to the fight against parliamentary control of patronage," Weber insisted, "but a strong material interest in official prebends, allied to the capitalist exploitation of 'connections'" (194). The German term *Pfründe*, usually translated into English as "prebend," played a significant role in the sociological studies that Weber was composing at roughly the same time. A prebend was an office, granted by a ruler to his official, that yielded a rent payment or usufruct in exchange for service. It represented one of the primary methods of funding the administration of religious communities and patrimonial societies (Weber [1920] 1951, 33–62, 126–27, 138; [1921] 2000, 68–77, 229–30, 263, 282–84, 328; [1922] 1978, 235, 966–67, 1032–38, 1073–77). Weber took some liberties with the term in his wartime journalism and applied it to German civil service positions that generated material benefits for their occupants (Weber 1994, 377–78). As he saw it, the competition for offices among the political parties of Wilhelmine Germany generated a dynamic that helped maintain the political status quo: "Officialdom benefits from the arrangement by being free to operate *without* personal *control*, in return for which it pays gratuities to the parties which count in the form of the patronage of *minor* prebends" (Weber [1918] 1994, 167). This kind of "*unofficial* patronage," he thought, was "the most pernicious form of parliamentary patronage of all, since it favors mediocrity" (194).

Weber believed that enthusiasm for the "German ideas of 1914" served to occlude and perpetuate a system of office patronage that implicated all of Germany's major political actors. At the same time, he refrained from reducing this dynamic to a simple struggle of economic or class interests. The "literati" who criticized parliamentarism were serving the "vested interests" of particular parties and institutions in maintaining or extending their political power. While individual office holders were undoubtedly pleased to receive the financial benefits that came with their positions, the agents whom Weber foregrounded in these machinations were not primarily individuals or classes in search of economic privilege but rather political parties intent on strengthening their power by securing a supply of offices for their followers. "By its nature *every* party strives for *power*," he observed, "which is to say, to share in the *administration*, and hence to influence appointments to official posts" (Weber [1918] 1994, 167). For Weber, the political efficacy of the "German ideas of 1914" had to be explained through reference to a variety of power interests: Bismarck's striving for personal power, the officialdom's desire to secure its "uncontrolled rule," the conservative Prussian landowners' efforts to maintain their social preeminence, and the political parties' determination to dominate the distribution of offices. While material interests in the form of prebends lay at the bottom of Weber's analysis, he ultimately offered something far more complex than a mere reduction of ideology to economic interest.

The first reader to comment on these specific passages was the sociologist and journalist Albert Salomon (1891–1966), a noted interpreter of Weber's thought during the Weimar Republic and one of his earliest popularizers in the United States. In an article published in 1926 in *Die Gesellschaft*, a leading cultural journal affiliated with the Social Democratic Party, Salomon commented on the parallels between Weber's and Marx's approaches to interpreting the world. "No bourgeois scholar has applied the method of the economic perspective more ruthlessly than Weber himself, indeed one could say that he transported Marx's work into new areas and continued his work," Salomon observed. What struck him as particularly Marxian about Weber's analysis was its ability to reveal the interests lurking beneath political ideologies, a process he associated with the concept of demagification:

> For while Marx's analysis of the socioeconomic structure achieved above all the demagification of the bourgeois social order, Weber went further and divested the state-political sphere of all its ideological magic, exposing the drives and motives of sociopolitical action in their unadorned constellations of interests – not unlike Balzac in that regard. Like no one else in Germany, Weber unmasked the ideology of the "German idea of the state," as opposed to the "Western" conception of the state, for what it is: a legend purveyed by bureaucrats who wished to remain undisturbed in the unsupervised exercise of power. He picked apart the motives behind the draft of the Prussian entailed estate law and ruthlessly uncovered the prebendary and rentier interests, which, together with the desire to secure Conservative party dominance, determined the draft. And his scholarly works likewise demonstrate an unyielding eye for the real motives of political and social action. (Salomon 1926, 142)

Salomon identified Weber's polemical texts, such as "Parliament and Government" and his objections to the Prussian entailed estate law (Weber [1904] 1988), as the primary venues in which this Marxian style of demagification took place. But he also drew attention to the points at which Weber's methodological assumptions and worldview departed from historical materialism. In contrast to Marxist social scientists, Weber refused to assume a "*unity* and connection of the entire historical social process." Where they saw a meaningful totality, Weber perceived ceaseless conflict among different spheres of life. "*Struggle* is [for Weber] the basis of all life, even cultural life," Salomon explained. "But how this struggle might end in each case, no one can say" (Salomon 1926, 144).

Marianne Weber was displeased to learn that Salomon had identified her late husband as a "bourgeois Marx" (Salomon 1926, 144; Matthiesen 1988, 318). Nevertheless, she was prepared to accept that Marx and Weber shared a similarly debunking attitude toward politics. In the biography of Max Weber that she published in the same year, Marianne Weber depicted him as a demagifier when he strode into the political fray. "Weber did not base his proposals on ideological political theories but presented them, explicitly and intentionally, as something practical and utilitarian, the need of the moment," she observed in reference to his wartime political journalism. His aversion to ideology translated into a scathing critique of the "political metaphysics" purveyed by his opponents to defend the status quo:

> He regarded the state only as the framework for the life of the *nation*; people had to be free to change it if its structure led to large numbers of people losing their sense of belonging to the nation. And Weber suspected all political metaphysics up to that time as a kind of mimicry by which the privileged classes protected themselves against a rearrangement of the spheres of power. In this respect he shared Karl Marx's conception of the state and its ideology. (Marianne Weber [1926] 2003, 587)

It is important to note that neither Salomon nor Marianne Weber equated Max Weber's approach with vulgar historical materialism. They recognized that Weber was broadly interested in understanding how ideology served "the unsupervised exercise of power" (Salomon) and the arrangement of the "spheres of power" (Marianne Weber), not simply the ability to control the means of production.

One scholar who directly benefited from Salomon's efforts to popularize Weber was the radical young historian Eckart Kehr (1902–33). A student of Friedrich Meinecke and Hans Rothfels's at the University of Berlin, Kehr was a precocious scholar whose first book, *Battleship Building and Party Politics*, caused a stir in the German historical profession. In the introduction to the book, Kehr thanked Salomon, his editor at *Die Gesellschaft* and colleague at the German College of Politics, for introducing him to the sociology of Max Weber and Carl Brinkmann and "the problematic of the economic and social imbrication of political activity" (Kehr 1930, vii). Weber's determination to reveal the elective affinities between the economy, society and politics resonated powerfully with Kehr (Wehler 1980, 245). More to the point, Kehr came to regard his own historical scholarship as a work of political demagification in precisely the mode that Salomon associated with Weber. In *Battleship Building and Party Politics* and a series of related articles, Kehr set out to challenge the "primacy of foreign policy," a favorite dictum of German historiography, which held that international relations constituted an autonomous sphere of politics governed by considerations of *raison d'état* (Kehr 1930, 448; [1928] 1965a, 149–50). Wilhelmine Germany's perplexing and oftentimes self-defeating foreign policy could not be fully understood, Kehr argued, without considering the domestic political and economic interests that lay behind it. Though he was treated as an outsider by the German historical profession during his brief lifetime, Kehr became an inspirational figure for younger West German historians in the 1960s and 1970s, who admired his social-scientific and critical approach to political history. Following in his footsteps, historians such as Hans-Ulrich Wehler ascribed crucial historical agency to a Wilhelmine ruling elite, led by aristocratic agrarians with a feudalized and unassertive bourgeoisie in tow, who promoted social imperialism as a means to suppress constitutional reform and forestall the rise of Social Democracy. For the "Kehrites," as well as for the revisionist historians who challenged their interpretation of Germany's political and social structure, Kehr's Weimar-era engagement with Weber's thought constituted a foundational moment in the development of modern German historiography (Sheehan 1968; Mommsen 1973; Eley 1978; Hobson 2002, 312–24; Berghahn 2005, xii–xvi).

Kehr's most important research concerned the history of German naval expansion at the turn of the twentieth century and, in particular, the political maneuvering that surrounded the passage of two naval bills in 1898 and 1900. The construction of a battle fleet was a signal event in the development of Wilhelmine Germany's "world policy" (*Weltpolitik*) and a factor that contributed to international tensions in the decades leading up to the First World War. The origins of this misguided policy were not to be found in geopolitical calculations, Kehr argued, but in the domestic alliances struck by Germany's ruling elites. The driving force behind the naval program was the government's "policy of rallying-together" (*Sammlungspolitik*), which sought to bring large agricultural landlords and industrialists into a parliamentary alliance on the basis of their mutual fear of the working class. Since the economic interests of agrarians and industrialists usually stood in opposition to each other, the alliance required each partner to make concessions. The agrarians agreed to support the second naval bill even though the construction of a battle fleet primarily served the industrial and commercial interests of the German bourgeoisie. In return, the industrialists pledged to support higher tariffs on Russian grain (1902), whose importation had threatened the economic and social position of large landlords. The alliance between agrarians and industrialists, as Kehr sometimes depicted it in his articles, was a lopsided one. Agency and initiative lay primarily with the agrarians: it was their successful demand for trade protection that had originally redirected German capitalist investment away from Russia and toward overseas competition with the British Empire.

Power imbalances aside, both agrarians and industrialists were capable of rallying around the fleet as a tool of social imperialism, which they thought would bolster the regime's prestige and distract the restive working class. The outcome of this domestic bargain among elite ruling groups, mediated by a state that aimed to maintain the political status quo, was a policy of navalism and protectionism that alienated both Britain and Russia, Germany's future opponents in the First World War (Kehr 1930, 173–74, 205, 262–65, 314–18, 330–31; [1928] 1965a, 168–70).

In his analysis of Wilhelmine politics, Kehr cited and largely affirmed the critique of agrarians and Conservatives that Weber had put forward in his political writings. Kehr emphasized that the agrarians' professed patriotic ideology no longer corresponded to their actual behavior. Their attempts to stave off inevitable economic decline were endangering Germany's political interests as a nation-state: pro-agrarian demands for protectionism hampered commercial development, while their predilection for hiring seasonal Polish laborers weakened the military security of Germany's frontier regions (Kehr 1930, 249, 265–72, 311–12, 410, 446; cf. Weber [1895] 1994). When a Munich newspaper solicited Weber's opinion (along with those of other prominent individuals) on the first naval bill, he expressed his support for the fleet's construction but warned that an authoritarian government engaged in demonizing the Left and "rallying-together" to preserve the domestic status quo would invariably make a mess of foreign policy. The expansion of Germany's maritime power made little sense, he argued, so long as pro-agrarian policies were constraining the nation's economic development (Weber [1898] 1988; see also Mommsen 1984, 77, 137–40). Kehr quoted Weber's remarks at length in *Battleship Building and Party Politics* (Kehr 1930, 436). As one historian has observed, Kehr's admiration for Weber's insights into the pathologies of German policy making "gave rise to the strange paradox that the obsessions of a committed Wilhelmine imperialist inspired a leftist critique of Wilhelmine imperialism" (Hobson 2002, 320).

Like Salomon, Kehr appreciated how Weber's political analysis elucidated the power interests that lay submerged beneath the surface of everyday politics. Kehr repeatedly cited a passage from Weber's discussion of imperialism in *Economy and Society* that exemplified the methodological approach he wished to emulate: "Every successful imperialist policy of coercing the outside normally – or at least at first – also strengthens the domestic prestige and therewith the power and influence of those classes, status groups and parties, under whose leadership the success has been attained" (Weber [1922] 1978, 920). Weber made this remark in the context of explaining why the working class tended to display a lack of interest in foreign investment or overseas colonies: the fact that the capitalist class appeared – at least initially – to benefit from such imperial ventures dissuaded workers from voicing their support. As a young, politically engaged scholar, Weber had hoped that German workers could be convinced to abandon what he considered to be a narrow and inaccurate class perspective. Their future livelihood, he argued, depended on Germany's continued commercial and imperial expansion (Beetham 1985, 134–35, 144–46; Mommsen 1980, 19–21; 1984, 77–84). But Kehr derived a different message from this passage in *Economy and Society*. Weber's insight was, as he understood it, a powerful heuristic for understanding the causal determinants of imperialism. German imperialism did more than merely fortify the power and prestige of the country's leading classes, status groups and parties. The fin-de-siècle naval program had come into being, Kehr argued, primarily in order to gratify those very power interests. As a gloss on his quotation from Weber, Kehr declared, "The fleet construction was supposed to provide the power-political basis for a successful foreign policy, and this foreign policy was supposed to stabilize the domestic and social position of the ruling strata, which were threatened by Social Democracy" (Kehr [1928] 1965b, 135–6; see also [1928] 1965a, 165; 1930, 314). Kehr thus equated Weber's argument with the central thesis of his own book.

The central section of *Battleship Building and Party Politics*, titled "classes, parties, status groups" in reference to the quotation from *Economy and Society*, examined how the various economic, political and social sectors of the German population responded to the fleet's construction (Kehr 1930, 208–379). Kehr maintained that the class interests of agrarians and industrialists constituted the driving force behind the passage of the second naval bill (174). At the same time, he acknowledged that the power interests served by the naval program were not exhausted by purely economic ones (Ferguson 1998, 27). Alfred von Tirpitz, the naval secretary and mastermind of the battleship construction program, was driven by a desire for professional and military aggrandizement; the Center Party, which cast a decisive vote in favor of the first naval bill, hoped to achieve "political hegemony" by making itself indispensable to the government's policies; status groups such as the civil service and professoriate derived their social dignity from supporting state-sanctioned goals (Kehr 1930, 167, 205, 287, 343, 349, 365–79, 380–81). When Kehr trained his eye on the panorama of Wilhelmine politics, he, like Weber, saw power struggles taking place over a variety of objects: the means of production, the distribution of party offices, as well as the acquisition of social ranks and prestige. Each, in his analysis, had contributed in its own way to the development of German naval policy.

Kehr admired how Weber's justification for building a battle fleet, his "political ideology," remained faithful to his methodological principles (Kehr 1930, 403). Weber, who viewed the state as simply "the form of human community that (successfully) lays claim to the *monopoly of legitimate physical violence* within a particular territory" (Weber [1919] 2004a, 33), was no less fixated on the importance of power when it came to international relations. Citing Salomon's article, Kehr called attention to the similarities between Weber's and Marx's methodological approaches. "Weber was like Marx in his soberness, in his rationality, which was at the same time suffused with passion and will to power," Kehr observed. "He was not like Marx in his inquiry into the foundations of culture." Weber's fundamental agonism extended from his scholarly work into his political convictions: just as he believed that culture was composed of autonomous and sometimes warring spheres, he saw "competition among powers as the essence of politics," and harbored no hopes that the future would bring the fulfillment of either a classless society at home or a harmonious international society abroad (Kehr 1930, 403, 404). "After a transitional period of outwardly peaceful competition," Weber warned, the efforts of capitalist nations to expand their international trade had reached the point "where *only power* will decide the extent of each nation's participation in the economic domination of the earth, and hence the scope for acquisition on the part of its population, particularly its working class" (Weber [1898] 1988, 30; cited in Kehr 1930, 404).

Kehr was deeply impressed by Weber's reasoning, which he considered "by far the most sober and far-seeing among the academic positions on the fleet" (Kehr 1930, 404). Weber did not believe that the fleet would guarantee a peaceful and prosperous future, nor did he regard it as the vehicle of any alleged civilizing mission. Germany needed a powerful navy simply to project power and defend commercial interests in a world of relentless global economic competition:

> As far as [Weber] was concerned, the German fleet had no "mission" to fulfill in the world, but was simply power to be used to overwhelm an economic or political opponent and set Germany's life in the place of its life. Politics was a biological process and not a moral discourse. He eliminated subjective interests not only from scholarship, but also from politics, and saw in it only a struggle over power that was divested of any inner warmth. Politics, too, was subject to the law of demagification. The state was not an ethical entity, but rather a pure power association: the relationships between power associations could only stand under the law of power. (403–4)

To subject politics to demagification meant, as Kehr understood it, to relentlessly lay bare the power relationships beneath the surface of domestic and international politics. This technique was part and parcel of a "heroic-skeptical conception of politics" that Kehr admired (405). But it was also an approach that reduced political life to a "biological process," a struggle for survival that was potentially devoid of any higher meaning for the individual. In the same way that scientific demagification had vitiated the "ethical postulate that holds the world to be a divinely ordered and thus somehow ethically *meaningful* cosmos" (Weber [1915] 1946a, 351), political demagification threatened to extract all noble purposes from the world of human affairs. If rigorous analysis reduced all ideology to hypocrisy or, at best, naïveté, it remained unclear what vocation the profession of politics could still possess.

Kehr did not linger over these troubling ramifications of the demagification of politics. He saw his task in *Battleship Building and Party Politics* as primarily a critical one: to demolish the myths surrounding Wilhelmine imperialism and expose the actual power interests that motivated it. Since he revealed so little about his specific goals or ideals in the process, the most appropriate way to situate him politically might simply be to say that he was "an innovating historian of rather indeterminate radical views" (Eley 1978, 738). Kehr called attention to the critical dimension of Weber's political thought, but he did not indicate what kind of new values might arise from this blasted landscape. The idea that demagification represented only the path – but not the final destination – of Weber's political thought was articulated by another Weimar intellectual, the philosopher Karl Jaspers (1883–1969). What was left after Weber had dispelled the optimistic illusions and ideologies of nineteenth-century politics was not a mindless "biological process," Jaspers argued, but rather an opportunity to find new sources of meaning in individual self-cultivation and national greatness.

Politics and Faith

Like his role model, Max Weber, Jaspers was a wanderer between academic worlds. As a boy he fell in love with philosophy but resolved against pursuing it for a university degree. He began his studies in law, then switched to medicine and wrote a dissertation on "Homesickness and Crime." Afterwards he found work at the University of Heidelberg's psychiatric clinic, first as an intern and later as a voluntary research assistant. His preoccupation with the methodological foundations of psychopathology inspired him to seek out Max Weber, a reclusive but much admired figure in Heidelberg. Jaspers developed a close rapport with Max and Marianne Weber and their circle in the years before the First World War. With Weber's help as an intermediary, Jaspers was able to switch disciplines and find a teaching position in psychology at Heidelberg. At the end of the First World War Jaspers chose to reinvent himself once again, this time as a philosopher. He succeeded in obtaining a chair in philosophy at

Heidelberg and eventually established himself as one of Germany's leading intellectuals and a founding father of modern existential philosophy.

Jaspers was raised in a well-to-do, liberal family, the son of a bank director who served as president of the local city council and representative to the regional parliament. "Until 1914 my basic attitude was strictly non-political," he recalled in his memoirs. "Everything seemed to be definitive" (Jaspers [1957] 1981, 55). The First World War shattered his sense of complacency. No political party or ideology appeared capable of instilling optimism in the face of the awful realities of the war. "The likes of us can see no future political current which we would affirm," he wrote in a letter to his father on 11 July 1915:

> There's no prevailing idea which one could follow. In your youth, liberalism was something like that, but it's finished as a political possibility and force. Socialism hasn't yet found the form, principles or goals that would make it into a positive, ideal force. [...] Sometimes I have such dark feelings, as if socialism could produce something that appeals to our worldview, just as liberalism suitably dressed it in 1870: justice and solidarity must be decisive, as well as the aversion to luxury, mere hedonism, and the abstract impulse to acquire consciousness, spirit and enjoyment. – But every consideration simply makes the complete darkness of the future visible to us. Human life at the present time is dreadful: charged with injustice, violence and brutishness – except for the fact that everywhere in this vortex there are *individuals* who are sensitive, humane and philosophical. The world as a whole is unconditionally and entirely ruled by power considerations and, as [the Swiss historian Jacob] Burckhart says, "power as such is evil." I often have this feeling of horror in the face of the human world. (Jaspers Nachlass, Familienarchiv, Box 133)

In the midst of this political confusion, Max Weber became Jaspers's point of orientation and trusted source of news and analysis. Jaspers listened attentively to his political monologues during their Sunday teas, and often received reports from Marianne Weber about his visits to meet with officials in Berlin. Jaspers filled his wartime letters to his parents with summaries of Max Weber's pronouncements on the progress of the war and even recommended his articles to read.

Weber's political thought mattered to Jaspers because it offered a solution to the problem he expressed to his father: How could one reconcile the reality of power politics with the importance of individuals and the cultivation of their sensibility? Jaspers sketched out the solution in a short book titled *Max Weber: German Essence in Political Thought, Research and Philosophizing*, published in 1932. Jaspers acknowledged that Weber saw power struggles as the central element in all political life. In his wartime article "Between Two Laws," Weber had gone so far as to identify the "pragmatics of power" as "the law [...] that governs all political history." But in "Politics as a Vocation" he insisted that "some faith must be *there* [in political action], for otherwise even what seem outwardly to be the most glorious political successes will be cursed – and rightly so – with the meaninglessness of the natural world" (Weber [1916] 1994, 78; Weber [1919] 2004a, 78–79; cited in Jaspers 1932, 31, 32–33). What, then, was Weber's own political faith, the vision that legitimized and gave meaning to the pursuit of power politics? Jaspers found its purest expression in Weber's Freiburg inaugural address, where Weber hammered home the necessity of Germany's involvement in world politics. There Weber declared:

> The question which stirs us as we think beyond the grave of our own genera-tion is not the *well-being* human beings will enjoy in the future but what kind of people they will *be*, and it is this same question which underlies all work in political economy. We do not want to breed well-being in people, but rather those characteristics which we think of as constituting the human greatness and nobility of our nature. [...] Even our highest, our ultimate ideals in this life change and pass away. It cannot be our ambition to impose them on the future. But we *can* want the future to recognize the character *of its own ancestors* in us. Through our work and our nature we want to be the forerunners of that future race. (Weber [1895] 1994, 15)

As Jaspers understood it, the ultimate calling of political power for Weber – the sense of purpose that distinguished it from the struggles of the animal kingdom – lay in the intention to create conditions that were conducive for human greatness. Weber's "faith in politics" was manifested in his "will to serve the outward goals of everyday life while thinking about humankind – not only about our well being, but about the nobility of our nature" (Jaspers 1932, 32–33). Here, for Jaspers, lay the essence of Weber's political thought: the determination to serve the higher ideals of human nobility through engag-ing in power politics. Weber prized "the nobility of the human being and the world-political prestige of the nation – not one without the other." It was a powerful idea. But what did it actually mean? Why did modern politics need to address the conditions for human nobility? And how could the German nation-state serve the cause of human greatness? "His ultimate goal," Jaspers admitted, "disappears into vagueness" (35). Though Jaspers offered no further explanation in this book, he had already come to the conclusion that only exis-tential philosophy was capable of lending clarity to Weber's vision. Jaspers's own foray into political philosophy, *The Intellectual Situation of the Age*, published in the previous year, had attempted to articulate Weber's faith in this new philosophical idiom.

Jaspers spent over a decade thinking about the meaning of modern philosophy before he produced his three-volume magnum opus *Philosophy* in 1932. In the course of finishing the manuscript he decided to remove the sections on current events and publish them separately as a work of cultural criticism (Jaspers [1957] 1981, 60). The resulting book, *The Intellectual Situation of the Age*, first published in late 1931 and then reissued in a revised edition the following year, became a philosophical bestseller in late Weimar Germany and found its way "into the hands of almost all educated people in the shortest period of time, even though it is in no way easy reading," as the philosopher Karl Löwith noted (Saner 1973, 142). Well-informed readers were capable of recognizing Weber's rhetoric and distinctive concepts throughout the book. Kurt Blumenfeld, a leading figure in the German Zionist movement, wrote to the publisher Salman Schocken on 9 November 1931 to recommend *The Intellectual Situation of the Age*, noting that "everywhere [in the book] one recognizes the student of Weber, and it's a pleasure every time Max Weber is openly or surreptitiously cited" (Blumenfeld 1976, 114). Jaspers's efforts to make sense of Weber's concept of demagification, and its consequences for those who wished to pursue politics as a vocation, constituted one of the book's central themes.

The opening sections of *The Intellectual Situation of the Age* identified three sets of principles that formed the core of the "Western individual" (*der abendländische Mensch*): the rationality of Greek science, Roman law and economic calculation; the subjectivity of the Hebrew prophets, Greek philosophers and Roman statesmen; and finally the conception of the world as a "factual reality" to be confronted and changed (Jaspers [1932] 1999, 17–18). This thumbnail sketch incorporated all the key elements of "Western rationalism" as identified by Weber in *The Economic Ethics of the World Religions*, especially in his prefatory remarks (Weber [1920] 2002; [1920] 1951, 226–49; [1921] 1952, 267–335; [1921] 2000, 329–43; cf. Jaspers 1932, 41). Like Weber, Jaspers suggested that modern Western culture had given rise to a series of developments that threatened to undermine its own conceptions of individuality and subjectivity. One of the defining characteristics of the modern period, Jaspers asserted, was the phenomenon that the poet Friedrich Schiller had called the "de-divinification of the world" (*die Entgötterung der Welt*). Jaspers interpreted de-divinification in much the same sense as Weber's demagification: it signified a process that divested the natural world of divinities and demons, thereby transforming nature into the kind of inanimate matter that could be the subject of human knowledge. Judaeo-Christian religion, in positing the existence of a supernatural God who created all matter, contained the seeds of de-divinification; Protestantism, with its "affinity" for natural science, accelerated the development. As religious faith attenuated in the nineteenth century, the notion of a creator God eventually disappeared, leaving natural science as the only remaining mode of comprehending Being. The consequence was a profound and widely experienced sense of nihilism (Jaspers [1932] 1999, 20–21; cf. Weber [1919] 2004b, 14–17; [1920] 1951, 226–49; [1922] 1978, 551–56).

Over the course of the nineteenth century, de-divinification and technical progress had unleashed a population boom that necessitated the creation of an "existence-order" (*Daseinsordnung*) to provision the masses. The existence-order was constituted by modern capitalist enterprises, communication and transport networks, rational law and state administration, which sustained the expanding population of the industrialized world. In the interests of greater efficiency, the existence-order sought to maximize the rationalization and mechanization of all forms of human life. "State, community, factory, business, everything has been made into an enterprise [*Betrieb*] through bureaucracy," Jaspers declared in a typically Weberian turn of phrase (Jaspers [1932] 1999, 47; cf. Weber [1918] 1994, 146–49). The ensuing massification of society placed priority on the will of the majority; average talents and pleasures dominated popular culture, and public opinion came to exert an oppressive force on individual convictions. Individuals were dissociated from their traditional norms and roles with unprecedented force. "That which has produced our material existence, and has thus become indispensable for us, endangers man's own Being," Jaspers warned (Jaspers [1932] 1999, 41). Yet Jaspers, like Weber, did not contemplate the possibility of overturning the bureaucratic structure of the modern world. Despite its dehumanizing effects, the existence-order provided an unprecedented level of prosperity and safety. Instead of demanding a utopian transformation of the existence-order, Jaspers sought to disclose its limits, to illustrate the points at which the existential needs of mankind remained unfulfilled by the social organization that guaranteed its physical survival. *The Intellectual Situation of the Age* surveyed contemporary government, entertainment, culture and scholarship, pointing out their propensity to homogenize or essentialize the human spirit and appealed to individuals to look deep within themselves for the source of their own authentic Being. Jaspers sought to reclaim the essence of Western subjectivity associated with the Greek philosophers and Hebrew prophets and make it viable in the modern world.

One of the chief demands of modern politics, as Jaspers saw it, was to find a sense of meaning in the state after its existential inadequacies and limitations had been revealed. After divine justification for political authority had lost its plausibility, modern individuals had come to see the "actuality of power" as the core of all social orders, and the state as the association that "claims for itself the monopoly on the legitimate use of force (Max Weber)" (81, 79). The existential task facing modern individuals was to come to terms with a state that "neither has the luster of an authority which could grant objective metaphysical justification for its present concrete actions, nor which can be established as a rationalizable center for the planned provision of all human needs" (83). He equated this condition with the phenomenon of demagification: "In the aftermath of the demagification of the world, which first brought the state under the spotlight of inquiry and the will to know, the intellectual situation of the present enables every individual to enter into this space of collective human existence. The awful reality of human action in the world of state affairs will seem pitiless and relentless to them." Some individuals might respond to the danger of political nihilism with apathy or fanaticism. But there were ways to find meaning in the state without clinging to utopian expectations or universalizing ideologies. By facing up to the "reality of human action and decision making," individuals could "attain clarity about what they themselves want, not universally and everywhere, but historically with those people who represent authentic humanity to them" (82). If man's selfhood had been forgotten in the modern existence-order, then it fell to the state to ensure that fundamental decisions concerning the possibilities of human greatness would still be made. Availing himself of the language of existential philosophy, Jaspers interpreted political power as constituting a kind of existential decision, a determination of purpose that ran counter to the means-ends imperatives of the economy and the welfare state, on the one hand, and the claims of universal and homogeneous humanity, on the other (Turner and Factor 1984, 125; Thornhill 2002, 59–73). Participation in the activities of the state was not the path by which individuals could disclose their own, most personal Being, but it could enable them to rise above the purely instrumental considerations of the existence-order to articulate their culturally specific visions of human flourishing (Jaspers [1932] 1999, 76, 77, 78, 101, 104).

Jaspers identified himself as a "Westerner" (*Abendländer*), an admirer of classical humanism and a defender of the subjectivity exemplified by the Hebrew prophets and Greek philosophers (107, 177). When he paraphrased Weber's famous declaration from the Freiburg inaugural address in *The Intellectual Situation of the Age*, he emphasized that the form of humanity whose continuity he wished to maintain was rooted in a millennia-old tradition:

> The fundamental question is: What kind of human beings will live in the future? They concern us only if they possess a value and dignity that stands in continuity with the humanity that has developed in us over the past millennia; future

generations should be able to know us as their forefathers, not necessarily in a physical sense, but in a historical one. (188)

The only mission for German national power that Jaspers could conceive was a negative, defensive one: to serve as a defender of "Western" culture and individuality against the onslaught of Bolshevism. He concurred with Weber's assessment that Russian hegemony posed the greatest existential danger for Germany (Max Weber [1916] 1988, 169; Marianne Weber [1926] 2003, 636–37). The Soviet threat was so grave, Jaspers concluded, that Germany would need to work together with Western European countries to counteract it. He encouraged politicians to consider the "future interests of humanity," whose fate would be determined by "the contrasts between Western and Asiatic essence, European freedom and Russian fanaticism." A foreign policy that was "sustained by a comprehensive historical consciousness," he insisted, was one that remembered "the profound human and intellectual solidarity between the German, Anglo-Saxon and Romance essences" (Jaspers [1932] 1999, 103).

Conclusion

In addition to helping us understand why Weber mattered to his contemporaries, the early reception of "demagification" illuminates two significant tensions in his thought. The first concerns the relation between his sociological writings on religion, where demagification functions as an empirical and "value-free" concept, and his political writings, which enact many of the same processes associated with religious and scientific demagification. In the former texts, Weber generally sought to empathetically understand religious beliefs; in the latter, he was quick to reduce political convictions to a mere reflection of power interests. What accounts for the disjuncture between Weber's treatment of religious and political beliefs? One possible explanation is that Weber practiced the methodological distinction that he preached in "Science as a Vocation": that while scholarship operates through contemplative inquiry, the essence of politics is unremitting struggle, and the rules of comportment in one domain of human life do not necessary apply in another. On this interpretation, Weber felt obligated to treat the religious views of his sociological subjects with understanding, but when it came to the clash of political ideals he gave himself license to resort to the most effective rhetorical tactics (Baehr and Gordon 2012, 389; see Weber [1919] 2004b, 20). Another possible explanation is also worth considering: that Weber was capable of dismissing religious as well as political beliefs, provided he found them inauthentic, even though political beliefs were the ones that tended to bear the brunt of his criticism.

"Science as a Vocation" was an occasion when he took the opportunity to dismantle what he considered ersatz religious or mystical beliefs among his contemporaries:

> Never has a new prophecy come into being because (and I deliberately repeat a metaphor that some have found offensive) many modern intellectuals experience the need to furnish their souls, as it were, with antique objects that have been guaranteed genuine. They then recollect that religion once belonged among these antiques. It is something they do not happen to possess, but by way of a substitute they are ready to play at decorating a private chapel with pictures of the saints that they have picked up in all sorts of places, or to create a surrogate by collecting experiences of all kinds that they endow with the dignity of a mystical sanctity – and which they then hawk around the book markets. This is simply fraud or self-deception. (Weber [1919] 2004b, 29–30)

Weber refused to acknowledge the New Age beliefs of his German contemporaries as authentic religious experience. While he did not seek to reduce the content of their beliefs to "interest situations," his charges of "fraud or self-deception" were reminiscent of the treatment accorded to the "literati" in his wartime journalism.

Sincerity mattered greatly to Weber. Though he frequently savaged the political views of his contemporaries, he implied that he could – at least in principle – admire the convictions of a political opponent, so long as they were authentic and responsibly held. In "Politics as a Vocation," he admitted that he found it "immeasurably moving when a *mature* human being – whether young or old in actual years is immaterial – who feels the responsibility he bears for the consequences of his own actions with his entire soul and who acts in harmony with an ethics of responsibility reaches the point where he says, 'Here I stand, I can do no other'" (Weber [1919] 2004a, 92). These passages suggest that Weber's empathetic approach to religious beliefs may have only extended to traditional world religions, and that his debunking approach to politics was intended to spare – or even inspire – the idealist who was both committed and mature (a rare bird, as far as Weber was concerned). In *The Intellectual Situation of the Age*, Jaspers argued that the demagification of the state made it possible for individuals to confront the limitations of political action and nonetheless pursue their anti-utopian projects with open eyes and renewed convictions. One does not have to accept *The Intellectual Situation of the Age* as a "faithful" rendition of Weber's political thought to see how it tried to make sense of a powerful theme that he raised: the notion that the demagification of the world and the cultivation of political maturity could go hand in hand.

The second tension in Weber's thought, as illuminated by these Weimar-era interpretations, concerns the nature of his own normative standpoint. In *Battleship Building and Party Politics*, Kehr commented on Weber's "icy style, through which, paradoxically, [his] passion radiated" (Kehr 1930, 404). Weber believed that all great leaders were required to combine these Apollonian and Dionysian qualities. "The heart of the problem [of political leadership]," as he explained in "Politics as a Vocation," "is how to forge a unity between hot passion and a cool sense of proportion in one and the same person" (Weber [1919] 2004a, 77). This unstable admixture of opposing elements in Weber's own persona was susceptible to widely diverging interpretations, depending on which features of his oeuvre or personality were adduced as evidence. For some contemporaries, Weber's ethos signified a responsible and committed acceptance of the ineluctable realities of modern life; to others, it exemplified the search for profound, nonuniversalizable values in an age when traditional values and ideologies had lost their legitimacy (Derman 2010). The attempt to reconcile these tensions – to forge a unity between Weber's scholarship and his politics and make sense of his own normative stance toward the world – preoccupied many of his contemporaries. Nearly a century after his death, these puzzles have lost none of their ability to fascinate.

Works Cited

Standard English translations of Weber's work have been quoted whenever possible. On some occasions, I have amended these translations in the interests of fidelity to the original German texts. I am very grateful to Peter Baehr for his comments on an earlier version of this chapter.

Baehr, Peter, and Daniel Gordon. 2012. "Unmasking and Disclosure as Sociological Practices: Contrasting Modes for Understanding Religious and Other Beliefs." *Journal of Sociology* 48 (4): 380–96.

Beetham, David. 1985. *Max Weber and the Theory of Modern Politics*. Cambridge: Polity.

Berghahn, V. R. 2005. *Imperial Germany, 1871–1918: Economy, Society, Culture, and Politics*. 2nd ed. New York: Berghahn.

Blumenfeld, Kurt. 1976. *Im Kampf um den Zionismus: Briefe aus fünf Jahrzehnten*. Edited by Miriam Sambursky and Jochanan Ginat. Stuttgart: Deutsche Verlags-Anstalt.

Derman, Joshua. 2010. "Skepticism and Faith: Max Weber's Anti-Utopianism in the Eyes of his Contemporaries." *Journal of the History of Ideas* 71 (3): 481–503.

———2012. *Max Weber in Politics and Social Thought: From Charisma to Canonization*. Cambridge: Cambridge University Press.

Eley, Geoff. 1978. "Capitalism and the Wilhelmine State: Industrial Growth and Political Backwardness in Recent German Historiography, 1890–1918." *Historical Journal* 21 (3): 737–50.

Ferguson, Niall. 1998. *The Pity of War*. London: Penguin.

Hennis, Wilhelm. 1987. *Max Webers Fragestellung: Studien zur Biographie des Werks*. Tübingen: Mohr Siebeck.

Hobson, Rolf. 2002. *Imperialism at Sea: Naval Strategic Thought, the Ideology of Sea Power, and the Tirpitz Plan, 1875–1914*. Boston: Brill.

Jaspers, Karl. (1932) 1999. *Die geistige Situation der Zeit*. Berlin: De Gruyter.

————1932. *Max Weber: Deutsches Wesen im politischen Denken, im Forschen und Philosophieren*. Oldenburg: Stalling.

————(1957) 1981. "Philosophical Autobiography." In *The Philosophy of Karl Jaspers*, pp. 5–94, edited by Paul Arthur Schilpp. La Salle, IL: Open Court.

————Nachlass. Deutsches Literaturarchiv, Marbach.

Kehr, Eckart. (1928) 1965a. "Englandhaß und Weltpolitik." In *Der Primat der Innenpolitik: Gesammelte Aufsätze zur preußisch-deutschen Sozialgeschichte im 19. und 20. Jahrhundert*, pp. 149–75, edited by Hans-Ulrich Wehler. Berlin: De Gruyter.

————(1928) 1965b. "Soziale und finanzielle Grundlagen der Tirpitzschen Flottenpropaganda." In *Der Primat der Innenpolitik: Gesammelte Aufsätze zur preußisch-deutschen Sozialgeschichte im 19. und 20. Jahrhundert*, pp. 130–48, edited by Hans-Ulrich Wehler. Berlin: De Gruyter.

————1930. *Schlachtflottenbau und Parteipolitik 1894–1901: Versuch eines Querschnitts durch die innenpolitischen, sozialen und ideologischen Voraussetzungen des deutschen Imperialismus*. Berlin: Ebering.

Lehmann, Hartmut. 2009. *Die Entzauberung der Welt: Studien zu Themen von Max Weber*. Göttingen: Wallstein.

Matthiesen, Ulf. 1988. "'Im Schatten einer endlosen großen Zeit': Etappen der intellektuellen Biographie Albert Salomons." In *Exil, Wissenschaft, Identität: Die Emigration deutscher Sozialwissenschaftler 1933–1945*, pp. 299–350, edited by Ilja Srubar. Frankfurt am Main: Suhrkamp.

Mommsen, Wolfgang J. 1973. "Domestic Factors in German Foreign Policy before 1914." *Central European History* 6 (1): 3–43.

————1980. *Theories of Imperialism*. Translated by P.S. Falla. Chicago: University of Chicago Press.

————1984. *Max Weber and German Politics, 1890–1920*. Translated by Michael S. Steinberg. Chicago: University of Chicago Press.

————1990. *Der autoritäre Nationalstaat: Verfassung, Gesellschaft und Kultur im deutschen Kaiserreich*. Frankfurt am Main: Fischer.

Salomon, Albert. 1926. "Max Weber." *Die Gesellschaft* 3, Part I: 131–53.

Saner, Hans, ed. 1973. *Karl Jaspers in der Diskussion*. Munich: Piper.

Schluchter, Wolfgang. 2009. "'Die Entzauberung der Welt': Max Webers Sicht auf die Moderne." In *Die Entzauberung der Welt*, pp. 1–17. Tübingen: Mohr Siebeck.

Sheehan, James J. 1968. "The Primacy of Domestic Politics: Eckart Kehr's Essays on Modern German History." *Central European History* 1 (2): 166–74

Thornhill, Chris. 2002. *Karl Jaspers: Politics and Metaphysics*. London: Routledge.

Turner, Stephen. 2004. "Morgenthau as a Weberian." In *One Hundred Year Commemoration to the Life of Hans Morgenthau (1904–2004)*, pp. 88–114, edited by G. O. Mazur. New York: Semenenko Foundation.

Turner, Stephen P., and Regis A. Factor. 1984. *Max Weber and the Dispute over Reason and Value: A Study in Philosophy, Ethics, and Politics*. London: Routledge & Kegan Paul.

Weber, Marianne. [1926] 2003. *Max Weber: A Biography*. Translated and edited by Harry Zohn. New Brunswick, NJ: Transaction.

Weber, Max. [1895] 1994. "The Nation State and Economic Policy." In *Political Writings*, pp. 1–28, edited by Peter Lassman and Ronald Speirs. Cambridge: Cambridge University Press.

————[1896] 1988. "Zur Gründung einer national-sozialen Partei." In *Gesammelte Politische Schriften*, pp. 26–29, edited by Johannes Winckelmann. Tübingen: Mohr Siebeck.

————[1898] 1988. "Stellungnahme zur Flottenumfrage der Allgemeinen Zeitung." In *Gesammelte Politische Schriften*, pp. 30–32, edited by Johannes Winckelmann. Tübingen: Mohr Siebeck.

————[1904] 1988. "Agrarstatistische und sozialpolitische Betrachtungen zur Fideikommißfrage in Preußen." In *Gesammelte Aufsätze zur Soziologie und Sozialpolitik*, pp. 323–93, edited by Marianne Weber. Tübingen: Mohr Siebeck.

————[1910] 2002. "A Final Rebuttal of Rachfahl's Critique of the 'Spirit of Capitalism.'" In *The Protestant Ethic and the "Spirit" of Capitalism and Other Writings*, pp. 282–339, edited and translated by Peter Baehr and Gordon C. Wells. New York: Penguin.

————[1915] 1946a. "Religious Rejections of the World and Their Directions." In *From Max Weber*, pp. 323–59, edited and translated by H. H. Gerth and C. Wright Mills. New York: Oxford University Press.

————[1915] 1946b. "The Social Psychology of the World Religions." In *From Max Weber*, pp. 267–301, edited and translated by H. H. Gerth and C. Wright Mills. New York: Oxford University Press.

————[1916] 1994. "Between Two Laws." In *Political Writings*, pp. 75–79, edited by Peter Lassman and Ronald Speirs. Cambridge: Cambridge University Press.

————[1916] 1988. "Deutschland unter den europäischen Weltmächten." In *Gesammelte Politische Schriften*, pp. 157–77, edited by Johannes Winckelmann. Tübingen: Mohr Siebeck.

————[1918] 1994. "Parliament and Government in Germany under a New Political Order." In *Political Writings*, pp. 130–271, edited by Peter Lassman and Ronald Speirs. Cambridge: Cambridge University Press.

————[1919] 2004a. "Politics as a Vocation." In *The Vocation Lectures*, pp. 32–94, edited by David Owen and Tracy B. Strong, translated by Rodney Livingstone. Indianapolis: Hackett.

————[1919] 2004b. "Science as a Vocation." In *The Vocation Lectures*, pp. 1–31, edited by David Owen and Tracy B. Strong, translated by Rodney Livingstone. Indianapolis: Hackett.

————[1920] 2002. "Prefatory Remarks to *Collected Essays in the Sociology of Religion*." In *The Protestant Ethic and the "Spirit" of Capitalism and Other Writings*, pp. 356–72, edited and translated by Peter Baehr and Gordon C. Wells. New York: Penguin.

————[1920] 2009. *The Protestant Ethic and the Spirit of Capitalism*. In *The Protestant Ethic and the Spirit of Capitalism with Other Writings on the Rise of the West*, pp. 61–159, edited and translated by Stephen Kalberg. New York: Oxford University Press.

————[1920] 1951. *The Religion of China: Confucianism and Taoism*. Edited and translated by Hans H. Gerth. Glencoe, IL: The Free Press.

————[1921] 1952. *Ancient Judaism*. Edited and translated by Hans H. Gerth and Don Martindale. New York: The Free Press.

————[1921] 2000. *The Religion of India: The Sociology of Hinduism and Buddhism*. Edited and translated by Hans H. Gerth and Don Martindale. New Delhi: Munshiram Manoharlal.

————[1922] 1978. *Economy and Society: An Outline of Interpretive Sociology*. Edited by Guenther Roth and Claus Wittich. Berkeley: University of California Press.

————1994. *Political Writings*. Edited by Peter Lassman and Ronald Speirs. Cambridge: Cambridge University Press.

Wehler, Hans-Ulrich. 1980. "Eckart Kehr." In *Historische Sozialwissenschaft und Geschichtsschreibung: Studien zu Aufgaben und Traditionen deutscher Geschichtswissenschaft*, pp. 227–48. Göttingen: Vandenhoeck & Ruprecht.

Weiß, Johannes. 1991. "Max Weber: Die Entzauberung der Welt." In *Grundprobleme der großen Philosophen: Philosophie der Gegenwart*, Vol. 4, pp. 9–47, edited by Josef Speck. Göttingen: Vandenhoeck & Ruprecht.

———1992. *Max Webers Grundlegung der Soziologie*. Munich: Saur.

Winckelmann, Johannes. 1980. "Die Herkunft von Max Webers 'Entzauberungs'-Konzeption: Zugleich ein Beitrag zu der Frage, wie gut wir das Werk Max Webers kennen können." *Kölner Zeitschrift für Soziologie und Sozialpsychologie* 32: 12–53.

Chapter 11

THE RELEVANCE OF MAX WEBER FOR POLITICAL THEORY TODAY

Terry Maley

There are a number of overlapping or interlocking theoretical, philosophical, historical and political contexts in which I want to situate my discussion of Max Weber's relevance for political theory today. The first is the (latest) revival in Weber scholarship that has gained momentum since around the time of the fall of the Berlin Wall. This has as its historical backdrop the dramatic changes wrought by globalization as well as the rise of cultural/identity politics in the 1980s and 90s. This era has also seen a resurgence of far right and far left politics in Europe and in the United States. We have seen eruptions of social and anti-capitalist protest movements in the global North and South in the 1990s and again since the financial crisis of 2008. Demonstrators have protested against the growing global social and economic inequality symbolized by the Occupy movement's slogan of the 99% vs the 1%. Far-right nationalist politics have reappeared across Continental and Eastern Europe, and now, disturbingly in the US Presidential election campaign in the form of Donald Trump.

These shifts have produced fractious debates about the relationship between liberalism and democracy in the postcommunist era. Among democratic theorists there is no consensus about the continuing viability of liberal democracy or what new political ideals or institutions should replace it. The foundations of modern democracy have once again become problematic at a time when the fundamental assumptions about Western liberal democracies are being questioned. One of the key issues animating recent debates in democratic theory has been the meaning of the "political," or what the foundations of modern politics can be today. Tracy Strong, after Hannah Arendt, says that doing political theory in the twenty-first century means thinking "without a bannister."

In the past 15 years democratic theorists have made new connections between Weber's view of democracy, leadership and the political. It is significant that these analyses of Weber have taken place alongside discussions of mid-twentieth-century thinkers who are critical of liberalism such as Carl Schmitt and Hannah Arendt. These engagements have complicated and enriched our appreciation of Weber's contribution to democratic theory.

The Weber Revival(s)

Before I comment on some of the most recent interventions in democratic theory involving Weber I want to briefly touch on previous "phases" of his complex reception history in US social theory since World War II. I will then discuss "parallel" developments in political and democratic theory. I want to show that looking at these closely related disciplinary traditions (social and political/democratic theory) can illuminate key issues in Weber's democratic politics and our own. They each illustrate Robert Antonio's view that "just when he (Weber) seems to have lost relevance, like a phoenix, he appears again on the horizon" (Antonio 2005, 1). In focusing on Weber's reception history I will discuss some theorists as much as Weber, whose "model" of democracy I have recently explored in a book-length study.

In the 1980s poststructural thought migrated from Continental Europe to the United States, permeating American literary and social theory. Poststructural or postmodern thought criticizes what philosophers call the metaphysics of presence – that natural phenomena are universally accessible to individual consciousness. Poststructural theorists are often critical of the eighteenth-century Enlightenment, modern liberal and socialist ideals such as the individual, the working class, the sovereignty of the "people" and Western ideals of freedom, liberty and equality. Thinkers (Derrida, Lyotard, Deleuze, Baudrillard) launched devastating critiques of the universal foundations of modern philosophy, liberal-democracy, representation, social scientific knowledge and modern ideas of subjectivity. As Antonio notes, modern theories that claim legitimacy for universal "macro-subjects" as agents of historical change have been subjected to withering critiques as "essentialist" – claiming to be universal when they are not. Criticisms of "strong-program" postmodernists reflect an anxiety about "the erosion of the post-war [World War II] system and ... the decline of its chief mode of legitimation, modernization" (Antonio 2005, 15).

Yet after the fall of the Berlin Wall not everyone was enamored with post-modernism. Other social theorists (re)turned to Weber. At a time when Marx was temporarily set aside by Western social theory, interest in Weber surged. In the 1980s Anglo-American scholars who explored Weber's thought such as Lawrence Scaff, Alan Sica, David Beetham, Charles Turner, Stephen Turner, Sam Whimster, Harvey Goldman, Peter Lassman, Robert Eden, Edward Portis and others did pioneering work in recovering aspects of Weber's historical, cultural intellectual and political contexts. They followed German scholars such as Wilhelm Hennis, Guenther Roth, Friedrich Tenburck and Wolfgang Schluchter.

The turn of the new millennium also brought new translations by Stephan Kalberg and Peter Baehr marking the one hundredth anniversary of *The Protestant Ethic and the Spirit of Capitalism* (Kalberg, 2002; Baehr, 2002). New translations of the famous lectures *Science* and *Politics as a Vocation* came out in 2004 (Strong, 2004). In 2004 an issue of the new journal *Max Weber Studies* explored "Max Weber's Relevance as a Theorist of Politics." In 2007 Laurence McFalls, editor of a volume of essays on Weber's social scientific "objectivity," reminded us of the complex "reception history" (*Rezeptionsgeschichte*) of Weber's work by social and political scientists in different cultural and historical contexts. (McFalls 2007, 24n38) Work by Wolfgang Mommsen, Sam Whimster and others on the *Gesaumptaussgabe*, the collective project to assemble all of Weber's work, brought previously untranslated writings to the English-speaking audience.

Antonio argues that the Weber revival is a complex phenomenon that has its roots in "phases" after World War II. He sees Weber's American reception history gathering around the theme of "homogenization-regimentation." This theme was developed by American and émigré social theorists on the left and the right who were critical of American-led modernization. Through this lens Antonio traces the "shifting interpretations of Weber's work in different phases of postwar American culture, society and politics" (Antonio 2005, 1–2).

Yet the "early" liberal form of this theme was put forward uncritically by Talcott Parsons after he introduced Weber to the Anglo-American audience with his translation of the *Protestant Ethic and the Spirit of Capitalism* (Parsons 1930/1992). The *Protestant Ethic* celebrates the origins of modern Western capitalism in the religious individualism of the early American Puritan sects. Parsons read Weber through a Durkheimian lens that emphasizes social cohesion with "a functionalist twist that was absent in Weber" (Antonio 2005, 2). In *The Structure of Social Action* (Parsons 1937/1968, 14) Parsons developed a theory of social action that emphasizes integration. As Antonio notes, Parsons generalizes the American example as a model of universal development in the West (Antonio 2005, 3). This reflects the prosperity of the "long economic boom" after World War II. Parsons's optimistic reading of the *Protestant Ethic* and social integration "legitimated the early postwar era's "liberal consensus," or the view that US capitalism's secularized Protestantism, managerial firms, advanced technology and modest Keynesian regulatory and welfare state policies unlocked the secret of continuous growth, (and) ended class warfare" (Antonio 2005, 3).

C. W. Mills's more critical interpretation (Gerth and Mills 1975) emphasizes affinities between Weber and Marx. Mills argues that the two thinkers are complementary in their historical analyses of capitalism. Mills and Hans Gerth provided the first English translations of the famous lectures *Science* and *Politics as a Vocation*. For Mills the contours of the "homogenization–regimentation" theme emerge in Weber's sociology of domination and in his discussions of disenchantment and bureaucracy in *Science as a Vocation* (Weber 2004). Mills also notes Nietzsche's influence on Weber, arguing that for Weber disenchantment as a philosophical problem emerges in a world in which, as Nietzsche said, "god is dead." In a secular modern world without dominant religious value systems individuals are left on their own to deal with a plurality of values – what Weber calls the "warring gods." The texts Gerth and Mills translated, which include parts of *Economy and Society*, the *Sociology of Religion*, and some of Weber's World War I political writings, revealed a Weber who was much more ambivalent about modernization than Parsons. Weber's concepts of disenchantment, meaning, science, objectivity, values, modern capitalism and democracy would not be accessible today as ideas of *critical social, political and philosophical analysis* without these texts.

In Germany Weber's post-World War II reception was shaped by different historical concerns. Wolfgang Mommsen and Jürgen Habermas are critical of what they see as Weber's obsession with charismatic leadership and its effects on German politics leading up to the Nazi era. Mommsen calls Weber's leadership politics "decisionist" and (initially) argued that his views helped pave the way for Hitler's ascent to power (Mommsen 1984). In the 1970s, after two decades of prosperity and the social/cultural turmoil of 1968, Wolfgang Schluchter and Habermas explored the ethic of responsibility and rationalization in the modern West. Friedrich Tenbruck asked whether there was a central theme in Weber's work. (Schluchter 1979; Habermas 1984; Tenbruck, 1989) These assessments revised the more pessimistic side of Weber's version of the "homogenization–regimentation" theme, retrieving the positive legacy of the Enlightenment in his work.

The work of émigré social philosophers such as Leo Strauss on the right and Frankfurt School thinkers Herbert Marcuse, Max Horkheimer and Theodor Adorno on the "New Left" complicated Weber's post–World War II reception history. Strauss and the Critical Theorists who fled Nazi Germany are critical of what they see as Weber's liberal "relativism" and the Enlightenment legacy in his work. As Horkheimer and Adorno said in *Dialectic of Enlightenment* in 1947:

> Enlightenment, understood in the widest sense as the advance of thought, has always aimed at liberating human beings from fear and installing them as masters. Yet the wholly enlightened earth is radiant with triumphant calamity. Enlightenment's program was the disenchantment of the world. (Horkheimer and Adorno 2002, 1)

Disenchantment is to "dispel myths, to overthrow fantasy with knowledge" (Horkheimer and Adorno 2002, 1). But the domination of nature and society, even the barbarism of the Nazi tyranny, are, for the critical theorists, inherent in Reason. In modernity Reason, manifested in the rational scientific and technical knowledge that underpins the modern bureaucratic state and capitalist economy, is totalizing (Wolin 1994, 164). Marcuse's *One Dimensional Man* (1964) sees American modernization as the triumph of a corporate culture of standardized mass production and regimented consumption. Marcuse calls this the "administered" society and sees its conformity as culturally totalizing. It is one-dimensional because the uniformity of this new phase of what Marcuse called monopoly capitalism effectively neutralizes all opposition, eliminating the "second" dimension of any kind of critical thinking about fundamentally different ways of organizing the economy, the state, culture or our relationship with nature.

The Critical Theorists' critique of modernization is grounded in Continental philosophy. This includes a holistic Hegelian vision of history as a totality and a reduced Marxism that accepts the disappearance of the working class as the universal agent of change. It also argues that the culture industries – Hollywood, popular music and advertising – repress our instinctual desires for happiness, channeling them into aggressive pursuits such as escapist consumerism and military/imperial competition.

The homogenization–regimentation theme takes a different form in Leo Strauss's conservative critique of Weber's methodological individualism. In *Natural Right and History* (1953) Strauss argues that for Weberian social science "there cannot be any genuine knowledge of the Ought" (Strauss 1953, 41) because of the equality of values under modern liberalism. Modern value pluralism means that for Weber "there is no possible social order or cultural order that can be said to be *the* right or rational order." Values are about individual choice and nothing higher. In Strauss's view this "leads to nihilism or to the view that every preference, however base, evil or insane, has to be judged before the tribunal of reason to be as legitimate as any other preference" (Strauss 1953, 42).

For the ancient Greek philosophers such as Plato and Aristotle, only Reason provided objective knowledge of natural right, or the proper ends of human and political life. For Strauss, "Natural right in its classic form is connected with a teleological view of the universe. All natural beings have a natural end... which determines what kind of operation is good for them ... reason determines what is by nature right" (Strauss 1953, 7).

Social science's role is to "search for the proper means to those ends; it would lead up to objective ... value judgments regarding policies" (Strauss 1953, 42). But it is only a select few philosophers who are capable of under-standing ends. I think Jeremy Valentine is right in seeing Strauss's view as a "pre-modern nostalgia" for hierarchy and order (Valentine 2006, 506).

Antonio sees in these critiques an exaggeration of the "dark side of Weber's account of rationalization, in isolation from other parts of his work that affirm modernity" (Antonio 2005, 6). This echoes Habermas's argument in *Theory of Communicative Action* (Habermas 1984) that the Frankfurt theorists' one-sided reading of Weber's idea of instrumental rationality did not leave open possibili-ties for the creation of a public sphere based on communication and solidarity, a potentiality made possible by modern economic, cultural and democratic developments. How to create a new "political" today that realizes this potenti-ality is a key issue for the democratic theorists I will discuss later in the chapter.

The developments I have been discussing influenced Weber scholarship for a decade after the mid-1990s. Peter Breiner's *Max Weber and Democracy* and his subsequent discussions are some of the most promising works on Weber's demo-cratic thought to emerge from the revival. (Breiner 1996, 2005, 2007) Breiner's work shifts the focus from the relationship between leadership and liberalism to the role of political judgment in Weber's thought. David Beetham had looked critically at Weber's liberalism in the 1980s (Beetham 1988, 1994). Breiner argues that for Weber the judgment of political actors is a link between histori-cal contingency, on the one hand, and the irreversibility of modern bureaucracy that Weber saw (famously at the end of the end of the *Protestant Ethic*) as an iron cage or "steel-hard casing" (*stahlhartes Gehäuse*), on the other. Breiner argues that Weber exploited both sides of this tension. Against left-leaning political oppo-nents, for example, Weber argued that direct democracy was not *feasible* because of the "inevitability" of bureaucracy in modern states. Building on Breiner's view I argue that in using this strategy, Weber tries to define not only the limits of modern democracy but the limits of the political (Maley 2011, 41).

Kari Palonen, in his discussion of Weber's ideas of freedom and democracy sees Weber as a theorist of contingency, though not in the strong postmodern sense that everything is always contingent and without foundations. Rather,

3

Palonen links contingency in Weber's democratic thought to the freedom to act, seeing freedom as critical to Weber's democratic politics. Sung Ho Kim's work on *Max Weber's Politics of Civil Society* reconstructs Weber's theory of democratic legitimacy, emphasizing the central role civil society associations play as spaces for citizen/leadership training that tests and legitimizes the ethically disciplined citizen. Kim traces the origin of this citizen training to the early American puritan sects. He sees the influence of this unique cultural legacy extending into the twentieth-century American experience of pluralism and strong civil society associations. These attempts to retrieve aspects of Weber's democratic thought have been made without postmodern critics' assumptions regarding the inauthenticity of representation or critical theory's view of the totalizing nature of instrumental rationality. Their work signals a shift away from the homogenization–regimentation thesis toward the historical origins and current implications of democracy in Weber's thought.

Over the last 15 years democratic theorists have also been spurred by critiques of the pluralist- or competitive-elitist model of democracy. The model was popularized by Joseph Schumpeter and Robert Dahl (Schumpeter 1976, Dahl 1961, 1971). For a generation after World War II, it was the dominant explanation of how democracy worked. According to democratic theorist C. B. Macpherson, the plural-elitist model "starts from the assumption that the society which a modern democratic system must fit is a plural society ... consisting of individuals each of whom is pulled in many directions by his many interests." It is elitist because "it assigns the main role in the political process to a self-chosen group of leaders" (Macpherson 1977, 77). The model assumes that democracy "consists of a competition between two or more self-chosen sets of politicians (elites), arrayed in political parties, for the votes which will entitle them to rule until the next election." Further, "the voters' role is not to decide political issues and then chose representatives who will carry out ... decisions: it is... to choose the men who will do the deciding." Democracy "is ... a market mechanism: the voters are the consumers; the politicians are the entrepreneurs" (Macpherson 1977, 78–79). As Breiner rightly argues, gone from this model is Weber's concern with the character of leaders (Breiner 2005).

David Held argues that in this model "the role of ordinary citizens is ... highly delimited" and even seen "as an unwanted infringement on the smooth functioning of 'public' decision-making." Held joins Schumpeter's view with Weber's in the following remark:

Along with Max Weber, Schumpeter too hastily closed off the exploration of other possible models in democratic theory and practice, beyond those posed by the control of public affairs by all citizens or by competitive elites. Along with Max Weber, he registered significant trends in modern politics – the development of the competitive party system, the ability of those in power to set agendas, the domination of elites in national politics – and uncritically cast them into rigid patterns: a basis for the claim that, ultimately, only one particular model of democracy is appropriate to the contemporary age. (Held 1996, 198)

The model of parliamentary democracy Weber proposed during and after World War I was the precursor to Schumpeter's view. The role Weber assigned to ordinary citizens conforms to this view closely. This is so even though Weber, as a progressive liberal in Germany, wanted equal suffrage as a central component of a new parliamentary system after the post-World War I collapse of the authoritarian monarchy and its three-tiered voting system. (Weber 1994; Maley 2011) Even though the context of post–World War I Weimar Germany was very different from post–World War II United States, the tendencies that Weber and Schumpeter identified became central to the competitive-elitist or realist model that became dominant after World War II.

After coming under heavy criticism by democratic theorists a version of the realist view has had a revival recently. In *The Eyes of the People* Jeffrey Green argues that "Democracy hitherto has been conceived as an empowerment of the People's voice." Green issues "a call to consider the People's *eyes* as an organ that might more properly function as a site of popular empowerment" (Green 2010, 3). Democratic theory has been largely grounded on the assumption that it is the people's voice that defines their sovereignty. Green finds that "by itself, this focus is too narrow and too productive of a democratic theory out of touch with the way politics is experienced by most people most of the time and by the People itself (the mass of everyday, non-office-holding citizens in their *collective* capacity) all of the time. The fact is that for most of us, our political voice is something we exercise rarely if at all" (Green 2010, 3–4). Green addresses the pervasive citizen *spectatorship* in modern liberal democracies. He redefines the problem of political passivity that observers today see as part of the "democratic deficit." Green sees spectatorship as "a problem that indicates the distinctive difficulties besetting democratic life at the dawn of the twenty-first century." Mass communications technologies and television (and now the internet) have turned the majority of citizens into a permanent spectator class. It is a hierarchical, top-down relationship with "little rotation between actor and spectator" (Green 2010, 4). There is little room for response by ordinary citizens.

Green's response to "the specific pathologies and dysfunctions that have accompanied democratic development over the course of the last century" is to revive "a forgotten alternative within democratic theory: …plebiscitary democracy" (Green 2010, 5). He traces this back to Weber, claiming that today it can "develop political principles that ... respect the everyday structure of political experience. Taking spectatorship seriously is a way of respecting the political lives of ordinary people." He argues that an "ocular" model of democracy "represents a new ethical paradigm that would reshape the way the moral meaning of democracy is approached"(Green 2010, 6,7). The hard question Green asks is how can modern democracies, which are governed by elites who control huge complex institutions, come to terms with existing, very low democratic capacities of ordinary citizens. Those capacities are largely reduced to watching politics by institutional, cultural and other barriers in the competitive-elite system. The only realistic way of correcting this today, Green suggests, is to shift the focus of democracy from the people, who are not sovereign and do not govern in any meaningful way, back to leaders. In doing so he wants to revive some of the plebiscitary practices he sees in Weber's emphasis on leaders in the *Profession and Vocation of Politics* (Weber 2004).

Green's proposal for correcting the defects of mass democracy is to subject leaders to more visible public scrutiny. He suggests that prominent forums (such as presidential debates) where party leaders are not in control of events or their own public appearances are the appropriate venues for this. By compelling them to respond to "spontaneous" events the people will be able to decide whether leaders are capable of governing. This will have a "disciplinary" effect on leaders; they will behave publicly with more "candor" and accountability. Green argues that he turns the work of Michel Foucault "on its head"; Foucault's idea of the disciplinary surveillance of populations (Foucault 1995) can be turned back onto political leaders (Green 2010, 154).

While democratic theorists have been critical of realist models like Green's, he notes that they have not agreed on what to replace it with. Green is critical of deliberative democrats who want citizens to rationally discuss issues and arrive at a consensus – this now occurs very rarely even in smaller settings. He is also critical of pluralist democrats who emphasize the "multiplicity of civic ties" and want a wider range of voices to be heard. Pluralist's arguments cannot deal with existing institutional inequalities of power (Green 2010, 57, 73). Working from a more mainstream institutional view of political science, Green seems to accept an implicit version of the homogenization–regimentation thesis. He accepts the uniform citizen apathy of the competitive-elite model as a given. He does not mention the "latest" stream in democratic theory, radical democrats who are critical of both representative democracy and its relationship to global capitalism. There is no critical discussion by Green of the effects of corporate power on democracy today. Weber was keenly aware of this in his criticisms of the power of the "ruthless barons of heavy industry" in German politics (Maley 2011). Theorists such as Bruce Ackerman and

Sheldon Wolin want the people to retain their autonomy and capacity for self-legislation. Ackerman talks about exceptional moments of crisis such as constitutional founding (Ackerman, 1991, 1998) while Wolin argues that under existing competitive-elite democracy moments of true democratic solidarity can only be created by citizens in "fugitive" moments that are noninstitutionalized (Wolin, 1996, 2004). Nor does Green acknowledge that significant changes have come about through protest and civil disobedience.

A basic problem with Green's view is that there is so much that leaders, parties, and officials already do through their control of the bureaucratic means of politics (parties) and administration (of the state) *away from* the eyes of the people. Even if the people can compel leaders to be more candid in rare unscripted moments, they still, under the current arrangements, cannot control leaders very effectively most of the time (to turn Green's argument "on its head"). Green argues that citizens as spectators can develop capacities for critical judgment in his "ocular" model. How effective they would be is an open question. Citizens can still participate in their communities, groups and associations. But Green's ocular model leaves the core sources of postmodern power – the state, the commanding heights of corporate power in the global economy and the symbolic power of the culture and media industries – untouched. Green's view also does not take into account some of the more "authoritarian" features of the modern state today (i.e., information and "big data" gathering). Still, Green asks some tough questions to which democratic theorists have to respond.

Green is critical of democratic theorists for not specifying alternatives to his plebiscitary/realist model. The lack of consensus is perhaps not surprising, given the resilience of a crisis-ridden global capitalism and (at least in the global north) representative democracy. Both systems have proved very adaptable. The world in which we live is not quite Fukuyama's triumphant liberalism (Fukuyama 1992). There are cracks; the legitimacy of the global economic order and the Western democracies that created it after World War II has come under serious strain. We have seen the return of old warring gods such as religion and the proliferation of new ones in the form of ecological and other social movements. It is harder to argue for the dominance of a seamless homogenization–regimentation thesis today. Yet the institutional and symbolic pillars of the competitive-elite order, while sporadically contested, remain entrenched.

These historical realities provide the context for current discussions in political theory about not only democracy but the idea of the "political" itself. Jeremy Valentine argues that the distinction between the "political" and politics "designates a difference between on the one hand 'normal,' ordinary and routinized activities which are occupied by the production and distribution of power … including the contested and disputed nature of these activities, and on the other, that which is supposed to ground, explain ... and locate these activities as a specific sphere of thought and action" (Valentine 2006, 15). The meaning of the political is hotly contested today by democratic theorists who see modernization (the state, representative democracy, liberalism and the global economic system) as a flawed political project. These debates parallel and often overlap with those in social theory traced by Antonio.

Debates over the political are most pressing when the hegemonic ideas or models that are used to *explain and contain* the complexities and contradictions of a given historical reality no longer effectively do so for significant parts of the population. This occurs when the dominant cultural "paradigms" and ideological lenses – cultural/symbolic, political, economic – come to be seen as no longer legitimate, when they are no longer accepted unquestioningly. Conceptions of the *political* rule seemingly naturally during different epochs. They appear to be self-evident when they are accepted as the relatively unquestioned foundation of how everyday politics work. (Valentine 2006, 508) Recent work by political theorists Tracy Strong and Andreas Kalyvas question the competitive-elite view and try to "see" beyond it. Their reflections on democracy and a new political emerge from a dialogue with Weber. That dialogue also forms the immediate background of the recent discussion by Ronald Beiner of the grounds of twentieth-century political thought (Beiner, 2014).

Tracy Strong, in *Politics without Vision: Thinking without a Bannister in the Twentieth Century*, argues that the last century saw conflicting visions of the political. These have often been forged in moments of crises such as those Weber experienced in Germany after World War I. Doing political theory was not been easy in the tumultuous twentieth century. Political theory today, Strong argues, has to "think without a bannister" in Hannah Arendt's phrase (Strong, 2012). Strong follows (mostly) twentieth-century thinkers who have been key participants in debates over what the political can mean in modernity without a vision of universal foundations. He looks at Kant, Nietzsche, Freud, Weber, Lenin, Schmitt and Arendt. I will restrict myself to his comments on Weber. But first, to give Strong's remarks some context, here is his own summary of his main themes.

Without going into the details of Strong's argument further here, he encapsulates his approach in the following six steps:

1) The so-called death of God ... refers not (simply) to the decay of Christianity but to a set of problems that ... correspond to the gradual unavailability of authoritative foundations for human knowledge and action.
2) This problem is conceptualized as the necessity of thinking without reliance on preexisting authority.

3) In the course of such thought, the world is conceived of in terms that reflect a vision of art, a vision of the world revealed to humans precisely because it is an artifact.

4) In the pursuit of this, knowledge on its own is understood to be insufficient to accomplish the construction of a new foundation.

5) The political realm will, to the extent that it responds to these developments (to which it must respond over time), manifest the above qualities.

6) Central attention will, therefore, be paid to the particular qualities that the agent must have in order to be the creator of a world and of an understanding. (Strong 2012, 14–15)

Here I will focus on Strong's last point, the centrality of the qualities the agent must have to define the political (skipping over Strong's detailed arguments, for example, about the aesthetic basis of judgment in the third point). Strong sets this against the same background that he provides for his discussion of the political in Weber – the modern disenchanted world. The modern politician and the social scientist live in the same world in which overarching meaning is no longer given by the authority of religion, philosophy or history. Not only is the disenchanted world devoid of intrinsic meaning. It also compels the politician and the social scientist to accept the limitations placed on them by history. This includes the modern division of labor, specialization and the other characteristics of twentieth-century modernity. Strong argues that as a social scientist this means accepting one's position as a member of the bourgeois, or professional middle classes. Strong asks, "What kind of person must one be – what must one have acknowledged about one's historicity – in order to be ... entitled to make, objective claims about our condition? It is a question he [Weber] will also ask about the person who truly has politics as a vocation: 'what kind of human being must one be to have the right to grasp the spokes of the wheel of history'" (Strong 2012, 121; Weber 2004, 76). Strong focuses on Weber's discussion of the qualities of the exemplary heroic politician in the PVP lecture. The lecture was given in January 1919, shortly after the November 1918 revolutions in Bavaria and Berlin – a period of extraordinary turmoil and uncertainty.

While the politician is thrown into the same world as the social scientist and citizens in modern democracies, there is something distinctive for Weber about her/his relationship to the political. While both must choose their values, the politician has the further task of being responsible for decisions that affect millions. In order to accept this responsibility for the consequences of their actions, politicians must, Strong argues (as does Weber), balance passionately held convictions and 'cool-headed' judgment. The main quality that someone with a vocation for politics must have is maturity. For Strong,

"Maturity – being an adult – is the recognition that any action taken is taken under circumstances where the consequences of that action, not only are not apparent, but also do not over the long term add up to make sense." In a famous passage from PVP, Weber describes "the qualities of character of those who have faced up to their historical position" (Strong 2012, 130) as follows:

> It is immeasurably moving when a mature man – whether old or young in years – who truly feels this responsibility for consequences and acts with his whole soul in terms of the ethic of responsibility, arrives at some point where he says: "I can do no other: here I stand."...For this situation must be truly possible at some point for each of us who is not inwardly dead. Insofar as the ethics of disposition [usually translated as ethics of conviction – my addition] and the ethics of responsibility are not absolute contraries, but complements, which only in combination constitute genuine persons, one who can have the calling for politics. (Strong 2012, 130–31; Weber 2004, 92)

I have argued that there is a tension in this passage between the idea that it may be possible for ordinary citizens to take a position and say: " Here I stand, I can do no other," and the more traditional reading of PVP, which says, as Strong does, that "having a calling for politics is not available to anyone ... at any time" (Strong 2012, 133). The self-knowledge gleaned from this for Weber is that the heroic politician must, paradoxically, have "measured up to the world as it really is in its everyday routine" before taking a stand (Strong 2012, 133; Weber 2004, 93). For Strong, "the important and often missed point here is that, for Weber, for most humans life is, or should be, routine; the most dangerous thing that people can do is to think that they can do more than what is before them – to have a modern version of hubris or original sin" (Strong 2012, 133). By this Strong means that "Weber sought to grasp the full significance of his historical thrownness into the world as a western bourgeois without ever seeking to escape from his historical condition. He understood the world to be ultimately chaos that had to be tamed by the person of knowledge" or politics (Strong 2012, 137). Weber thought only an exceptional few were capable of this "taming" or setting limits in the modern world of conflicting values. At the same time Strong notes that "From his inaugural lecture [in 1895] to the end of his life, [in 1920] Weber sought to recover the political, that is, the magical, the non-rationalized" (Strong 2012, 144). The question this raises is "who is capable of, or should, be doing this?" Who can *re-enchant the world by giving it limits*, and under what circumstances?

The relation between the political, the nonrational and the symbolic is also at stake in Andreas Kalyvas's 2008 book *Democracy and the Politics of the Extraordinary: Max Weber, Carl Schmitt and Hannah Arendt*. It is an example of democratic theory and the political coming together. I will also focus on Kalyvas's discussion of Weber. But the fact that Kalyvas, like Strong, discusses Weber, Schmitt and Arendt signals a significant shift in recent democratic theory debates that go beyond liberalism in the search for a new political (Strong 2013, 8). These thinkers are not promoters of a smaller state, unrestricted individual rights and freedoms, equality of opportunity or an unregulated market economy. They are critics of the competitive-elite model of liberal-democracy. Yet they are not postmodern either; they do not think that any attempt to ground the political is merely a cynical or instrumental exercise on the part of privileged elites to accumulate power.

Kalyvas begins his discussion with a distinction he sees in Weber's work between a narrow conception of politics and a broader one. The narrow one has to do with more traditional interpretations of Weber's view of politics and the state. As Weber famously said in the 1919 lecture *The Profession and Vocation of Politics*, "We shall use the term politics only to mean the leadership of a political association, ... which today means a state" (Weber 2004, 309–10). For Weber "the modern state is a compulsory organization which organizes domination." This includes the state's monopoly of the legitimate use of violence. For decades after World War II, this view was very influential in political science among students of political theory and international relations. Yet, for Kalyvas those realists who accept this version of Weber's view of the state "are far from exhausting the complexity and richness of Weber's political thought ... they do not fully capture his theory of the political." Kalyvas argues that on one level "Weber's view of the modern Occidental bureaucratic state and the struggle for state power" are "a depiction of normal politics" (Kalyvas 2008, 33). By normal politics Kalyvas means the everyday business side of politics under relatively stable conditions in which the state's legitimacy is largely unquestioned. In the post–World War II period normal politics in the global north was "characterize by civic privatism, depoliticization and passivity and carried out by political elites, professional bureaucrats and social technicians" (Kalyvas 2008, 6). These correspond to Schumpeter's competitive-elite model or to the conditions that prevail today under Green's ocular model.

But normal politics only "refers to one dimension of politics, that of state legality, everyday lawmaking, and the utilitarian politics of interests" (Kalyvas 2008, 33). Besides this narrower view of politics, Kalyvas argues that there is another broader dimension of politics that he calls extraordinary. Instead of the settled routines of everyday politics extraordinary politics challenges the stable structures, institutions and symbols of the state and legal authority. This takes place not only on the level of material or individual interests. Here Kalyvas follows Weber in being critical of both Marxism and liberalism for reducing the political to either individual or collective/class economic interests. Drawing on Pierre Bourdieu, Kalyvas argues that there is a symbolic dimension to the political that involves culture and subjective perceptions of the world and one's place in it. A political "community is always more than an economic group" as Weber said in *Economy and Society* (Weber 1978, 902) As Kalyvas argues, "Weber sought to demonstrate that the political realm transcends purely instrumental economic considerations centered on the market economy" (Kalyvas 2008, 39). The "ends" of politics are constituted by nonmaterial values. Kalyvas thus follows Weber in distinguishing the realm of the political from the economic and the social.

The influence of Bourdieu on Kalyvas's view is evident again when he says, "the formation of collective subjectivities is possible only with the presence of symbolic representations that transform actors from economic agents into conscious political actors." It is not that material interests or the economic realm are unimportant, but "the political is the site of identities" (Kalyvas 2008, 44). Based on Weber's critical dialogue with Marxism, "the political can be redefined as the central field where collective subjectivities are constructed and actors struggle for the determination of the dominant world view that will enable individuals to identify with larger collectivities." It is this "symbolic and constitutive dimension of politics" that allows individuals to "be a member of a broader ethical-political community" (Kalyvas 2008, 45).

With this in mind, Kalyvas's aim is to "uncover and reconstruct the political, conflictual processes whereby a worldview becomes institutionalized after emerging victorious from a struggle with its rivals" (Kalyvas 2008, 46). Kalyvas looks to Weber's sociology of religion and charisma for an explanation of how this historical/political process works. Rather than seeing a certain vision of the political as having been blocked, as was the case with the Frankfurt thinkers or Strauss, Kalyvas's sees the political as a dynamic and contested process whose outcomes are contingent and never permanently fixed. Kalyvas looks at the political through the lens of how the symbolic perception or legitimacy of a predominant worldview is transformed. He reconstructs Weber's sociology of charismatic authority through this lens and finds that "Weber's description of charismatic politics consisting of competing religious movements striving to control their communities by challenging the existing dominant beliefs, representations and institutions and seeking to create a new collective will before engaging in the transformation of the structure of political power" (Kalyvas 2008, 47).

Kalyvas is interested in two things. First, his discussion shifts the focus from concern with the charisma of individual leaders. Second Kalyvas, drawing on Cornelius Castoriadis, is concerned with the founding or "instituting" moment of politics, or what he calls the extraordinary (Kalyvas 2008, Castoriadis,

1997, 320). His discussion draws out the tension inherent in Weber's explanation of the founding of new charismatic religious communities and identities, on one hand, and the hegemony (and tenacity) of the existing order, its institutions and values, on the other. Through his discussion of founding dynamics in Weber's discussion of charismatic communities Klayvas tries to show that no system's legitimacy is ever airtight, unassailable or permanently closed. "The moment of perfect closure and total stability never arrives. Absolute legitimation is impossible … there will always be room for new contestation, struggles and counter-hegemomic forces" (Kalyvas 2008, 55).

These struggles emerge out of the fact of domination. Domination always involves subordination, "which always breeds inarticulate feelings of dissatisfaction, distress and suffering." Kalyvas suggests that "[n]o instituted order, however legitimate it may appear at any one historical period, can extinguish these feelings" completely (Kalyvas 2008, 55). This means that the potential for change or new foundings always exists.

In addition, Kalyvas alerts us to another important implication. That is that founding, or the attempt to mobilize the subordinate masses and create new symbolic meanings out of their dissatisfaction with the status quo, also necessarily involves delegitimizing the existing order, its foundational values, its symbols and institutions. "In order to succeed in its delegitimizing project a charismatic movement has to launch a counter-hegemonic cultural attack against the dominant world-view." It has to begin by "attacking their symbolic and motivational foundations … in order to weaken the sources of internal obedience and tacit consent upon which the existing order is based" (Kalyvas 2008, 58).

In addition, charismatic movements must do two things to succeed. First, they must appeal to people from across the social spectrum, and not simply members of a particular class. "A charismatic movement 'cuts vertically through all strata' and aspires to regulate the practical conduct of the entire population" (Kalyvas 2008, 59; Weber 1978, 1180). Second, they must also not only try to change external political and economic conditions, but more importantly they must "revolutionize men from within," as Weber said, by offering a rival worldview that can be seen as redemption from suffering, inequality and the injustices of the existing order. Only extraordinary movements are capable of this in extraordinary times. "Especially in times of tension, such as political crises, war, economic disruptions and geopolitical changes, where widespread insecurity and dislocation arise these feelings will make the subjected masses more attentive to … promises of … emancipation and more receptive to rival visions of the world and alternative ethical doctrines expounded by prophetic charismatic leaders" (Kalyvas 2008, 56). Emissary prophets in particular, whom Weber discusses in *Religious Rejections of the World and Their Directions,* hold out the promise of redemption from injustice and suffering because their prophecy is closely connected to "the regulation of social conduct in the world, to collective mobilization and to the radical transformation of the established order" (Kalyvas 2008, 56). Once victorious these new rulers will try to consolidate their own visions in new hegemonic institutions, laws and norms or a new form of normal politics. But before that they must be able to exploit or create breaks with or within the existing order.

Kalyvas argues that even though we can find this view of the collective force of charisma in the *Sociology of Religion,* Weber renounces it in his political writings and speeches such as *The Profession and Vocation of Politics.* The charismatic politician in the PVP speech, famous among Weber scholars, is often taken to be an antidote to the rationalization of the state and the disenchanted world in which the normal business of modern politics takes place. Kalyvas argues, however, that the politician or leader Weber discusses in PVP is already de-charismatic: "The plebiscitarian Caesarist president of the Reich is neither a founder of a legislator, but simply an institutional means for counter-balancing legal formalism, bureaucratic rule, instrumental rationality, weak parliaments and the politics of interest" (Kalyvas 2008, 65).

Kalyvas asks why Weber would reduce charisma to an individual property and not try to mobilize charisma as a collective force for social change. Kalyvas's answer is that in Weber's time new collective charismatic visions had gravitated to the far left of the political spectrum. The revolutionary syndicalism Weber criticizes in PVP was a new movement with an emancipatory vision of extraordinary politics. It arose during the destabilizing period of rapid industrial growth in Germany at the end of the nineteenth century and then erupted again after Germany's catastrophic defeat in World War I.

As Kalyvas argues, picking up on the theme of Weber's elite liberalism, Weber distrusted the working classes and the Many deeply. He did so because he thought they were ruled by unruly emotional impulses and not a disciplined, rational conduct of life. "Weber identified mass society with the rue of irrational emotions, uncontrollable impulses and dangerous passions. He considered participatory democracy susceptible to the 'unregulated rule of the street'" and "the manipulations of demagogues" (Kalyvas 2008, 70; Weber 1994a, 231). This distrust led Weber to confine charisma to leaders within the parliamentary system, where it was institutionally contained. Thus, for Kalyvas, "Weber abandoned the instituting, founding dimension of charismatic politics" (Kalyvas 2008, 73).

I have argued that Weber uses a somewhat different distinction between politics and the political. Kalyvas sees this through the lens of Bourdieu's concern with the symbolic. I follow Sheldon Wolin in his view that "[t]he political ... is an expression of the idea that a free society composed of diversities can

nonetheless enjoy moments of commonality when, through public delibera-
tions, collective power is used to promote or protect the well-being of a col-
lectivity" (Wolin 1996, 31). Politics, by contrast, is "the public contestation, by
organized and unequal powers" over collective resources; the stuff of "normal"
politics (Wolin 1996, 30). In his definition of the political Wolin holds open a
key tension in modern democracies; that the "collective power" of the people
(or portions of the demos) can still be used to create moments of commonality
in diverse, pluralistic societies in which an unequal distribution of power and
resources is considered normal and legitimate. Despite inequalities in power
and resources, for Wolin "ordinary individuals are capable of creating new
cultural patterns of commonality at any moment" (Wolin 1996, 36). Members
of the demos have the potential to come together to create new experiences
of democratic solidarity that are noninstitutionalized, more egalitarian and
participatory than those available to them under the existing institutional
arrangements of the competitive-elite order. Yet Wolin also has, in *Democracy
Inc.* (Wolin, 2008) his own version of the homegenization-regimentation thesis. He looks at the predominance of what he calls the Mega-state and global
capitalism in the current era. The nearly one-dimensional predominance of
these great powers in modern democratic societies means that fuller experiences of democracy are fleeting or "fugitive" (Wolin 1996, 2004).

Following Wolin's distinction between politics and the political, I have
argued that Weber's vision of heroic leaders, who were seen by Weber to be
bearers of the political, were designed to *contain* a rebellious, unruly working class after World War I. Workers were torn between competing radical
visions of how to change the political system and the authoritarian culture of
Wilhelmine Germany that collapsed after the war. In my view Weber pushed
the political 'up' to leaders in his search for a new vision of the political, a new
founding moment that could galvanize the population. Yet Weber wanted this
to occur in the context of a new system of parliamentary democracy with
a directly elected, plebiscitary president added on top. These leaders were
to negotiate the difficult compromises demanded in a parliamentary system.
Only they could be trusted to achieve the difficult balance between reason and
emotion, or cool-headed responsibility and passionate conviction to a cause
that the mature politician needs to be successful.

The flip side of this is that Weber, as Kalyvas also sees, thought the working class was too emotional and immature to be trusted with political power.
They had a role for Weber, but it was limited to supporting organized parties
within a parliamentary system of representative democracy. Weber made a
case, in his political writings during and after World War I, for the orderly
participation of the German Social Democratic Party in electoral politics.
By the beginning of World War I the SPD was the largest party in the lower

house of the German parliament, the *Reichstag*. Weber thought they should be included in any new system that arose after the war. Yet I argue that there is a clear distinction, in the same writings, between the orderly participation of working-class party on the one hand, and the unruly "politics of the street" of the syndicalist and other revolutionaries of November 1918, on the other. Weber used the hierarchical privileging of reason over emotion as a strategy of argument in trying to discredit his overly "emotional" political opponents on the radical left and right. The way Weber uses this dichotomy of reason versus emotion is closely related to his own politics at the time, where he publicly battled more radical views of a new political on both the far left and far right. This, in turn, was part of his effort to make the positive case for a system of parliamentary democracy in the precarious circumstances right after World War I. It is interesting to note that a number of commentators have recently cited this phrase – the "politics of the street" – in Weber's stinging criticism in PVP of the revolutionaries of 1918. Perhaps it is a sign of democratic tensions today finding their way into the recent literature of the Weber revival.

The hierarchical distinction between reason and emotion is as old as Western political philosophy. Wendy Brown, in her book *Manhood and Politics* (Brown 1988), first noted this in the 1980s in relation to Weber and other thinkers in the Western tradition going back to Plato and Aristotle. Feminist critics such as Susan Hekman and Rosalyn Bolough (Hekman 1983, 1994; Bolough 1990) note that Weber, like the vast majority of (male) thinkers in the Western canon prior to the twentieth century, privileges reason as mastery, self-control and objectivity, the stuff of the public sphere. Emotions, on the other hand, are feminine and irrational, closer to uncontrolled nature.

Volker Heins takes this argument in another direction. Heins agrees that one can find ample evidence in Weber's political writings of the reason vs. emotion dichotomy (Heins 2007, 717). Heins cites Weber's famous discussion from the PVP speech, that "successful democratic politics are conducted with the head" and a cool, clear head at that (Heins 2007, 717; Weber 2004, 353). Heins notes that Weber, "in his political criticism of the contemporary Left ... devotes much space to a rejection of its *Affektpolitik*" or emotion-driven politics. Heins notes that Weber paints an interesting picture of the political activity of the revolutionary masses: "what the masses do is described in terms of "surging," "erupting" and "flaring up" – recurrent themes in Weber, suggesting both the violent an ephemeral nature of such experience" (Heins 2007, 718). Heins is correct to note that, for the same reasons, Weber is critical of "Wilhelmine monarchists" (and nationalists) on the right, as well as "other literati" or "the deracinated strata of urban intellectuals" (Heins 2007, 722). He also worried about how this volatile interplay of emotional politics would

affect the bourgeoisie, and "whether such explosions unleash yet again the …
usual fear of the propertied classes … it depends on whether the emotional
effect of undirected mass fury [of the revolutionary working class] produces
the equally emotional and equally undirected cowardice of the bourgeoisie"
(Heins 2007, 721; Weber 1994, 232).

But Heins also suggests that this view is more complex than a simple split
between reason and emotion and that it has implications for modern democratic politics. He argues that "Weber's discovery of the role of the prophets
in Ancient Judaism … led him to reevaluate the place of emotions and 'dema-
gogy' in the public sphere" (Heins 2007, 716). In *Economy and Society* Weber
discusses the Hebrew prophets Amos and Jeremiah, who had "no official position" and who were "unrelentingly hostile to magic." Their charismatic vision
of politics, Heins argues, was a "delicate balance consisting of abstinence from
the world, lay ecstasy and apocalyptic hopes." Jesus and the Christian Apostles
employed similar arguments. Heins notes that for Weber "Jesus's 'wrathful
speeches' against the Pharisees and subsequently the propaganda techniques
used by Paul are interpreted as media with which to create communal institutions based on a strong, value-oriented rationality" (Heins 2007, 718–19).

From the perspective of democratic theory today, it is interesting that both
Heins and Kalyvas focus on how charismatic prophecy seeks to create "communal institutions" outside of "existing hierarchies" (i.e. the state) based on
an emotional critique of suffering and social injustice. In this analysis, "Weber
shows no inclination to think of the emotions and emotionally charged discourses merely as factors disrupting rational political processes" (Heins 2007,
719). This is further evidence of the idea that Weber's use of "emotional"
arguments is varying; it depends on the context and his own political purposes.
Here the prophet's use of "surging," eruptive arguments is seen in a positive
light, as part of a new founding, or in Kalyvas's terms, an extraordinary political moment. Weber's "positive counter-image" of Hebrew prophecy is rooted
in "the fact that the prophets were the first to create an awareness of the state
of the nation and the need for a moral change of the existing hierarchies from
outside (my italics) and solely through the medium of an emotionally tinged
public discourse." Heins also provides a reading of the context in which to
place Weber writings on Hebrew prophecy: "Weber saw the Germany of the
Empire [prior to World War I] and the subsequent revolutionary period in
the grip of emotional epidemics, as … diseases of the soul. According to his
analysis, irrational passions were whipped up by demagogues facing a population rendered emotionally susceptible by deprivation and the hardships of
war" (Heins 2007, 719–20).

We can see both Heins's and Wolin's views in the context of Kalyvas's explanation of a "three-level model of democratic politics." The first level consists

of a founding moment in which a new legitimate political emerges after challenging the existing state and beliefs. The second moment occurs as the new regime is stabilized and its norms are institutionalized in normal lawmaking. But a third level continues to occur on the margins of the second. It consists of an ongoing "politics of spontaneous and unpredictable forms of popular mobilization and informal participatory agitations." (Kalyvas 2008, 12)

Kalyvas goes on to argue that Schmitt and Arendt also offer versions of this tripartite model. Without being able to go into greater detail here, Kalyvas argues that Schmitt, who wrote during and after the Weimar and Nazi eras, tries to recover the basis of the extraordinary constituting power of the people from the "normal" politics of conflicting individual interests that characterize liberal democracies. Schmitt was critical of the system of parliamentary democracy that Weber had helped found in Germany after World War I. That system, characterized by formal political equality, the rule of law and the parliamentary representation of conflicting economic and societal interests, was too pluralist for Schmitt. His concern was with order and unity. Parliamentary politics was not consistent with democracy, which entailed a greater unity or even identity between the rulers and ruled in order to be legitimate. That unity was spelled out, for Schmitt, in a fuller notion of constitutions. Liberal-democratic constitutions were concerned with procedurally limiting government and state power as a way of protecting individual rights and freedoms. For Schmitt, constitutions embodied and legitimated the founding moments of democracy. They embody the unity of the people's sovereign will, which is "represented" by the leader/president. This idea of sovereignty is the secularized, modern version of an old theological concept – that the unity of the will comes from one source, God (Kalyvas 2008, 215).

Kalyvas's discussion tries to recover the democratic moment of "constituent power," separating it from Schmitt's authoritarian decisionism in which leaders mobilize the people around "friends and enemies." As Kalyvas notes, Schmitt is not an advocate of extensive citizen deliberation (Kalyvas 2008, 86). For Schmitt, the friend/enemy distinction galvanizes the political, constituting it. It paradoxically creates the unity of the sovereign democratic will but leaves the people in the passive role of acclaiming the leaders plebiscites. From the perspective of a participatory model of democracy, there are a host of issues with Schmitt; his very conservative views are ultimately closer to Strauss's. Schmitt's is a version of premodern nostalgia in a more realist form that accepts Weber's analysis of disenchantment and the modern state while wanting the "constituent power," represented by the leader, to be supreme in the name of order (Valentine 2006).

In his discussion of Arendt Kalyvas argues that Arendt tries to replace "Schmitt's decisionistic model of constitutional politics with her own ...

version of an original, horizontal founding contract" (Kalyvas 2008, 233). Kalyvas argues that Arendt's *On Revolution* is important in its discussion of how to reconcile the first two moments or levels of democracy, the extraordinary and the normal. Though Arendt's thought was also shaped by the Weimar era and its splintering of the political into radical right and left, she sought a third way beyond the split of politics into the normal and the extraordinary. Arguing that the sovereignty of the people echoed arguments in the Western theological tradition regarding a "limitless divine power located outside of human laws" (Kalyvas 2008, 214; Arendt 1990, 183), Arendt wants to see a plurality of powers and possibilities of new beginnings, not ones associated only with the "people" or privileged "universal" agents in extraordinary revolutionary moments of rupture. This is what Kalyvas calls her "dual" vision of freedom. She has a notion of the extraordinary instituting of politics that for Kalyvas sets the "boundaries that delineate the proper frontiers of the political" (Kalyvas 2008, 202). But this should not, he argues, preclude new beginnings that are not absolute ruptures *within* the established system (Kalyvas 2008, 232; Arendt 1969, 79). Arendt argued that this could be accomplished by instituting two things within normal politics that are bound by constitutional limitations. The first is a "combination of a council system of elementary republics and a powerful judiciary." This is "an unusual theory of republican federalism and ordinary politics" combined (Kalyvas 2008, 264). As Kalyvas notes, however, these councils can also be limited by "hierarchical and elitist structures" (Kalyvas 2008, 288).

The other consists of movements of civil disobedience. In *Civil Disobedience* Arendt proposed a constitutional amendment to create an enhanced right of association that would include civil disobedience (Kalyvas 2008, 287; Arendt 1969, 95). She and Kalyvas have in mind social movements that

> are free form the entaglments of representation … and operate apart from the existing mechanisms of organized power. They are based on the premise of a more direct, democratic form of participation, where citizens are able to speak and act for themselves. Finally, whereas movement for civil disobedience are non-institutionalized collective subjects, they are not disorganized or amorphous. … even though they are characterized by more or less fluid internal structures … they are not completely lacking in organizational and political forms. They are extra-institutional but not anti-constitutional. (Kalyvas 2008, 288)

Creating these extra-institutional forms of politics creates spaces that are on the borderline between the formal structures of state power/electoral representation and civil society. For democratic theorists today, it is not a matter of choosing between reforming the state, on the one hand, or taking politics to the street in local or global protest movements, on the other. The search for a new political by democratic theorists must encompass both. Only then can a new (perhaps charismatic/collective) democratic political move beyond critical theory's impasse, Green's acceptance of the apathy of the competitive-elite framework or Weber's (at the time perhaps understandable) reliance on party/state leaders. Democratic theorists must be mindful, as Kalyvas and Strong are, of the tension or fine balance Weber brought to light between the maturity of recognizing the world as it is, in its historical "objectivity," and the desire to change it.

Bibliography

Ackerman, Bruce. 1998. *We the People: Transformations*. Cambridge, MA: Harvard University Press.

———1991. *We the People: Foundations*. Cambridge, MA: Harvard University Press.

Antonio, Robert. 2005. "Max Weber in the Post-WWII US and After." *Ethics and Politics*, 2: 1–94.

———2000. "After Postmodernism: Reactionary Tribalism". *American Journal of Sociology*, 106(2): 40–87.

Arendt, Hannah. 1990. *On Revolution*. New York: Penguin Books.

———1969. "Civil Disobedience" in *Crises of the Republic*. New York: Harvest Books.

Beetham, David. 1994. "Max Weber and the Liberal Political Tradition" in *The Barbarism of Reason: Max Weber and the Twilight of Enlightenment*. eds. Asher Horowitz and Terry Maley. Toronto: University of Toronto Press.

———1988. *Max Weber and the Theory of Modern Politics*. 2nd ed. Cambridge: Cambridge University Press.

Beiner, Ronald. 2014. *Political Philosophy: What It Is and Why it Matters*. New York: Cambridge University Press.

Bolough, Rosalyn. 1990. *Love or Greatness: Max Weber and Masculine Thinking – A Feminist Inquiry*. Boston: Unwin Hyman.

Breiner, Peter. 2007. "Ideal Types as 'Utopias' and Impartial Political Clarification: Weber and Mannheim on Sociological Prudence" in *Max Weber's Objectivity Reconsidered*. ed. Laurence McFalls, Toronto: University of Toronto Press.

———2005. The Origins of the Puritan Capitalist and the Vocational Politician – A Series of Just-So-Stories? Or Why Is Weber's Genealogy of the Vocational Politician So Uncontroversial?" *Max Weber Studies* 6(1): 3–31.

———1996. *Max Weber and Democratic Politics*, Ithaca, NY: Cornell University Press.

Brown, Wendy. 1988. *Manhood and Politics: A Feminist Reading in Political Theory*. Lanham: Rowan and Littlefield.

Castoriadis, Cornelius. 1997. "Radical Imagination and the Social Instituting Imaginary," in *The Castoriadis Reader*, ed. David Ames Curtis, Oxford: Blackwell Publishers.

Dahl, Robert. 1961. *Who Governs: Democracy and Power in an American City*. New Haven, CT: Yale University Press.

———1971. *Polyarchy: Participation and Opposition*, New Haven, CT: Yale University Press.

Eden, Robert. 1983. *Political Leadership and Nihilism: A Study of Weber and Nietzsche*. Tampa: University of Florida Press.

Eliason, Sven and Kari Palonen. 2004. "Max Weber's Relevance as a Theorist of Politics." *Max Weber Studies*, 4(2): 135–42.

Foucault, Michel. 1995. *Discipline and Punish: The Birth of the Prison*, trans. Alan Sheridan. New York: Pantheon.

Fukuyama, Francis. 1992. *The End of History and the Last Man*. New York: Avon.

Gerth, Hans and C. W. Mills, eds. 1948 [1975]. *From Max Weber: Essays in Sociology*. New York: Oxford University Press.

Goldman, Harvey. 1990. *Max Weber and Thomas Mann: Calling and the Shaping of the Self*. Berkeley: University of California Press.

Habermas, Jürgen. 1984. *The Theory of Communicative Action*, trans. Thomas McCarthy. Boston: Beacon Press.

Green, Jeffrey. 2010. *The Eyes of the People: Democracy in an Age of Spectatorship*. New York: Oxford University Press.

Heins, Volker. 2007. "Reasons of the Heart: Weber and Arendt on Emotion in Politics." *European Legacy* 12(6): 715–28.

Hekman, Susan. 1994. "Max Weber and Post-Positivist Social Theory" in *The Barbarism of Reason: Max Weber and the Twilight of Enlightenment*, eds. Asher Horowitz and Terry Maley. Toronto: University of Toronto Press.

———1983. *Max Weber, The Ideal Type, and Contemporary Social Theory*. Notre Dame: University of Notre Dame Press.

Held, David. 1996. *Models of Democracy*. 2nd ed. Stanford: Stanford University Press.

Hennis, Wilhelm. 2000. *Max Weber: Essays in Reconstruction*. Translated with a new Introduction by Keith Tribe, London: Threshold Press.

Horkheimer, Max and Theodor Adorno, 2002. *Dialectic of Enlightenment: Philosophical Fragments*. Stanford: Stanford University Press.

Kalyvas, Andreas. 2008. *Democracy and the Politics of the Extraordinary: Max Weber, Carl Schmitt and Hannah Arendt*. New York: Cambridge University Press.

Kim, Sung Ho. 2004. *Max Weber's Politics of Civil Society*. Cambridge: Cambridge University Press.

Lassman, Peter. 2004. "Political Theory in an Age of Disenchantment: The Problem of Value Pluralism: Weber, Berlin, Rawls." *Max Weber Studies* 4(2): 253–71.

Macpherson, C. B. 1977. *The Life and Times of Liberal Democracy*. New York: Oxford University Press.

Maley, Terry. 2011. *Democracy and the Political in Max Weber's Thought*. Toronto: University of Toronto Press.

Marcuse, Herbert. 1964. *One Dimensional Man: Studies in Advanced Industrial Society*. Boston: Beacon Press.

McFalls, Laurence. 2007. "Introduction" in *Max Weber's Objectivity Reconsidered*, ed. Laurence McFalls. Toronto: University of Toronto Press.

Mommsen, Wolfgang. 1984. *Max Weber and German Politics, 1890–1920*, trans. Michael S. Steinberg. 2nd ed. Chicago: University of Chicago Press.

Parsons, Talcott. 1937 [1968]. *The Structure of Social Action: A Study in Social Theory with Special Reference to a Group of Recent Writers*, two vols. New York: Free Press.

Portis, Edward. 1986. *Max Weber and Political Commitment*. Philadelphia: Temple University Press.

Roth, Günther. 1993. "Weber the Would-be Englishman" in *Weber's Protestant Ethic: Origins,' Evidence, and Contexts*. Helmut Lehman and Günther Roth eds. Washington/ Cambridge, MA: German Historical Institute / Cambridge University Press.

———*The Social Democrats in Imperial Germany*. Salem: Ayer, 1984.

Scaff, Lawrence. 1989. *Fleeing the Iron Cage: Culture, Politics, and Modernity in the Thought of Max Weber*. Berkeley: University of California Press.

Schluchter, Wolfgang. 1989. *Rationalism, Religion, and Domination*. Berkeley: University of California Press.

————1981. *The Rise of Western Rationalism*, trans. Günther Roth. Berkeley: University of California Press.

Schumpeter, Joseph. 1976. *Capitalism, Socialism, and Democracy*, 3rd ed. New York: Harper Torchbooks.

Sica, Alan. 2004. *Max Weber and the New Century*. New Brunswick: Transaction.

Strauss, Leo. 1953. *Natural Right and History*. Chicago: University of Chicago Press.

Strong, Tracy B. 2012. *Politics without Vision: Thinking without a Bannister in the Twentieth Century*. Chicago: University of Chicago Press.

Tenbruck, Friedrich. 1989. "The Problem of Thematic Unity in the Works of MaxWeber" in *Reading Weber*, ed. Keith Tribe. London: Routledge.

Turner, Charles. 1992. *Modernity and Politics in the Works of Max Weber*. London: Routledge.

Turner, Stephen. 2000. *The Cambridge Companion to Weber*. Cambridge: Cambridge University Press.

Turner, Stephen, and Regis Factor. 1984. *Max Weber and the Dispute over Reason and Value*. London: Routledge and Kegan Paul.

Valentine, Jeremy. 2006. "The Political." *Theory, Culture and Society*, 23(2–3): 505–11.

Weber, Max. 2004. "Science as a Vocation" in *The Vocation Lectures*. eds. David Owen and Tracy B. Strong. trans. Rodney Livingstone. Indianapolis: Hackett.

————2002. *The Protestant Ethic and the "Spirit" of Capitalism*. trans. Stephen Kalberg. Los Angeles: Roxbury.

————2002. *The Protestant Ethic and the "Spirit" of Capitalism and Other Writings*. trans. Peter Baehr and C.G. Wells. New York: Penguin.

————1994a. "The Profession and Vocation of Politics" in *Weber: Political Writings*, eds. Peter Lassman and Ronald Speirs. Cambridge: Cambridge University Press.

————1994b "Parliament and Government in Germany under a New Political Order" in *Weber: Political Writings*, ed. Peter Lassman and Ronald Speirs. Cambridge: Cambridge University Press.

————1994c. "Suffrage and Democracy in Germany" in *Weber: Political Writings*, ed. Peter Lassman and Ronald Speirs. Cambridge: Cambridge University Press.

————1930 [1992]. *The Protestant Ethic and the Spirit of Capitalism*, trans. Talcott Parsons, intro. Anthony Giddens. New York: Scribner.

————1978. *Economy and Society: An Outline of Interpretive Sociology*, eds. Günther Roth and Claus Wittich. Berkeley: University of California Press.

Whimster, Sam. 2004. *The Essential Weber*. London: Routledge.

Wolin, Sheldon S. 2008. *Democracy Incorporated: Managed Democracy and the Specter of Inverted Totalitarianism*. Princeton, NJ: Princeton University Press.

————2004. *Politics and Vision: Continuity and Innovation in Western Political Thought*, expanded ed. Princeton: Princeton University Press.

————1996. "Fugitive Democracy" in *Democracy and Difference: Contesting the Boundaries of the Political*, ed. Seyla Benhabib. Princeton, NJ: Princeton University Press.

————1994. "Reason in Exile: Critical Theory and Technological Society" in A. M. Melzer, J. Weiberger, & M. R. Zinman, eds. *Technology in the Western Political Tradition*, pp. 162–189.

CONTRIBUTORS

Christopher Adair-Toteff earned his PhD degree in philosophy but for the last two decades has focused primarily on classical German sociology. He is the author of *Sociological Beginnings* (2005), *Fundamental Concepts in Max Weber's Sociology of Religion* (2015) and *Max Weber's Sociology of Religion* (2016). His articles have appeared in numerous journals, including *Journal of Classical Sociology*, *History of the Social Sciences*, *Max Weber Studies*, and *European Journal of Cultural and Political Sociology*. He is a contributor to the *Anthem Companion to Karl Mannheim* (forthcoming 2017) and the editor of the *Anthem Companion to Troeltsch* (forthcoming 2017). He is currently working on a book about Troeltsch.

Jack Barbalet is chair professor in sociology and head of the Department of Sociology at Hong Kong Baptist University. He has published extensively in the sociology of emotions, economic sociology and sociological theory. His contribution to Weber studies includes *Weber, Passions and Profits: 'The Protestant Ethic and the Spirit of Capitalism' in Context* (2008) and many articles in *British Journal of Sociology*, *European Journal of Sociology*, *Journal of Classical Sociology* and *Max Weber Studies*. Barbalet is currently researching social relations and social structure in mainland China, including family relations, *guanxi* networks and wealth migration.

Joshua Derman is associate professor of humanities at the Hong Kong University of Science and Technology. He received his PhD in modern European history from Princeton University, and his AB in philosophy from Harvard University. Prior to joining HKUST, he was a Max Weber postdoctoral fellow at the European University Institute in Florence. His research focuses on modern German history and, in particular, the international dimensions of German political and social thought. His book, *Max Weber in Politics and Social Thought: From Charisma to Canonization* (2012), is the first comprehensive history of Weber's early impact in Germany and the United States.

Sven Eliaeson is a PhD in political science from Uppsala University. He was a docent at Stockholm University in 1996 and a visiting professor in sociology at the Centre for Social Studies of the Institute for Philosophy and Sociology, Polish Academy of Science, Warsaw. He was also a senior research fellow at Uppsala Centre for Russian and Eurasian Studies. He is the author of *Max*

Weber's Methodologies (2002) and has edited several volumes on East of the Elbe affairs and problems of post-1989 tranformations.

Lutz Kaelber is associate professor of sociology at the University of Vermont. His publications include S*chools of Asceticism* (1998) and an edited volume entitled *The Protestant Ethic Turns 100: Essays on the Centenary of the Weber Thesis* (with William Swatos, 2005). His translations include Max Weber's dissertation (*The History of Commercial Partnerships in the Middle Ages*, 2003) and recent essays by the German legal scholar Gerhard Dilcher. His current research focuses on collective memory and commemoration in Europe, specifically of medical crimes against the disabled in Nazi Germany.

Stephen Kalberg teaches classical theory, contemporary theory, and comparative political cultures in the Sociology Department at Boston University. He is the translator of Max Weber's *The Protestant Ethic and the Spirit of Capitalism* (2001, 2011) and editor of *Max Weber: Readings and Commentary on Modernity* (2005) and *The Protestant Ethic and the Spirit of Capitalism with Other Writings on the Rise of the West* (2009). He is the author of *Max Weber's Comparative-Historical Sociology* (1994), *Les Idees, les Valeurs et les Interets: Introduction á la Sociologie de Max Weber* (2010), *Max Weber's Comparative-Historical Sociology Today* (2012), *Deutschland und Amerika aus der Sicht Max Webers* (2013), *Searching for the Spirit of American Democracy: Max Weber's Analysis of a Unique Political Culture* (2014), and *The Social Thought of Max Weber* (2016). His *Max Weber's Sociology of Civilizations* is forthcoming. In addition, he has written numerous studies that compare German and American societies.

Terry Maley teaches in the Political Science and Graduate Social and Political Thought programs at York University, Toronto, Canada. His book, *Democracy and the Political in Max Weber's Thought* (2011) critically examines the relation between Weber's heroic view of agency and democracy. Maley's first book on Weber, *The Barbarism of Reason: Max Weber and the Twilight of Enlightenment* (1994), co-edited with Asher Horowitz, dealt critically with Weber's relationship to Enlightenment thought. Maley's research now situates Weber's thought in relation to current debates in democratic theory and Critical Theory.

Lawrence A. Scaff is professor emeritus of political science at Wayne State University, Detroit. He is the author of *Fleeing the Iron Cage* (1989), *Max Weber in America* (2011; German trans., 2013) and *Weber and the Weberians* (2014).

Alan Sica is professor of sociology and founding director of the Social Thought Program at Pennsylvania State University. He was editor of two journals owned by the American Sociological Association, *Sociological Theory* and *Contemporary Sociology*. He has written or edited a dozen books, many of them about Max Weber, including *Weber, Irrationality and Social Action* (1988) and *Max Weber: A Comprehensive Bibliography* (2004).

David Norman Smith (PhD, Sociology, Wisconsin, 1988) is professor and chair of the Sociology Department at the University of Kansas. He publishes on classical and critical theory, class, charisma, capitalism, authoritarianism, prejudice, and genocide. His most recent book is *Marx's Capital Illustrated* (2014), and he is currently editing Marx's late manuscripts on global society.

Stephen P. Turner is Distinguished University Professor of Philosophy at the University of South Florida. He has written extensively on Weber, including *Max Weber and the Dispute over Reason and Value* (1984) and *Max Weber: The Lawyer as Social Thinker* (1994), both with Regis Factor. He edited the *Cambridge Companion to Weber* (2000), and in addition has published articles and chapters on Weber's methodology and his political, constitutional and legal thinking. His most recent article is "Deflating the Rule of Law: Weber and Kelsen," in *Lo Stato*.

INDEX

Knies, Karl 29
Knight, Frank 177–80, 191
Kommanditgesellschaft partnerships 31–33
Kon, Igor S. 203–04
Konfession und Soziale Schichtung. Eine
Studie über die Wirtschaftliche Lage der
Katholiken und Protestanten in Baden
(Offenbacher) 61–62
Konfuzianismus und Taoismus (Weber) 213
Kongzi (Confucius leader) 208–12
Kracauer, Siegfried 182–83

Laband, Paul 29–30
labor
    German agrarian crisis and shortages
        of 49–50
    Weber's analysis of 53–61
Lachmann, Karl 12–13
Landauer, Carl 180–83
Landwirtschaftliche Hochschule 51–52
Lassman, Peter 258–59
Lastig, Gustav 29–30
law and legal studies
    in China, Weber's discussion of 220–25
    multi-causal embeddedness of social
        action and 130–32
    sociological approaches in Weber's study
        of 33–34
    Weber's participation in 28–33
Lazarsfeld, Paul 180–83
leadership
    mass democracy and 264–66
    role of the political for 266–74
    Weber on political responsibilities
        of 162–64, 166–68, 172–73,
        260–62, 274–75
League of Nations 147–52
Lederer, Emil 181–82
legacies, Weber's discussion of 132–40
Legge, James 209–10, 218–19
legitimation
    charisma and 202–03
    in democratic politics 262–63
    domination and 123
Leibniz, Gottfried 209–10
Lengerke, Alexander von 53–55
Lenin, Nikolai 267
    Weber and 203–04

Lepsius, M. Rainer 191
Lepsius, Susanne 29–30
Leviné, Eugene 200
liberalism
    modern relevance of Weber concerning
        257–58, 262
    Weber's interest in 199
Liddel, Peter 12–13
Lipset, S. M. 183
Loewenstein, Karl 180–83
Losch, H. 52
Lossache. See sacred lottery, of Moravian
    Brotherhood
Low, Polly 12–13
Löwith, Karl 247
Luckau, Alma 20–21, 151–52, 159
Luddendorf, Eric 147, 159
Ludwig Maximilian University 200
Luther, Martin
    Beruf principle of 108–12
    capitalism and 73–75
    Protestant Reformation and 77
Lyotard, Jean-François 258

Macpherson, C. B. 263
magic. *See also Entzauberung*
    (demagification)
    charisma and 106–12
    in China 91–94, 103–06
    in India 98–103
    Weber's discussion of 86–91, 231–35
Mahayana Buddhism 102n. 112
Maley, Terry 23–24, 257–79
Malinowski, Bronislaw 178
"Manchester Liberalism" 50–51
Manhood and Politics (Brown) 275–76
Mann, Michael 203–04
Mannheim, Karl 178, 180–83
Marcuse, Herbert 260–62
Marett, Robert Ranulph 91–94
market development in China, Weber's
    analysis of 220–25
Martindale, Don 181
Marut, Ret 200
Marx, Karl 39, 201–02
    postmodern dismissal of 258–59
    Weber and 117–19, 190, 200, 233–35,
        238–39, 241–44

CPSIA information can be obtained at www.ICGtesting.com
Printed in the USA
BVOW04*1948231016

465810BV00003B/15/P